Anxiety in Sports

The Series in Health Psychology and Behavioral Medicine

Charles D. Spielberger, *Editor-in-Chief*

Chesney, Rosenman Anger and Hostility in Cardiovascular
 and Behavioral Disorders
Elias, Marshall Cardiovascular Disease and Behavior
Hackfort, Spielberger Anxiety in Sports: An International Perspective
Hobfoll The Ecology of Stress
Lonetto, Templer Death Anxiety
Morgan, Goldston Exercise and Mental Health
Pancheri, Zichella Biorhythms and Stress in the Physiopathology
 of Reproduction

IN PREPARATION

Byrne, Rosenman Anxiety and the Heart
Elias, Elias, Robbins, Schultz Cognitive Psychology of Essential
 Hypertension

Anxiety in Sports:
An International Perspective

Edited by

Dieter Hackfort
University of Heidelberg
Heidelberg, Federal Republic of Germany

Charles D. Spielberger
University of South Florida
Tampa, Florida

⬤ HEMISPHERE PUBLISHING CORPORATION
A member of the Taylor & Francis Group

New York   Washington   Philadelphia   London

ANXIETY IN SPORTS: An International Perspective

1 2 3 4 5 6 7 8 9 0   B C B C   8 9 8 7 6 5 4 3 2 1 0 9 8

This book was set in Times Roman by Hemisphere Publishing Corporation. The editor was Mark A. Meschter, the production supervisor was Miriam Gonzalez, and the typesetter was Sandi Stancil. Cover design by Tammy Marshall.
Book Crafters Inc. was printer and binder.

Library of Congress Cataloging-in Publication Data

Anxiety in sports : an international perspective / edited by Dieter
    Hackfort and Charles D. Spielberger.
        p. cm.—(The Series in health psychology and behavioral
    medicine)
        Bibliography: p.
        Includes index.
        1. Sports—Psychological aspects. 2. Anxiety. I. Hackfort,
    Dieter. II. Spielberger, Charles Donald. III. Series.
    GV706.4.A58 1988
    796'.01—dc 19
ISBN 0-89116-754-4
ISSN 8756-467X

Contents

II
ANXIETY AND PERFORMANCE IN SPORTS

III
ANXIETY CONTROL IN SPORTS

Contributors

Apitzsch, Erwin   Nordmannavägen 4, S-223 75 Lund, Sweden

Ellickson, Kathleen A.   Sport Psychology Laboratory, University of Wisconsin-Madison, 2000 Observatory Drive, Madison, WI 53706, USA

Fuchs, C. Zvi   Zinman College of Physical Education, The Wingate Institute, Natanya, Israel 42902

Hackfort, Dieter   Institut für Sport und Sportwissenschaft der Universität Heidelberg, Im Neuenheimer Feld 710, D-6900 Heidelberg, FRG

Hahn, Erwin   Bundesinstitut für Sportwissenschaft, Carl-Diem-Weg, D-5000 Köln 41, FRG

Hanin, Yuri L.   Podvoskogo Str. 14/1, Leningrad - 193313, USSR

Hosek, Vaclav   FTVS UK, Ujezd 450, 11807 Praha, Czechoslovakia

Kerr, John H.   Department of Physical Education, Nijenrode University, Nijenrode, The Netherlands

Machac, Milos   Nad Hercovkou 9, 18200 Praha 8, Czechoslovakia

Machacova, Helena   Nad Hercovkou 9, 18200 Praha 8, Czechoslovakia

Mahoney, Michael J.   Personal Development Laboratory, Counseling Psychology, University of California, Santa Barbara, CA 93106, USA

Man, Frantisek   Pedagogical Faculty, Department of Psychology, Ceske Budejovice, Jeronymova 10, Czechoslovakia

Meyers, Andrew W.   Center for Applied Psychological Research, Department of Psychology, Memphis State University, Memphis, TN 38152, USA

Morgan, William P.   Sport Psychology Laboratory, University of Wisconsin-Madison, 2000 Observatory Drive, Madison, WI 53706, USA

Nideffer, Robert M.   12468 Bodega Way, San Diego, CA 92128, USA

Sanderson, Frank H.   Department of Sport and Recreation Studies, Liverpool Polytechnic, Byrom Str., Liverpool L 33 AF, England

Schulz, Peter   Fachbereich I der Universität Trier, Postfach 3825, D-5500 Trier, FRG

Schwenkmezger, Peter   Fachbereich I der Universität Trier, Postfach 3825, D-5500 Trier, FRG

Smith, Ronald E.   Psychology Department, NI-25, University of Washington, Seattle, WA 98195, USA

Spielberger, Charles D.   Center for Research in Behavioral Medicine & Health Psychology, University of South Florida, Tampa, FL 33620, USA

Suinn, Richard M.   Department of Psychology, Colorado State University, Ft. Collins, CO 80523, USA

Weinberg, Robert   Physical Education and Dance, College of Education,
North Texas State University, P.O. Box 13857, Denton, TX 76203-3857, USA

Zaichkowsky, Leonard D.   School of Education, Division of Instructional
Development, Boston University, 605 Commonwealth Avenue, Boston, MA
02215, USA

Foreword

Research on the effects of anxiety and other personality factors on athletic performance has been of major interest to the European Federation of Sports Psychology/Federation Europeéne de Psychologie des Sports et des Activites Corporelles (FEPSAC) since the founding of the society in the late 1960s. The primary goals of FEPSAC are to stimulate scientific work in sports psychology and to encourage social and scientific relations among individuals and groups in this field. In keeping with these objectives, FEPSAC strives to promote closer working relationships between coaches and behavioral and medical scientists working in sports psychology.

As the president of FEPSAC (G.S.) and the director of the FEPSAC Anxiety-in-Sport Project (E.A.) at the time work on this volume began, we are especially pleased to see the publication of a book that so clearly exemplifies the goals of the society. We are also grateful for this opportunity to note several significant landmark events relating to the FEPSAC Anxiety-in-Sport Project that contributed to the preparation of this volume.

Many coaches are intensely interested in understanding the personality of their athletes, especially how emotions and personality enhance or inhibit performance in competitive sports. To stimulate cooperation and to help bridge the gap between coaches and psychologists, FEPSAC's first international project on personality and sports was initiated in 1973. It was determined at the outset that the instruments and techniques for personality assessment should not be limited to certain languages and that test administration must be relatively brief and objective in order to collect a large amount of data. The Minnesota Multiphasic Personality Inventory (MMPI; Hathaway & McKinley, 1933) was selected as the major instrument to be used in the FEPSAC project because this test was the most widely used objective measure of personality throughout the world. The MMPI was adapted for the FEPSAC project by Peter Blaser and Annemarie Gehring; the total number of items was reduced from 556 to 221.

The abbreviated MMPI was administered in 10 different languages to 294 football players and 213 track-and-field athletes from 9 countries. The results of the FEPSAC MMPI study were discussed at a research workshop in Magglingen, Switzerland, in March 1975 and at the FEPSAC Congress in Edinburgh in September of the same year. On both occasions there was general agreement that the society should continue to collect and evaluate data on the use of psychological tests in sports. It was also concluded that the best way to further stimulate and facilitate international cooperation would be for FEPSAC to initiate a new research project.

During the 1978 IAAP International Congress of Psychology in Munich, the FEPSAC Managing Council met with Charles D. Spielberger to discuss recent applications of his State-Trait Anxiety Inventory (STAI) in research on athletic competition and motor behavior. The STAI seemed well suited for research in sports psychology because it was relatively brief (40 items), easily administered, and objectively scored (Spielberger, Gorsuch, & Lushene, 1970) and had been used successfully in a number of studies of motor skills and athletic performance (Spielberger, 1971, 1983). Could the STAI provide answers to coaches' questions about the anxiety of athletes? How does anxiety affect sports performance? Should the FEPSAC start an international project on anxiety in sports? These questions were discussed further at the FEPSAC Congress at Varna in 1979 and at the meeting of the Managing Council in Budapest in 1980. It was decided that FEPSAC would initiate and sponsor a new cooperative project on anxiety in sports and that the project would examine applications of the STAI and other tests used to measure anxiety in sports-related contexts. Erwin Apitzsch was appointed as project director.

The goal of the first phase of the FEPSAC Anxiety-in-Sport Project was to conduct a survey of the use of anxiety tests in sports psychology. A questionnaire was sent to the representatives of the FEPSAC member countries and to all persons known to be using anxiety measures in sports psychology research. Partly as a result of the stimulation provided by the FEPSAC project, anxiety in sports has been a theme at many international conferences, including the FEPSAC Congress in Varna in 1979 and the Congress of the International Society of Sport Psychology (ISSP) in Ottawa in 1981. This theme was also the topic of a symposium at the West German Society of Sport Psychology (ASP) in Kiel in 1982.

In responding to the FEPSAC survey, researchers were asked to submit one-page summaries of their investigations. From the returned questionnaires a list of investigations of anxiety in sports—either completed, ongoing, or planned—was compiled. The list of studies was first distributed by FEPSAC to all participants in this collaborative effort in July 1981, systematically updated, as information about new studies was received, and distributed again in January 1983. Thus, everyone involved in the FEPSAC project was informed about current research on anxiety in sports. Contacts among investigators, and between researchers and interested coaches, was also stimulated, encouraged, and facilitated.

A detailed report based on the information collected in the Anxiety-in-Sport Project was compiled by Apitzsch (1983) and distributed to the participants in the 1983 FEPSAC Congress held in Magglingen, Switzerland, in September 1983. The Apitzsch Report included summaries of 44 investigations carried out in 13 languages in 11 different countries. In addition, several theoretical and research papers relating to the general theme invited from leading authorities in these fields were included. The distribution of the Apitzsch Report at the 1983 FEPSAC Congress stimulated extensive dialogue among the participants. An interesting opportunity was also provided at the conference for the participants to "get in touch with" their own anxiety by making a parachute jump. Several participants jumped for the first time in their lives! Afterwards there were panel discussions about the experience of the jumpers.

The publication based on the 1983 Magglingen Congress Proceedings, entitled *Excellence and Emotional States in Sport* (Schilling & Herren, 1985), completed the FEPSAC Anxiety-in-Sport Project. Although much progress was made, we know that we are just beginning to understand the influence of anxiety in sports.

Moreover, it is apparent that further progress will require intensive and continuing discussion among anxiety researchers, coaches, and athletes and between sport psychologists and other behavioral and medical scientists.

We are extremely pleased that the Magglingen Congress provided an opportunity for Professors Spielberger and Hackfort to initiate planning for this volume on *Anxiety in Sports: An International Perspective*. The work was actually begun in 1985 during an extended visit by Professor Hackfort to Professor Spielberger's Center for Research in Behavioral Medicine and Health Psychology at the University of South Florida. This state-of-the-art volume is comprised of original theoretical papers and reports of empirical studies by outstanding investigators from Europe and North America in the fields of anxiety and sports psychology research. Its publication in the Series on Health Psychology and Behavioral Medicine brings research on sports psychology to the attention of behavioral and medical scientists who may not be familiar with this relatively new field.

Work on sports-related anxiety stimulated by the FEPSAC project was brought to the attention of the general scientific community at a conference on stress and emotions in Budapest in 1986. Also, at this meeting Professor Paul Kunath, president of FEPSAC, invited Professor Hackfort to serve as the director of a new project on emotions in sports. We trust that the fruitful collaboration between Professors Hackfort and Spielberger will continue in this new project. We also welcome the cooperation of the International Society for Sport Psychology (ISSP) in helping us to extend this collaborative research program throughout the world.

REFERENCES

Apitzsch, E. (Ed.) (1983). *Anxiety in Sport.* Magglingen: ETS.

Hathaway, S. R., & McKinley, J. C. (1933). *Manual for the Minnesota Multiphasic Personality Inventory.* New York: Psychological Corporation.

Schilling, G., & Herren, K. (Eds.) (1985). *Proceedings of the VIth FEPSAC Congress.* Magglingen: ETS.

Spielberger, C. D. (1971). Trait-state anxiety and motor behavior. *Journal of Motor Behavior, 3,* 265–279.

Spielberger, C. D. (1983). *Manual for the State-Trait Anxiety Inventory (Form Y).* Palo Alto, CA: Consulting Psychologists Press.

Spielberger, C. D., Gorsuch, R. L., & Lushene, R. E. (1970). *The State-Trait Anxiety Inventory (Test Manual).* Palo Alto, CA: Consulting Psychologists Press.

Guido Schilling
Zurich, Switzerland

Erwin Apitzsch
Lund, Sweden

Preface

This volume brings together the current theory and research on sports-related anxiety of leading investigators from a number of western and socialist countries. Individual chapters bridge different cultures and research traditions, while describing diverse applications of a wide range of concepts, methods, and research strategies. The contributors include authors from nine countries: Czechoslovakia (CSSR), Federal Republic of Germany (FRG), Great Britain (GB), Israel, The Netherlands, the Soviet Union (USSR), Sweden, Switzerland, and the United States (USA).

The historical background and the *zeitgeist* factors that contributed to the development of this volume are described in the foreword by Guido Schilling (Switzerland) and Erwin Apitzsch (Sweden). The volume itself is divided into four major parts: Theory and Assessments, Anxiety and Performance, Anxiety Control in Sports, and Perspectives in Sport Psychology. In the final chapter (Part IV), the editors examine trends in anxiety theory and research in sports psychology that are reported in the other chapters and endeavor to relate these to relevant research in personality, social, clinical, and health psychology.

The five chapters in Part I present varying theoretical perspectives and report the findings of a number of empirical investigations of stress and anxiety in sports contexts. Charles D. Spielberger (USA) and Frank H. Sanderson (GB), in Chapters 1 and 4, examine the influence of the trait-state model in sports psychology research and describe several different approaches to measuring anxiety as an emotional state and individual differences in anxiety proneness as a personality trait. In Chapter 2, Yuri L. Hanin (USSR) introduces the concepts of "interpersonal" and "intragroup" anxiety as major components of the emotional reactions of athletes in sports practice and competition. Dieter Hackfort and Peter Schulz (FRG), in Chapter 3, differentiate between worry and emotionality as components of state anxiety, outline the assumptions of Action Theory that pertain to anxiety in sports, and report research findings of studies carried out in laboratory and real-life sports settings. Methodological problems encountered in measuring sports-related anxiety are considered in Chapter 5 by Dieter Hackfort and Peter Schwenkmezger (FRG).

The five chapters in Part II examine anxiety-performance relationships that are of central interest to sports scientists and practitioners. In Chapter 6, Michael J. Mahoney and Andrew W. Meyers (USA) compare traditional and "cognitive-developmental" approaches to sports psychology. Robert Weinberg (USA), in Chapter 7, describes a new orientation in sports psychology research that focuses on movement as a process and the patterning of neuromuscular energy. Robert M. Nideffer (USA) endeavors in Chapter 8 to bridge the gap between sports research and practice, demonstrating the influence of attention and interpersonal processes on anxiety and performance. In Chapter 9, John H.

Kerr (The Netherlands) discusses several applications of Reversal Theory in sports psychology research. A broad framework for evaluating the effects of various emotions in sports is proposed by Erwin Hahn (FRG) in Chapter 10.

Theoretical concepts, empirical findings, and intervention strategies relating to the control of anxiety and athletic burnout are considered in Part III. William P. Morgan and Kathleen A. Ellickson (USA), in Chapter 11, examine possible anxiolytic effects of exercise on physical and mental health. In Chapter 12, Richard M. Suinn (USA) discusses, from a behavioral perspective, specific stress management approaches that have proved effective in reducing the anxiety of athletes, while in Chapter 13 Leonard D. Zaichkowsky (USA) and C. Zvi Fuchs (Israel) describe biofeedback-assisted self-regulation procedures that they have successfully used to help athletes manage stress.

Innovative procedures for controlling anxiety in sports competition are reported by two groups of investigators from Czechoslovakia. Impressive research findings on applications of a Relaxation-Activation Method specially designed to control anxiety in prestart situations are described by Milos Machac and Helena Machacova (CSSR) in Chapter 14. In Chapter 15, Vaclav Hosek and Frantisek Man (CSSR) report findings from their studies in which achievement motivation training and psycho- and sociodrama were used to reduce anxiety in top athletes. In the final chapter of Part III, Ronald E. Smith (USA) proposes a theoretical framework for interpreting the cumulative effects of stress and emotions on athletic burnout and presents evidence of the usefulness of two specific intervention strategies for preventing burnout.

The contents of *Anxiety in Sports: An International Perspective* will be of interest to behavioral and medical scientists and practitioners in a number of disciplines who are concerned with sports-related anxiety, anxiety-performance relationships, and emotions and health. Many of the innovations reported by colleagues from Europe have not previously been published in English-language sources. We hope this volume will serve to stimulate further basic and applied research in sports psychology and facilitate the integration of theory and research on anxiety in sports with relevant theory in psychology and the social and medical sciences.

We would like to express our deepest appreciation to Guido Schilling for his role in stimulating and encouraging the development of this volume, to the European Federation of Sports Psychology (FEPSAC) for inviting us to participate in its anxiety research program, and to the authors of the individual chapters whose expertise, enthusiasm, and dedication ensure a bright future for sports psychology. We also thank Susan Krasner and Virginia Berch of the University of South Florida for their assistance in preparing the manuscript for publication.

Dieter Hackfort
Charles D. Spielberger

I

ANXIETY IN SPORTS: THEORY AND ASSESSMENT

1

Stress and Anxiety in Sports

Charles D. Spielberger

The importance of anxiety and other emotional and personality factors in sports competition has been recognized for many years (e.g., Kroll, 1970; Martens, 1971, 1975; Singer, 1975). Consider the following observation of Howard S. Slusher in his influential book, *Man, Sport and Existence* (1967, p. 192):

> *As it is in most aspects of life, anxiety is present in sport. . . Each time man "takes the field," he not only lives with anxiety, he embraces it. It allows him and, in fact, motivates him, toward greater realization of his skill in the contest. . . Sport encourages man to live with anxieties as opposed to the psychiatric school advocating the "cure" of anxiety.*

In a similar vein, Rainer Martens (1977, p. 3) has raised cogent questions regarding the influence of anxiety-related cognitive processes on performance in sports competition: "What causes athletes to become uptight? Why do some athletes 'rise to the occasion' in intense competition while others 'buckle under the pressure?' What's 'in the head' is just as important in determining a winner, and in having competitive sports be an enjoyable experience."

Interest in the role of anxiety in sports competition has stimulated a substantial amount of research among sports psychologists over the past twenty years. Moreover, research in sports psychology has kept abreast of advances in

This chapter is based in part on invited papers that were presented at: The Sixth Congress of the European Federation of Sports Psychology, Magglingen/Macolin, Switzerland, September 5–9, 1983; the First Israeli National Congress on the Psychology and Sociology of Sport and Physical Eduction, The Wingate Institute, Netanya, Israel, April 11–13, 1982; and the Annual Meeting of the North American Society for the Psychology of Sport and Physical Activity, Tallahassee, Florida, May 23, 1978. The questions, and comments of the participants at these conferences are acknowledged with appreciation. I would also like to thank Dr. Guido Schilling for his role in initiating and organizing the FEPSAC Anxiety Project (Apitzsch, 1983), and arranging for me to participate in the Congress at which the findings of research on anxiety in sports were presented.

relevant psychological theory. For example, although the state-trait distinction has been only recently accepted in personality research, Professor Ema Geron made this a central theme more than a decade ago in her keynote address at a Wingate Institute Symposium on Psychological Assessment in Sport. Specifically, Geron called for identifying and investigating ". . . individual traits, personality profiles and interpersonal relations of athletes before, during and after competition" (1978, p. 5). With regard to the assessment of anxiety in sports, it is especially pleasing for the writer to note that the *State-Trait Anxiety Inventory* (STAI: Spielberger, 1983; Spielberger, Gorsuch & Lushene, 1970) has been used in numerous investigations in a variety of sports, including research on basketball, football, tennis, gymnastics, swimming, rowing, wrestling, and running — from recreational jogging to professional marathons.

The main goal of this chapter is to present a conceptual framework for examining the extensive research literature on stress and anxiety in sports. Recent psychometric developments in the measurement of anxiety as a transitory emotional state and individual differences in anxiety proneness as a personality trait are also discussed. The findings of several representative studies in which the STAI was used to assess anxiety are briefly reviewed to provide examples of contemporary research on stress and anxiety in sports settings. A bibliography of sports psychology studies in which the STAI was used to assess state and trait anxiety is provided in the Appendix to this chapter.

STRESS, THREAT, AND ANXIETY: DEFINITIONS AND CONCEPTS

Stress refers to a complex psychobiological process that consists of three major elements: stressors, perceptions or appraisals of danger (threats), and emotional reactions. The stress process is generally initiated by situations or circumstances (stressors) that are perceived or interpreted (appraised) as dangerous, potentially harmful, or frustrating. If a stressor is perceived as dangerous or threatening, irrespective of the presence of an objective danger, an emotional reaction (anxiety) is evoked. Thoughts or memories that are perceived as threatening can also evoke anxiety reactions as readily as real dangers in the external world.

Anxiety as an emotional state (S-Anxiety) consists of subjective, consciously experienced feelings of tension, apprehension, nervousness and worry, and heightened arousal or activation of the autonomic nervous system. Since perceived threat mediates the relationship between a stressor and the intensity of an anxiety reaction, anxiety states vary in intensity and fluctuate over time as a function of the amount of perceived threat. Thus, the relationship among the three major elements of the stress process may be conceptualized as consisting of the following temporal sequence of events:

Stressor → Perception and appraisal of threat → S-Anxiety

The term *stressor* refers to situations or circumstances that are characterized by some degree of objective physical or psychological danger. Stressful circumstances are ubiquitous; they are encountered every day and at every stage of human development. There is even evidence that stress before birth influences both the mother and the fetus, and may contribute to obstetric complications and birth defects (Spielberger & Jacobs, 1979). Infants and young children meet unavoidable pressures in weaning and toilet training, and in the process of learning social skills and acquiring a formal education. Pressures at work and the stress inherent in marriage and family relationships present new challenges to contend with throughout the life span. Retirement and old age are not only stages of life, but are themselves among the pervasive sources of stress in modern society.

The concept of *threat* refers to an individual's perception or appraisal of a situation as potentially dangerous or harmful. Reactions to a particular stressor will depend on the degree to which it is seen as threatening. Threat appraisals are influenced, of course, by the objective characteristics of a situation, and objectively dangerous stressors are realistically appraised as threatening by most people. But the thoughts and memories stimulated by a particular event, along with an individual's coping skills and previous experience with similar circumstances, may often have an even greater impact. Consequently, the same stimulus may be seen as a threat by one person, a challenge by another, and as largely irrelevant by a third.

The experience of threat is, essentially, a state of mind which has two main characteristics: (1) It is future oriented, generally involving the anticipation of a potentially harmful event that has not yet happened; (2) It is mediated by complex mental processes, i.e., perception, thought, memory and judgment, which are involved in the appraisal process. Threat appraisals of present or future danger serve an important function in producing emotional reactions that mobilize an individual to take action to avoid harm. But even when there is no objective danger, the perception or appraisal of a situation as threatening transmits the essential message of stress, which results in the arousal of an *anxiety state*.

Anxiety states are emotional reactions that consist of a unique combination of: (1) feelings of tension, apprehension and nervousness; (2) unpleasant thoughts (worries), and (3) physiological changes. An important characteristic of S-Anxiety is that it varies in intensity and fluctuates over time. Calmness and serenity indicate the absence of S-Anxiety; tension, apprehension, nervousness and worry accompany moderate levels; intense feelings of fear and fright, catastrophic thoughts, and disorganized panic behaviors are associated with very high levels of S-Anxiety.

The physiological changes associated with increased S-Anxiety include: elevated heart rate and blood pressure; faster, shallower, more intense breathing; dryness of the mouth; dilation of the pupils; erection of the hair; and increased perspiration. In addition, many muscles tense and contract to prepare the body for rapid and vigorous action; more white corpuscles are produced to help fight infection; and low priority functions, like eating and the digestion of food, are suspended.

The term anxiety is also used to refer to relatively stable individual differences in anxiety proneness as a personality disposition or trait. In contrast to S-Anxiety, *trait anxiety* (T-Anxiety) may or may not be manifested directly in behavior, but can be inferred from the frequency that an individual experiences elevations in S-Anxiety. People who are high in T-Anxiety are more anxiety-prone, i.e., they perceive and/or appraise a wider range of situations as more dangerous or threatening than do individuals who are low T-Anxiety. Since high trait anxious people are more vulnerable to stress, they experience S-Anxiety reactions more frequently, and with greater intensity, than do individuals who are low in T-Anxiety.

Empirical evidence supporting the state-trait distinction in anxiety research was first demonstrated in the factor analytic studies of Cattell and Scheier (1961). It is now generally accepted that a comprehensive theory of stress and anxiety must distinguish between anxiety as a transitory emotional state, and individual differences in anxiety as a relatively stable personality trait. An adequate theory must also differentiate between the stimulus conditions (stressors) that evoke anxiety states, the mental processes that mediate the perception or appraisal of particular stressors as threatening, and the psychological defenses that serve to reduce the intensity of S-Anxiety reactions once they have been aroused.

Trait-State Anxiety Theory provides a general framework for examining the major variables in research on stress and anxiety, and suggests possible relationships among these variables (Spielberger, 1966a, 1972, 1979). In addition to delineating the properties of S-Anxiety and T-Anxiety as psychological constructs, the theory specifies the characteristics of stressful situations that evoke differential levels of S-Anxiety in persons who differ in T-Anxiety, recognizes the centrality of cognitive appraisal in evoking anxiety states, and notes the important role of defense mechanisms in serving to eliminate or reduce S-Anxiety.

High levels of S-Anxiety are experienced as intensely unpleasant. Therefore, if an individual cannot avoid a stressor or lacks the skills needed to cope with a threatening situation, he/she may be overwhelmed with S-Anxiety, and may initiate defensive processes to reduce this intensely unpleasant emotional state. *Defense mechanisms* involve psychobiological processes that in some way modify or distort the perception or appraisal of a situation. To the extent that a defense mechanism is successful, the circumstances that evoke anxiety are seen as less threatening, and there is a corresponding reduction in S-Anxiety. But the individual pays the price of investing large amounts of energy in psychobiological processes devoted entirely to reducing S-Anxiety while the actual source of the perceived danger, i.e., the underlying circumstances that caused the S-Anxiety reaction, remains unchanged.

In sum, the concept of stress refers to a complex psychobiological process that consists of a sequence of temporally ordered events. This process may be initiated by any external event or internal stimulus that is perceived or appraised as dangerous or threatening. The appraisal of a particular circumstance as threatening is influenced by a person's ability, coping skills and past experience, as well as by the objective danger inherent in the situation. Situations or circumstances in which personal adequacy is evaluated are likely to be perceived as more threatening by high T-Anxiety individuals than by persons low in trait anxiety. Once a stimulus or situation is appraised as threatening: (1) an S-Anxiety reaction will be evoked; (2) the intensity of this reaction will be proportional to the amount of threat the situation poses for the individual; and (3) S-Anxiety will remain elevated until the appraisal of the situation as threatening is altered by effective coping or defensive operations.

MEASUREMENT OF STRESS AND ANXIETY

Over the past 20 years, the *Social Readjustment Rating Scale* (SRRS) has been widely used to investigate the relationship between stressful life events and physical illness, with impressive results (e.g., Holmes & Rahe, 1967; Harman, Masuda, & Holmes, 1970), but these findings are only of marginal significance for sports psychology. Several new scales designed to assess stressful life events (Sarason, Johnson, & Siegel, 1978) and the 'hassles' that are experienced in daily life (Kanner, Coyne, Schaefer, & Lazarus, 1981) may eventually prove more useful in sports psychology than the SRRS. Although most studies of the stress process in sports have focused on the athletes' emotional reactions rather than the characteristics of the stressor situation, Martens (1977; Martens & Gill, 1976) has developed the Sports Competition Anxiety Test (SCAT) which was specifically designed to assess the anxiety experienced in sports settings.

The extensive research literature on the relation between anxiety and performance has especially important implications for sports psychology. In psychological research on learning and performance, the Taylor (1953) Manifest Anxiety Scale (MAS), one of the earliest measures of trait anxiety, has been used in numerous studies. In general, persons with high MAS scores perform more poorly on difficult learning tasks than persons with low anxiety, but on simple or easy tasks the performance of individuals with high anxiety was at times better than that of those with low anxiety (Spielberger, 1966b).

The IPAT Anxiety Scale was constructed by Cattell and Scheier (1963) to assess anxiety in clinical situations, but this scale has also been widely used in research. Despite differences in the definitions of anxiety that guided the development of the MAS and the IPAT Anxiety Scale, and in the methods of test construction and item format, these scales are highly correlated, providing evidence that T-Anxiety is a stable construct, and that the MAS and the IPAT scales are essentially equivalent measures.

The Affect Adjective Check List (AACL) was developed by Zuckerman and his associates to measure both state and trait anxiety (Zuckerman, 1960; Zuckerman & Lubin, 1965). The "General" form of the AACL measures T-Anxiety; respondents check adjectives such as tense, nervous and calm to indicate how they *generally* feel. In responding to the "Today" form of the AACL, which measures S-Anxiety, subjects check the same adjectives according to how they feel on the day the test is given. There is substantial evidence of the validity of the AACL "Today" form as a measure of S-Anxiety, but the AACL General Form typically correlates only moderately with other standard measures of T-Anxiety, such as the MAS and the IPAT. Therefore, the validity and usefulness of the AACL as a measure of T-Anxiety seems questionable.

The State-Trait Anxiety Inventory (STAI) was developed to provide reliable, relatively brief self-report measures of state and trait anxiety (Spielberger et al., 1970). The items for the STAI T-Anxiety scale were selected on the basis of their concurrent validity with the best available measures of T-Anxiety. Each of the 20 STAI T-Anxiety items correlated significantly with total scores on the MAS and the IPAT anxiety scales. In responding to the STAI T-Anxiety scale, subjects are instructed to report how they generally feel by rating the *frequency* that they have experienced symptoms of anxiety on the following 4-point scale: "Almost never";

"Sometimes"; "Often"; "Almost always." Representative STAI T-Anxiety items are:

I feel nervous and restless.
I worry too much over something that really doesn't matter.
I lack self-confidence.

Three important criteria guided the selection of items for the STAI S-Anxiety scale: (1) The primary criterion was construct validity. Each item was required to have a higher mean in *a priori* stressful situations, and a lower mean in relaxed situations than in nonstressful (neutral) situations; (2) Strong internal consistency was required for each item, and for the scale as a whole, as measured by item-remainder correlations and alpha coefficients; (3) Ease and brevity of administration were desired. Since rapid fluctuations in S-Anxiety may occur in a changing environment, a lengthy test might be insensitive to such variations and would also be unsuitable for assessing S-Anxiety in situations in which the time required to take the test might interfere with performance.

Representative items from the STAI S-Anxiety scale are: "I feel tense," "I feel upset," "I feel nervous." In responding to these items, subjects are asked to indicate how they feel *right now,* or at a specified time, by rating themselves on the following 4-point scale: (1) "Not at all," (2) "Somewhat," (3) "Moderately so," (4) "Very much so." Scores on the STAI S-Anxiety scale define a continuum of increasing intensity. Low S-Anxiety scores indicate calmness and serenity; intermediate scores indicate moderate levels of tension and nervousness; high scores reflect intense apprehension and fearfulness, approaching panic.

Over the past decade, the STAI has been used in more than 2500 studies (Spielberger, 1984), and has become the standard international measure of state and trait anxiety (Spielberger & Diaz-Guerrero, 1976, 1983, 1986). Translations and adaptations of the scale are available in more than 40 languages, and standardized editions are published commercially in Dutch, German, Italian, Portuguese and Spanish. A children's form of the scale is also available in many of these languages.

RESEARCH ON STRESS AND ANXIETY IN SPORTS

Research on stress and anxiety in sports has increased dramatically over the past decade (Apitzsch, 1983). This research has included investigations of anxiety effects on football, basketball, badminton, racquetball and tennis players, swimmers, runners, gymnasts, fencers, jugglers, and persons engaged in a wide variety of physical activities, ranging from routine exercise to climbing ladders, riding bicycles, and performing on treadmills. Individual differences in anxiety among participants in different sports and the impact of various forms of exercise on anxiety level have also been examined (e.g., see Hanin, Chapter 2; Sanderson, Chapter 4; Morgan & Ellickson, Chapter 12, Hosek & Man, Chapter 17, this volume).

The findings in sports psychology research provide substantial evidence that the STAI S-Anxiety scale is a sensitive index of the changes in anxiety level produced by practice, physical activity, perceived or experienced success or failure, and level of competition. While T-Anxiety has also been found to be related to some of these variables, situational factors and the skill and experience of an athlete seem to have greater impact on performance than individual differences in general anxiety proneness.

A number of investigators have reported that higher levels of S-Anxiety are experienced under game conditions than during practice. Decreases in S-Anxiety have also been reported as a function of practice (e.g., Hollingsworth, 1975; Milillo, 1976). For example, Klavora (1974) observed that S-Anxiety was lower in preseason practice than prior to competition in high school and college basketball and football players, and that S-Anxiety increased for college basketball players from regular season games to playoff competition. Similarly, Gill (1980) reported that S-Anxiety was higher for competitive volleyball players immediately prior to competition than during practice sessions, and Milillo (1976) observed that S-Anxiety was higher for marathoners, tennis players and archers just prior to competition than during practice, and was lower following competition.

Milillo also found a positive relationship between the amount of strenuous motoric activity required in a particular sport and level of S-Anxiety. State anxiety was highest in marathoners and lowest for archers, with tennis players falling in between these groups. In contrast, Morgan and his colleagues (Bahrke & Morgan, 1978; Morgan, 1973; Morgan & Horstman, 1976) have consistently observed that S-Anxiety decreases as a function of various physical activity, and similar findings have been reported by other investigators (Driscoll, 1975; Mitchum, 1976; Rhodes, 1980).

The experience of failure in sports activities generally results in higher levels of S-Anxiety. Noyes (1971) observed that S-Anxiety increased in college students given feedback that implied failure on two physical performance tasks. Scanlan (1977) and Martens and Gill (1976) have also reported increases in S-Anxiety following failure experiences. On the other hand, Sanderson and Ashton (1981) observed a significant decrease in S-Anxiety in female badminton players following a winning match.

Tannenbaum and Milgram (1978) compared the state and trait anxiety of students who voluntarily participated in competitive sports with the anxiety of noncompetitors. Three groups of Israeli physical education students (competitors in individual sports; competitors in group sports; noncompetitors) were evaluated. Both groups of competitive athletes scored substantially lower in T-Anxiety than the noncompetitors. Additionally, a large positive correlation ($r = .83$) was found between S-Anxiety and the *increase* in heart rate evoked by the stress of competition, i.e., the number of heart beats measured immediately prior to a competitive sports event was much higher than the competitors' heart rate when relaxed.

Over the past decade, Hanin and his colleagues (e.g., Hanin, 1977; Hanin, 1980; Hanin, 1986) have carried out extensive experimental investigations and clinical studies with Soviet athletes. This work has included the development of a sequence of diagnostic procedures for determining each athlete's zone of optimal functioning (ZOF), that is, the optimal level of S-Anxiety before a forthcoming contest, and the anticipated level of S-Anxiety on the first day of the contest. Each athlete's schedule of training activities was ". . . organized to facilitate optimalization of anxiety level according to the individual's ZOF" (Hanin, 1986, p. 61). These investigators found that the management of stress for most athletes required a reduction in the actual level of S-Anxiety, rather than increasing anxiety, which was accomplished by modifying the athletes' attitudes toward training and competition. Managing stress by regulating the athletes' anxiety level so that it falls within the ZOF generally facilitated achieving a superior performance level (see also Hanin, Chapter 2, this volume).

In most of the studies briefly described above, the impact of situational factors on S-Anxiety has been emphasized. It should be noted, however, that many sports psychologists are interested primarily in the effects of stress and anxiety on performance. Although a comprehensive review of this research is beyond the scope of the present chapter, it can be noted that high levels of S-Anxiety typically interfere with performance, whereas persons with very low S-Anxiety often lack the motivation to do well. In general, the relationship between anxiety and performance in sports competition approximates the inverted U-shaped function described many years ago by Yerkes and Dodson (1908). The recent work by Hanin and his colleagues further demonstrates that superior performance is associated with an "optimal level" of precompetition anxiety (see Hanin, Chapter 2, this volume).

SUMMARY

This chapter presents a conceptual framework for examining the growing research literature on stress and anxiety in sports psychology. Stress is viewed as a complex psychobiological process. The perception or appraisal of a situation or circumstance (stressor) as threatening results in the arousal of an anxiety state, which consists of feelings of tension, apprehension, nervousness and worry, and activation of the autonomic nervous system. Recent psychometric developments in the assessment of anxiety as a transitory emotional state and individual differences in anxiety proneness as a personality trait were discussed. The findings of a number of representative studies of stress and anxiety in sports settings were also reviewed. A bibliography of sports psychology studies in which anxiety was assessed with the *State-Trait Anxiety Inventory* is provided in an Appendix.

REFERENCES

Apitzsch, E. (Ed.). (1983). *Anxiety in sport.* Magglingen, Switzerland: Guido Schilling, ETS.

*Bahrke, M. S., & Morgan, W. P. (1978). Anxiety reduction following exercise and meditation. *Cognitive Therapy and Research, 2,* 323–333.

Cattell, R. B., & Scheier, I. H. (1961). *The meaning and measurement of neuroticism and anxiety.* New York: Ronald Press.

Cattell, R. B., & Scheier, I. H. (1963). *Handbook for the IPAT Anxiety Scale* (2nd ed.). Champaign, IL: Institute for Personality and Ability Testing.

*Driscoll, R. H. (1975). Exertion therapy: Rapid anxiety reduction using physical exertion and positive imagery. Unpublished doctoral dissertation, University of Colorado. *Dissertation Abstracts, 35,* 4647B.

*The asterisks identify exercise and sports psychology studies in which the State-Trait Anxiety Inventory (STAI) was used to measure anxiety. More than 100 additional studies in which the STAI was employed in sports psychology research are listed in the Appendix to this chapter. Detailed information about the psychometric properties of the STAI is reported in the Test Manuals for the adolescent and adult (Spielberger, 1983; Spielberger et al., 1970) and the children's (STAIC): Spielberger, 1973) forms of the scale.

Geron, E. (1978). Opening remarks. In U. Simri (Ed.), *Proceeding of an International Symposium on Psychological Assessment in Sport.* Netanya, Israel: Wingate Institute, pp. 5–6.

*Gill, D. L. (1980). Comparison of three measures of pre-competition arousal. *Perceptual and Motor Skills, 51,* 765–766.

*Hanin, Y. L. (1977). Social psychological problems of pre-competition preparation of athletes. In Y. Y. Kisseleu (Ed.), *Psychological problems of pre-competition preparation of qualified athletes.* Leningrad, LNIIFK, 86–97. (In Russian)

*Hanin, Y. L. (1980). Contemporary status and perspectives of psychological studies in sport. In V. M. Vydrin (Ed.), *Sport in contemporary society.* Moscow: Physical Culture and Sport Publishers, 124–173. (In Russian)

*Hanin, Y. L. (1987). Anxiety research in sports. In C. D. Spielberger, I. G. Sarason, & P. B. Defares (Eds.), *Stress and anxiety* (Vol. 11). New York: John Wiley & Sons.

Harman, D. C., Masuda, M., & Holmes, T. H. (1970). The Social Readjustment Rating Scale: A cross-cultural study of Western Europeans and Americans, *14,* 391–400.

Holmes, T. H., & Rahe, R. H. (1967). The Social Readjustment Rating Scale. *Journal of Psychosomatic Research, 11,* 213–218.

*Hollingsworth, B. (1975). Effects of performance goals and anxiety on learning a gross motor task. *Research Quarterly, 46,* 162–168.

Kanner, A. D., Coyne, J. C., Schaefer, C., & Lazarus, R. S. (1981). Comparison of two modes of stress management: Daily hassles and uplifts versus major life events. *Journal of Behavioral Medicine, 4,* 1–39.

*Klavora, P. (1974). State anxiety and athletic competition. Unpublished doctoral dissertation, The University of Alberta-Edmonton.

Kroll, W. (1970). Current strategies and problems in personality assessment of athletes. In L. E. Smith (Ed.), *Psychology of motor learning.* Chicago: Athletic Institute.

*Martens, R. (1971). Anxiety and motor behavior: A review. *Journal of Motor Behavior, 3,* 151–179.

Martens, R. (1975). The paradigmatic crises in American sport personology. *Sportwissenschaft, 5,* 9–24.

Martens, R. (1977). *Sport Competition Anxiety Test.* Champaign, IL: Human Kinetics Publishers.

*Martens, R., & Gill, D. L. (1976). State anxiety among successful and unsuccessful competitors who differ in competitive trait anxiety. *Research Quarterly, 47,* 698–708.

*Milillo, M. D. (1976). A study of trait anxiety, state anxiety, defense mechanisms and personality in three individual sport groups. Unpublished doctoral dissertation, University of Minnesota. *Dissertation Abstracts, 36,* 3058B.

*Mitchum, M. L. (1976). The effect of participation in a physically exerting leisure activity on state-anxiety level. Unpublished master's thesis, Florida State University.

*Morgan, W. P. (1973). Influence of acute physical activity on state anxiety. *Proceedings, National College Physical Education for Men, January,* 113–121.

*Morgan, W. P., & Horstman, D. H. (1976). Anxiety reduction following acute physical activity. *Medicine and Science in Sports, 8,* 62.

*Noyes, R. C. (1971). The effects of success and failure in physical performance upon state anxiety and bodily concern of college students varying in anxiety proneness. Unpublished doctoral dissertation, Florida State University. *Dissertation Abstracts, 31,* 4529A.

*Rhodes, D. L. (1980). Mens sana, corpore sano: A study of the effect of jogging on depression, anxiety and self concept. Unpublished doctoral dissertation, Duke University, 1980. *Dissertation Abstracts International, 41,* 1500A.

*Sanderson, F. H., & Ashton, M. K. (1981). Analysis of anxiety levels before and after badminton competition. *International Journal of Sports Psychology, 12,* 23–28.

Sarason, I. G., Johnson, J. H., & Siegel, J. M. (1978). Assessing the impact of life changes: Development of the Life Experience Survey. *Journal of Consulting and Clinical Psychology, 46,* 932–946.

*Scanlan, T. K. (1977). The effects of success-failure on the perception of threat in a competitive situation. *Research Quarterly, 48,* 144–153.

Singer, R. N. (1975). Sports psychology. *American Corrective Therapy Journal, 29,* 115–120.

Slusher, H. S. (1967). *Man, sport and existence.* Philadelphia: Lea & Febiger.

Spielberger, C. D. (1966a). Theory and research on anxiety. In C. D. Spielberger (Ed.), *Anxiety and behavior.* New York: Academic Press.

Spielberger, C. D. (1966b). The effects of anxiety on complex learning and academic achievement. In C. D. Spielberger (Ed.), *Anxiety and behavior,* pp. 361–398. New York: Academic Press.

Spielberger, C. D. (1972). Anxiety as an emotional state. In C. D. Spielberger (Ed.), *Anxiety: Current trends in theory and research.* (Vol. 1). New York: Academic Press.

Spielberger, C. D. (1979). *Understanding stress and anxiety.* London: Harper & Row.

Spielberger, C. D. (1983). *Manual for the State-Trait Anxiety Inventory (Revised).* Palo Alto, CA: Consulting Psychologists Press.

Spielberger, C. D. (1984). *State-Trait Anxiety Inventory: A Comprehensive Bibliography.* Palo Alto, CA: Consulting Psychologists Press.

Spielberger, C. D., & Diaz-Guerrero, R. (Eds.). (1976). *Cross-cultural anxiety* (Vol. 1). Washington, DC: Hemisphere.

Spielberger, C. D., & Diaz-Guerrero, R. (Eds.). (1983). *Cross-cultural anxiety* (Vol. 2). Washington, DC: Hemisphere.

Spielberger, C. D., & Diaz-Guerrero, R. (1986). *Cross-cultural anxiety* (Vol. 3). Washington, DC: Hemisphere.

Spielberger, C. D., Gorsuch, R. L., & Lushene, R. E. (1970). *STAI Manual for the State-Trait Anxiety Inventory ("Self-Evaluation Questionnaire").* Palo Alto, CA: Consulting Psychologists Press.

Spielberger, C. D., & Jacobs, G. A. (1979). Maternal emotions, life stress and obstetric complications. In L. Zichella & P. Pancheri (Eds.), *Psychoneuroendocrinology in reproduction.* Amsterdam: Elsevier/North-Holland Biomedical Press.

Spielberger, C. D., Jacobs, G. A., Russell, S., & Crane, R. S. (1982). Assessment of anger: The State Trait Anger Scale. In J. N. Butcher & C. D. Spielberger (Eds.), *Advances in personality assessment* (Vol. 2). Hillsdale, NJ: LEA.

Taylor, J. A. (1953). A personality scale of manifest anxiety. *Journal of Abnormal and Social Psychology, 48,*. 285–290.

*Tenenbaum, G., & Milgram, R. M. (1978). Trait and state anxiety in Israeli student athletes. *Journal of Clinical Psychology, 34,* 691–693.

Yerkes, R. M., & Dodson, J. D. (1908). The relation of strength of stimulus to rapidity of habit formation. *Journal of Comparative and Neurological Psychology, 18,* 459.

Zuckerman, M. (1960). Development of an Affect Adjective Check List for the measurement of anxiety. *Journal of Consulting Psychology, 24,* 457–462.

Zuckerman, M., & Lubin, B. (1965). *Manual for the multiple affect adjective checklist.* San Diego, CA: Educational & Industrial Testing Service.

APPENDIX: STAI/SPORTS PSYCHOLOGY REFERENCES

Abood, D. A. (1982). The effects of acute physical exercise on the state anxiety and mental performance of college women (Doctoral dissertation, University of Tennessee, 1981). *Dissertation Abstracts International, 42,* 3640B.

Allawy, M. (1983). Anxiety among Egyptian athletes as measured by the Arabic *State-Trait Anxiety Inventory.* In E. Apitzsch (Ed.), *Anxiety in sport* (p. 26). Magglingen, Switzerland: Federation Europeenne de Psychologie des Sports et des Activites Corporelles (FEPSAC).

Allawy, M., & Hassan, Z. (1983). Differences in competitive trait and state anxiety among track and field competitors according to some selected variables. In E. Apitzsch (Ed.), *Anxiety in sport* (p. 28). Magglingen, Switzerland:FEPSAC.

Andres, F. F. (1978). Changes in state anxiety and urine catecholamines produced during treadmill running (Doctoral dissertation, University of Pittsburgh, 1977). *Dissertation Abstracts International, 42,* 4178B.

Apitzsch, E. (1973). Pre-start anxiety in competitive swimmers. Paper presented at the meeting of the *Third International Congress of Sport Psychology,* Madrid, Spain, June 25–29.

Bahrke, M. S. (1978). Influence of acute physical activity and non-cultic meditation on state anxiety (Doctoral dissertation, University of Wisconsin-Madison, 1977). *Dissertation Abstracts International, 38,.* 5987A.

Balog, L. F. (1983). The effects of exercise on muscle tension and subsequent muscle-relaxation training. *Research Quarterly for Exercise and Sport, 54,* 119–125.

Barton, K. (1970). Block manipulation by children as a function of social reinforcement, anxiety, arousal, and ability pattern (Doctoral dissertation, George Peabody College for Teachers, 1969). *Dissertation Abstracts, 30,* 5219B.

Basler, M. L., Fisher, A. C., & Mumford, N. L. (1976). Arousal and anxiety correlates of gymnastic performance. *Research Quarterly, 47,* 586–589.

Berg, H., & Ebel, H. C. (1976). Anxiety, task-experience, and vocal-style of judges as determinants of performer confidence. *Perceptual and Motor Skills, 43,* 515–521.

Blacksmith, W. C. (1977). The effect of systematic desensitization of prematch anxiety among collegiate wrestlers (Doctoral dissertation, West Virginia University, 1977). *Dissertation Abstracts International, 38,* 1974A.

Blumenthal, J. A., Williams, R. S., Needels, T. L., & Wallace, A. G. (1982). Psychological changes accompany aerobic exercise in healthy middle-aged adults. *Psychosomatic Medicine, 44,* 529–536.

Brodie, D. A., et al. (1983). STAI changes during the preparation for a parachute drop. In E. Apitzsch (Ed.), *Anxiety in Sport* (p. 30). Magglingen, Switzerland: FEPSAC.

Burton, E. C. (1971). State and trait anxiety, achievement motivation and skill attainment in college women. *Research Quarterly, 42,* 139–144. Based on doctoral dissertation, submitted to the Department of Psychology, Ohio State University, 1970.

Chait, H. N. (1974). Stress and task performance: A comparison of physical and psychological stressors. Unpublished doctoral dissertation, Indiana University.

Cheun, S. Y. (1985). *Relaxation training and precompetition anxiety levels of young gymnasts.* Unpublished master's thesis, Springfield College, Springfield, MA.

Corbin, C. B., Barnett, M. A., & Matthews, K. A. (1979). The effects of direct and indirect competition on children's state anxiety. *Journal of Leisure Research, 11,* 271–277.

Deikis, J. G. (1983). Stress inoculation training: Effects on anxiety, self-efficacy, and performance in divers (Doctoral dissertation, Temple University, 1983). *Dissertation Abstracts International, 44,* 303B.

Diddle, T. (1973). The effects of physical conditioning programs on self-esteem and state-trait anxiety in college women. Unpublished master's thesis, University of Colorado.

Dorsey, J. A. (1977). The effects of biofeedback assisted desensitization training on state anxiety and performance of college male gymnasts (Doctoral dissertation, Boston University, 1976. *Dissertation Abstracts International, 37,* 5680A.

Douglas, R. L. (1976). Differences in anxiety levels, neuroticism, and extraversion associated with three levels of physical fitness in females (Doctoral dissertation, University of Southern Mississippi, 1975). *Dissertation Abstracts, 36,* 4150–4151B.

Fabian, L. A. (1974). Effects of coeducational environment and sex of instructor on anxiety and achievement of students in college beginning swimming classes. Unpublished master's thesis, Pennsylvania State University.

Faulkner, M. K. (1983). A study of pre-match state anxiety in Northhamptonshire County women's hockey teams. In E. Apitzsch (Ed.), *Anxiety in sport,* (p. 34). Magglingen, Switzerland: FEPSAC.

Griffin, M. R. (1972). An analysis of state and trait anxiety experienced in sports competition by women at different age levels (Doctoral dissertation, Louisiana State University, 1971). *Dissertation Abstracts, 32,* 3758A.

Griffiths, T. J., Steel, D. H., & Vaccaro, P. (1978). Anxiety levels of beginning scuba students. *Perceptual and Motor Skills, 47,* 312–314.

Griffiths, T. H., Steel, D. H., & Vaccaro, P. (1979). Relationship between anxiety and performance in scuba diving. *Perceptual and Motor Skills, 48,* 1009–1010.

Hall, E. G., Church, G. E., & Stone, M. (1980). Relationship of birth order to selected personality characteristics of nationally ranked Olympic weight lifters. *Perceptual and Motor Skills, 51,* 971–976.

Hanin, Y. L. (1978). The problem of psychological tension of environmental influences in the process of management of athletes preparation. *The management of the process of athletes preparation: Materials of the 4th All-Russian Scientific Methodological Conference.* Leningrad: LNIIFK, 100–103.

Hanin, Y. L. (1980). A study of anxiety in sports. In W. F. Straub (Ed.), *Sport psychology: An analysis of athlete behavior* (2nd Ed.). Ithaca, NY: Movement Publications.

Hanin, Y. L. (1980). Methods of assessment of pre-contest and interpersonal anxiety in athletes. In *Sport in the contemporary society: Pre-Olympic Congress in Tblisi.* Moscow: Pedagogics and Psychology, 218 (In Russian).

Hanin, Y. L. (1980). *Psychology of communication in sport.* Moscow: Physical Culture and Sport Publishers (In Russian).

Hanin, Y. L. (Ed.) (In press). *Stress and anxiety in sport.* Moscow: Physical Culture and Sport Publishers (In Russian).

Hanin, Y. L., & Bulanova, G. V. (1979). Emotional state of students in sports and study groups. *Theory and Practice of Physical Culture, 4,* 45–47 (In Russian).

Hanin, Y. L., & Bulanova, G. V. (1981). Status and anxiety state of students in groups of varying social maturity. *The Questions of Psychology, 5,* 124–129 (In Russian).

Hanin, Y. L., & Kopysov, V. S. (1977). A-State of competing athletes during communication with different seconds. *Theory and Practice of Physical Culture, 2,* 37–39 (In Russian).

Hanin, Y. L., & Kopysov, V. S. (1978). Anxiety state of competing athletes during communication with various seconds. In *Weightlifting.* Moscow: Physical Culture and Sport Publishers, 49–52 (In Russian).

Harrigan, J. M. (1981). A component analysis of yoga: The effects of diaphragmatic breathing and stretching postures on anxiety, personality and somatic/behavioral complaints (Doctoral dissertation, Pennsylvania State University, 1981). *Dissertation Abstracts International, 42,* 1489A.

Hilyer, J. C., Wilson, D. G., Dillon, C., Caro, L., Jenkins, C., Spencer, W. A., Meadows, M., & Booker, W. (1982). Physical fitness training and counseling as treatment for youthful offenders. *Journal of Counseling Psychology, 29,* 292–303.

Holmes, D. S., Solomon, S., & Rump, B. S. (1982). Cardiac and subjective response to cognitive challenge and to controlled physical exercise by male and female coronary prone (Type A) and non-coronary prone persons. *Journal of Psychosomatic Medicine, 26,* 309–316.

Huddleston, S., & Gill, D. L. (1981). State anxiety as a function of skill level and proximity to competition. *Research Quarterly for Exercise & Sport, 52,* 31–34.

Janak, V., Mazurov, O., Kopecka, T. (1983). Trait and situational anxiety influence upon a sport performance. In E. Apitzsch (Ed.) *Anxiety in sport,* (pp. 36–37). Magglingen, Switzerland: FEPSAC.

Jones, G. E., & Hollandsworth, J. G. (1981). Heart rate discrimination before and after exercise-induced augmented cardiac activity. *Psychophysiology, 18,* 252–257.

Kauss, D. R. (1977). The effects of anxiety and activation on athletic performance (Doctoral dissertation, University of California, Los Angeles, 1976). *Dissertation Abstracts International, 37,* 5814B.

Klavora, P. (1975). Application of the Spielberger trait-state anxiety theory and STAI in pre-competition anxiety research. Unpublished manuscript. (Assistant Professor, School of Physical and Health Education, University of Toronto, Canada.)

Klavora, P. (1975). Optimal pre-competition emotional arousal of high school football players. Unpublished manuscript. (Assistant Professor, School of Physical and Health Education, University of Toronto, Canada.)

Kopysov, V. S., Prilepin, A. S., & Hanin, Y. L. (1979). The problem of assessment and regulation of emotional arousal in weightlifters. In *Weightlifting.* Moscow: Physical Culture and Sport Publishers, 37–40 (In Russian).

Lay, C. M. (1974). The influence of trait anxiety, knowledge of results, and physical working capacity upon the amount of learning and final performance of a gross motor skill among male college students (Doctoral dissertation, East Texas State University, 1973). *Dissertation Abstracts, 34,* 5690–5691A.

Martens, R., & Simon, J. A. (1976). Comparison of three predictors of state anxiety in competitive situations. *Research Quarterly, 47,* 381–387.

Mattli-Baur, B. (1983). Trait anxiety of gymnasts. In E. Apitzsch, *Anxiety in sport* (p. 40). Magglingen, Switzerland: FEPSAC.

McKelvie, S. J., & Hubard, D. E. (1980). Locus of control and anxiety in college athletes and non-athletes. *Perceptual & Motor Skills, 50,* 819–822.

Morgan, W. P. (1970). Influence of acute physical activity on state anxiety. In W. P. Morgan (Ed.), *Contemporary readings in sport psychology.* Springfield, IL: Charles C Thomas.

Morgan, W. P. (1973). Psychological factors influencing perceived exertion. *Medicine and Science in Sports, 5,* 97–103.

Morgan, W. P. (1979). Prediction of performance in athletics. In P. Klavora, (Ed.). *Proceedings of the Applied Sciences Symposium of the Canadian Society for Psychomotor Learning and Sport Psychology Congress.* Toronto.

Morgan, W. P. (1979). Anxiety reduction following acute physical activity. *Psychiatric Annals, 9,* 36!45.

Morgan, W. P. (1981). Psychophysiology of self-awareness during vigorous physical activity. *Research Quarterly for Exercise and Sport, 52,* 385–427.

Morgan, W. P., & Brown, D. R. (1981). Interaction of anxiety, perceived exertion and dyspnea in the person-respirator interface. *Medicine and Science in Sports and Exercise, 13,* 73.

Morgan, W. P., & Horstman, D. H. (1978). Psychometric correlates of pain perception. *Perceptual and Motor Skills, 47,* 27–39.

Morgan, W. P., & Horstman, D. H., Cymerman, A., & Stokes, J. (1980). Exercise as a relaxation technique. *Primary Cardiology, 6,* 48–67.

Morris, P. R., & Peacock, H. (1983). Anxiety and the effects on competitive performance. In E. Apitzsch (Ed.) *Anxiety in sport* (p. 41). Magglingen, Switzerland: FEPSAC.

Moulds, E. E. (1979). Selected physiological measures of arousal of high and low trait-anxiety females during competition (Doctoral dissertation, Louisiana State University, 1978). *Dissertation Abstracts International, 39,* 6635A.

Norcross, F. (1983). An investigation into the relationships between levels of anxiety and competitive games. In E. Apitzsch (Ed.) *Anxiety in sport* (p. 46). Magglingen, Switzerland: FEPSAC.

O'Connor, F. J. (1977). Trait-state anxiety and the effects of exposure to a high anxiety sport (Doctoral dissertation, Boston University, 1976). *Dissertation Abstracts International, 37,* 4960–4961A.

Onwuka, G. T. (1979). Effects of competition on motor skill performance and preference in relation to achievement motivation and anxiety (Doctoral dissertation, University of California, Los Angeles, 1979). *Dissertation Abstracts International, 40,* 3205A.

Otto, J. (1984). Self-awareness and coping style: Differential effects of mild physical exercise. In R. Schwarzer (Ed.), *The self in anxiety, stress and depression.* North-Holland: Elsevier Science Publishers BV.

Peacock, H. (1983). An investigation into personality and anxiety of canoeists. In E. Apitzsch (Ed.) *Anxiety in sport* (p. 47). Magglingen, Switzerland, FEPSAC.

Pink, R. J. (1976). The relationship of state-trait anxiety levels and basketball free-throw shooting proficiency among selected college women basketball players. Unpublished manuscript, Florida State University.

Poteet, D., & Weinberg, R. (1980). Competition trait anxiety, state anxiety and performance. *Perceptual & Motor Skills, 50,* 651–654.

Price, C. S., Pollock, M. L., Gettman, L. R., & Kent, D. A. (1977). *Physical fitness programs for law enforcement officers: A manual for police administrators.* Washington, DC: U.S. Government Printing Office.

Raglin, J. S., & Morgan, W. P. (1985). Influence of vigorous exercise on mood states. *The Behavior Therapist, 8,* 179–183.

Ramsburg, I. D. (1978). Anxiety, locus of control, and attributions to success/failure in a competitive tennis situation. *Dissertation Abstracts International, 39,* 1420–1421A.

Raviv, S. (1981). Reactions to frustration, level of anxiety and locus of control in marathon runners. In E. Apitzsch (Ed.) *Anxiety in sport* (p. 52). Magglingen, Switzerland: FEPSAC.

Reiter, M. A. (1981). Effects of a physical exercise program on selected mood states in a group of women over age 65 (Doctoral dissertation, Columbia University Teachers College, 1981). *Dissertation Abstracts International, 42,* 1974A.

Ribisl, E. F. (1980). Relationship among personality, physical fitness, coronary heart disease, and causal attributions in cardiac patients beginning rehabilitation (Doctoral dissertation, Fordham University, 1980). *Dissertation Abstracts International, 40*,. 5735–5736A.

Rohaly, K. A. The relationships between movement participation, movement satisfaction, self-actualization, and trait anxiety in selected college freshmen women (Doctoral dissertation, Ohio State University, 1971). *Dissertation Abstracts, 32*, 3766A.

Sanderson, F. H., & Reilly, T. (1983). Trait and state anxiety of cross-country runners. In E. Apitzsch (Ed.) *Anxiety in sport* (p. 54). Magglingen, Switzerland: FEPSAC.

Saul, T. T. (1981). Effects of physical exercise and stress management training on Type A individuals participating in a physical fitness program (Doctoral dissertation, University of Oklahoma, 1980). *Dissertation Abstracts International, 41*,. 3562B.

Scanlan, T. K., & Passer, M. W. (1978). Anxiety-inducing factors in competitive youth sports. In F. L. Small and R. E. Smith (Eds.), *Psychological perspectives in youth sports*. New York: Wiley.

Schwartz, G. E., Davidson, R. J., & Goleman, D. J. (1978). Patterning of cognitive and somatic processes in the self regulation of anxiety effects of meditation versus exercise. *Psychosomatic Medicine, 40*, 321–328.

Sime, W. E. (1977). A comparison of exercise and meditation in reducing physiological response to stress. *Medicine & Science in Sports, 9*,. 55.

Simon, J. A. (1978). Children's anxiety in sport and nonsport evaluative activities (Doctoral dissertation, University of Illinois at Urbana-Champaign, 1977). *Dissertation Abstracts International, 38*,. 5997B.

Sinyor, D., Schwartz, S. G., Peronnet, F., Brissor, G., & Seragani, P. (1983). Aerobic fitness level and reactivity to psycho-social stress: Physiological, biochemical, and subjective measures. *Psychosomatic Medicine, 45*, 205–217.

Sipos, K., & Kara, M. (1983). Data on the application of STAI (STAIC), SCAT-A and SCAT-C for the psychological examination of sportsmen. In E. Apitzsch (Ed.) *Anxiety in sport* (p. 56). Magglingen, Switzerland: FEPSAC.

Sipos, M., Sipos, K., Kara, M., Buda, B., & Bodo, M. (1979). A study on the relevance of the STAI/STAIC scores in the estimation of competition-effectiveness of sportsmen. V. *European Congress for Sports Psychology, 17*–22.

Sipos, K., & Vura, M. (1983). Study of the relevance of methods characterizing the affective states of sportsmen in "basal" and "precompetitive" situations. In E. Apitzsch (Ed.) *Anxiety in sport* (p. 60–61). Magglingen, Switzerland: FEPSAC.

Slevin, R. J. (1971). The influence of trait and state anxiety upon the performance of a novel gross motor task under conditions of competition and audience (Doctoral dissertation, Louisiana State University, 1970). *Dissertation Abstracts, 31*, 3941A.

Sparrow, F. (1983). Anxiety measures among national standard male hockey players and male and female elite fencers. In E. Apitzsch (Ed.) *Anxiety in sport* (p. 62). Magglingen, Switzerland: FEPSAC.

Spielberger, C. D. (1971). Trait-state anxiety and motor behavior. *Journal of Motor Behavior, 3*, 265–279.

Spielberger, C. D. (1982). Stress and anxiety in sports. In E. Geron & A. Mashiach (Eds.), *Proceedings of the First National Conference on Psychology and Physical Education*, (pp. 190–198). Netanya, Israel: Wingate Institute.

Spielberger, C. D. (1983). State-trait anxiety and sports psychology. In E. Apitzsch (Ed.) *Anxiety in sport* (p. 74–85). Magglingen, Switzerland: FEPSAC.

Stocker, J. M. (1974). Motor performance and state anxiety at selected stages of the menstrual cycle (Doctoral dissertation, Temple University, 1973). *Dissertation Abstracts, 34*, 3971A.

Vines, R. H. (1972). The influence of race and anxiety level upon performance of novel motor tasks under varying stressful conditions (Doctoral dissertation, Louisiana State University and Agricultural and Mechanical College, 1971). *Dissertation Abstracts, 32*, 3770A.

Vura, M., Növényi, N., Sipos, K., & Sipos, M. (1983). Anxiety analysis of a first class wrestling team. In E. Apitzsch (Ed.) *Anxiety in sport* (p. 63). Magglingen, Switzerland: FEPSAC.

Vura, M., Sipos, K., & Sipos, M. (1983). Commitment to running: Contributing psychological, anthropometrical and sport achievement factors. In E. Apitzsch (Ed.) *Anxiety in sport* (p. 64). Magglingen, Switzerland: FEPSAC.

Weinberg, R. S. (1972). An electromyographic study of anxiety and motor performance. Unpublished master's thesis, University of California, Los Angeles.

Weinberg, R. S., & Genuchi, M. (1980). Relationship between competitive trait-anxiety, state anxiety and golf performance: A field study. *Journal of Sport Psychology, 2*, 148–154.

Wilson, V. E., Berger, B. G., & Bird, E. I. (1981). Effects of running and of an exercise class on anxiety. *Perceptual and Motor Skills, 53,* 472–474.

Wilson, V. E., & Bird, E. I. (1981). Effects of relaxation and/or biofeedback training upon hip flexation in gymnasts. *Biofeedback and Self-Regulation, 6,* 25–34.

Wilson, V. E., Morley, N. C., & Bird, E. I. (1980). Mood profiles of marathon runners, joggers and non-exercisers. *Perceptual and Motor Skills, 50,* 117–118.

Wolfson, S. (1983). The use of the STAI in a study of table tennis players. In E. Apitzsch (Ed.) *Anxiety in sport* (p. 65). Magglingen, Switzerland: FEPSAC.

Wood, D. T. (1977). The relationship between state anxiety and acute physical activity. *American Corrective Therapy Journal, 31,* 67–69.

Yousif, S. F. (1983). Anxiety and volleyball players. In E. Apitzsch (Ed.) *Anxiety in sport* (p. 66). Magglingen, Switzerland: FEPSAC.

2

Interpersonal and Intragroup Anxiety in Sports

Yuri L. Hanin

The main goal of this chapter is to examine a number of complex conceptual and methodological issues encountered in assessing the impact of situational and social factors on state-anxiety (S-Anxiety) in sports settings. Research findings and practical experience in the evaluation of S-Anxiety associated with individual and team athletic performance will be described. In these studies, the Russian adaptation (Hanin & Spielberger, 1983) of the State-Trait Anxiety Inventory (STAI: Spielberger, Gorsuch, & Lushene, 1970) was used in a *non-traditional* manner to assess three aspects of S-Anxiety that appear to influence performance in sports competition: Interpersonal S-Anxiety (S-A$_{int}$), intragroup S-Anxiety (S-A$_{gr}$), and performance S-Anxiety related to *zones of optimal functioning* (ZOF).

Most of the observations and experimental findings that are reported in this chapter were obtained in real-life sports settings. Prior to describing the findings of our studies, the theoretical assumptions that guided this work are briefly considered. Then, pragmatic issues in the operational assessment of the theoretical concepts noted above are examined and the specific assessment procedures are described in some detail. Finally, implications for future research and clinical practice are discussed.

SOCIAL PSYCHOLOGY OF EMOTIONAL EXPERIENCE

Emotional reactions are an important component of adaptive behavior in organism-environment interactions. According to L. S. Vygotsky (1926, 1984), three patterns of interchangeable relationships are possible: (a) The predominance of the organism (person) over the environment, which results in relatively easy task performance; (b) A balance between person and environment; and (c) A person-environment imbalance, manifesting itself in a high level of tension due to the inability of an individual to cope with task demands and/or the expectations of partners. In all three cases, emotional behavior is triggered by a person's appraisal of her/his relationships with the environment and strong emotional reactions occur at critical moments of imbalance in person-environment interactions. These ideas were first formulated by Vygotsky more than fifty years ago, and are now well represented in most major cognitive theories of stress and anxiety (e.g., Arnold, 1960; Lazarus, 1966; Schachter, 1964; Spielberger, 1966, 1972, 1979; Weiner, 1980).

Given the importance of the social environment as a primary determinant of emotion, it seems strange that, until quite recently, stress and anxiety were studied in a vacuum devoid of social elements, especially, in sports settings (Vallerand, 1983). An important exception is Trait-State Anxiety Theory (Spielberger, 1966, 1972), which identifies social psychological factors (interpersonal or group evaluative situations) as stressors that differentially evoke S-Anxiety in persons who differ in trait anxiety (T-Anxiety). There is also excellent research on the impact of stressful social environments on emotions and performance (e.g., Sears, 1967), and a number of scales have been developed to assess T-Anxiety in social contexts (e.g., Friedrich, 1970; Gilkinson, 1942; McCrosky, 1970, 1978, 1984). But the study of the psychosocial determinants of S-Anxiety in sports situations has thus far received relatively little attention (Hanin, 1986).

S-Anxiety has been defined as a "temporal cross-section in the emotional stream-of-life of a person, consisting of subjective feelings of tension, apprehension, nervousness, and worry, and activation or arousal of the autonomic nervous system" (Spielberger, 1985, p. 10). In most studies, only the parameters of S-Anxiety for a particular time period have been investigated, but not the setting or the social context. The study of S-Anxiety from a social psychology perspective would require treating subjective emotional experience as a unit of consciousness in which the meaning of the environment is reflected in a person's emotional reactions (Vygotsky, 1984). Thus, in the analysis of emotional reactions, situations and personality should be represented in a relative form; environment in its relationship to the person, and the person in his/her relationship to the environment.

According to Vygotsky, person-environment unity is an indivisible whole, not two separate entities. One cannot study the unity of something by first dividing it into parts, studying them separately, and then trying to integrate the obtained results. A person's involvement in a task, and with other people, is manifested in the person-environment interaction. Emotional experience (subjective feelings) must be examined as one of the principal units of study in research on person-environment interactions.

In clinical studies of the emotional experiences of airplane pilots, F. D. Gorbov (1971) suggested that self-observations in relation to one's environment are generally accompanied by self-reflection and by changes in what he called "self-sensations." Such processes are consciously perceived, involuntary, and constantly changing (Ganzen, 1984). Since the individual is aware of these processes, it is theoretically possible to assess subjective feelings by focusing his/her attention on a particular aspect of the environment. Recent developments in self-report methodology demonstrate that this focusing procedure is quite feasible. Thus, the critical question is: "What aspects of the social environment should be selected for focused attention in evaluating S-Anxiety for a particular time interval?"

A person's relationships with other people seem to have a greater impact on his/her emotional reactions than the objective characteristics of the physical environment (Rubinstein, 1946). From a social psychological perspective, Myaissischev (1965) contends that it is unproductive to attempt to explain behavior under real-life conditions entirely in terms of abstract personality traits or specific qualities of the social environment. For example, it would be a mistake, both psychologically and pedagogically, to try to explain a child's behavior without paying attention to the particular people with whom he/she interacts at a given moment, and the nature of his/her relationships with them.

It should be noted that Myassischev's position corresponds quite well with an interactionist perspective, and with observations of communication patterns in small groups (James, 1951; Bales, 1950, 1970, 1981). Interpersonal and intragroup interactions (individual-individual and individual-group, in Myassischev's terms) are easy to identify; interpersonal contacts are predominant, comprising about 70% of all interactions in various samples. In social-skills training, there is a trend toward identifying not only the type of skill (communication, leadership, decision-making), but also toward matching specific skills with particular types of contact situations, e.g., dyadic and intragroup interactions, intergroup relations, etc. (Berger & Harrison, 1976).

The social psychological theoretical perspective described above led us to consider two new S-Anxiety concepts: *Interpersonal S-Anxiety* (S-A$_{int}$) and *Intragroup S-Anxiety* (S-A$_{gr}$). Both constructs refer to the emotional reactions experienced by a person at a given moment in time as a function of his/her *involvement* with a particular partner (S-A$_{int}$), and/or as a member of a group or team (S-A$_{gr}$). In accordance with these concepts, the intensity of S-Anxiety is assessed *relative* to present, anticipated, or past interactions with specific individuals or groups.

ASSESSMENT OF INTERPERSONAL AND INTRAGROUP ANXIETY

The assessment of interpersonal and intragroup anxiety involves evaluating a temporal cross-section in the emotional stream-of-life of a person as related to interpersonal and intragroup aspects of the social environment. S-A$_{int}$ and S-A$_{gr}$ were assessed with the Russian adaptation of Spielberger's (1983; Spielberger et al., 1970) State-Trait Anxiety Inventory (STAI-R: Hanin, 1976; Hanin & Spielberger, 1983). In addition, a visual analogue S-Anxiety measure, called the "Psychological Discomfort/Comfort" (D/C) scale, was used to assess immediate fluctuations in S-Anxiety experienced while performing on a task. This measure correlated .64 and −.56, respectively with the STAI state anxiety present and absent items in a sample of 45 college students (22 females, 23 males).

Instructions for the STAI S-Anxiety scale may be modified to refer to any situation or time interval of interest to an experimenter or clinician (Spielberger et al., 1970). In actual practice, however, such assessments are usually carried out by directing the respondents' attention to a particular time interval or situation without specifying the environmental context. For example, in a study of 22 female gymnasts, the standard instructions for the STAI S-Anxiety scale were modified to ask these athletes to report how they ". . . think they would feel before the start of a forthcoming competition." This anticipated (predicted) level of S-Anxiety was assessed 5 days before a forthcoming contest, and was found to be moderately correlated with actual S-Anxiety scores obtained one hour before the contest began ($r = .50$, $p < .05$). The anticipation of elevated S-Anxiety several weeks before an important competition provides an indirect measure of the degree to which a future situation is presently perceived as threatening.

Interpersonal S-Anxiety is assessed by asking a person to evaluate how he/she felt at a particular moment while in actual or anticipated contact with a particular person (partner, coach, trainer, sports administrator, rival, referee, etc.). The focus of appraisal in assessing intragroup anxiety is a group situation in which the individual is a member of a team. The subject is asked to evaluate "how he/she feels (felt, would feel) at a particular moment as a team member. In clinical work, the assessment of S-A_{int}. and S-A_{gr} can be augmented by requesting subjects to report, in their own words, *why* they feel a particular way while communicating with a particular partner (S-A_{int}), or as a team member (S-A_{gr}). Content analysis of the reasons given by subjects in explaining their S-A_{int} and S-A_{gr} provides valuable additional information about personality-environment interactions as perceived by the participant. Before describing experimental findings and clinical observations demonstrating the utility in sports settings, of the concepts of interpersonal and/or intragroup anxiety, several additional anxiety-related concepts that have proved useful in working with top Soviet athletes will be briefly examined.

RETROSPECTIVE AND PREDICTIVE MEASURES OF S-ANXIETY

Performance anxiety refers to the emotional reactions experienced while working on a particular task. *Optimal S-Anxiety.* (S-A_{opt}) is defined as the level of performance S-Anxiety that enables a particular athlete to perform at his/her *personal best.* In the assessment of S-A_{opt} two procedures have proved useful: (a) systematic measurement of individual levels of pre-start and performance S-Anxiety, associated with performance level, and (b) retrospective measures of anxiety associated with a successful previous performance. In the second approach, the athlete is instructed to evaluate how he/she felt before his/her most successful contest or how he/she feels when performing with greatest ease and efficiency.

Retrospective assessment of an individual's optimal anxiety level has been investigated in correlational studies and in clinical work. The optimal level of S-Anxiety turned out to be extremely variable, with individual scores of 250 top athletes ranging from 26 to 67 and mean values for different samples varying from 39 to 43 points. Given the range of individual differences in optimal levels of S-Anxiety, a *zone of optimal functioning* (ZOF) was conceptualized to take into account errors in reporting S-Anxiety after an unsuccessful performance. The upper and lower boundaries (thresholds) of the ZOF are established for an individual athlete by adding and subtracting 4 points to his/her optimal pre-start S-Anxiety level. This value corresponds, approximately, to half of the average SD of pre-contest scores.

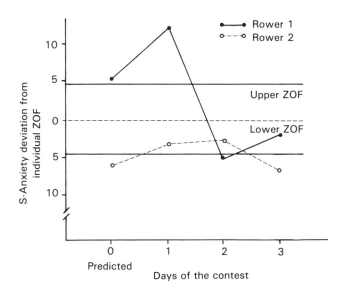

Figure 1 Actual and predicted S-Anxiety for two one-person rowing crews as compared to the Zone of Optimal Functioning.

To demonstrate the practical utility of the ZOF concept in clinical work with top athletes, Figure 1 presents the predicted S-Anxiety scores of members of two one-person rowing crews. The S-Anxiety measures were taken one week in advance, and these scores were compared to the individual's optimal S-Anxiety level (ZOF). The S-Anxiety of both rowers was about the same, but the coaches of these boats were clearly confronted with quite different tasks: To increase pre-start S-Anxiety in one case, and to decrease it in the other. Minimizing the contacts between the rowers having high and low anxiety relative to their own ZOF was also desirable.

Predicted (anticipated) S-Anxiety can also be elevated by comparing scores obtained from athletes and coaches, and by contrasting such scores with actual and predicted measures in other settings (speech anxiety, test anxiety, behavior therapy). In essence, the concepts of performance anxiety and zone of optimal functioning provide relevant reference points for identifying stressors that evoke $S-A_{int}$ and $S-A_{gr}$ and for the management of anxiety in a manner that will facilitate better performance for individual athletes and teams.

RESEARCH ON INTERPERSONAL AND INTRAGROUP ANXIETY

Clinical (single-case) and correlational studies of top athletes, coaches, managers, and college students were undertaken to evaluate the utility of the concepts of interpersonal and intragroup anxiety, and the methodology for their assessment. In this research, measures of $S-A_{int}$ and $S-A_{gr}$ proved to be valid indices of emotional involvement on group tasks with a particular partner and/or team. More than 150 groups, consisting of approximately 2000 subjects, participated in the research on the assessment of S-A$_{gr}$. One-time and repeated measures of S-A$_{gr}$ were obtained in order to compare the interindividual, intragroup, and intergroup S-Anxiety for athletes on the same and on different teams.

Personality and environmental determinants of S-A$_{gr}$ were evaluated by contrasting the intragroup S-Anxiety of extreme group members. Briefly, the influence of selected personality characteristics on the level of intragroup S-Anxiety was demonstrated in the elevated S-A$_{gr}$ scores of males with high T-Anxiety, neuroticism and social desirability. High S-A$_{gr}$ was associated with low self-esteem, Fiedler's Aso scores, and low social desirability in females. For a small sample of college volleyball players, the athletes who were less experienced and insufficiently prepared for a contest had higher levels of S-Anxiety, as might be expected. It is also interesting to note that the reserves were higher in S-A$_{gr}$ than the starters (principal players), both during training and in competition.

The combined effects of personality and environmental factors were manifested in team members experiencing elevated levels of S-A$_{gr}$ who negatively evaluated the team's "psychological atmosphere" as measured by the Seashore (1954) Group Cohesiveness Index. Conversely, athletes with a more favorable view of a particular team in comparison with other teams experienced less S-A$_{gr}$. Team members who thought that they were "treated worse than others," or who did not know the attitudes of other group members towards them, usually experienced higher levels of S-Anxiety. In socially mature groups, the level of S-A$_{gr}$ of high and low status members were similar, whereas in immature groups the leaders (high status members) felt more comfortable psychologically, as reflected in lower S-A$_{gr}$ scores, than their lower status counterparts.

Activity factors and level of S-A$_{gr}$ were related in a study involving 154 college students, who were asked to evaluate how they felt in academic study and sports groups. The 20-item STAI S-Anxiety scale was used to assess S-A$_{gr}$, and the students were asked to explain, in their own words, why they felt that way. Content analysis of the students' responses revealed that elevated S-A$_{gr}$ was associated with insufficient class preparation, poor task-oriented study group relationships, and poor attitudes toward future professional activity. Differences between males and females in the relative importance of these factors, and in physical well-being and outside activity, were not significant. In another study, high levels of S-A$_{gr}$ in young workers were associated with rejection by the group, lack of positive interpersonal relationships, and adequate group support.

Interpersonal S-Anxiety, reflecting emotional reactions while interacting with a particular partner, was studied in a number of different samples involving more than 400 subjects (athletes, coaches, college students, sports administrators, top level executives, etc.). The findings indicated that S-A$_{int}$ was determined by four groups of factors: (1) Situational characteristics; (2) The respective performance levels of interacting partners; (3) Status and role relationships of the participants; and (4) Personality traits.

Elevated S-A$_{int}$ was usually observed in uncertain situations in which the interpersonal relationship between partners was not well-established. Communication apprehension, a form of T-Anxiety measured by McCrosky's Personal Report of Communication Apprehension (PRCA), and S-A$_{int}$ were considerably higher in interactions with unfamiliar partners than with familiar ones. In a study of 34 top Soviet weight-lifters (Hanin & Kopyssov, 1977), competing athletes reported maximum comfort while assisted by their own coach, whereas maximum psychological discomfort was highest with unfamiliar coaches. It is interesting to note that these top level competitors were stressed not only by actual communication, but also by the unexpected behavior and actions of people around them, and by the anticipation of unfavorable contacts and/or the absence of desired (or habitual) support. Given such "unexpected barriers" (Kisselev, 1965), these top athletes could not cope effectively on their own in the majority of cases.

In sports competition, $S\text{-}A_{int}$ may be observed in the communication of partners with well-established status and interpersonal relationships. Moderate to highly negative correlations ($r = -.34$ to $-.73$) were found between the level of $S\text{-}A_{int}$ and positive interpersonal choices. In some cases, however, no correlation was found, suggesting that the emotional reaction to a partner in a specific situation might be influenced by attitudes based on past experience. The complexity of the relationship between $S\text{-}A_{int}$ and interpersonal relations is clearly demonstrated when the level of $S\text{-}A_{int}$ in positive, neutral, and negative pairs is compared in positive, neutral and negative situations, as can be seen in Table 1. In a conflict-situation, high levels of $S\text{-}A_{int}$ are observed in all three pairs irrespective of their interpersonal relationship. Such findings substantiate, theoretically and practically, the importance of taking into account both interpersonal relationships and situational factors in measuring $S\text{-}A_{int}$.

The influence of status relationships among partners in producing elevated levels of $S\text{-}A_{int}$ was examined in several studies. The findings indicated that: (a) Low-status volleyball players, both in training and in competition, experienced higher levels of $S\text{-}A_{int}$ than their high-status counterparts; (b) Starters felt less $S\text{-}A_{int}$ while communicating with other team members in training and competition, as compared with reserves; (c) Higher levels of $S\text{-}A_{int}$ were experienced by soccer and ice-hockey players in contacts with coaches than with their team members; (d) Female handball players felt more $S\text{-}A_{int}$ in contacts with their head coach than with either a second coach or team administrator.

Table 1 Interpersonal S-Anxiety as a Function of Partners' Relationships and Situation of Communication[a]

	Partners' relationships			
Communication situation	Positive	Neutral	Negative	X_r^2
1. Favorable	6.2	7.9	11.8	16.35**
2. Neutral	6.7	9.7	14.1	10.06*
3. Conflict	14.4	14.8	17.0	3.95
H^2	15.8**	15.35**	3.72	

[a]The level of significance was determined using the Friedman two-way analysis of variance (X_r^2) and Kruskal-Wallis one-way analysis of variance (H^2). Siegel (1956).
*$p < .01$.
**$p < .001$.

The effect of role and status on S-A$_{int}$ was examined in a study of coaches and executives. The findings revealed that, in communication and interaction with another person, the higher the status of one's partner the higher the level of S-A$_{int}$ that was experienced in interacting with him/her. The highest S-A$_{int}$ was observed when partners disagreed about their relative status and/or were fighting for an "upper hand." The most comfortable contacts were observed in colleagues of equal status in situations of functional interdependence. In general, role-status relationships in group activities appear to activate a social-comparison process that may evoke considerable fluctuations in interpersonal S-Anxiety levels.

In order to clarify the meaning of interpersonal and intragroup S-Anxiety, these concepts must be compared and contrasted with one another. Since interpersonal contacts are an integral part of person's group experience, the basic question is: How are intragroup and interpersonal S-Anxiety related? A special study was undertaken to examine this question. All members of a sports class attended by college students specializing in gymnastics were requested to report how they felt in the group, and in their relationships with *each* group member. They were also asked to evaluate their interpersonal and working relationships with group members by rating the attractiveness of each group member as a partner. The mean for each member, and the mean S-A$_{int}$ for each member with his PT instructor (S-A$_{int-I}$) were determined. The following regression equation (reliability 83.5%) was computed:

$$S\text{-}A_{gr} = .95\ SA_{int\text{-}I} + .85\ SA_{int\text{-}P} + .71\ SA_{int\text{-}R} - 9.5$$

The results of the regression analysis indicated that S-A$_{gr}$ consists of the S-A$_{int}$ experienced in contact with the gymnast's PT instructor (S-A$_{int-I}$), a first-choice partner (S-A$_{int-P}$), and a significant referent member of the group (SA$_{int-R}$). Thus, disruptions in the contacts with these key persons cause the greatest intragroup S-Anxiety. Contrary to expectation, S-A$_{int}$ was *not* related to the level of interpersonal S-Anxiety felt in communicating with less preferred group members. Nor was it equivalent to the average S-A$_{int}$ experienced in contact with other group members. Rather, contacts in this type of group activity appear to be highly selective and not forced by task demands. Although additional studies of intergroup and interpersonal S-Anxiety are needed for a variety of teams, the preliminary findings that have been reported throw some light on the complex relationships between S-A$_{int}$, S-A$_{gr}$ and performance S-Anxiety.

SUMMARY AND CONCLUSIONS

Advances in research on anxiety and other stress-related emotions appear to be closely linked to understanding the stressful impact of social psychological and environmental factors on state anxiety. In this chapter, S-Anxiety was conceptualized as reflecting the "emotional stream of life" of a person within a broad context of significant task requirements and interpersonal contacts. Several new concepts proposed for the study of such personality-environment and predictive approaches to assessing interpersonal and intragroup S-Anxiety, and levels of S-Anxiety for defining the zones of optimal functioning (ZOF) that facilitate the performance of individual athletes.

Sports settings provide a unique context for studying real-life emotional experience in situations where training, competition, and leisure are closely related. A social psychological approach to the study of stress and anxiety in sports requires the investigation of both new and traditional concepts. For example, anxiety may be evoked by the perception of danger or threat not only to an individual, but also to his/her partners and the group as a whole. Emotional experience needs to be examined in the context of interpersonal and group behavior which can be described within the three-dimensional space suggested by Bales, Cohen, and Williamson, (1979). Studies are needed to determine the degree to which subjective feelings are isomorphic with interpersonal and group behavior (Mehrabian, 1980; Bales et al., 1979).

The research findings and clinical observations presented in this chapter provide evidence of the limitations of global measures of anxiety in evaluating emotional reactions in sports activities and other real-life groups where multiple factors are operating. Nevertheless, many tests in current use are potentially valuable for evaluating individuals with single-case experimental designs, traditional laboratory methodology, and in longitudinal approaches, as was shown with Spielberger's STAI. Moreover, such procedures are likely to be most useful when used in conjunction with an in-depth analysis of the reasons for experiencing particular stress emotions, as Sanderson and Ashton (1983) have shown. Examining subjectively perceived determinants of emotions is also therapeutic, in that the individual is encouraged to develop more sophisticated self-insights and more effective coping behaviors.

The concepts and methodology for the assessment of interpersonal and intragroup anxiety presented in this chapter have special significance when viewed in the context of the extreme task demands of sports competition and the mutual responsibility involved in team sports. The search for psychologically healthy ways of increasing human potential is of greatest importance with rising interpersonal and intragroup tensions. Finding cooperative approaches among group members for coping with stress is a challenging task in the study of emotional reactions to the stressful conditions of modern life.

REFERENCES

Arnold, M. B. (1960). *Emotion and personality.* Baltimore: Penguin.

Bales, R. F. (1950). *Interaction process analysis: A method for the study of small groups.* Cambridge, MA: Addison-Wesley.

Bales, R. F. (1970). *Personality and interpersonal behavior.* New York: Holt, Rinehart and Winston.

Bales, R. F., Cohen, S. P., & Williamson, S. A. (1979). *SYMLOG: A system for the multiple level observation of groups.* New York: The Free Press.

Berger, M., & Harrison, K. (1976). A new approach to interpersonal skills development. In C. L. Cooper (Ed.), *Developing social skills in managers: Advances in group training* (pp. 128–137). London: The Macmillan Press.

Friedrich, G. W. (1970). An Empirical Explication of a Concept of Self-Reported Speech Anxiety. Speech Monographs, 37, 67–72.

Ganzen, V. A. (1984). *Systemnye opissaniya v psykhologuii [System descriptions in psychology].* Leningrad: University Press.

Gilkinson, H. (1942). Social Fears as Reported by students in College Speech Classes. Speech Monographs, 9, 141–160.

Gorbov, F. D. (1971). Determinatsiya psykhicheskikh sostoyanii (On the determination of psychological states). *Voprosy psykhologuii, 50,* 20–29.

Hanin, Y. L. (1976). Emotsional noye sostoyaniye litchnosti v collective [Personality's emotional state in a collective]. *Problems of Child and Pedagogical Psychology* (pp. 20–22). Moscow: Research Institute of General and Pedagogical Psychology, USSR Academy of Pedagogical Science.

Hanin, Y. L., & Spielberger, C. D. (1983). The development and validation of the Russian Form of the State-Trait Anxiety Inventory. In C. D. Spielberger & R. Diaz-Guerrero (Eds.), *Cross-cultural anxiety* (Vol. 2, pp. 15–26). Washington: Hemisphere.

James, J. A. (1951). A preliminary study of the size determinant in small group interaction. *American Sociological Review, 16,* 474–477.

Kisselev, Y. Y. (1965). Psikhologuichesky analiz prepyatstviy neozhidanno voznikayuschchikh v sorevnovaniyakh po bor be i tyazholoy atletike [Psychological analysis of unexpected barriers encountered in wrestling and weightlifting competition]. In *Psychological preparation of athlete.* Moscow: Physical Culture and Sports Publishers.

Lazarus, R. S. (1966). *Psychological stress and the coping process.* New York: McGraw-Hill.

McCrosky, J. C. (1970). Measures of communication-bound anxiety. *Speech Monographs, 37,* 269–277.

McCrosky, J. C. (1978). Validity of the PRCA as an index of oral communication apprehension. *Communication Monographs, 45,* 192–203.

McCrosky, J. C. (1984). The Communication Perspective. In J. A. Daly & J. C. McCrosky (Eds.), *Avoiding communication: Shyness, Reticence, and communication apprehension.* London: Sage Publications.

Mehrabian, A. (1980). *Basic dimensions for a general psychological theory.* Cambridge, MA: Oelgeschlanger, Gunn and Hain.

Myassischev, V. N. (1965). Sotsial naya psikhologuiya i psikhologuiya otnoshenii [Social psychology and psychology of relationships]. In V. N. Kolbanovsky & B. F. Porshnev (Eds.), *Problems of social psychology* (pp. 273–285). Moscow: Mysl.

Rubinstein, S. L. (1946). *Osnovy obschey psikhologuii [The Foundations of General Psychology].* Moscow.

Sanderson, F. H., & Ashton, M. K. (1983). Analysis of anxiety levels before and after badminton competition. In E. Apitzsch (Ed.), *Anxiety in sport.* Magglingen: G. Schilling.

Schachter, S. (1964). The interaction of cognitive and physiological determinants of emotional state. In L. Berkowitz (Ed.), *Advances in experimental social psychology.* New York: Academic Press.

Sears, J. O. (1967). Social anxiety, opinion structure and opinion change. *Journal of Personality and Social Psychology, 7,* 142–151.

Seashore, S. E. (1954). *Group cohesiveness in the industrial work group.* Ann Arbor: Survey Research Center, Institute for Social Research, University of Michigan.

Siegel, S. (1956). *Nonparametric statistics for the behavioral sciences.* New York: McGraw-Hill Book Company.

Spielberger, C. D. (1966). Theory and research on anxiety. In C. D. Spielberger (Ed.), *Anxiety and behavior.* New York: Academic Press.

Spielberger, C. D. (1972). Anxiety as an emotional state. In C. D. Spielberger (Ed.), *Anxiety: Current trends in theory and research* (Vol. 1). New York: Academic Press.

Spielberger, C. D. (1979). *Understanding stress and anxiety.* London: Harper & Row.

Spielberger, C. D. (1985). Assessment of state and trait anxiety: Conceptual and methodological issues. *The Southern Psychologist, 2,* 6–16.

Spielberger, C. D., Gorsuch, R. L., & Lushene, R. E. (1970). *Manual for the State-Trait Anxiety Inventory.* Palo Alto, CA: Consulting Psychologists Press.

Vallerand, R. J. (1983). On emotion in sport: Theoretical and social psychological perspectives. *Journal of Sport Psychology, 5,* 197–215.

Vygotsky, L. S. (1926). *Pedagoguicheskaya psykhologuiya [Pedagogical psychology].* Moscow: Rabotnik prosvescheniya.

Vygotsky, L. S. (1984). Detskaya psykhologuiya [Child psychology]. In *Selected works* (Vol. 4). Moscow: Pedagoguika.

Weiner, B. (1980). *Human motivation.* New York: Holt, Rinehart, and Winston.

3

Competence and Valence
as Determinants of Anxiety

Dieter Hackfort and Peter Schulz

Worry and emotionality are usually (see Spielberger, Gonzalez, Taylor, Algaze, & Anton, 1978) regarded as two components of anxiety. Within an action concept of anxiety we further differentiate three aspects of emotionality: (1) emotionality as an increase in autonomic arousal, (2) emotionality as an affective-physiological experience, and (3) emotionality as a source of interference. From an action theory perspective the development of emotionality and worry cognitions are a result of the interaction of competence and valence appraisals. This paper will review the relationship of worry and emotionality with competence and valence. First a brief review of action theory is necessary with particular attention given to the concepts of competence and valence.

THEORETICAL BACKGROUND

Valence

The term valence of outcome refers essentially to the importance of an outcome, i.e., the significance an outcome has for a subject (Wortman & Brehm, 1975). Based on the arguments of Vroom (1964) it is apparent that valence results from the connection between an outcome of an action and the consequences of this outcome, e.g., an exam lection is failed (outcome) leading to the consequence of repeating the course. Thus the development of valence is equivalent with the coupling of outcomes with consequences which can be of differing strength. Thorndike (1911) already demonstrated that motivation can result from the goal (1) to reach positive consequences or (2) to avoid negative consequences. On the basis of this distinction we can postulate two qualitatively different motivational states, which are called (1) appetitive motivational state and (2) aversive motivational state (e.g., Fowles, 1982; Gray, 1976).

Appetitive motivational state occurs in situations where the subject intends to achieve a positive consequence by a certain outcome. This implies that no negative consequences result, if the outcome is not achieved. The higher the personal advantage associated with the positive consequences, the stronger the appetitive motivation (appetence) to reach the outcome, assuming there is a relationship between outcome and consequences.

Aversion, on the other hand, occurs in situations where the subject intends to avoid a negative consequence. This implies that no positive consequences result, if the subject succeeds in achieving the intended outcome. The greater the disadvantage associated with the negative consequence, the higher the necessity to reach an outcome which avoids this negative consequence (see also Nitsch, 1981).

The valence of an outcome can vary with regard to its quality and quantity. This means that the valence of an outcome and thus the motivation for an action can result from a high/low appetence or from a high/low aversion.

Competence

Concerning the elaboration of the concept of competence (Nitsch & Hackfort, 1981) two relationships are important: (1) competence with regard to the intended action and (2) competence with regard to situational demands. A person can predict whether (s)he can reach positive or negative consequences of an action outcome depending on the appraisal of one's competence. In situations where there is the potential for strain a positive prediction is equivalent to the anticipation of situational control by avoidance. Negative prediction means that there is essentially no chance to organize effective behavior to avoid negative results. Under the condition of appetence a positive prediction is identical with the anticipation of reaching positive consequences associated with certain outcomes. Negative prediction on the other hand is identical with the anticipation of not reaching positive consequences.

Uncertainty is at its maximum if the anticipation to reach or not to reach positive consequences is of equal probability to avoid or not avoid negative consequences (Schulz & Schönpflug, 1982). Uncertainty is characterized by the conviction of the subject that all personal abilities and efforts in combination with favorable circumstances are necessary to avoid negative consequences or to reach positive consequences. In other words: the person doesn't know if (s)he has the required ability and can utilize them when needed.

Valence and Competence as Determinants of Worry and Emotionality

Because we are dealing with anxiety the further considerations are concentrated on aversive motivational states. Now let us outline the hypothesis concerning the relationship between uncertainty under the condition of aversion on the one hand and emotionality and worry on the other hand (Figure 1). As the upper section of Figure 1 shows, under the conditions of positive and negative

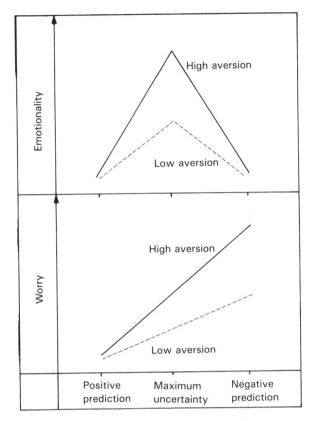

Figure 1 Emotionality and worry as a function of the amount of aversion and the degree of uncertainty (theoretical model).

predictions, low emotionality scores were expected. However, the more the uncertainty increases, the more emotionality rises. The gradient depends on the personal disadvantages associated with the negative consequence not reaching the intended outcome. The reason for this relationship might be seen in the functional usefulness of further activation if it is of very high or low probability to avoid negative consequences.

The lower part of Figure 1 illustrates the hypothesis concerning the relationship between uncertainty and worry. As can be seen in the figure, under the condition of an aversion motivation, worries arise, as the prediction of negative consequences become more certain, e.g., the more the predictions become negative the more worries are to be expected. Again the gradient depends on the amount of anticipated disadvantages associated with the negative consequences, in short: the amount of aversion. That means: The higher the aversion the higher is the influence of uncertain or negative predictions on worries.

EMPIRICAL INVESTIGATIONS

A Laboratory Study

An experiment wa carried out to test the hypothesis concerning the relationship between emotionality on the one hand and uncertainty of prediction on the condition of aversion on the other hand.

In the experimental group two subjects had to solve a common task together. Subject "A," who collaborated with the experimenter, was given a slide with a so-called total-task, simulating features of clerical work. This task contained a sub-task, which was first to be solved by the other subject "B," before subject "A" could accomplish a solution of common task. In addition, the subject "B" first had to solve the sub-task within a time limit of 50 seconds. After 50 seconds, the task presentation was terminated automatically, and the subject "B" was instructed to communicate the solution to the subject "A." The solution was communicated via a digital counter, which could be seen by both subjects. With the solution of the sub-task, the subject "A" now could complete the total-task, again within a time-limit of 50 seconds. Meanwhile the subject "B" had to wait for feedback, whether his solution was right or wrong. After subject "A" also had communicated its solution, both subjects got feedback. Only the joined result, if it was right, was rewarded with money. Both subjects got 1,—DM for a right solution. If the task solution was wrong, 1,—DM was subtracted. A digital-counter displayed the common premium. When the joined task solution was wrong, the subjects were informed who made the mistake. The purpose of this experimental condition was to induce high aversion, because the subjects of this group were responsible for the loss of the premium of their co-workers. Eighteen pairs of subjects were tested within this condition.

In the control group another 18 pairs worked at the same tasks, but a joined solution was not demanded. A feedback and a premium was not provided. In the control group low aversion was induced because the subjects of this group got no premium and the subjects were not responsible for the mistakes of their co-workers.

Only the reactions of subject "B" were analyzed, because subject "A" was a collaborate of the experimenter, who was familiar with the tasks. The subjects—students of the University of Trier—were recruited by announcement. The sample consists of 24 males and 12 females. The mean age was 26 years. The total experimental work was arranged in two blocks of 10 tasks. Thus, all 36 pairs of subjects had to solve 20 tasks, with a three minute time break after 10 tasks.

In order to vary the uncertainty of prediction we measured the IQ prior to the experiment with the Amthauer test and assigned the subjects to two groups according to their demand/capacity ratio: (1) Uncertain prediction group: Demand and capacity were balanced ($IQ > \bar{x}$). (2) Negative prediction group: Demand outbalanced capacity ($IQ < \bar{x}$). Thus, a 2 × 2 factorial design was obtained (high vs. low aversion; uncertain vs. negative predictions).

As dependent variables were measured: (1) Physiological arousal by heart rate, (2) state anxiety before and after the experiment with the STAI-G (Laux, Glanzmann, Schaffner, & Spielberger, 1981), and (3) introspective reports concerning the experience of anxiety cognitions by self rating.

Results

As mentioned above analyses was made of emotionality according to three different aspects:

(1) Emotionality as an increase in autonomic arousal,
(2) Emotionality as an affective-physiological experience, and
(3) Emotionality as a source of interference.

To analyze emotionality as an increase in autonomic arousal the cardiac signal (ECG) during the various activity periods were taken continuously. This cardiovascular response was recorded by a "Cardiovascular-Monitor-System" based on a Z-80 microprocessor. The cardiac signal was converted to a step function measure of heart rate. Figure 2 shows the data from the heart rate (HR) measures. The values represent the different scores of HR-level between the baseline, obtained to the experimental work, and the period of information processing.

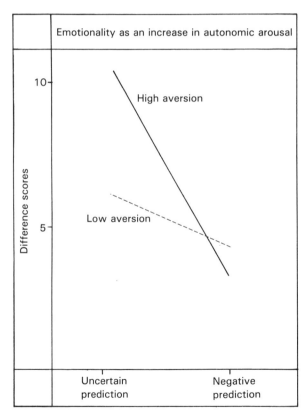

Figure 2   Increase in heart rate for uncertain and negative prediction during high and low aversion.

As can be seen in Figure 2 subjects in the high aversion condition had the highest increase in HR but only when they were uncertain about their outcome consequences. The negative prediction groups had the lowest HR-increase irrespective whether they worked under the condition of high or low aversion. A two-way ANOVA revealed a significant difference between the prediction-groups (F (1.32) = 4.61; p ≤ .05). This result is in line with the model outlined above (see Figure 1).

To evaluate emotionality as an affective-physiological experience state anxiety was measured prior to and after the experiment. Prior to the experiment the mean state anxiety score was 40.2 (high aversion group = 39.7; low aversion group = 40.7), after the experiment the score was 38.7 (high aversion group = 41.1; low aversion group = 36.3). Since state anxiety was measured at two points in time, it was possible to evaluate the effect of the competence valence interactions on changes of emotionality scores. According to Laux et al. (1981) six items were selected, which are said to measure emotionality. A two-way ANOVA

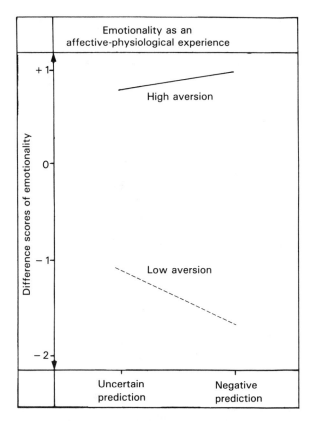

Figure 3 Changes of self-reported emotionality during the experiment as a function of uncertain and negative predictions for high and low aversion.

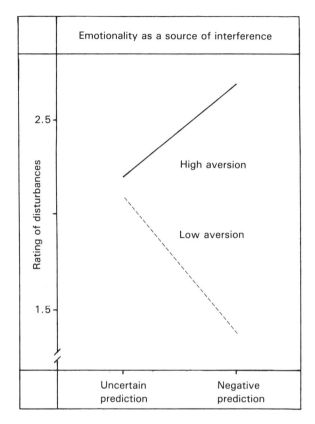

Figure 4   Interference by emotionality as a function of
uncertain and negative predictions for high and low aversion.

based on the sum of these items revealed a significant difference between the experimental and control group (F = 7.61, p ≤ .01), but no differences were identified between the prediction groups (Figure 3).

As can be seen in Figure 3 the measures of perceived emotionality are also in line with our model (Figure 1), except the values of the subjects in the high aversion condition with negative predictions. For these sub-groups we expected—according to the model—a decrease of self-reported emotionality. But the emotionality component of anxiety has still another aspect: The disturbances caused by the perception of changes in autonomic arousal. To analyze this aspect of emotionality we asked, after the experiment was finished, for an answer to the following statement: "In the waiting periods I was disturbed by perceiving my bodily sensations." The groups mean of answers from a four level rating scale differs between the groups. The analysis of variance yielded a main effect for aversion (F (1,32) = 3.92, p = .06) and an effect for the prediction condition (F (1,32) = 2.72, p = .10; see Figure 4). Analyzing emotionality as a source of interference subjects in the high aversion negative prediction condition had the highest values as Figure 4 indicates.

A Field Study

To test the relationship between competence on the one hand and worry on the other hand under the conditions of low and high aversion two investigations were carried out in which self report data have been collected by informal (self-constructed) questionnaires.

Subjects were 52 male students of physical education in Cologne (West Germany) who participated in gymnastics. The mean age of this group was 26 years. The first investigation was carried out with 25 students during a training lesson. We assume that by a training situation low aversion was imposed (quantitative aspect of valence). The second investigation was carried out with 27 students during a physical fitness test situation in gymnastics. We assume that this situation represents a high aversion condition. Prior to the lessons we measured the subjective competence asking in one item of an informal questionnaire for the actual ability to cope with the actual motor tasks. The answer category was a ten-point rating scale (0 = very little, 10 = very high). Subjects were divided post hoc into two groups: High and low subjective competence. As dependent variable we measured worry and emotionality with 8 items from STAI-G (Laux et al., 1981; Worry items: nrs. 4, 7, 11, 17; Emotionality items: nrs. 3, 9, 13, 14).

As can be seen in Figure 5, only in the test situation, which represents a high aversion condition, an increase in worries was observed from high competence to low competence. In the test situation the high competent subjects were sure to reach a good mark low competent subjects were sure to reach a bad mark. An

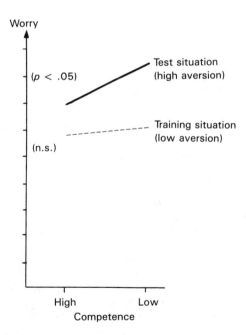

Figure 5 Worry cognitions by persons with high and low subjective competence in two different situations.

uncertainty group could not be obtained, because the subjects were able to judge their abilities reliably, because they learned it on the bases of their experiences in training lessons. Thus, the differentiation between high and low competence in this case was identical with the positive and negative prediction condition. From this point of view the results are in line with the theoretical model outlined above.

Out of the perspective of action psychology two aspects are fundamental in the development of anxiety (Hackfort, 1983): (1) competence, e.g., the competence to cope with the tasks at hand, and (2) valence which reflects the anticipated outcome-consequence-relationship. Anxiety only occurs under the condition of an aversive motivational state. Aversion is characterized by the anticipation of negative consequences. But—as was pointed out—aversion only leads to anxiety if it is combined with uncertain or negative predictions. A negative prediction, however, is less probable if the subjects' competence is high. The higher the aversion the more the uncertain or negative prediction affects anxiety. If there are low degrees of aversion no or only moderate anxiety will occur, although uncertain or negative predictions are present.

In theoretical respect emotionality and worry are components of anxiety. In methodical respect in the operationalization of emotionality and worry this are indicators of anxiety. For both indicators a model was introduced (Figure 1) that predicts the increase in different anxiety components as a function of the amount of aversion on the one hand and the degree of uncertainty on the other. The data of the two studies presented above confirm this model. But—and this is a main result of these investigations—emotionality is a rather ambiguous concept, which needs further theoretical and empirical investigations.

The data suggest that emotionality can be analyzed in respect to three different aspects. Analyzing emotionality as an increase in autonomic arousal, e.g., as an increase in heart rate level, the empirical data of the two studies fits the model perfectly (see Figures 1 and 2). However, analyzing emotionality cognitions, e.g., by the emotionality items of the STAI (Laux, Glauzmann, Schaffner, & Spielberger, 1981), it does not (see Figure 3). Measuring emotionality as a source of interference, the data of the reported studies even contradict the outlined model (see Figure 4). We assume in the later case there are to analyze rather worry than emotionality cognitions. According to this point of view, emotionality as an affective-physiological experience mediated the objective physiological changes during anxiety on the one hand and the interferences caused by those changes on the other. We believe that emotionality cognitions as sources of interference are most important to anxiety research.

In summary, the data of the two experimental studies are in line with the outlined theoretical model if it is considered to analyze (1) emotionality as autonomic arousal and (2) emotionality as cognitions about ones autonomic arousal. Under the second aspect it is suggested to regard emotionality as an indicator which releases cognitions about, e.g., possible negative consequences of the high arousal. These are typical worry cognitions. In this way the differences in the worry gradient and the emotionality gradient would be explainable. There is agreement in anxiety theories that state anxiety is an emotional syndrome with physiological, behavioral and cognitive components. From the perspective of a cognitive approach the appraisal process is fundamental for the development of anxiety. As was pointed out of an action theoretical point of view two aspects as determinants of anxiety can be distinguished: competence and valence. Because cognitions can be understood as symptoms of anxiety and two kinds of cognitions are differentiated, namely worry and emotionality, it is reasonable to test their connections with these two determinants. The presented studies are first steps to clarify the status of worry and emotionality as indicators of certain interactions of competence and valence appraisals.

SUMMARY

In this chapter emotionality and worry as components of anxiety were analyzed out of the perspective of action theory. The main assumptions of this theoretical approach in respect to anxiety were briefly outlined. The concept of emotionality was differentiated and the cognitions of emotionality and worry were regarded as results of an interaction of competence and valence appraisals. The concepts of valence and competence were explained and the conceptualizations were operationalized in two investigations: (1) a laboratory study and (2) a field study. The empirical data fits the outlined model on one hand and suggests further differentiations on the other.

REFERENCES

Fowles, D. C. (1982). Heart rate as an index of anxiety: Failure of a hypothesis. In J. T. Capioppo & R. E. Petty (Eds.), *Perspectives in cardiovascular psychophysiology.* New York: Guilford Press.

Gray, J. A. (1976). The neuropsychology of anxiety. In I. G. Sarason & C. D. Spielberger (Eds.), *Stress and anxiety* (Vol. 3), Washington, DC: Hemisphere.

Hackfort, D. (1983). *Theorie und Diagnostik sportbezogener Ängstlichkeit. Ein situationsanalytischer Ansatz.* Unveröff. Diss. DSHS Köln.

Laux, L., Glanzmann, P., Schaffner, P., & Spielberger, C. D. (1981). *Das State-Trait-Angstinventar. Theoretische Grundlagen und Handanweisung.* Weinheim: Beltz.

Nitsch, J. R. (1981). Streßtheoretische Modellvorstellungen. In J. R. Nitsch (Hg.), *Streß.* Bern: Huber.

Nitsch, J. R., & Hackfort, D. (1981). Stress in Schule und Hochschule—Eine handlungspsychologische Funktionsanalyse. In J. R. Nitsch (Hg.), *Streß.* Bern: Huber.

Schulz, P., & Schönpflug, W. (1982). Regulatory activity during states of stress. In L. Laux & H. W. Krohne (Eds.), *Achievement, stress and anxiety.* Washington, DC: Hemisphere.

Spielberger, C. D., Gonzalez, H. P., Taylor, C. J., Algaze, B., & Anton, W. D. (1978). Examination stress and test anxiety. In C. D. Spielberger & I. G. Sarason (Eds.), *Stress and anxiety* (Vol. 5). New York: Hemisphere.

Thorndike, E. L. (1911). *Animal Intelligence: Experimental Studies.* New York: Macmillan.

Vroom, V. H. (1964). *Work and motivation.* New York: Wiley.

Wortman, C. B. & Brehm, J. W. (1975). Responses to uncontrollable outcomes: An integration of reactance and the learned helplessness model. In L. Berkowitz (Ed.), *Advances in experimental and social psychology* (Vol. 8). New York: Academic Press.

4

Analysis of Anxiety Levels in Sport

Frank H. Sanderson

INTRODUCTION

Over the past few years there has been an increasing awareness amongst sportsmen and coaches of the importance of psychological factors in sports. The world of sport abounds with examples of unexpected success or failure which on closer analysis suggests that psychological phenomena were at least partly responsible, e.g., the sometimes remarkable performances of lowly teams in championship matches. The recognition of this influence is exemplified in many ways: by the acknowledgement of psychological factors in the analysis of sport in the media, by the efforts of coaches and sportsmen to gain knowledge of psychology and, significantly, by the active involvement of sports psychologists in the preparation of sportsmen for competition. This last development has taken many forms, ranging from the individual athlete independently seeking assistance, to the full-time employment of a psychologist by a team of athletes, e.g., the Brazilian soccer team and many sports teams in Eastern Europe.

Many, if not all, "psychological" influences in sport can be directly related to the sportsman's experience of stress and his subsequent reaction to it. Stress has been defined in many ways but in the present context, it is perhaps best described as "a *perceived* situation which threatens the gratification of needs." This implies strong ego-involvement in the "stressed" individual, and emphasizes both the link between stress and the emotional reaction and the fact that this reaction can have positive or negative effects. For example, anxiety, a frequent consequence of stress, could lead to a deterioration in performance—a player "losing his cool"—or an increased determination to perform well. Hence, although the terms "stress" and "anxiety" are not synonymous, they both can exhibit an inverted 'U' relationship with performance. The present chapter is concerned with problems and possibilities of anxiety measurement in sport as revealed by research at Liverpool Polytechnic in recent years.

It is widely accepted that anxiety, both trait and particularly state, plays an influential role in the sports performance of individuals. At a trait level, it has frequently been found that the best athletes tend to be relatively low in anxiety (e.g., Booth, 1958). Anxiety-prone individuals, identified by questionnaire methods are not well represented among elite sports groups. Whilst this is of general interest it is perhaps more relevant to understand the kinds of relationship which exist between sports performance and the anxiety which it transiently generates.

With objectivity in mind, early investigators tended to employ psychophysiological measures of state anxiety in the sports context (Harmon and Johnson, 1952). However, more recent research has highlighted the inherent unreliability of such measures which has given a new status to the questionnaire approach (Levitt, 1971). Of particular interest in this regard is Spielberger's State-Trait Anxiety Inventory (Spielberger, et al., 1970) which has the advantages of incorporating a state questionnaire along with the more usual trait aspect, and can be administered very quickly with minimal disruption of the preoccupied athlete. Such is not possible with psychophysiological monitoring.

The difficulties of obtaining psychophysiological measures of anxiety are well indicated by Reilly et al's. (1985) study of anxiety and thrill on a fair-ground ride. Heart-rates of individuals strapped into a "roller-coaster" were monitored by means of radio-telemetry, and since the individuals were in a "resting" state, a fairly pure measure of "emotional reaction" was generated. However, there was no means of knowing from the heart-rate data whether the individual was anxious, thrilled, both or neither. Post-ride questionnaires considerably aided the interpretation of the heart-rate data; most subjects' heart-rate appeared to be elevated by the relatively unrelated emotional reactions of anxiety and enjoyment. The conclusion is that if information is required about an individual's emotional reactions, an excellent means is to ask him, providing he has no interest in giving misleading information.

ANXIETY BEFORE AND AFTER BADMINTON COMPETITION

The usefulness of the Spielberger inventory in the sporting context was investigated in a pilot study in April, 1977, when 64 of the best 18–21 year old badminton players in England assembled at the National Sports Centre at Lilleshall for an inter-regional tournament. The weekend of badminton took place right at the end of the season. Most players had surpassed their peaks after completing 9 months of training and competition. Consequently, the tournament was to be treated by most players as a non-serious winding-down after the rigors of the competitive season. However, several players were keen to make an impression with the coaches for possible National Youth Squad selection.

Every player had several matches and the intention was that each should complete an A-State inventory immediately before and after each match. This would allow two complementary predictions to be tested:

1. A-State postmatch will be higher than prematch A-State when the player loses.

2. A-State postmatch will be lower than prematch A-State when the player wins.

It was considered that basal (uncontaminated) A-States could not be assessed during the weekend and A-traits were also not measured.

Seventeen (10 females and 7 males) of the 64 players agreed to fill in the questionnaires and as many had more than one match, 39 sets of before-after A-States were recorded. The results were divided about equally between "winning" and "losing" matches, there being 19 losers and 20 winners.

Pre-match and post-match A-States of males/females and match winners and match losers were calculated and subjected to analysis.

Matched pairs 't' tests on the before-after A-State data revealed only one significant change, i.e., a significant decrease (P < .05) in the female players' anxiety after winning matches. The figures suggest other differences might exist but no significance can be attached to these, largely as a result of the combination of the small samples and the relatively large variances. For example, the apparent increase in male A-State after winning can primarily be attributed to one individual whose A-State score more than doubled probably because he had beaten a highly rated player against all expectations.

It is also possible that his remarkably low "before" A-State score of 22 indicated the presence of the "denial" defense mechanism, particularly as he was aware of the status of his opponent. On the other hand, the lack of anxiety may have been a reflection of his resigned expectation of defeat. This situation served to highlight the fact that the A-State score does not reveal *why* an individual is more or less anxious.

Examination of the individual before-after data discloses decreases and increases in A-States under all conditions and suggested the need for more sophisticated hypotheses about A-State changes in this kind of situation. Some of the "nuisance variables" which need to be considered are listed below:

1. The existence of "denial" sets in some players—representing an attempt on the part of the individual to convince himself that he is not anxious—an understandable and maybe subconscious strategy.

2. Increased A-State after winning could have resulted from a phenomenon broadly associated with success phobia. The personality of the player would be a key factor in determining the emotional reaction to victory. A high A-trait individual would possibly find unexpected victory quite traumatic.

3. Decreased A-State after losing could have resulted from the feeling that "the ordeal is over" or that certain subgoals had been successfully achieved, e.g., managing to take a game off the eventual winner.

4. Prior knowledge of the opponent's standard of play may have been an important factor in both before and after A-State level. Predicting what these levels might be on this evidence alone would be problematical.

5. It became apparent that the timing of the post-match administration is important. The psychophysiological reverberations persist for some time after the match, having the effect of counteracting the deactivation process. Concerning pre-match anxiety measurement Huddlestone and Gill (1981) demonstrated that A-State increases as time to competition nears with a substantial increase being

noted from the "pre-meet" (45 min prior to the meet) to the event (5 min before the event) measure. This finding serves to emphasize the importance of collecting A-State data as close as possible to the start of the competition.

6. The perceived importance of the competition appeared to be a significant factor governing A-State reactions. There was some anecdotal evidence from this tournament that female players took the tournament much more seriously than the males.

It was clear from this study that the possible combinations of factors which will determine A-State at any time are numerous, suggesting caution in the use of state measures to predict performance. Largely on the basis of this limited evidence, Sanderson and Ashton (1981) argued that A-State measures would be likely to be more useful when used in conjunction with in-depth analysis of the *reasons* for the existence of particular anxiety states. Such an approach, they maintained would be likely to encourage in the individual a sophisticated self-insight and more effective coping behavior in situations of stress.

An important omission of the above investigation was Spielberger's complementary A-trait questionnaire, which would have allowed measurement of the relationship between transient and dispositional anxiety reactions, as well as the links between these measures and performance. Additionally, although it was found that reduction in post-competitive A-State appeared to be contingent upon success for ego-involved badminton players, it is also recognized that the criteria for "success" in sport may be complex and individual-specific.

For instance, if the probability of winning is assumed to be $\frac{1}{N}$ then the badminton player is clearly more hopeful of absolute success than, say, the cross-country runner. This raises questions about the nature of the relationship between performance in situations where there is one winner and many "losers" and state/trait anxiety measures. Accordingly, a study was undertaken of trait and state anxiety reactions of cross-country runners (Sanderson & Reilly, 1983).

TRAIT AND STATE ANXIETY IN MALE AND FEMALE CROSS-COUNTRY RUNNERS

In this investigation, the performance of cross-country runners was examined in the light of both trait and anxiety state scores, the latter being administered both pre- and post-race. In correlating anxiety and performance data, competitive success was equated with absolute performance proficiency, i.e., a direct function of finishing position. It was hypothesized that both trait and state anxiety would be positively related to this index of performance. Because of the greater impact match outcome was found to have had on state anxiety of female badminton players (Sanderson & Ashton, 1981) it was decided to monitor both male and female competitors in this study.

Subjects consisted of 38 randomly selected female runners aged between 18 and 41 years who were competing in the English Womens' Cross-Country Championships in February, 1978, and 26 males aged 19 to 31 (randomly selected from a field of 102) from the Hollymount International Road Race in November, 1978. In each case, runners completed a Spielberger trait questionnaire 1 hour before the race as indicated by circumstantial constraints and a state questionnaire within 15 minutes of the start of the race. A-State was again measured immediately after the athletes finished the race. The results were as follows:

1. *Women's National Championships:* Correlation analysis revealed that A-trait was significantly related to pre-race A-state (r = 0.47; P < .01), which in turn was marginally related to race performance on the basis of the unidirectional hypothesis (r = 0.29; P < .01). This suggests greater control and composure in the better runners. Pre- and post-race A-states were significantly related (r = 0.34; P < .05). Unlike the badminton research a useful distinction could not be made between winners and losers, but an attempt was made to distinguish between more or less proficient runners. To this end, subjects were divided into 2 approximately equal groups: Group A, consisting of 20 athletes who finished in the first 55 places and Group B, consisting of 18 athletes who finished between 68th and 158th place. Pre-race A-states of the groups (49.7/8.8 and 46.0/11.8 respectively) did not differ significantly. Similarly, post-match A-States (33.1/12.0 and 41.0/12.4 respectively) did not differ, but matched pairs analysis revealed a significant post-race A-state reduction for the more successful group (P < .01). The mean A-trait scores of the groups approximated to the combined mean score of 39.8.

2. *Hollymount Road Race:* It was found that A-trait was significantly correlated with race performance (r = 0.43; P < .05) and, as was the case with the women, pre-race A-state was related to A-trait (r = 0.43; P < .05). Pre- and post-race A-states (42.4/10.7 and 33.3/11.0 respectively) were found to be significantly different. The average A-trait of 37.1/7.6 compares closely with the average A-trait for the female runners.

The major finding is that there were clear post-race reductions in A-state for the high finishers in the women's race and for the whole group in the men's race. For the top five men, it was noticed that the A-state reduction was even more marked. In the light of previous findings that A-state reductions are associated with absolute success in badminton and basketball (Sanderson & Ashton, 1981; Gruber & Beauchamp, 1979) it is clear that cross-country running is in a different category in that winning is not the sole criterion of success. The hypothesis that cross-country runners are likely to assign importance to and find comfort in the achievement of individual specific sub-goals, which leads to A-state reduction, irrespective of absolute achievement level, is given some support. A qualifying factor seems to be that low finishers in large fields of runners may have more difficulty in perceiving their performance as having redeeming features. Perhaps too it reflects ill-defined criteria of "success" amongst such individuals and/or unrealistic levels of aspiration. It is also likely that age and/or experience will affect subjective interpretations of quality of performance.

Elevated A-state levels post-competition would suggest that specific attention of coaches and mentors might need to be directed to athletes recognized as poor losers. The aim would be to develop positive coping behavior in the athlete which would enable him to recover quickly from any competitive trauma associated with performing poorly.

ANXIETY AND CAUSAL ATTRIBUTIONS

Relevant here is Sanderson and Gilchrist's (1981) study which examined relationships between match outcome, anxiety reactions and causal attributions of squash players. The subjects of the study were 26 seasoned county standard players participating in important league matches; hence, ego-involvement could be assumed. This assumption was supported by the anxiety reactions of players—significant pre-post match decreases in state anxiety for winning players contrasted with significant increases in anxiety for losing players. No relationship was found between pre-match anxiety and performance. Correlational analysis of pre- and post-match state anxiety scores revealed a non-significant correlation for losers and a significant correlation for winners ($r = 0.58$, $P < 0.005$). This suggests that, in spite of the significant increase in state anxiety for losers, the magnitude of the increase is individual specific. Winners on the other hand demonstrate significant reductions in state anxiety which are proportional to the pre-match levels.

It was interesting to observe the way in which the squash players ascribed responsibility for success and failure. Previous research has suggested that individuals take credit for positive outcomes by attributing success to internal factors such as personal ability and effort. Conversely, they tend to deny responsibility for negative outcomes by attributing responsibility to external factors beyond their control, such as luck or task difficulty. Hence, a winning athlete is quite happy to accept that his ability is instrumental in the outcome whereas a losing athlete is much less likely to explain his defeat in terms of his lack of ability. On the contrary, it is an unusual loser who does not have several excuses to explain his lack of success. Thus individuals tend to display "self-serving biases" in competitive ego-involving situations.

The players were asked to attribute causality for competitive outcomes to nine selected internal factors and nine selected external factors by completing a causality questionnaire which was administered 30 min after the match. The main hypotheses were that winners would tend to attribute internally and losers would tend to attribute externally. It was found that although winners indeed attributed more internally and less externally than losers, the latter still assessed internal attributes to be the most important determinants of match outcome and this was in spite of the significantly elevated post-match anxiety levels of losers with the associated need to protect self-esteem. In line with predictions from attribution theory it was noted, however, that there was a tendency for post-match anxiety to correlate significantly and negatively with internal attribution score, irrespective of match outcome i.e., there was a reduced tendency for those with high post-match anxiety to attribute internally. For the winners, lower post-match anxiety was associated with a reduced tendency to make external attributions. Nevertheless, it is probable that social norms/constraints associated with squash tend to limit the acceptability of external attributions. Perhaps losing players were sufficiently realistic to realize that, even though they were disposed to make excuses, such a "coping strategy" would lack credibility with observers. Also pertinent is the fact that the attribution questionnaire was administered 30 min after the match, whereas the state anxiety inventory was administered immediately after the match. It seems reasonable to suppose that attributions immediately post-match would be more external than those made 30 min later when reason is more likely to prevail. In this sense, external attribution may be temporarily functional for the loser, allowing the threatened ego to negotiate the painful aftermath of the match. The time it takes for the pain and anxiety to reduce to acceptable proportions varies across individuals but it seems that for many, this will have been accomplished within 30 min. of the match. Thus high anxious unrealistic individuals who tend to be consistent in their external attributions should be encouraged to be more internal in their attributions. If excuses are always made in defeat, there is the possibility that the athlete will not learn from his mistakes. He can gain superficial comfort from external attribution without considering his own role in preventing the recurrence of defeat. In team sports, the situation could be made worse in the sense that an individual in a losing team may attribute the outcome to team mates, which could be damaging to team morale, cohesion and efficiency. Accordingly, the following advice to coaches and athletes is offered:

a) The coach should encourage, by example, an internal attribution perspective amongst the athletes. Such an example should also be set by, for example, the team captain and senior players.
b) In physical preparation of the athlete the cause and effect relationship between skill, quality of training and success should be emphasized. The aim should be for optimum event motivation linked with functional post-match coping strategies following defeat.
c) Levels of aspiration of athletes should be realistically set. The means by which aspirations can be achieved should be discussed.
d) Although the relationship between athlete behavior and subsequent success should be noted and acknowledged the apportionment of blame should be avoided.

PSYCHOLOGICAL CORRELATES OF PERFORMANCE IN MALE CROSS-COUNTRY RUNNERS

Having made the link between post-event anxiety and loss of self-esteem in the squash study, it was decided to refocus attention on cross-country running and investigate psychological correlates of performance, including anxiety and attribution.

It has already been demonstrated that the criteria of "success" are more subtle than in 1 v 1 sports, with the consequence that there is no straightforward relationship between anxiety reactions and success as determined by finishing position. It was argued that the individual's criteria for success might be more readily identified with the aid of more psychologically comprehensive pre- and post-event questionnaires. The major aim of the study was to investigate the relationship between finishing position and the athlete's expectations, satisfactions, feelings and attributions by means of pre- and post-race questionnaires. The questionnaires addressed themselves only partly to state anxiety, as opposed to solely, as was the case with the previous investigation into cross-country running (Sanderson & Reilly, 1983).

Accordingly, two questionnaires were developed to be administered immediately pre-race and immediately post-race respectively.

The pre-race questionnaire (see Appendix A) contained the competitive short form CSAI of the Spielberger State Anxiety Inventory (Martens, 1977). On evidence presented by Martens (1977) CSAI provides a good indication of changes in A-state as a function of competition. The 'activation' questions, measuring high levels of A-state are: 3, 9, 11, 15 and 21 and the deactivation questions, emphasizing low A-states are 2, 6, 10, 13 and 19. As well as the CSAI, the pre-race questionnaire contained questions related to the athlete's state of fitness (Q7 and Q17); whether he ran in the race for enjoyment (Q4, Q8 and Q12); questions concerning race-related anxiety (Q1, Q14, Q16 and Q20); whether or not the athlete was taking the race seriously (Q23) and whether or not he felt team pressure (Q18 and Q22).

The post-race questionnaire (see Appendix B) included the CSAI measure of state anxiety with 4, 9, 12, 18 and 21 being the activation questions and 1, 6, 10, 15 and 20 being the deactivation questions. Other questions related to: whether the athlete enjoyed participating in the race (Q2); whether he thought he had performed well (Q3 and Q13); whether he was glad the race was over (Q8); whether he took the race seriously (Q11) and other questions broadly pertaining to attributional factors (Q7, Q14, Q16, Q17, Q19 and Q22). Question 5—"I ran better than in my last league race" was used as a reliability check to see if the subjects were answering correctly and not randomly ticking boxes. A four-point Likert-type scale was used in the manner of Spielberger's state anxiety inventory.

The statements used in the questionnaire were all written positively to avoid confusion with double negatives, e.g., it may have been confusing to answer a statement "I didn't take the race seriously" with "not at all" if the respondent *did* take the race seriously.

Forty male cross-country runners were used in the study. All of the subjects had run in at least one of the previous 8 league races during the 1982–83 season. All were regular runners in full training.

The pre-race questionnaire was administered approximately 15 min before the race, immediately prior to the athlete's warm-up period. The idea of administering the questionnaire immediately prior to the race was rejected on several grounds:

1. There was a risk of taking advantage of the athlete's willingness to cooperate to the detriment of the athlete.

2. It was possible that the warm-up and immediate pre-race preparation would induce catharsis, which would have the effect of reducing the emotional variance across athletes.

3. Some athletes may have objected to an intrusion at a late stage.

The post-race questionnaire was administered to the athletes as they entered the changing rooms and before showering. The fact that the investigator was known to the athletes ensured that full cooperation was gained, even from those athletes who were disappointed in their performances.

RESULTS AND DISCUSSION

Correlation analysis revealed that 4 pre-race items were significantly related to performance, indexed in terms of finishing position. The results suggested that more successful runners were more satisfied with the way training had been going (Item 7; r = −0.32; P < 0.05), more inclined to be looking forward to the race (Item 8; r = −0.40; P < 0.01), more tense (Item 9; r = −0.41; P < 0.01) and more likely to be participating for enjoyment (Item 12; r = −0.47; P < 0.01). These results suggest a somewhat closer connection between absolute success and psychological variables than had been hypothesized. It would appear that in competitive races, the poorer performers, far from finding comfort in the achievement of individual sub-goals, are more likely to see the race as an ordeal to be negotiated than to be enjoyed. The better runners on the other hand, appear to anticipate the race with pleasure. By implication and contrary to expectations intrinsic motivation (i.e., participating for enjoyment) appears to be linked with absolute success. The "also ran" can gain little comfort from these findings.

It is interesting to note the significant correlation between tension (Item 9) and finishing position, i.e., higher finishers claimed to be more tense pre-race than the lower finishers. It is possible that variations in pre-race tension are connected with the idea of arousal optimization and that higher tension is conducive to subsequent optimal performance. On the other hand, higher pre-race tension could relate to the pressure on the better performer to confirm or protect his racing reputation. Conversely, the "also ran" with no reputation to protect feels less tense.

As was expected a greater number of significant correlations were found between post-race questionnaire items and race performance. The better the performance, the more the athlete was likely to be at ease (Item 1; r = 0.33; P < 0.05), relaxed (Item 15; r = −0.51; P < 0.01), and calm (Item 20; r = −0.39; P < 0.01). He was also more likely to believe that he performed well (Item 3; r = −0.43; P < 0.01), more likely to be pleased with his performance (Item 13; r = −0.47; P < 0.01), less likely to be glad the race was over (Item 8; r = 0.43; P < 0.01) and less likely to claim that he made tactical mistakes (Item 22; r = 0.42; P < 0.01). The results tend to confirm the implicit pre-race evidence that absolute performance is an important determinant of race enjoyment, and that less successful runners are more likely to view the race as an "ordeal to be negotiated." Furthermore there is some evidence that lower finishers are more inclined to make excuses (i.e., claim to have made tactical mistakes), presumably as a means of protecting self-esteem. It is less damaging to attribute "failure" to an *unstable* internal factor which could conceivably be remedied on a future occasion than to a *stable* internal factor relating to absolute ability as a runner.

As mentioned above, the competitive short form of the SAI was incorporated into the pre- and post-race questionnaires. A significant pre-post reduction in anxiety was noted (t = 3.94; P < 0.001) and correlation analysis revealed a non-significant relationship between pre-race CSAI and finishing position but a significant relationship post-race (r = +0.27; P < 0.05), i.e., a tendency for anxiety to increase with decreasing absolute performance. Pre- and post-race CSAI scores were not significantly correlated. Incidentally, analysis of individual CSAI items generally revealed high significant correlations amongst the deactivation items, but not amongst the activation items. One interpretation of this is that a greater range of identifiable psychological states is encompassed by the activation items of CSAI.

As a means of clarifying the pattern of relationships amongst the questionnaire items, the data was factor analyzed. For the pre-race analysis, the rotated factor matrix produced 7 factors with eigen values in excess of 1. On the basis of the item-loading, each factor was tentatively named as follows:

		Loading
I.	RACE ANXIETY	
	I feel at ease	−0.79
	I feel nervous	+0.69
	I am tense	+0.66
	I am relaxed	−0.73
	I get nervous waiting to start the race	+0.78
	I am jittery	+0.62
	I feel calm	−0.63
II.	ENJOYMENT	
	Competing against others is socially enjoyable	+0.82
	I am looking forward to the race	+0.81
	I participate in the race for enjoyment	+0.88
III.	OVER-AROUSAL	
	I usually get up-tight pre-race	−0.88
	I feel over-excited and rattled	−0.83
IV.	PREPAREDNESS	
	I am satisfied with the way training has been going	+0.84
	I feel secure	+0.66
	I feel anxious	−0.51
	I am fit enough to give a true representation of my ability	+0.69
V.	CONFIDENCE	
	I expect to run better than in my last league race	+0.80
	I feel comfortable	+0.51
VI.	TEAM PRESSURE	
	I have a queasy feeling in my stomach	+0.47
	There is pressure on me as a team member to do well	+0.49
	I run for myself rather than the team	−0.68
VII.	CONCERNEDNESS	
	I am worried about performing well	+0.83
	I am taking the race seriously	+0.61

The same procedure was adopted for the post-race data, with the resulting rotated factor matrix producing 7 factors. The factors were named as follows:

		Loading
I.	RELAXEDNESS	
	I feel at ease	+0.84
	I enjoyed competing in the race	+0.59
	I feel comfortable	+0.69
	I am relaxed	+0.89
	I am calm	+0.85
II.	TENSION	
	I am tense	+0.78

I was too nervous before the race   +0.82
III. EXCUSES
    I took the race seriously   +0.66
    The course was not to my liking   −0.70
    I finished the race with plenty in hand   −0.60
IV. NERVOUS REGRET
    I feel nervous   −0.41
    I was satisfied with my pre-race build up   +0.74
    I am glad the race is over   −0.73
    I feel over-excited and rattled   −0.52
V. CONTENTMENT
    I have performed well   −0.81
    I ran better than in my last league race   −0.74
    I am pleased with my performance   −0.83
    I think my finishing position is a true reflection of my ability   −0.77
VI. ANXIETY
    I feel secure   −0.45
    I feel anxious   −0.68
    I am jittery   −0.81
VII. TACTICAL MISTAKES
    I made tactical mistakes in the race   −0.91

Item scores were combined appropriately under the 14 identified factors which were then subjected to correlation analysis together with the performance data. Two pre-race factors were significantly related to finishing position, i.e., enjoyment ($r = 0.38$; $P < 0.05$) and preparedness ($r = 0.38$; $P < 0.05$). Specifically, the more prepared they were and the more they identified enjoyment as an important factor in racing, the better they were likely to fare in the race. In order to examine the predictive potential of the pre-race variables, a regression of finishing position on the variables was undertaken (See Table 1).

Table 1   Regression of Finishing Position on Pre-race Variables

Factors	Standardized regression coefficients	't' value
Race anxiety	−0.36	−2.43*
Enjoyment	0.39	2.62*
Over arousal	−0.02	−0.15
Preparedness	0.33	2.32*
Confidence	0.20	1.45
Team pressure	0.13	0.90
Concernedness	0.31	2.10*
Multiple R	0.66	
Coefficient of determination	0.42	
F ratio (df = 7,39)	3.86*	

*$P < 0.05$.

The pre-race factors accounted for 42 percent of variance in subsequent performance. A 't' test of the individual regression coefficients revealed that race anxiety, enjoyment, preparedness and concernedness were contributing significantly to the performance variance. A stepwise regression analysis demonstrated that these particular variables accounted for 37 percent of the variance, made up of 6, 15, 9 and 7 percent respectively.

Concerning the post-race correlation analysis several factors were significantly related to finishing position. Relaxedness significantly correlated with performance (r = 0.57; P < 0.01), as did nervous regret (r = 0.33; P < 0.05), contentment (r = 0.42; P < −0.01) and, as mentioned earlier, tactical mistakes. As might be expected, the better the performance, the more likelihood of the athlete being relaxed, not showing nervous regret and showing contentment.

With reference to the overall "predictive" potential of post-race questionnaire data, it was found, perhaps not surprisingly, that more variance was accounted for than was the case pre-race (Table 2). It would seem that predictive potential would increase because subjects know the performance outcome which is assumed to have influenced their post-race questionnaire responses.

It was found that over 50 percent of the variance in performance was accounted for by the 7 post-race factors. A 't' test indicated that it was relaxedness and tactical mistakes which were contributing significantly to the variance in outcome. Stepwise regression analysis revealed that these variables predicted 42 percent of the variance in performance outcome, with the contributions being 33 percent and 9 percent respectively. The fact that as much as 42 percent of the variance was accounted for was remarkable in that it had been assumed that post-race responses would be strongly influenced by subjective judgments of success which would not necessarily be related to finishing position in the race.

It would appear then that, contrary to the subjective success hypothesis, the individuals psychological state is strongly affected by the absolute success achieved in a race. The lower the finishing position the less likely it is for the athlete to be experiencing satisfaction and gaining fulfillment. Rather, it is the high achiever who is intrinsically motivated even though he is clearly more exposed to extrinsic motivational factors such as praise and material gain. Indeed, intrinsic and extrinsic motivation, far from being mutually exclusive, appear to be

Table 2 Regression of Finishing Position on Post-race Variables

Factors	Standardized regression coefficients	't' value
Relaxedness	0.44	2.61 (P < 0.02)
Arousal	0.07	0.48 –
Effort	0.08	−0.55 –
Regret	0.13	0.89 –
Contentment	0.25	1.54 –
Anxiety	−0.24	−1.47 –
Mistakes	0.33	2.51 (P < 0.02)
Multiple R	0.71	
Coefficient of determination	0.50	
F ratio (df = 7,39)	4.46 (P < 0.002)	

complementary for the high achiever. The more comprehensive analysis of psychological states both pre- and post-event has proved to be worthwhile. Although the criteria for success may be more subtle than in 1 v 1 sports, a surprising correspondence has been found between absolute performance and psychological state. Broadening the forms from "anxiety" to include factors such as "enjoyment" and "preparedness" was useful in increasing the predictive potential of the questionnaires; additional factors which would need to be examined would include level of aspiration, attribution (only hinted at in the present investigation) and extrinsic motivation. Ultimately, it is hoped that a more sensitive and coherent framework for the analysis of psychological state and performance will be produced. Monitoring anxiety in sports situations has proved useful in the past, but if the complex reasons for particular anxiety states are to be investigated realistically and performance is to be more sensitively predicted, then a more psychologically comprehensive approach needs to be adopted.

SUMMARY

The present chapter is concerned with problems and possibilities of anxiety measurement in sport as revealed by research at Liverpool Polytechnic in recent years. Research into the anxiety of badminton players before and after competition demonstrated both the advantages and limitations of using anxiety questionnaires with athletes. Subsequent research examined the more complex relationships between performance in cross-country running, where there is one winner and many "losers," and anxiety. It was found that the criteria of success are ill-defined which complicates the relationship between anxiety and absolute performance.

Since it was found that measuring anxiety per se raised many questions, causal attribution was introduced as an additional dimension in a study which examined the relationships between match outcome and anxiety reactions of squash players. The main finding was that both winners and losers, despite different post-match anxiety reactions, tended to attribute internally.

A final study again focused on cross-country runners, but with a more comprehensive monitoring of psychological states, including anxiety, both pre- and post-race. Including such factors as "enjoyment" and "preparedness" was useful in increasing the predictive potential of the questionnaires. It is concluded that if the complex reasons for particular anxiety states are to be investigated realistically and performance is to be more sensitively predicted, then more psychologically comprehensive approaches need to be adopted.

REFERENCES

Booth, E. (1958). Personality traits of athletes as measured by the MMPI. *Research Quarterly, 29,* 127–138.

Gruber, J. J., & Beauchamp, D. (1979). Relevancy of the competitive state anxiety inventory in a sport environment. *Research Quarterly, 50,* 207–214.

Harmon, J., & Johnson, W. (1952). The emotional reactions of college athletes. *Research Quarterly, 23,* 391–397.

Huddleston, S., & Gill, D. L. (1981). State anxiety as a function of skill level and proximity to competition. *Research Quarterly, 52,* 31–34.

Levitt, E. E. (1971). *The psychology of anxiety.* London: Paladin.

Martens, R. (1977). *Sport competition anxiety test.* Champaign, IL: Human Kinetics Publishers.

Reilly, T., Lees,A., MacLaren, D., & Sanderson, F. H. (1985). Thrill and anxiety in adventure leisure parks. In D. J. Osborne (Ed.), *Contemporary Ergonomics* (pp. 210–214). London: Taylor and Francis.

Sanderson, F. H., & Ashton, M. K. (1981). Analysis of anxiety levels before and after badminton competition. *International Journal of Sports Psychology, 12,* 23–28.

Sanderson, F. H., & Gilchrist, J. (1982). Anxiety and attributional responses of squash players. *British Journal of Sports Medicine, 16,* 115.

Sanderson, F. H., & Reilly,T. (1983). Trait and state anxiety in male and female cross-country runners. *British Journal of Sports Medicine, 17,* 24–26.

Spielberger, C. D., Gorsuch, R. L., & Lushene, R. E. (1970). *Manual for the State-Trait Anxiety Inventory.* Palo Alto, CA: Consulting Psychologists Press.

APPENDIX A

NAME:_____

PRE-RACE QUESTIONNAIRE

	Not at all 1	Somewhat 2	Moderately so 3	Very much so 4

Please tick *one* box for every statement.
1. I am worried about performing well.
2. I feel at ease.
3. I feel nervous.
4. Competing against others is socially enjoyable.
5. I expect to run better than in my last league race.
6. I feel comfortable.
7. I am satisfied the way training has been going.
8. I am looking forward to the race.
9. I am tense.
10. I feel secure.
11. I feel anxious.
12. I participate in the race for enjoyment.
13. I am relaxed.
14. I get nervous wanting to start the race.
15. I am jittery.
16. I have a queasy feeling in my stomach.
17. I am fit enough to give a true representation of my ability.
18. There is pressure on me as a team member to do well.
19. I feel calm.
20. I usually get 'up-tight' pre-race.
21. I feel over excited and rattled.
22. I run for myself rather than the team.
23. I am taking the race seriously.

APPENDIX B

NAME_____

POST-RACE QUESTIONNAIRE

	Not at all 1	Somewhat 2	Moderately so 3	Very much so 4

Please show how *true* the statements below
are, by ticking *one* box for every statement.

1. I feel at ease.
2. I enjoyed competing in the race.
3. I have performed well.
4. I feel nervous.
5. I ran better than in my last league
     race.
6. I feel comfortable.
7. I was satisfied with my pre-race
     build-up.
8. I am glad the race is over.
9. I am tense.
10. I feel secure.
11. I took the race seriously.
12. I feel anxious.
13. I am pleased with my performance.
14. The course was not to my liking.
15. I am relaxed.
16. I was too nervous before the race.
17. I think my finishing position is a true
     reflection of my ability.
18. I am jittery.
19. I finished the race with 'plenty in
     hand'.
20. I feel calm.
21. I feel over-excited and rattled.
22. I made tactical mistakes in the race.

5

Measuring Anxiety in Sports: Perspectives and Problems

Dieter Hackfort and Peter Schwenkmezger

INTRODUCTION

Diagnostic methods developed in general anxiety research cannot simply be taken over uncritically and used in investigations in the field of sport psychology. Many sport scientists tend to reject methods from general psychology, recommending instead that specific instruments be developed for questions concerning the area of sport psychology (e.g., Nitsch, 1975; Martens, 1977). There are, however, several arguments which speak against such a methodological specificity. Because the development of adequate methods is a very long and painstaking undertaking, the first and most obvious reason for retaining these methods is economy. Everyone involved with research in sport psychology is interested in getting results that can be used in education and training practice as quickly as possible, with a minimum of time-consuming experiments dealing exclusively with methodology. For this reason it seems necessary to combine methods that have already been developed and validated in general anxiety diagnostics and then to develop these for applications to sport-specific fields.

Even if one takes the standpoint that sport science and sport psychology are independent scientific disciplines and therefore need to develop their own specific research instruments, then one is faced with new problems, since it then follows that measurement methods also have to be developed for all the different kinds of sport. For example, Martens' (1977) sport-anxiety questionnaire cannot be applied to team sports without first undergoing some modifications, since certain of the items do not seem to be relevant to this particular field.

In addition, some psychologists maintain that sport psychology is threatening to break away from its parent discipline and become an applied sport science. The consequences of this would be a loss in quality for the parent discipline and, for both psychology and sport psychology alike, reduced feedback for the research process. As an alternative it is recommended that sport be regarded as a field of study in which many originally psychological hypotheses can be tested, modified or rejected (Nitsch, 1978; Heckhausen, 1979; Browne & Mahoney, 1984).

The following article will begin by summarizing the various possible methods of measuring anxiety and questions about convergence and divergence among the various levels of measurement. This will then be followed by a discussion of more recent approaches and findings in the field of anxiety diagnosis, concluding with sport-specific implications.

MULTILEVEL APPROACHES TO THE MEASUREMENT OF SPORT-SPECIFIC ANXIETY: POSSIBILITIES AND PROBLEMS

Before one begins to discuss measurement-theoretical problems of anxiety assessment it is first necessary to draw a distinction between the different approaches for assessing anxiety and anxiety reactions. In general one distinguishes between assessing anxiety on the cognitive level (self-assessment and assessment by others), records of physiological parameters, and behavioral and non-verbal or expressive indices. On each of these levels there is something different that must be taken into account, which in part prevents a high degree of covariation between parameters of the various measurement levels.

MEASURING ANXIETY ON THE COGNITIVE LEVEL

One example of classifying anxiety measures on the cognitive level is McReynold's (1968) system, which distinguishes between three major categories:

(1) Anxiety scales can attempt to assess either (a) a person's situation-independent, general anxiety level (anxiousness), or (b) his or her anxiety level under situation-specific conditions. Cattell and Scheier (1961) were the first to suggest such a distinction and to study it systematically. Spielberger (1966, 1975) took this one step further and formulated an interactional theory of anxiety. According to him, a person's current anxiety level depends upon the duration and intensity of the threatening stimulus (situation). The number and types of situations which cause any individual person anxiety depends upon his personality-specific level of anxiety: The more anxious a person is, the more situations he will interpret as being personally threatening.

(2) If anxiety is regarded as a hypothetical construct, then the array of instruments for measuring anxiety can assess either (a) previous conditions or (b) subsequent consequences of anxiety. Previous conditions can include, for example, person-specific factors that are either genetically determined or are acquired during the course of socialization and reflect stabilized behavioral dispositions. Other previous conditions occur in specific situations—for example, when subjectively threatening stimulus constellations generate anxiety. Consequences of anxiety include those reactions that are traditionally characterized as anxiety symptoms. Here, too, one can distinguish between direct and long-term manifestations of anxiety reactions. Direct consequences of threatening situations can include, for example, a diminished sense of well-being or specific physiological reactions; long-term consequences include expectations of failure following an extended series of failures.

(3) A third category, according to McReynolds, is the question of the *generality* of the measuring instrument. Depending upon one's purpose, one can attempt either to (a) obtain a value for a person's general anxiety or (b) assess only specific aspects of anxiety (for example, fear of physical injury or ego-threat). The majority of instruments introduced for measuring anxiety are very heterogeneous with regard to their methodology. In their theoretical conception and formal design they take into account different aspects of anxiety measurement. With regard to methodological aspects, one can distinguish between ratings, personality inventories and questionnaires. For a number of measures one must also take into account the theoretical foundations. And, under the aspect of application, the sport-specific relevance of each of the measures has to be discussed.

Anxiety questionnaires always contain some items related to physiological manifestations as indicators of activation: for example, the item "I frequently have strong heartbeats" for Wieczerkowski et al.'s (1979) AFS, or the item "I seldom notice my heartbeat and rarely get out of breath" from Spreen's (1961) "Saarbrücker Liste," a German translation of Taylor's (1953) MAS.

In sports a response to this kind of item has a completely different interpretation than, for example, in everyday cognitive demands, in school, or in a psychological experiment on attention. In sports high physiological activation is often a prerequisite for optimal performance and is regarded as a positive factor, whereas in the other situations it tends to be disruptive.

This raises the question of whether the questionnaire method is an optimal method for diagnosing sport-related anxiety, both in general and as far as specific groups, particularly children, are concerned.

A major objection to the traditional use of questionnaires to measure fear or anxiety is that they require the respondent to perceive anxiety-related cognitions for himself, to quantify these and to report them to other people—and all of this, sometimes, in a state of heightened anxiety. Problems of anxiety repression and willingness to disclose information cannot be overlooked. Another related problem is that of social desirability which, according to Nickel (1976, pp. 111 ff.), is particularly acute in younger subjects. Response tendencies always come into play when an item is not answered solely on the basis of its contents but when other variables distort the measurement intentions. This is particularly true for anxiety questionnaires, where the measurement dimensions and/or intentions can be easily discerned in the item formulation. The validity of these instruments depends significantly on such factors as openness, honesty, accurate self evaluation and, finally, on the self-awareness of the respondent.

An additional problem with children is that they don't understand certain statements, or that they understand them differently from adults. Moreover, the STAI, currently the best-known general instrument, and other measures based on the STAI are symptom-oriented. This does not, however, mean that individual symptom preferences (e.g., in "somaticizers") are taken into account, nor is there a description of symptoms balanced over all three levels (physiological, psychological and motoric); with additively registered degrees of anxiety this sows the seeds of quantification problems which so far have not been discussed.

The personal instructions focus the person's attention on his own affective state (current or general); this can result in an intensification of affect processes, something which doesn't necessarily occur during ordinary dealing with a task and which can cause evaluation problems (cf. also Wicklund, 1979, p. 158 for related statements concerning the theory of self-awareness).

For the reasons listed above neither a simple transfer of usual anxiety tests to the field of sports nor the sole use of the questionnaire technique seems very promising.

The question of whether to use general or sport-specific questionnaires will also depend upon the topic being studied. If, for example, one wants to compare the personality structure of athletes to that of a control group or to population norms (Vanek & Hosek, 1977), one will usually choose a questionnaire that is not specific to sports and that also measures the personality trait "anxiousness." Of course, in interpreting the results it is necessary to bear in mind that top athletes possibly encounter labilizing situations (e.g., extreme training situations or competitions) more often than other groups of people, with the result that they also more often experience the labilizing symptoms listed in questionnaire items, and for this reason alone will have higher anxiety scores. Nitsch (1978) concludes that athletes' higher anxiety scores possibly represent a methodological artefact, in that the validating sample is scarcely comparable to the athlete sample.

Taking a general look at questionnaire techniques, one has to conclude that their significance is too often misjudged; this is true at both extremes. Whereas some psychologists tend to overrate the validity and value of questionnaires, others reject them out of hand without naming any alternatives. In order to avoid both unrealistically high and low expectations, it is recommended that questionnaires be used only in those areas where empirical evidence for their validity has been demonstrated (cf. Guilford, 1964; Häcker & Schwenkmezger, 1984). One will then be able to obtain information that, using other methods, would have been incomplete or much less precise.

PHYSIOLOGICAL INDICATORS

Physiological indicators can be roughly classified as (1) respiratory and cardiovascular indicators, (2) biochemical indicators and (3) electrophysiological indicators. They can be related to one of three systems in the human organism: the muscular system, the vegetative, autonomic nervous system and the central nervous system. Parameters frequently studied with regard to anxiety include pulse rate, blood pressure, rate of respiration, biochemical indicators like adrenaline and noradrenaline, and electrophysiological measures such as EEG correlates, muscle potentials and skin resistance. For a detailed discussion see Fahrenberg (1977) or Lang (1977).

What advantages do physiological measurements bring to anxiety research? First, they are not tied to verbal statements and are therefore independent of verbal expressive ability. Secondly, they can be used with almost all kinds of people because the ability of self-observation is not a prerequisite. Thirdly, almost all can be assessed continuously, parallel to behavior; in contrast, with self-observation, the behavior has to be interrupted, particularly in actions which are not yet automatic and in standardized self-ratings.

The disadvantages, however, seem to balance out the advantages. Even analyses which are based on physiological measures are for the most part method-dependent. For example, two different physiological indicators (e.g., heart rate and action potential in an electromyogram), both of which are indices of general arousal or activation, show only slight correlations with each other.

Although it is agreed that physiological side-effects of emotional processes can be measured, up to now only a few specific reactions of qualitatively different emotions have been found. This means that an increase in heart rate can occur both in the context of the emotion anxiety and in reactions of joy or anger. Which of these emotional reactions occurs is determined by a cognitive evaluation of the stimulus situation. For example, parallel bars might induce the emotion anxiety due to associations with an unhappy previous experience or the emotion joy as a result of victory in a previous competition. Because of the non-stimulus-specific physiological effects of both emotions, however, there will be an increase in heart rate in both situations. In more general terms, specific systems have different functions, that is under each condition in mobilizing for a reaction or in concentrating on vegetative functions certain structures will become active, others will reduce their activity, and still others will remain unaffected (see Lang, 1977, p. 48).

Can physiological indicators of anxiety also be applied in sport psychological investigations? It is important to note that mainly indicators of the peripheral circulatory system but also biochemical indicators cannot legitimately be used when the organism is physically activated in any way. These parameters change much more as a result of physical activity than as a result of stress- or anxiety-inducing situations. In addition, they are very susceptible to artifacts and are method-dependent. There is indeed some evidence to suggest (1) that physical stress is accompanied by increased adrenaline levels and mental stress by increased noradrenaline levels and (2) that the ratio of adrenaline to noradrenaline is a good index of the existence of emotional strain (cf. Frankenhäuser, 1969; Lehmann & Keul, 1981). However, getting exact measurements of catecholamines in experimental settings—especially in field settings—appears to be a complex technical problem. And we shall have to wait and see what comes of the possibility of analyzing catecholamine levels in saliva (cf. Hellhammer, Kirschbaum, & Belkien, 1987).

So far the only approach remaining for assessing physiological indicators is to record physical activity using structured observational methods. A sport-specific example is provided by Schwenkmezger, Voigt, and Müller (1979). Volleyball players were observed in neutral (training games) and stress-inducing (examination games) situations; among other measures, the distance covered in walking and running, number of actions made during play, and the number of maximal jumps were carefully and precisely recorded. Comparison of telemetrically recorded heart rates in test and neutral situations was confined to those subjects who had the same number of ball actions, the same number of walking and running steps, the same number of maximal jumps, etc. in both situations over a series of time intervals. The results in Figure 1 show that, despite an equal amount of physical stress in both situations, heart rate during the test situation is higher than in the neutral situation. These results were confirmed by self-reports in the State scale of the STAI (Spielberger et al., 1972), recorded before and after each observation segment. Although the method used here represents only a very rough control index of physical stress and it remains unclear whether, for example, the increased heart rate might not be a consequence of increased muscle tension during the test situation, the study does

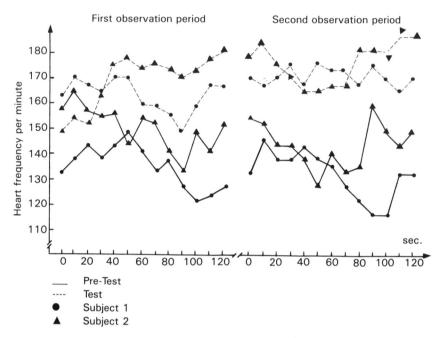

Figure 1   Heart rate of two subjects during two-minute observation periods before and during an examination (Schwenkmezger et al., 1979).

point out a possible means of interpreting physiological measures as indicators of emotional processes (e.g., here the anxiety reaction). At the same time this study also illustrates the methodological problems that need to be overcome if physiological parameters used as indicators of mental stress are to be considered as being independent of physical stress (Schwenkmezger, 1979).

The problems of interpreting physiological data are not confined to assigning quantities to qualities and to methodological difficulties in assessment. There are particular problems related to the principle of autonomic *reactions specificity* (Lacey, 1950; Lacey & Lacey, 1958). This general principle, which must also be taken into account in sport psychological studies, describes the existence of individual ways of reacting to certain stimuli or stimulus constellations. These were confirmed in studies by Lazarus and Opton (1966), who found different physiological reactions to constant anxiety-inducing situations. There is also some controversy with regard to hormonal processes, which are closely related to the nervous system. Whereas some authors suggest it may be possible unequivocally to determine the presence of fear and anxiety and to distinguish between them on the basis of catecholamine, adrenaline and noradrenaline levels (e.g., Schildkraut & Kety, 1967), other authors feel that catecholamine secretion can only be regarded as an indication of the size of the emotional reaction and not as an indicator of the quality of the emotion (e.g., Levi, 1967; Frankenhäuser, 1969). The *specificity problem* can be subdivided into three subprinciples (Fahrenberg, 1968, 1977): the principle of individual-specific reaction, the principle of stimulus-specific reaction and the principle of motivation-specific reaction. All three principles influence the general and generalizable interpretation of physiological indicators of anxiety.

Physiological measures assess something that can be termed an indication of physiological excitation; their relationship to that which they are an indication of needs to be clarified, and cannot be related to the construct without resorting to a theory; and the researcher brings the two into contact. Moreover, there are also problems in gathering and interpreting physiological data. For example, the influence of the act of collecting physiological data itself is still unclear. Nitsch points out that we don't know whether one has assessed the reaction to the stressor being studied or the person's specific stress sensitivity toward physiological-medical procedures (Nitsch, 1981a, p. 153). In psychophysiological stress and anxiety research physiological values are registered and interpreted as "indicators" without first having a sufficiently worked-out and tested physiological model or even a psychophysiological model available. The correlation-statistical activation research is still too superficial; although it can help to generate hypotheses; it cannot be used to test them. Moreover, physiological processes can be influenced by climate, general well-being or fitness, different biological rhythms (e.g., daily rhythm), and not least by the activity itself. For these reasons alone the low correlations with other data are not surprising (cf. Hackfort & Schwenkmezger, 1985, pp. 84 ff.). In some cognitive-psychological contexts it is assumed that physiological excitation only represents one source of information among others for the individual, but cognitions are almost exclusively responsible for the origin of emotions (see Valins, 1966, 1967; Heckhausen, 1977; Liebhart, 1978; Weiner et al., 1978).

From this point of view it isn't necessarily a contradiction to view emotions such as anxiety as syndromes. However, physiological processes are only of secondary importance: it isn't the physiological processes *per se* that are important, but rather the perception of physiological processes as information for the subjective evaluation of one's own state, the way he feels. Lazarus (see Lazarus, 1966, 1981; Lazarus & Launier, 1978) emphasizes the role of subjective assessment, which influence both emotional reactions and further actions and he assumes that this process of action guidance, which is put into gear by mental processes, has substantiated effects on somatic processes (an interaction commonly termed psychosomatic) (see Lazarus, 1981).

BEHAVIORAL INDICATORS OF ANXIETY

What was said earlier about physiological processes with respect to their ambiguity is also true for behavior data. Although anxiety as a construct is related to certain kinds of behavior (particularly expressive behavior and avoidance behavior), it seems extremely questionable to claim that anxiety can be regarded in movement behavior. In scientific theory anxiety is an abstraction for which behavior *may* be *one* empirical indicator, insofar as a particular behavior can be connected theoretically to anxiety. This always has to take place within a hypothetical net, however, since context dependency on the one hand and the content ambiguity of a single behavior (Nitsch, 1981a, p. 156) on the other hand both have to be taken into account. An example: If one observes a skier trembling in front of a steep downhill slope, one doesn't know whether the skier is trembling because he's afraid or because he's cold. Observing further, if the skier is seen to begin his run in a cramped, tense and awkward position, one doesn't know whether he really is freezing, whether he's not a particularly good skier but a brave one, trying this difficult run in spite of his lack of skill, or whether his posture is a sign of anxiety. The answer only becomes clear when one has additional information—for instance, that it isn't cold, or that, although he has completed skiing lessons he isn't really confident about this run and is only doing it because his friends have brought him along and are waiting for him. Observation of behavior is problematic because one cannot distinguish between anxious behavior and coping behavior—something that people have been pointed out since Freud's time.

It is true both for expressive behavior and for performance behavior that the situation has to transmit an interpretative background so that behavior data can be adequately evaluated. For this reason the analysis of behavior data in anxiety research cannot concentrate exclusively on the execution of the movement; it also has to take into account the person within the particular situation. If one chooses to use movement actions as the subject of analysis and tries to deduce anxiety from movement regulation, then it is essential that the actor's self statements be recorded; otherwise it is impossible for an observer to know whether, for example, inadequate action plans or anxiety has led to disruptions in the action process. Observation of behavior and behavioral data do not seem to be superfluous or inconsequential for an action-theoretical movement analysis, but neither are they sufficient in themselves. Observation methods become useful only in conjunction with procedural data, and observational data only in conjunction with self statements.

Assessment of anxiety on the behavioral level is usually discussed in the literature for the sake of completeness, less often for its specific relevance. This is surprising in view of the fact that behavior diagnostic approaches are available but are only seldom discussed in anxiety diagnosis. One reason for the relatively few references to behavior diagnosis might lie in the not unproblematical realization of data collection methods on this level. For example, if one wants to take up Birbaumer's (1977) suggestion that, when assessing avoidance or flight reactions, expressive behavior, simple motor sequences like conditioned repression, micro- and macrotremors be used to measure anxiety on the behavioral level, the question of how to ensure objectivity, reliability and validity arises. Also in this connection one must bear in mind that, with regard to their function as indicators of a particular process, behavior characteristics can be a long way removed as explanations from that which they are reflecting (Hackfort, 1983b). If classes of anxiety reactions on the behavioral level cited in the literature are ordered according to their causal distance, a distinction has to be drawn between expressive behavior, avoidance and flight behavior, and achievement behavior.

We cannot go into details about specific methods of assessment here. With regard to expressive behavior, the reader is referred to studies by Ekman and Oster (1979; see also Hackfort & Nitsch, 1988); behavioral indicators are described by Hackfort and Schwenkmezger (1985). Although the assessment of expressive behavior seems obvious as an index of anxiety reactions in sport, it may be appropriate to make a few remarks on certain flight and avoidance reactions. Avoidance behavior is particularly apparent in the case of encountering a feared opponent. It is relatively easy to identify simulated illnesses and aggravation in such situations as avoidance behavior. In sport classes flight and avoidance behavior is often manifested very subtly. Sometimes sport teachers are confronted with a flood of doctors' excuses which can be viewed as symptoms of pupils' dislike for sport. The spectrum of avoidance behavior extends into the lessons themselves and becomes evident when, for example, someone breaks out of the lineup, a sport action (take-off) is interrupted, or a simple exercise is suddenly substituted for a more complex one. Still another variant of avoidance behavior might occur when a threatened failure or fear of losing leads to a blind, relatively hopeless attack.

Assessment and understanding of flight and avoidance behavior is particularly important in sports because trainers, coaches and teachers with little or not training in psychology tend to rely on their own observation of anxiety symptoms rather than employing questionnaires or physiological methods.

CONVERGENCE OF THE DIFFERENT LEVELS OF MEASUREMENT

One important reason why many theories of anxiety are unable to provide satisfactory explanations lies in the low covariation reported in many empirical studies between the range of measures at the three levels. Several causes have been identified:

(1) The relationships between measurement levels can only be described as satisfactory on the subjective-psychological level. Within the group of physiological indicators of anxiety and anxiety reactions on the behavioral level, covariations are minimal. As long as no qualitatively different reactions can be identified within these measurement levels, no convergent relationships can be expected between them.

(2) The probable cause of this low covariation within the physiological level or within the behavioral level is failing to take into account the course patterns of physiological reactions or behavioral indices. Once again we would like to point out that individual, situational and motivational stereotypes of reaction patterns can occur in physiological measures. A similar explanation could be applied to behavior reactions, where idiosyncratic learning processes have to be taken into account.

(3) A third argument is presented by the different temporal latencies of anxiety reactions shown on the various levels of measurement. Whereas one is dealing with latencies of a few milliseconds in EEG reactions to anxiety-inducing stimuli, changes in peripheral circulatory measures take seconds or minutes, and biochemical indicators can vary over minutes or even hours. Little information is available about temporal latencies of behavioral changes and reactions on the subjective level. Whereas fine motoric reactions can often be observed in fractions of a second, gross motor reactions occur only after much longer intervals. Even less is known about the level of cognitive reactions, because cognitive processes can produce short, middle or long latencies depending upon the processing of threatening situations. In sport psychological studies, too, time shifts have been demonstrated in reactions on different measurement levels. For example, in a study carried out in our research group we investigated the convergence between respiration frequency and state anxiety reactions of

underwater divers in different stress situations in connection with level of experience. Twenty beginners, 22 advanced and 18 experienced deep-sea divers took part in a diving exercise in a 3.5-meter deep pool. They were subjected three times to anxiety-inducing situations (having to put on a blindfold, wearing a heavy lead belt, and having their air supply temporarily cut off). As dependent variables breathing rate was measured continuously and following each threat situation the state anxiety reaction (responses to the state-anxiety questionnaire by Spielberger et al. (1970) during the underwater dive) was recorded. The results are shown in Figure 2. Although there is a definite convergence between breathing rate and state anxiety for beginners and experienced divers (for beginners the arousal level is constantly high, for experienced divers constantly low), the values of breathing rate and subjective feelings of anxiety diverge for advanced divers. A probable explanation of this result is that advanced divers somewhat overestimate their diving abilities and for this reason feel less anxious, while autonomic indicators are still reflecting a strong state of excitement. With more experience this difference becomes less pronounced, as the control of autonomic functions also increases.

(4) Another aspect is put forward by Birbaumer (1977): Covariation between the three levels of measurement is dependent upon the intensity of the emotional

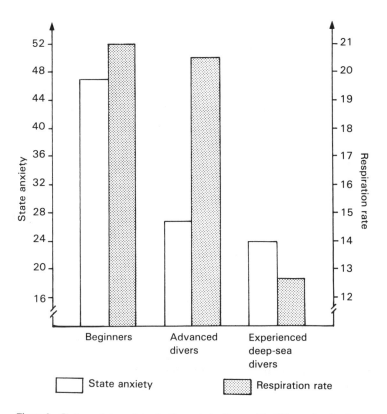

Figure 2   State anxiety and respiration rate in divers with different levels of experience.

activation. The more threatening the anxiety-inducing stimulus is perceived to be, the higher the convergence seems to be. Epstein's work (1973), too, shows that with increasing intensity of the stress stimulus, the convergence between the individual systems is also increased.

(5) Anxiety-coping theories (Byrne, 1964; Krohne, 1986) often stress the importance of coping mechanisms. Depending upon the extent of person-specific differences with respect to repression/sensitization, different latencies are expected in coping with anxiety-inducing stimuli. For example, repressers tend to avoid anxiety or to control it by interpreting anxiety-inducing situations as harmless, but sensitizers react to threatening situations with increased attention, because their threshold for anxiety-inducing stimuli is significantly lower. Such cognitive processing styles for anxiety seem, however, to function independently of the physiological reaction level; at least, no unequivocal correlates have yet been found. This could serve to lower any possible convergences.

(6) Also working against convergence of levels of measurement is the fact that anxiety control mechanisms and anxiety processing mechanisms influence reactions and processes on the different levels at different speeds and to different extents. Whereas cognitive processes and therefore reactions on the subjective level can be modified fairly quickly (cf. Meichenbaum, 1977), anxiety reactions of the autonomic nervous system and the behavior of individuals probably only change as a result of more long-term processes.

(7) Physiological psychology has traditionally been regarded as a research discipline whose task is to analyze convergence between physical and mental reactions. The basis for this is the conviction that mental reactions and processes represent causes and results of central nervous and hormonal processes. In the field of sport psychology, however, psychophysiological approaches are relatively rare because the dependency of physiological reactions on muscular strain overlaps the proportion of variance of physiological variables due to psychological causes (cf. Schwenkmezger, 1979). For this reason only a few sport-specific analyses have been able to demonstrate correlational relationships between psychological and physiological parameters.

(8) Finally, it can be observed that a large majority of the causes for low convergence between measurement levels can also be traced to inadequate methodology in the assessment of anxiety.

To summarize: If it can be demonstrated that anxiety reactions occur on the various measurement levels with different latencies, it follows logically that the many cross-sectional analyses of anxiety states should be supplemented by process analyses. In spite of the still inadequate connections the goal of anxiety research is convergence of the three levels of measurement, because optimal coping with anxiety will only be available when reduction of anxiety can be shown at all measurement levels.

SITUATION–SPECIFIC INSTRUMENTS

As a result of the so-called interactionism debate, there is an increased awareness of the importance of taking into account, both conceptually and methodologically, the way in which personality traits appear in different situations. This led to a demand for situation-specific personality tests.

In anxiety research there has been a trend toward situation-specific trait scales, in the hope that better predictions will result for state anxiety in the corresponding situational classes (cf. Mellstrom, Zuckerman, & Cicala, 1978).

Situation- or activity-specific instruments have been developed for measuring trait anxiety—for example, test anxiety scales (like the "Test Anxiety Inventory" by Spielberger et al., 1978) or speech anxiety scales (the "Speech Anxiety Inventory" by Lamb, 1973). In contrast to general anxiety tests (e.g., Taylor's "Manifest Anxiety Scale," 1953), in these situation-specific measures the relationship to a specific situation or to a class of situations is explicitly created by means of the instructions or item formulation (Laux, 1983, p. 72).

In sport anxiety research the demand for situation-specific trait scales was welcomed, in the hope of improving the prediction of state anxiety in certain sport situations. Based on Spielberger's (e.g., 1975, 1980) State-Trait concept, Martens (1977) developed a questionnaire for measuring trait anxiety in competitive sport situations.

The low correlation with the STAI Trait scale (about .40) clearly shows that this sport-specific test accounts for portions of the variance which are not covered by the general measure. Results obtained with the German translation of this scale also indicate, however, that the prediction of state anxiety reactions has not yet been greatly improved (cf. Hackfort & Schwenkmezger, 1985).

Schwenkmezger (1981), for instance, observed that the STAI Trait scale is able to predict state reactions in sport-related stress situations just as well as Martens' (1977; cf. Hackfort & Schwenkmezger, 1985) sport-specific trait anxiety scale. Similar results have been reported by Singer and Ungerer-Röhrich (1985).

Vormbrock's (1983) sport anxiety questionnaire ("Sportangstfragebogen," SAF) is also based on Spielberger's concept and Endler's (e.g., 1975, 1978) multidimensional anxiety model. This instrument distinguishes between three dimensions of sport anxiety, each related to different types of sport: (1) "Fear of the unknown, injury"; items related to gymnastics. (2) "Fear of failure in social situations"; items related to ball games. (3) "Fear of disgrace"; items related to dancing.

Test criteria of the SAF were investigated in a sample of university students, and the instrument was shown to be both valid and reliable. The question remains, however, whether the method of factor analysis used in the SAF for obtaining dimensions of sport anxiety is more appropriate than activity-specific subscale construction.

In the field of test anxiety research, classifications of cognitive relationships into task-relevant and solution-irrelevant cognitions (see Sarason, 1975, 1978, 1980) or into "worry" and "emotionality" aspects (see Liebert & Morris, 1967; Morris & Liebert, 1970) are now generalized into evaluation anxiety (see Wine, 1980, 1982). The usefulness of this concept of evaluation anxiety in the analysis of sport-related fears has been demonstrated by Schwenkmezger (1985) and Schwenkmezger and Laux (1986). Using an activity-specific scale construction of task-unrelated cognitions in a study of handball players, they found that high-anxious players tend to have more task-unrelated cognitions than low-anxious players. In evaluation situations (selection games with evaluation of personal performance) there was a significant increase in task-unrelated cognitions compared to training situations; these results support Spielberger's State-Trait Model of anxiety. In addition, highly significant relationships were found between frequency of task-unrelated cognitions and assessments of individual performance by independent raters.

Only recently have children and young people been included in research on the development of sport-specific anxiety inventories. Two instruments directed at this age group differ in several ways from the usual questionnaire construction.

Bös and Mechling (1983) developed an instrument (the "Sport Anxiety Picture Test"; SAPT) for measuring the self concept in anxiety-inducing movements in sport classes. The SAPT is aimed at male and female children between the ages of 9 and 11 and is available in German, English and Italian versions. Photographs of school sport situations are combined with answer categories in sentence form. The purpose of this method is to combine the advantages of projective and questionnaire techniques and to permit a quantitative statement about the self concept during anxiety-inducing movements.

The SAPT does not distinguish between different dimensions or possible connections with particular activities. However, factor analysis results suggest that activity-specific evaluations of competence do indeed play a role.

Based on situational analysis approach and the assumption that particular sport-specific anxiety dimensions might be effective in different sport activities (e.g., for gymnastics, fear of injury and/or fear of disgrace), Hackfort (1983a, 1986) distinguished between various fields of activity (ball games, fighting games, gymnastics, swimming/diving and track and field sports) in developing the "Sportangstdeutungsverfahren" (SAD; sport anxiety interpretation measure). He also distinguished five dimensions of sport anxiety according to their relationship to central motives, following Maslow's (1954) classification of motives: (1) "fear of disgrace," (2) "fear of competition," (3) "fear of failure," (4) "fear of the unknown" and (5) "fear of injury."

The SAD consists of 22 items in the form of drawings of different situations (picture series). The response categories are also nonverbal (sketches of facial expressions, portraying varying degrees of anxiety). The respondent makes a cross to indicate the extent to which his interpretation or definition of the situation is anxiety-thematic. The dimensions that are relevant to the individual are determined by means of a method developed expressly for that purpose, the dimension-decision-method (DEV). Test-retest reliabilities, important for trait anxiety, lie between .87 and .94. The test can be used in both group and individual diagnosis.

Although up to now the focus has primarily been on the diagnosis of trait anxiety, it should be pointed out that, along with situational and activity-specific factors the development of state-anxiety scales is also necessary. Particularly with regard to the two-component approaches, the relationships of cognitions to certain activities play an important role in item formulation. Anxiety diagnosis is left with the methodologically unsatisfactory technique of operationalizing anxiety and styles of anxiety control separately.

Another approach which may prove promising is scale combination in the development of specific instruments of diagnosing sport anxiety.

The methods discussed above could certainly provide inspiration for general anxiety research or anxiety research in other fields. The SAPT and SAD are child-appropriate methods in that they take into account the fact that visual perception is very important in this age group (cf. Nickel, 1976, p. 112) and the manner of item presentation corresponds well with intellectual ability. Questions that arise with other questionnaires for the same age group about how to mark an item like "I have heart palpitations" (since one always has heart palpitations) do not occur here. Another point to remember is that children have difficulty expressing their feelings and reactions, and this should be considered when constructing, for example, measures of school anxiety. Minimal connections with verbal ability, as found in the SAD, shows that there are alternatives to questionnaires, and this is desirable for other reasons as well.

FUNCTIONAL ANALYSES IN ANXIETY AND STRESS RESEARCH

There is no lack of definitions in stress and anxiety research. What is lacking is the willingness to analyze all of the definitions which have been proposed. Considering that the problem lies less in correctly defining these constructs than in defining them purposefully (see Nitsch, 1981b, pp. 39 ff.), it is important that (a) the construct be thoroughly anchored theoretically and (b) the construct be formulated so that at least its major aspects can be investigated empirically. The following discussion focuses mainly on the second requirement and the foundations of functional analyses in anxiety and stress research.

In recent years the search for nomological knowledge in stress and anxiety research has focused on studies in which data from a large number of subjects have been collected and compared, and laws derived on the basis of statistical procedures. The search for laws, or for statements in causal-deterministic form ("for all X it is true that: if $X = A$, then B") cannot be solved by large-sample studies. Statements arising from large-sample studies are the results of data aggregations and represent statements of averages; they cannot—although this is more the exception than the rule—be interpreted as general statements, or laws. Typical examples from stress research are provided by studies on the relationship between activation/stress/anxiety and performance. Exceptions to the generally accepted curvilinear relationship are possible—also in "if—then" formulations—only in statements specifying the type of task (e.g., task complexity), personality traits (e.g., anxiousness) or surrounding conditions (e.g., social environment). It is regarded as having been confirmed because it has been studied in many subjects and found to be statistically significant. The question remains (1) whether average results should not be regarded and interpreted exclusively as regularities and (2) whether such regularities cannot also—or perhaps even better—be found in single case analyses.

What prevents us in psychology (or, more generally: in the social sciences) from formulating laws? The precondition of sampling is important here: whereas in natural sciences today individual objects can be compared and classed according to *functional* aspects, in psychology this has up to now only been possible according to *descriptive* aspects. But it is not fundamentally possible to derive general statements about function on the basis of summaries of individual objects, which differ not only due to random errors of measurement but also in their functional course and in their kinds of reactions (see also Wottawa, 1981, p. 134).

This judgment refers to carrying out functional analyses. The first step would be to develop ideas about functional relationships. Based on the question, for example, "How does anxiety function?," functional models would be constructed, which had been generated and tested by single case studies. Using these "models for the single case," persons could be classified into groups for which certain assumptions of the model had been found to be true, people of the same functional type.

If one begins with the assumption that every person—more or less differentiatedly and consciously—has ideas about how he functions or how others function (cf. Laucken, 1974; Hackfort, 1979, 1981; Nitsch & Hackfort, 1979), then his actions can only be understood if one can perceive how he experienced or experiences the situation, how he feels this constellation of factors affects him and the extent to which he can affect them, etc.—in short, if one can discover his naive functional model (Hackfort, 1979). For example, differences in performance under stress conditions can also be explained by the fact that a person feels he isn't capable of performing under stress and therefore doesn't develop any will to perform, whereas another person believes that the only time he can perform well is under stress and for that reason really makes an effort when he perceives conditions to be stressful. In choosing this approach one is not looking for causes but for reasons following a final scheme of explanation and an epistemological model of human subjects.

With this concept laboratory studies, too, as classical arrangements of the causal scheme would be used differently than they have been up to now: instead of having the researcher decide what are the causes of a subject's actions, one would have to identify the factors perceived by the subject and how he processes them. That is, *cognitions about effect-relationships* under controlled conditions would be recorded, from which functional relationships can be inferred, the validity of which would need to be demonstrated in other situations—for example, in everyday situations. In this way, the problem of the external validity of laboratory studies would be somewhat diminished; if a person perceives conditions to be identical or very similar, then he will act the same way—provided such actions have proved successful in the past. Basically there is an implication here of context-specificity of hypotheses and theories (see Cronbach, 1975).

In functional analyses, expanding upon previous studies, the interest is on the course of performance (process orientation), as well as the performance result (product orientation). From this perspective it is important to note that

- the same or similar results can occur as a result of different processes (for example, when one person hardly needed to exert himself, experienced no anxiety-caused disturbance, whereas another person really had to push himself in order to achieve the same result in spite of anxiety-caused disturbance), something that has to lead to completely different evaluations;
- under certain conditions different results can form the basis of completely different performance courses (for example, when one person was able to perform to his best ability and was completely exhausted, whereas another person didn't ever "get into the swing," had no problems getting started and was only just beginning to unfold his performance ability), which also gives rise to differential judgments.

Questionnaire methods are probably less well suited to process-oriented analyses, because they don't permit data to be collected continuously *during* the course of an action; the action has to be interrupted. In a pre- or postactional application there is the additional problem of what cognitions one is dealing with: prospective or retrospective attributions, action-guiding or action-justifying cognitions. Periactional verbalization methods—for example, thinking aloud during the action—present an additional task which may interfere with coping with the original task, or may lead to commentaries instead of information about task-relevant thoughts. In any event, reports of cognitions irrelevant to task solution (see the attention hypothesis in anxiety research, especially Wine, 1980, 1982; Sarason, 1978) could be used in anxiety diagnosis; up to now they have been restricted exclusively to postactional reports (see e.g., Heckhausen, 1977, 1982; Schwenkmezger, 1980, 1985).

Nevertheless studies in the field of sport psychology have also been carried out using questionnaires which come close to fulfilling the requirements for functional analyses. An example will serve to illustrate this. In one of our own studies (see also Schwenkmezger, 1980, 1981), a field experiment, subjects were investigated while they learned a very difficult, complex task: skiing. All participants (N = 24) were absolute beginners. Measurements were taken at six different times during a beginner's ski course. On each date the subjects were given a general anxiety scale, a state scale, and asked to evaluate the difficulty of the task as a result of external conditions. Product-moment correlation coefficients between state anxiety on the one hand and trait anxiety or task-specific cognitions on the other are presented in Table 1. It was found that, at the beginning of the learning process, probably because of the lack of specific experience, state anxiety level was almost exclusively determined by the general trait "anxiousness." However, this influence weakens over the course of the learning process. Covariation with task-specific cognitions is just the opposite: thus, one might infer that at the beginning of the learning process the level of situation-specific anxiety is determined by general dispositions, but with increasing experience very specific, situational conditions determine the anxiety level.

Nonetheless, physiological measures and behavior observation seem better suited for process-accompanying data gathering (see also Weinberg in this volume). These data, however, differ in their ability to explain psychological constructs such as anxiety or stress.

Table 1   Correlations between anxiousness and task-specific cognitions and state anxiety at six different times during the learning of a gross motor, complex task

Time	1	2	3	4	5	6
Anxiousness	.55ss	.37s	.02	−.06	.08	.04
Task-specific cognitions (median)	.22	.17	.45ss	.57ss	.47ss	.36s

ss: p ≤ .01; s: p ≤ .05.

CONCLUSIONS

The foregoing reflections can be summarized in four major points:

(1) More emphasis on the single case approach seems desirable in stress and anxiety research, but not so much that the idiographic approach takes precedence over the nomothetic approach (cf. also Lazarus, 1981). In psychology the single case approach is conceivable from a nomothetic, nomothetic-idiographic or idiographic viewpoint.

(2) Descriptive approaches in anxiety research (e.g., in the form of correlational analyses) should be supplemented by functional approaches. The first priority here is to decide upon the theoretical prerequisites (see e.g., Nitsch & Hackfort, 1981). A beginning could be made in analyses of naive functional concepts.

(3) In studies on "anxiety and performance" more process analyses should be done and performance results interpreted against the background of the course of performance. In this context the procedural regularities, which can be translated into operative technological rules, are of particular interest.

(4) In constructing and applying methods in anxiety research more attention should be paid to the fact that anxiety as a subjective experience is bound up with subjective situational definitions. Important components of these situational definitions are subjective weightings and assignments of importance that underlie the relationships of the individual anxiety. Particularly for methods that aren't used solely as research instruments it is recommended that an analysis strategy be done with different procedural techniques.

SUMMARY

In this chapter are discussed possibilities to measure sport-related anxiety with nonsport-specific and sport-specific questionnaires and with further methods on different levels (the cognitive, behavioral and physiological level). Special consideration is given to multilevel approaches and the problems of convergence between the different levels as well as to basic methodological considerations and the problems of data interpretation. Sport-specific instruments are introduced and results of investigations carried out with these instruments are reported. Two main perspectives for future research in the field should be (1) to focus not only on the performance result (product orientation) but also on the course of performance (process orientation) and (2) to carry out functional analyses based not only on pre- and postactional methods of data collection but also on periactional methods which are suited for process-accompanying data gathering.

REFERENCES

Birbaumer, N. (1977). Angst als Forschungsgegenstand der experimentellen Psychologie. In N. Birbaumer (Hg.), *Psychophysiologie der Angst* (pp. 1–14). München: Urban & Schwarzenberg.
Bös, K., & Mechling, H. (1983). *Dimensionen sportmotorischer Leistungen.* Schorndorf: Hofmann.
Browne, M. A., & Mahoney, M. J. (1984). Sportpsychology. *Annual Review of Psychology, 35,* 605–625.

Byrne, D. (1964). Repression-sensitization as a dimension of personality. In B. A. Maher (Ed.), *Progress in experimental personality research* (Vol. 1, pp. 169–220). New York: Academic Press.

Cattell, R. B., & Scheier, J. H. (1961). *The meaning and measurement of neuroticism and anxiety.* New York: Ronald.

Cronbach, L. J. (1975). Beyond the two disciplines of scientific psychology. *American Psychologist, 30,* 116–127.

Ekman, P., & Oster, H. (1979). Facial expression of emotion. *Annual Review Psychology, 30,* 527–554.

Endler, N. S. (1975). The case for person-situation-interaction. *Canadian Psychological Review, 16,* 12–21.

Endler, N. S. (1978). The interaction-model of anxiety. In D. M. Landers & R. W. Christina (Eds.), *Psychology of motor behavior and sport—1977* (pp. 332–351). Champaign, IL: Human Kinetics Publishers.

Epstein, S. (1973). Versuch einer Theorie der Angst. In N. Birbaumer (Hg.), *Neuropsychologie der Angst* (pp. 184–241). München: Urban & Schwarzenberg.

Fahrenberg, J. (1968). Aufgaben und Methoden der psychologischen Verlaufsanalyse (Zeitreihenanalyse). In K. J. Groffman & K.-H. Wewetzer (Hg.), *Person als Prozeß: Festschrift zum 65. Geburtstag von Prof. Dr. phil. Robert Heiss* (pp. 41–82). Bern: Huber.

Fahrenberg, J. (1977). Physiological concepts in personality research. In R. B. Cattell & R. M. Dreger (Eds.), *Handbook of modern personality theory* (pp. 585–611). Washington, DC: Hemisphere.

Frankenhäuser, M. (1969). Biochemische Indikatoren der Aktiviertheit: Die Ausscheidung von Katecholaminen. In W. Schönpflug (Hg.), *Methoden der Aktivierungsforschung* (pp. 195–214). Bern: Huber.

Guilford, J. P. (1964). *Persönlichkeit.* Weinheim: Beltz.

Hackfort, D. (1979). *Grundlagen und Techniken der naiven Fremdbeeinflussung im Sport unter besonderer Berücksichtigung der Angstbeeinflussung.* Köln: bps.

Hackfort, D. (1981). Naive Vorstellungen und Techniken der Angstkontrolle. In W. Michaelis (Ed.), *Bericht über den 32. Kongreß der DGfPs in Zürich 1980* (Band II, pp. 681–686). Göttingen: Hogrefe.

Hackfort, D. (1983a). *Theorie und Diagnostik sportbezogener Ängstlichkeit. Ein situationsanalytischer Ansatz.* Unveröff. Diss. DSHS Köln.

Hackfort, D. (1983b). Methodische Ansätze und Probleme in der Angstforschung. In J. P. Janssen & E. Hahn (Hg.), *Aktivierung, Motivation, Handlung und Coaching im Sport* (pp. 77–85). Schorndorf: Hofmann.

Hackfort, D. (1986). Theoretical conception and assessment of sport-related anxiety. In C. D. Spielberger & R. Diaz-Guerrero (Eds.), *Cross-cultural anxiety* (Vol. 3, pp. 79–88). Washington: Hemisphere/Harper & Row.

Hackfort, D., & Nitsch, J. R. (1988, in press). *Das Sportangstdeutungsverfahren (SAD). Theoretische Grundlagen und Handanweisung.* Schorndorf: Hofmann.

Hackfort, D., & Schwenkmezger, P. (1985). *Angst und Angstkontrolle im Sport.* Köln: bps.

Häcker, H., & Schwenkmezger, P. (1984). Persönlichkeitsfragebogen. In L. R. Schmidt (Hg.), *Lehrbuch der Klinischen Psychologie* (pp. 220–246). Stuttgart: Enke.

Heckhausen, H. (1977). Achievement motivation and its constructs: A cognitive model. *Motivation and Emotion, 1,* 283–329.

Heckhausen, H. (1979). Sportpsychologie: Auf der Suche nach Identität in einem magischen Dreieck verschiedener Fachöffentlichkeiten. In J. R. Nitsch (Hg.), *Bericht über die 10-Jahres-Tagung der Arbeitsgemeinschaft für Sportpsychologie in Köln 1979* (pp. 43–61). Köln: bps.

Heckhausen, H. (1982). Task-irrelevant cognitions during an exam: Incidents and effects. In H. D. Krohne & L. Laux (Eds.), *Achievement, stress, and anxiety* (pp. 247–274). Washington, DC: Hemisphere.

Hellhammer, D. H., Kirschbaum, C., & Belkien, L. (1987). Measurement of salivary cortisol under psychological stimulation. In J. N. Hingtgen, D. H. Hellhammer, & G. Huppmann (Eds.), *Advanced methods in psychobiology* (in press). Toronto: Hogrefe.

Krohne, H. D. (1986). Coping with stress: Dispositions, strategies, and the problem of measurement. In M. H. Appley & R. Trumbull (Eds.), *Dynamics of stress* (in press). New York: Plenum.

Lacey, J. I. (1950). Individual differences in somatic response patterns. *Journal of Comparative and Physiological Psychology, 43,* 338–350.

Lacey, J. I., & Lacey, B. C. (1958). Verification and extension of the principle of autonomic response-stereotypy. *American Journal of Psychology, 71,* 51–73.

Lamb, D. H. (1973). The effects of two stressors on state-anxiety for students who differ in trait-anxiety. *Journal of Research in Personality, 7,* 116–126.

Lang, P. J. (1977). Die Anwendung psychophysiologischer Methoden in Psychotherapie und Verhaltensmodifikation. In N. Birbaumer (Hg.), *Psychophysiologie der Angst* (pp. 15–84). München: Urban & Schwarzenberg.

Laucken, U. (1974). *Naive Verhaltenstheorie.* Stuttgart: Klett.

Laux, L. (1983). Neuere Eigenschaftskonzeptionen in der Angst- und Stressforschung. In J. P. Janssen & E. Hahn (Hg.), *Aktivierung, Motivation, Handlung und Coaching im Sport* (pp. 69–76). Schorndorf: Hofmann.

Lazarus, R. S. (1966). *Psychological stress and the coping process.* New York: McGraw-Hill.

Lazarus, R. S. (1981). The stress and coping paradigm. In C. Eisdorfer, D. Cohen, A. Kleinman, & P. Maxim (Eds.), *Models for clinical psychopathology* (pp. 177–214). New York: Spectrum.

Lazarus, R. S., & Launier, R. (1978). Stress-related transactions between person and environment. In L. A. Pervin (Ed.), *Perspectives in interactional psychology* (pp. 287–327). New York: Plenum Press.

Lazarus, R. S., & Opton, E. M. (1966). A study of psychological stress: A summary of theoretical formulations and experimental findings. In C. D. Spielberger (Ed.), *Anxiety and behavior* (pp. 225–262). New York: Academic Press.

Lehmann, M., & Keul, J. (1981). Adrenalin- und Nor-Adrenalin-exkretion bei verschiedenen Belastungen. In P. E. Nowacki & D. Böhmer (Hg.), *Sportmedizin: Aufgaben und Bedeutung für den Menschen in unserer Zeit. 26. Deutscher Sportärztekongreß in Bad Nauheim* (pp. 348–353). Stuttgart: Thieme.

Levi, L. (1967). Biochemische Indikatoren bei verschiedenen experimentell hervorgerufenen Gefühlszuständen. In P. Kielholz (Hg.), *Angst* (pp. 83–102). Bern: Huber.

Liebert, R. M., & Morris, L. W. (1967). Cognitive and emotional components of test anxiety: A distinction and some initial data. *Psychological Reports, 29* 975–978.

Liebhart, E. H. (1978). Wahrgenommene autonome Veränderungen als Determinanten emotionalen Verhaltens. In D. Görlitz, W.-U. Meyer, & B. Weiner (Hg.), *Bielefelder Symposium über Attribution* (pp. 107–138). Stuttgart: Klett.

Martens, R. (1977). *Sport Competition Anxiety Test.* Champaign, IL: Human Kinetics Publishers.

Maslow, A. H. (1954). *Motivation and personality.* New York: Harper & Row.

McReynolds, P. (1968). The assessment of anxiety: A survey of available techniques. In P. McReynolds (Ed.), *Advances in psychological assessment* (Vol. 1, pp. 244–264). Palo Alto: Science and Behavior Books.

Meichenbaum, D. (1977). *Cognitive behavioral modification. An integrative approach.* New York: Plenum.

Mellstrom, M., Zuckerman, M., & Cicala, G. A. (1978). General versus specific traits in the assessment of anxiety. *Journal of Consulting and Clinical Psychology, 46,* 423–431.

Morris, L. W., & Liebert, R. M. (1970). Relationship of cognitive and emotional components of test anxiety to physiological arousal and academic performance. *Journal of Consulting and Clinical Psychology, 35,* 332–337.

Nickel, H. (1976). *Entwicklungspsychologie des Kindes- und Jugendalters,* Band II. Bern: Huber.

Nitsch, J. R. (1975). Sportliches Handeln als Handlungsmodell. *Sportwissenschaft, 5,* 39–55.

Nitsch, J. R. (1978). Grundbezüge der Sportpsychologie. In J. R. Nitsch & H. Allmer (Hg.), *Sportpsychologie—eine Standortbestimmung* (pp. 13–25). Köln: bps.

Nitsch, J. R. (1981a). Zur Problematik von Streßunterschungen. In J. R. Nitsch (Hg.), *Streß* (pp. 142–160). Bern: Huber.

Nitsch, J. R. (1981b). Zur Gegenstandsbestimmung der Stresforschung. In J. R. Nitsch (Hg.), *Streß* (pp. 29–51). Bern: Huber.

Nitsch, J. R., & Hackfort, D. (1979). Naive Techniken der Psychoregulation im Sport. In H. Gabler, H. Eberspächer, E. Hahn, J. Kern, & G. Schilling (Hg.), *Praxis der Psychologie im Leistungssport* (pp. 299–311). Berlin: Bartels & Wernitz.

Nitsch, J. R., & Hackfort, D. (1981). Streß in Schule und Hochschule—eine handlungspsychologische Funktionsanalyse. In J. R. Nitsch (Hg.), *Streß* (pp. 263–311). Bern: Huber.

Sarason, I. G. (1975). Anxiety and self-preoccupation. In I. G. Sarason & C. D. Spielberger (Eds.), *Stress and anxiety.* (Vol. 2, pp. 27–44). Washington, DC: Hemisphere.

Sarason, I. G. (1978). The Test Anxiety Scale: Concept and research. In C. D. Spielberger & I. G. Sarason (Eds.), *Stress and anxiety* (Vol. 6, pp. 193–216). New York: Hemisphere.

Sarason, I. G. (Ed.). (1980). *Test anxiety: Theory, research, and applications.* Hillsdale, NJ: Erlbaum.

Schildkraut, J. J., & Kety, S. S. (1967). Biogenic amines and emotion. *Science, 156,* 21–30.

Schwenkmezger, P. (1979). Psychophysiologische Ansätze in der Sportpsychologie. Probleme—Ergebnisse—Perspektiven. *Sportwissenschaft, 9,* 125–142.

Schwenkmezger, P. (1980). Untersuchungen zur kognitiven Angsttheorie im sportmotorischen Bereich (state-trait-anxiety). *Zeitschrift für Experimentelle und Angewandte Psychologie, 27,* 607–630.

Schwenkmezger, P. (1981). Eigenschafts- und Zustandsangst als Prädiktoren sportspezifischer Belastung. In *Proceedings of the V. European Congress of Sportpsychology, Varna, Bulgaria, 1979* (Vol. 2, pp. 303–309). Varna: University Press.

Schwenkmezger, P. (1985). *Modelle der Eigenschafts- und Zustandsangst.* Göttingen: Hogrefe.

Schwenkmezger, P., & Laux, L. (1986). Trait anxiety, worry and emotionality in athletic competition. In C. D. Spielberger & R. Diaz-Guerrero (Eds.), *Cross-cultural anxiety* (Vol. 3, pp. 65–77). Washington, DC: Hemisphere.

Schwenkmezger, P., Voigt, H.-F., & Müller, W. (1979). Über die Auswirkungen einer Prüfungssituation auf psychologische und physische Belastung und die Spielerleistung im Volleyball. Sportwissenschaft, 9, 303–317.

Singer, R., & Ungerer-Röhrich, U. (1985). Zum Vorhersagewert des State-Trait-Angstmodells. Eine empirische Untersuchung an Sportstudent(inn)en, Squash- und Tischtennisspielern. In G. Schilling & K. Herren (Eds.), *Proceedings of the VIth FEPSAC congress* (Vol. 1, pp. 129–138). Magglingen: ETS.

Spielberger, C. D. (1966). Theory and research on anxiety. In C. D. Spielberger (Ed.), *Anxiety and Behavior* (pp. 3–20). New York: Academic Press.

Spielberger, C. D. (1972). Anxiety as an emotional state. In C. D. Spielberger (Ed.), *Anxiety: Current trends in theory and research* (Vol. 1, pp. 23–49). New York: Academic Press.

Spielberger, C. D. (1975). Anxiety: State-trait-process. In C. D. Spielberger & I. G. Sarason (Eds.), *Stress and anxiety* (Vol. 1, pp. 115–143). Washington, DC: Hemisphere.

Spielberger, C. D. (1980). *Test Anxiety Inventory* ("Test Attitude Inventory"). Palo Alto, CA: Consulting Psychologists Press.

Spielberger, C. D., Gorsuch, R. L., & Lushene, R. E. (1970). *STAI. Manual for the State-Trait-Anxiety Inventory.* Palo Alto, CA: Consulting Psychologists Press.

Spielberger, C. D., O'Neil, H. F., & Hansen, D. N. (1972). Anxiety, drive theory and computer-assisted learning. In B. A. Maher (Ed.), *Progress in experimental personality research* (Vol. 6, pp. 109–148). New York: Academic Press.

Spielberger, C. D., Gonzales, H. P., Taylor, C. J., Algaze, B., & Anton, W. D. (1978). Examination stress and test anxiety. In C. D. Spielberger & I. G. Sarason (Eds.), *Stress and anxiety* (Vol. 5, pp. 167–191). Washington, DC: Hemisphere.

Spreen, O. (1961). Konstruktion einer Skala zur Messung der manifesten Angst in experimentellen Situationen. *Psychologische Forschung, 26,* 205–223.

Taylor, J. A. (1953). A personality scale of manifest anxiety. *Journal of Abnormal and Social Psychology, 48,* 285–290.

Valins, S. (1966). Cognitive effects of false heart-rate feedback. *Journal of Personality and Social Psychology, 4,* 400–408.

Valins, S. (1967). Emotionality and information concerning internal reactions. *Journal of Personality and Social Psychology, 6,* 458–463.

Vanek, M., & Hosek, V. (1977). *Zur Persönlichkeit des Sportlers.* Schorndorf: Hofmann.

Vormbrock, F. (1983). *Diagnostizierbarkeit von Angst. Untersuchungen zur Trait-Angst-Diagnostik für die Verhaltensvorhersage in Sportsituationen.* Köln: bps.

Weiner, B., Russel, D., & Lerman, D. (1978). Affektive Auswirkungen von Attributionen. In D. Görlitz, W.-U. Meyer, & B. Weiner (Hg.), *Bielefelder Symposium über Attribution.* (pp. 139–174). Stuttgart: Klett.

Wicklund, R. A. (1979). Die Aktualisierung von Selbstkonzepten in Handlungsvollzügen. In S.-H. Filipp (Hg.), *Selbstkonzeptforschung* (pp. 153–169). Stuttgart: Klett-Cotta.

Wieczerkowski, W., Nickel, H., Janowski, A., Fittkau, B., & Rauer, W. (1979). Angstfragebogen für Schüler. Göttingen: Hogrefe.

Wine, J. D. (1971). Test anxiety and direction of attention. *Psychological Bulletin, 76,.* 92–104.

Wine, J. D. (1980). Cognitive-attentional theory of test anxiety. In I. G. Sarason (Ed.), *test anxiety: Theory, research, and applications* (pp. 349–385). Hillsdale, NJ: Erlbaum.

Wine, J. D. (1982). Evaluation anxiety: A cognitive attentional construct. In J. W. Krohne & L. Laux (Hg.), *Achievement, stress, and anxiety* (pp. 349–385). Washington, DC: Hemisphere.

Wottawa, H. (1981). Allgemeine Aussagen in der psychologischen Forschung: Eine Fiktion. In W. Michaelis (Hg.), *Bericht über den 32. Kongreß der DGfPs in Zürich 1980* (Band 1, pp. 131–136). Göttingen: Hogrefe.

II

ANXIETY AND PERFORMANCE IN SPORTS

6

Anxiety and Athletic Performance: Traditional and Cognitive-Developmental Perspectives

Michael J. Mahoney and Andrew W. Meyers

"So now, here we go again. It has been a wonderful time off, and I should be so carefree, but I'm scared when I play tennis, I fear failure at every corner, and until I rid myself of that attitude, I know I'll never attain my goals, winning a Wimbledon or a U.S. Open" (Shriver, 1985, p. 48). This quotation from Pam Shriver, who has been ranked among the world's top ten women's tennis players for the last five years, illustrates the complexity of the relationship between anxiety and athletic performance. Shriver's admission suggests that anxiety is experienced by even the most skilled athletic performers, and that it is in all likelihood an almost universal athletic experience. But her consistently superior level of play indicates that anxiety in sport can be overcome or used by the athlete in an adaptive and even beneficial fashion.

Landers (1980) and many others have argued that the experience of anxiety in physiological, affective, cognitive and behavioral channels is central to motor performance. The breadth and impact of anxiety in sport is illustrated by a variety of research findings. Gould, Horn, and Spreeman (1983), for example, studied 458 wrestlers at a junior national championship. The young athletes (ages 13–19) reported experiencing anxiety in 66% of their matches. Over 25% of child athletes surveyed by Pierce (1980) indicated that worry and anxiety might prevent them from continued sports participation. Bramwell, Masuda, Wagner, and Holmes (1975) found that level of stress in an athlete's life was a significant positive predictor of time lost to injury. The impact of anxiety on performance can even be seen at the biochemical level. Beuter and Duda (1985) found that the ankle joint function of 8-year-old boys involved in a stepping task was impaired under a high arousal condition compared to performance under a low arousal condition.

This chapter is devoted to only a very limited aspect of the complex interface between sport and anxiety. For the most part, we will not address the importance of social/self-conscious anxiety in the child and adolescent athlete or the wider role of sports as an integral aspect of our contemporary and developing cultures. It is more than anxiety that is associated with athletic training and competition, and the role of sport in children's self-system development imbues public contests with a profound personal significance (Martens, 1978). We will, in this chapter, only address traditional and recent approaches to the relationship between anxiety and performance. The first part of the chapter will review traditional conceptions of anxiety-performance relationships. After presenting brief reviews of drive theory and the Yerkes-Dodson "Law" or inverted-U hypothesis, state-trait conceptions of anxiety will be discussed. The relationship between arousal, attention, and peak performance will preview the second part of the chapter, which is devoted to cognitive processes and models. The chapter closes with a comment on research issues and practical implications.

ANXIETY AND PERFORMANCE

Drive Theory

Perhaps the first impactful theoretical view of the arousal-performance relationship was drive theory (Hull, 1943). Spence and Spence (1966), in their modification of drive theory, argued that performance is a multiplicative function of habit strength and drive ($P = H \times D$). Habit strength was defined as the hierarchical ordering of correct and incorrect responses on a specific skill task. Drive has referred traditionally to a generalized state of arousal, typically physiological arousal, experienced by the performer. Drive theorists predict that as arousal or drive level increases, the probability of occurrence of behaviors that are dominant in the response hierarchy increases. This suggests that for well-learned behaviors or performance on simple tasks where the dominant responses in the hierarchy are correct, higher levels of arousal should facilitate skilled performance. When the dominant responses are incorrect or inefficient, increases in arousal should hinder performance.

Drive theory has received some corroboration by studies examining the arousal-performance relationship on simple tasks such as paired-associate learning or the classical conditioning of eye blinks (Sonstroem, 1984). Additionally, research on social facilitation has lent some convergent data on the hypothesized relationship between arousal and performance. As early as 1897, Triplett noted that the presence of others influenced performance of an athletic task. Zajonc (1965), in a classic review of social facilitation research, concluded that the presence of spectators or other participants facilitated performance of simple tasks or dominant responses, but that these audiences and coparticipants hampered the execution of complex or novel tasks. If we assume that the athlete generally responds to observers with an increase in arousal, then Zajonc's explanation of social facilitation effects fits well with drive theory.

However, drive theory and social facilitation have not fared as well as explanations of the anxiety-performance relationship on more complex motor skill tasks. One major problem has been the difficulty of specifying habit strength and habit hierarchies in applied sport settings. Even in those experiments where attempts have been made to define dominant responses, results have not always been consistent with drive theory (Wankel, 1984). In addition, evaluations of the social facilitation effects of observers and coactors has not consistently produced anxiety increases.

Drive theory posits an essentially linear relationship between arousal and performance. As arousal increases, the quality of performance should increase. An alternative conception argues that as arousal increases, so should performance efficiency—but only to the point where the high arousal level begins to interfere with skilled performance. This conception has been labeled the Yerkes-Dodson "Law" or inverted-U hypothesis (Landers, 1980).

Inverted-U Hypothesis

This view of the anxiety performance relationship suggests that the effects of arousal on performance are curvilinear. Extremely low and extremely high levels of arousal are hypothesized to impair performance, while moderate arousal levels are thought to facilitate performance. A study by Ahart (1973) examining free throw shooting by basketball players during a variety of game situations illustrated this possible curvilinear relationship. He assumed that the closer the score of the game, the greater the stress experienced by the players. From this assumption, Ahart predicted that free throw accuracy would be best when there was a moderate score discrepancy between the two teams. Close games with a wide point differential should produce the least accurate free throw shooting. These predictions were substantiated by Ahart's data.

While other studies have also corroborated the inverted-U hypothesis, Martens (1972) concluded that the literature is far from consistent. Indeed, he found no clear relationship between arousal and motor performance. These confusing findings may be due, in part, to methodological shortcomings (Landers, 1980). Few studies evaluating the inverted-U or drive theories have presented subjects with the three levels of stress necessary to adequately test the theories, and very few experiments have demonstrated that the situations or stimuli employed were actually stressful.

A number of authors have argued that the relationship between arousal and performance is far more complex than that presented by either drive theory or the inverted-U hypothesis. Task complexity and task difficulty appear to mediate the arousal-performance relationship. Optimal levels of arousal may be lower for more complex or more difficult athletic behaviors. Mahoney (1979) suggested that simple strength tasks such as weightlifting may profit from high levels of arousal or anxiety while more cognitive tasks such as golf may suffer from even moderate anxiety experiences. Landers (1978; 1980) made a similar point when he hypothesized that moderate levels of arousal would facilitate performance on tasks involving high information processing, complex motor integration, and low energy mobilization demands.

Oxendine (1970) has summarized the research on arousal and task complexity and generated the following rules:

1) A high level of arousal is essential for optimal performance in gross motor activities involving strength, endurance, and speed.

2) A high level of arousal interferes with performances involving complex skills, fine muscle movements, coordination, steadiness, and general concentration.

3) A slightly-above-average level of arousal is preferable to a normal or sub-normal state for all motor tasks.

Martens (1978) has acknowledged the practical benefits of Oxendine's generalizations, but questioned their ability to withstand empirical scrutiny. Martens suggested that Oxendine's analysis disregards the role of attentional processes and individual differences in response to stress (cf. Shelton & Mahoney, 1978).

Individual differences in skill levels and experience may also affect the relationship between arousal and performance. In an experiment comparing experienced and novice skydivers, Fenz and Epstein (1969) found—although anxiety was reported as a pervasive experience—the more competent divers reported reductions in their arousal levels immediately prior to the jump. In contrast, the anxiety level of novice jumpers continued to rise as performance became imminent. Similar findings were reported by Mahoney and Avener (1977) in their study of Olympic gymnasts and by Meyers, Cooke, Cullen, and Liles (1979) in their work with collegiate champion racquetball players. While the experimental results have not been consistent (cf. Gould, Weiss, & Weinberg, 1981), the pattern of results that has emerged suggests that more experienced or more skilled athletes—when compared with less experienced less skilled competitors—cope more effectively with high stress tasks and exhibit different temporal patterns of anxiety prior to and during performance. Whether these differences relate to differential skills or other psychological variables is not yet clearly elucidated.

Trait Anxiety

One of the oldest traditions in psychology is the search for an intrapersonal explanation for human behavior. In sport the trait psychology approach, or "personology," has been directed towards the identification of the "athletic personality" (Mahoney, 1979). Ogilvie (1968) concluded that the data "strongly support the tendency for certain personality traits to receive greater reinforcement within the competitive world of athletics. . . . We can state with some certitude that . . . (athletes) . . . have most of the following personality traits: ambition, organization, deference, dominance, endurance, and aggression." The implications of the athletic personality are obvious. If a global set of athletic personality traits can be identified, then guidelines for the selection and training of competitors should follow logically.

In sport personology, anxiety has received a great deal of research and clinical attention. Trait anxiety has been defined as "relatively stable, individual differences in anxiety proneness, that is . . . differences in the disposition to perceive a wide range of stimulus situations as dangerous or threatening . . . the tendency to respond to such threats with A(anxiety)-State reactions" (Spielberger, 1972). This is to be contrasted with state anxiety which is "a transitory emotional state or condition of the human organism that varies in intensity and fluctuates over time . . . characterized by subjective, consciously perceived feelings of tension and apprehension, and activation of the autonomic nervous system" (Spielberger, 1972). The state-trait view indicates that both high and low trait anxious individuals experience anxiety, but that the high trait anxious person's anxiety experience should be more frequent, intense, and prolonged.

Martens (1975) has cited the lack of non-correlational empirical work evaluating the trait position in the sport personality literature, and this is typical of the heavy fire that trait conceptions have come under throughout clinical, social, and personality psychology (cf. Mischel, 1968). Mischel (1968) launched the most damaging attacks against the trait position by acknowledging the stability of individual behavior patterns, but arguing that these patterns were not highly generalized across situations. The position adopted by Mischel (1979) and other social learning theorists was that individuals organize and pattern behavioral consistencies and discriminations in terms of subjectively perceived equivalencies and distinctions. Mischel argued that one should expect behavioral stability only to the extent that the individual's skills, encoding, expectancies, values, goals, and plans endure across situations. By ignoring this individual variability, the personality trait approach has severely limited value for understanding the athlete's performance.

One approach to dealing with these criticisms has been to identify a "situation-specific trait anxiety" (Passer, 1984). This assumes that some people tend to perceive competitive situations (but not necessarily other stress situations such as examinations and social evaluation) as threatening and respond with varying levels of state anxiety (Martens, 1977). Support for this position came from Scanlan's (1977) work with fifth and sixth grade boys competing on a motor maze task. She found that competitive trait anxiety was a significant contributor to precompetitive stress. However, post-competitive stress was, in the main, attributed to winning or losing the maze competition.

While further specification of the trait conception of anxiety may be valuable, competitive trait anxiety and other situation-specific traits remain vulnerable to Mischel's (1968; 1979) critique. Passer (1984) argued that competitive trait anxiety is mediated by one's perceived ability, and expectancy of success, failure and negative affect. Cottrell (1968) concluded that the presence of others during an athletic task would have arousing effects only to the extent that the competitor perceived the observer as evaluative and anticipated negative outcomes. The use of so-called specific traits is a step towards identifying functional relationships among person, situation, and performance. But this position stops short of identifying the reciprocal relationships among cognition, physiological arousal, behavior, and environment or task demands that will enable us to develop a comprehensive understanding of athletic performance.

This brief examination of theories relating anxiety, performance, and individual differences obviously leaves several major questions unanswered. Some partial clarification is offered, however, by sport psychologists who have investigated the mediating role of attention in the anxiety-performance relationship.

Arousal and Attention

Traditional perspectives on anxiety have not adequately explained the anxiety-performance relationship. Furthermore, these theories have not identified the factors that mediate between anxiety and performance. Several recent writers have argued that attention and cue utilization may be the crucial factors in understanding this relationship. In a review of experiments employing a dual-task paradigm, Landers (1980) concluded that, in general, subjects maintaining performance on a primary task were less able to respond to peripheral or secondary tasks while under stress. This finding seems to hold true under a variety of stressors including amphetamines, exercise stress, electric shock, sleep deprivation, incentives, hypoxia, and threat of personal injury. Landers (1978; 1980), relying on Easterbrook's (1959) cue utilization theory, hypothesized that as performance anxiety increases, perceptual selectivity will also increase. At optimal levels of arousal this should facilitate action by increasing perceptual selectivity and eliminating task-irrelevant cues. However, this is accomplished without an excessive narrowing of attention that might eliminate some task-relevant cues. At low levels of arousal the athlete may fail to eliminate irrelevant stimuli due to an uncritical perceptual focus, while at high arousal levels the perceptual range may narrow to the point of eliminating valuable cues. The ice hockey goalie whose arousal level is too low may be distracted by the crowd or bench activity; under extremely high arousal he may fail to attend to opposing skaters moving into the play from the periphery.

The effects of arousal on attention may serve to explain the curvilinear relationship observed between arousal and performance. However, we must also acknowledge that both individual and task differences influence attentional processes and their eventual effect on performance. Easterbrook (1959) argued that the range of essential task cues may be narrower for simple than for complex tasks. Yet each athletic task presents the individual with different attentional demands and often with constantly shifting demands. There is some evidence that attention to "internal" cues—especially anxiety cues—may detract from some performances (Borkovec & O'Brien, 1977; Sarason, 1975; Wine, 1971), but these findings were not replicated in a motor task involving hand steadiness (Carpenter & Mahoney, 1980). It would appear, however, that anxiety and attention are reciprocally interactive phenomena. High levels of anxiety may interfere with an individual's ability to shift attention among changing tasks demands, and attention to anxiety cues may further contribute to experienced arousal.

The consideration of attentional processes as mediators of the arousal-performance relationship also highlights the role of individual differences in response to stress. Athletes' ability to direct and control their attentional processes is clearly critical to their athletic performance. Nideffer (1976) has offered the most systematic analyses of the role of attention in sport behavior. He conceptualized attention along two dimensions—direction and breadth of focus. An individual's attention may be directed to either internal or external cues, while the breadth of focus may be either broad or narrow. Nideffer has employed these two bidirectional dimensions to develop a matrix of attentional styles which can be assessed using his Test of Attentional and Interpersonal Style.

Nideffer (1976) suggested that each sport requires a specific attentional style or pattern, and that the individual's attentional style may or may not fit with that sport. The functional value of this model lies in the practical implication that attentional style or skill should be trainable (Weinberg, 1984).

One well known example of attentional style or skill in sport is Morgan's work with endurance runners (Morgan & Pollock, 1977). Morgan reported that world class marathon runners often employed *associative* strategies during their long races. That is, they attended to the pain and fatigue experienced during the race,

race demands (e.g., terrain, weather), and competition. Morgan hypothesized that these associative cognitive strategies allowed the highly skilled runner to match his or her physical abilities to race demands. "Middle of the pack" runners most often reported using distraction or *dissociative* cognitive strategies during marathons. These strategies may distract less skilled runners from the pain of the marathon and allow them to continue competing (though they may fail to optimally match their physical abilities to the task demands). The significant point here is that both of these attentional strategies serve to benefit runners at different skill levels on the long distance endurance task. Morgan and Pollock (1977) and Okwumabua, Meyers, and Schleser (1983) have both presented evidence that the training or adoption of appropriate cognitive strategies can improve endurance performance.

The work by Nideffer, Morgan and others suggests that arousal may not operate only on breadth of attention as Easterbrook (1959) hypothesized in his cue utilization theory. Wachtel (1967) argued that high levels of arousal are also associated with increased attentional distractibility. Carver and Scheier (1981) pointed out that the athlete's perception of evaluative observers or coactors, demands for excellence or other anxiety-inducing stimuli may lead to misdirected attention rather than a narrowed attentional focus. Prime foci of misdirected attention are negative aspects of the self and molecular or minor components of the athletic task (e.g., a quarterback attending solely to the snap from the center rather than the defense and the play about to be performed).

The evidence that arousal may serve to misdirect attention and the studies on patterns of athletic anxiety cited earlier (Fenz & Epstein, 1969; Mahoney & Avener, 1977; and Meyers et al., 1979) all suggest that the crucial variable is not arousal, but how athletes perceive the anxiety-arousing sport situation and how they employ strategies and skills to handle competitive stress. The appropriate task may not be a search for "laws" relating anxiety to athletic performance. Rather, the task may be to develop a systemic approach to the identification of functional relationships that allow athletes to more effectively manage or "use" the arousal inherent in any meaningful competition. This creates the possibility that for some athletes heightened arousal and narrowed or "misdirected" attention may not serve counterproductive purposes. In the next section we discuss this possibility by examining the concept of peak performance.

Peak Performance

High levels of anxiety and arousal are typically conceptualized as having a negative influence on performance. However, the literature on attention as a mediator of the arousal-performance relationship, and the studies examining athletes' patterns of anxiety response to competitive events suggest something different. The anxiety pattern studies indicate that athletes at all skill levels experience similar levels of precompetitive stress and anxiety. Our review of the arousal and attention research (and the social learning literature in general) suggests that it is not arousal that is central to performance but the athlete's expectations, efficacy beliefs, and strategies for managing and using that arousal.

This perspective allows us to consider the potentially energizing properties of anxiety and arousal. Both Shelton and Mahoney (1978) and Weinberg, Gould, and Jackson (1980) found that subjects asked to "psych-up" prior to performing a motor task often reported employing preparatory arousal strategies. Gould et al. (1983), in their survey of champion high school wrestlers, not only found that two thirds of the young men reported prematch anxiety but that they often indicated that this anxiety was beneficial to their performance. Harris (1970) has labeled such positive stress from physical activity, "eustress." She observed that some individuals strive to raise their tension levels rather than maintain homeostasis and that this apparent paradox can be resolved "by the fact that pleasure and pain are both drawn from the same reservoir of underlying excitement." As an example, Harris cited the combination of joy and fear of a child's first trip down a long slide.

Special episodes of superior functioning or intense experience related to positive stress and arousal have been labeled peak performance (Privette, 1983), peak experience (Maslow, 1971; Ravizza, 1977), the "sweet spot in time" (Jerome, 1980), or flow (Csikszentmihalyi, 1975a). These experiences are typically characterized by an intense focused awareness on the act and on the self; distracting stimuli are completely eliminated from the attentional field. "One is very aware of one's actions, but not of the awareness itself" (Csikszentmihalyi, 1975a).

An element of risk is often associated with peak experiences. Csikszentmihalyi (1975b) argued that special experience occurs when feelings of control and competence predominate over voluntarily accepted risk. The danger and accompanying anxiety, what Harris (1970) has labeled "being on the brink of catastrophe," seem to function as compelling motivation to enforce an extremely high level of attention to the immediate task. "You're so involved in what you're doing that you aren't thinking about yourself as separate from the immediate activity. You're no longer a participant observer, only a participant. You're moving in harmony with something else you're part of (Csikszentmihalyi, 1975a, p. 86). Here, in contrast to the other models of arousal and performance thus far discussed, anxiety serves as a challenging ally.

COGNITIVE PROCESSES AND PERFORMANCE ANXIETY

The fact that some athletes find extremely high and low levels of anxiety helpful to their performance forces a reappraisal of our traditional views. There is more to be accounted for than level of arousal, type of task, and the presence of observers. As will be outlined in this section, the individual's relationship with his or her personal anxiety patterns appears to be a formative influence in the experience and effects of anxious episodes. Individuals assign personal meanings to their performance, to winning, losing, and trying, to being nervous, and so on. This suggests the need for accelerated research into the formation and change of such private belief systems. Illustrations will be drawn from published and unpublished studies of over 1,000 athletes in over 25 sports at all skill levels, with a subset of 24 who have been studied longitudinally over periods of 3–5 years. Treatment approaches to sports anxiety will be briefly examined in light of the proposed role of personal meaning systems in individual anxiety patterns. Although relaxation and anxiety management training may help some athletes, there is considerable room for improvement in our theories and services in this area.

Integration of Cognition, Emotion, and Behavior

This may be a good point at which to briefly broaden the scope of the present discussion. Our current models of the relationship between anxiety and performance are themselves embedded in larger contexts, tacit assumptions, and metatheories. One example is the increasing interface among the sport, behavioral, and cognitive sciences (Straub & Williams, 1984). It is probably not coincidental that cognitive theories and therapies have become more popular and populous in psychology, in general, and in sport psychology, in particular (Dember, 1974; Mahoney, 1977, 1979). But as psychology and sport psychology have increasingly employed cognitive models, those models have themselves matured and developed. Although the nature and nuances of these developments lie beyond the scope of this chapter (see Mahoney, in press), their relevance can be illustrated by a single example.

Consider the current and ongoing controversy regarding the primacy of cognition versus affect in human experience (Lazarus, 1982, 1984; Zajonc, 1980, 1984). The basic argument has focused on whether cognition or affect somehow dominate or "come first" as prime movers. Lazarus has emphasized the pervasiveness of "cognitive appraisal" in emotional experience, while Zajonc has defended emotional responding as more basic. The respective meanings of "cognitive" and "emotional" have been reappraised in the process of the debate, and commentaries on the argument have offered less dichotomous resolutions (cf. Guidano, 1984, in press; Mahoney, 1984, 1985a, in press).

In some ways, the debate about the primacy of cognition and affect is reminiscent of a parallel debate in the 1960s about the relative primacy of behavior and cognition (attitudes) (Bandura, 1969; Mahoney, 1974). It is as if psychology has gradually differentiated itself into at least three basic camps corresponding to beliefs about the relative power of thought, feeling, and action. In their respective corners of this conceptual triangle, cognitivists, 'somaticists,' and behaviorists have defended the primary importance of their angle on the triad. Cognitivists have focused on changing mental representations, somaticists have encouraged affective expression, and behaviorists have emphasized motoric performance.

Whether a paradigm shift is or is not underway in psychology, it is apparent that some fundamental assumptions are being publicly reviewed and conceptual refinements are being offered. The resurgence of structuralism and constructivism are cases in point, and movements toward theoretical convergence, developmental processes, and systems analyses reflect signs of conceptual developments (Bowlby, 1985; Goldfried, 1983; Guidano, 1984, in press; Joyce Moniz, 1985; Mahoney, 1985a,b, in press; Reda & Mahoney, 1984; Weimer, 1977, 1982). Among many other assertions, these works—which belong to a common superordinate metatheory one could call "*cognitive developmental*"—question the meaningfulness of separating cognition, affect, and behavior into such discrete classes. In their interpretations, for example, anxiety is recognized as a pattern of holistic or organismic activity distributed across systems that are dynamically interdependent. At some level, it is argued, the experience of anxiety presupposes an interactive system of systems (muscular, respiratory, cardiac, attention, memory, etc.) whose interface is expressed in the (conscious or tacit) anticipation of danger/pain and an active intent/attempt to avoid/control such a development. In other words, anxiety is imbued with the experience of time (memory/moments/anticipation), contexts or boundaries of valence (good/bad, safe/dangerous), and the sense of efficacy (Bandura, 1977, 1982, 1986; Beck, Emery, & Greenberg, 1985).

Personal Meanings, Anxiety, and Performance

One of the central tenets of cognitive developmental approaches is the extent to which experience is self-structured via the imposition of individual meanings. When meanings change, people change, and vice-versa. From this approach, meanings and beliefs are not confined to intellectual realms, but are also reflected in perceptual, emotional, and behavioral processes. They are highly individualized. Translated into a practical example, this would emphasize the importance of multisystem measures and, in the case of dysfunctional anxiety patterns, the assessment of relevant personal meanings.

The desire to reduce and control anxiety is frequently reported by athletes of all ages and skill levels. There is accumulating evidence that various forms of relaxation training and anxiety-management training can be helpful to some athletes. At the same time, however, it is clear that there is considerable room for improvement in our theories and services related to anxiety and sports. One such improvement may be the increasing focus on personal meanings, self-esteem, and attentional skills as factors involved in understanding individual patterns of anxiety and performance (Mahoney, Avener, & Avener, 1983). Skills in self-relaxation, rest, and arousal regulation ("psyching") are valuable on and off the playing field. From the perspective here termed cognitive developmental, a pattern of severe or dysfunctional performance anxiety would first invite an assessment of the athlete's "personal reality"—including the meanings of performance, anxiety and control. The meaning of anxiety for the athlete offers an illustration. Athletes across all age and skill levels report the experience of high intensity, adrenalization, and multisystem arousal before, during, and after competition. From these reports, sport scientists have tended to infer a monolithic prototype of anxiety built up from individual questions that actually inquired about convergent phenomena like tension, metabolic rate, thoughts, images, pulse, changes in breathing, etc. The experience of anxiety is just as diverse as the range of individual meaning associated with it. For one individual, it may be an uncomfortable annoyance; for another, a life-threatening terror.

Individual meaning systems also play a significant role in the experience of success, failure, setbacks, motivation, and so on. Whatever the dimensions of relevance to the athlete, such themes may offer valuable information regarding optimal foci of interest. Relaxation and basic coping skills may be helpful for athletes who struggle with moderate, acute, and topical anxieties. In cases of extreme, chronic, and general anxiety, however, more comprehensive interventions may be warranted.

Anxiety Patterns in Athletes

The available literature on anxiety and sports suggests considerable complexity beyond some very broad generalizations. The latter, however, would include the following:

1. athletes generally report lower levels of tension than nonathletes and
2. experienced and skilled athletes, relative to their less experienced and skilled peers, report different patterns and experiences of performance anxiety.

The first generalization is corroborated by extant research comparing athletes and nonathletes on measures of psychological distress and dysfunction. Morgan (1985) has recently proposed a "mental health model of performance" which contends that *success in sport is inversely correlated with psychopathology*" (p. 71). He reviews evidence consistent with the model and defends the "iceberg profile" of elite athletes. According to Morgan, the elite athlete tends to be relaxed, happy, energetic, and mentally clear. Whether the bold assertions of the mental health model can survive the scrutiny of adequate empirical trials poses an important question for contemporary researchers. Exceptions to these probabilistic generalizations also deserve closer attention and theoretical analysis. Likewise, the complex issue of causality presents itself. If the highly skilled athlete exhibits fewer or less intense "problems in living," what are the active sources of this association? Are more successful athletes 'naturally selected' by the rigors of competition and training and/or do those rigors provide a powerful context for the refinement of adaptive, stress-moderating skills?

Longitudinal data on skill refinement and psychological development in athletes have been relatively hard to find. Evidence for the second generalization is therefore confined to a few earlier works and two longitudinal studies in progress. Among other things, these data suggest that veteran athletes may have learned to regulate, tolerate, and "use" their anxiety more effectively than their less experienced peers. At present, it would appear that skilled athletes:

a. tend to view their anxiety as, at worst, a nuisance and, at best, an ally in their performance;
b. tend to "pace" their pre-competition anxiety more effectively; and
c. are less focused on their anxiety and more focused on momentary task demands during their performance.

The "pacing" of pre-competition anxiety has yet to be well documented across independent studies, but it is probably well known to the veteran athlete and coach. Although highly individualized, the pre-competition anxiety pattern that emerges in the skilled and experienced athlete tends to be much more efficient than those reported by less experienced athletes. Some athletes report that their anxiety starts later in the preparation sequence—e.g., several hours before competition rather than its original onset at days or weeks prior. Others report "getting nervous" earlier than they used to, but then inserting a disciplined calmness in the last 24–48 hours pre-competition. As performance approaches, of course, anxiety tends to mount, and the absolute level of pre-competition anxiety may not differ significantly between experience levels.

> . . . *although there were no apparent differences in overall anxiety between the gymnasts who qualified for the Olympics and those who did not, there was some indication that the more successful gymnasts were slightly more anxious prior to the competition and less anxious once the actual performance had begun. Likewise, it appeared that the two groups of athletes may have assigned a different meaning to their anxiety and to performance mistakes:*

> "*Supplementing their subjective reports of anxiety level, verbal interviews suggested that the more successful athletes tended to 'use' their anxiety as a stimulant to better performance. The less successful gymnasts seemed to arouse themselves into near panic states by self-verbalizations and images that belied self-doubts and impending tragedies (Mahoney & Avener, 1977, p. 140.''*

> *In a typical interview, the less successful gymnast would often report that he was concerned and frightened by his level of pre-competitive anxiety. Likewise, these athletes were more likely to get 'rattled' by minor breaks in performance and to either 'choke' and/or progressively deteriorate in their performance during the competition. . . .*

> *The more successful athletes tended to view and even label their anxiety as a kind of 'high energy' that was necessary to and facilitative of their optimal performance. One of the gymnasts in this group even worried that he might not be anxious enough to attain the 'psych' he needed for this level of performance (Mahoney, Avener, & Avener, 1983, pp. 62–63).*

Strategies for Coping with Anxiety

The foregoing generalizations, if they survive continuing scrutiny, would suggest that the personal meanings assigned to athletic performance and the experience of anxiety might be a fruitful focus for researchers and service providers in this area. Practical strategies for coping with performance anxiety would then include the following:

1. training and refinement of basic relaxation skills (via muscular, imaginal, respiratory, and other exercises);
2. training and refinement of coping skills (e.g., stress inoculation, self-instruction);
3. appraisal and refinement of personal meanings assigned to performance, anxiety, control, success, failure, etc.;
4. training and refinement of concentration skills; and
5. practice/implementation of the foregoing in actual or simulated competitive situations.

These last two strategies (concentration skills and in vivo/simulation practice) emerge from observations that (a) athletes often report that extreme anxiety interferes with their attentional skills, and (b) attentional strategies related to task demands have been reported by successful athletes during the stress of competition.

> *. . . the more successful gymnasts reported that they were, indeed, upset by their mistakes, but they uniformly stated that their strategy for optimal performance was to maintain their focus of attention on the current and upcoming demands of competition. . . . we encourage athletes to occasionally practice performing under high anxiety conditions. The best way to learn how to direct or 'channel' performance anxiety in such a way that it adds to (rather than detracts from) performance seems to be one in which conceptual learning and mental practice are followed by actual in vivo practice of working in a high anxiety state. This can be accomplished by open discussions of the experience of performance anxiety, mental practice in encountering and channeling high arousal energy, and participation in actual or simulated competitive situations (Mahoney, Avener, & Avener, 1983, p. 63).*

ISSUES AND IMPLICATIONS

We began this chapter with an acknowledgement of the pervasiveness of anxiety in sports and briefly reviewed traditional views of the relationship between emotional arousal and skilled performance. Investigations into the validity of drive theory, the inverted-U hypothesis, and trait-state levels of anxiety have offered valuable information and challenges for researchers in this area. More recent work on the relationship between arousal and attentional processes has also introduced heuristic complexities, and the phenomenon of "flow" or peak experiences emphasized the importance of individual, and perhaps skill, differences in optimal performance.

In the second part of the chapter we noted the recent acceleration of contacts among the sport, cognitive, and behavioral sciences. The search for a "most basic" category of causal influence was placed in an historical context, and more recent, holistic models of human experience were briefly acknowledged. The role of personal meaning systems in the experience of anxiety and in the modulation of the anxiety-performance interaction were also noted, with illustrations from extant studies on anxiety patterns in more and less experienced/skilled athletes. Finally, strategies for coping with performance anxiety were outlined.

In these, our closing remarks, our goal is not to summarize what has already been said so much as to suggest some of the research issues and practical implications that emerge out of those remarks. For example, the analysis offered here under the label of "cognitive developmental" approaches would question the relevance of research that does not acknowledge and explore the role of personal meanings in anxiety-performance interactions. Drive theory, the inverted-U hypothesis, and even much of the social facilitation literature have sought to identify universal generalizations that override individual differences. These differences, it would seem, loom far more important than has been recently acknowledged by psychological theories. Studies into the trait, state, and interactional factors in anxiety have offered more individualized speculations, as have the literatures on attentional processes and peak performance. It is clear, however, that a more adequate understanding of the complex relationship between anxiety and performance will require a more adequate understanding of the anxious performer and his/her individual strategies for adaptation.

An underlying theme throughout this chapter has been the assertion that our scientific study and understanding of anxiety and performance—in sports, but also in other areas—has been unnecessarily constrained by our theoretical traditions. All too often, in our opinion, anxiety has been selectively associated with psychopathology and treated as a potential enemy of the performer. Only with the recent acknowledgements of positive stress, anxiety in elite athletes, and peak performance has anxiety, as a concept, approached decriminalization in its technical usage.

A parallel theme has been the futility of "prime mover" arguments regarding the relative power of cognitive, affective, and behavioral processes. The point here goes well beyond an acknowledgment that each of these categories of experience is very difficult to differentiate from the others. We can, of course, operationalize our definitions, but this is no guarantee of their validity. Thoughts are very hard to separate from feelings and behaviors, and our neural organization further challenges their differentiation (Weimer, 1977, 1982). But it is not just a problem of conceptual demarcations among cognitive, affective, and behavioral processes. What has been emerging within the constructivistic models of recent cognitive developmental writings has been a complexly integrated system of independent and interdependent processes (Guidano, 1984, in press; Mahoney, 1984, 1985a, in press). Congruent with the earlier writings of Piaget (1981) and Kelly (1955) on these matters, recent developments have emphasized the fundamental inseparability of cognition, affect, and action into discrete and independent categories. Their facile, everyday differentiation by so many people may well reflect centuries of indoctrination into "carving experience at its joints."

Besides its widespread popularity in both scientific and lay populations, the division of human experience into discrete and causal categories is encouraged by dominant philosophies of science within psychology. Unfortunately, those philosophies are pervasively anachronistic when viewed from current approaches in epistemology (Mahoney, 1985b). Until recently, 20th century psychology has been dominated by perspectives espousing what might be called "billiard ball determinism," which posits absolute causal relationships among discrete particulars. This type of thinking is clearly Newtonian and Aristotelian in prototype. Billiard ball determinism was formally rejected by the physical sciences in 1927 (with the Copenhagen Interpretation of Quantum Mechanics), but it has remained a stubborn and pervasive influence in the behavioral sciences. Besides acknowledging the pervasive powers of relativity and the reactivity of observational methods, quantum physics and, later, thermodynamics have come to emphasize the importance of a system's development over time. In increasing numbers, the physical, biochemical, and social sciences have begun to generate theories that are *process-oriented.* In our opinion, it is time that psychology follow suit.

And, finally, with regard to the practical implications of our current and emergent understanding of the phenomenon of anxiety in sports, our conclusions are brief.

1. Anxiety is experienced and reported by virtually all athletes across all age and skill levels.

2. Experienced and skilled athletes report somewhat different attitudes toward and experiences of anxiety.

3. The intensity and effects of performance anxiety may be related to that individual's relevant personal meanings.

4. Basic training in relaxation, coping, and stress management skills are recommended.

5. When more comprehensive or extensive services are desired, personal meaning systems may offer heuristic themes for assessment and intervention.

Our goal, of course, is not simply to help the athlete perform better or more comfortably. The athlete who performs well under pressure but suffers chronically in the process soon learns that performance cannot be separated from training or from life circumstances. However they are conceptualized, the "everyday anxieties" of modern life play a significant role in our individual psychological well-being.

We conclude that the relationship between anxiety and athletic performance is complex and highly individualized. Continuing studies of this relationship will hopefully offer further insights into how individuals cope with stressful challenges and, in particular, how different styles of conceptualizing and responding to intense performance-related arousal may significantly influence the quality of both the performance and its experience. Coming full circle, such refinements in our understanding would aid us not only in working with other anxious individuals, but also with young athletes whose notions of self-worth, self-efficacy, and competence are often so formatively intertwined with their sports performance.

SUMMARY

The experience of anxiety by athletic competitors is pervasive and impactful. However, traditional unidimensional or trait-based explanations of the anxiety-athletic performance relationship have not adequately addressed this complex phenomenon. Contemporary interactional and skill-based perspectives offer a more useful conceptualization of the multivariate nature of the anxiety-performance relationship. Factors including physical skill level, sport experience, task demands and complexity, stress management skills, cognitive strategies, and attentional skills all serve to mediate stressful athletic performance. Indeed, the literature on peak performance and flow experience suggests that high levels of anxiety and risk may, in some cases, offer competitors a positive and valued experience that may benefit their physical performance.

The complexity of the anxiety-performance relationship emphasizes the crucial role of personal meaning systems in the experience of anxiety. The athlete's private beliefs and cognitive constructions of anxiety, performance, and the competitive environment may be key to understanding the effects of anxiety. A cognitive developmental model that acknowledges the personal and multisystemic nature of the anxiety experience should enable us to design and implement more effective anxiety management programs.

REFERENCES

Ahart, F. C. (1973). *The effects of score differential on basketball free throw shooting accuracy.* Unpublished master's thesis, Ithaca College, Ithaca, NY.

Bandura, A. (1969). *Principles of behavior modification.* New York: Holt, Rinehart, and Winston.

Bandura, A. (1977). Self-efficacy: Toward a unifying theory of behavioral change. *Psychological Review, 84,* 191–215.

Bandura, A. (1982). Self-efficacy mechanism in human agency. *American Psychologist, 37,* 122–147.

Bandura, A. (1986). *Social foundations of thought and action: A social cognitive theory.* Englewood Cliffs, NJ: Prentice-Hall.

Beck, A. T., Emery, G., & Greenberg, R. L. (1985). *Anxiety disorders and phobias: A cognitive perspective.* New York: Basic Books.

Beuter, A. & Duda, J. L. (1985). Analysis of the arousal/motor performance relationship in young children using motor kinematics. *Journal of Sport Psychology, 7,* 229–243.

Borkovec, T. D. & O'Brien, G. T. (1977). Relation of autonomic perception and its manipulation to the maintenance and reduction of fear. *Journal of Abnormal Psychology, 86,* 163–171.

Bowlby, J. (1985). The role of childhood experience in cognitive disturbance. In M. J. Mahoney & A. Freeman (Eds.), *Cognition and psychotherapy* (pp. 181–200). New York: Plenum.

Bramwell, T., Masuda, M., Wagner, N. N., & Holmes, T. H. (1975). Psychological factors in athletic experience: Development and application of the social and athletic readjustment rating scale (SARRS). *Journal of Human Stress, 1,* 6–20.

Carpenter, F. H., & Mahoney, M. J. (1980). Attentional processes and stress-related performance. *Cognitive Therapy and Research, 4,* 423–426.

Carver, C. S., & Scheier, M. F. (1981). *Attention and self-regulation: A control theory approach to human behavior.* New York: Springer-Verlag.

Cottrell, N. B. (1968). Performance in the presence of other human beings: Mere presence audience and affiliation effects. In E. C. Simmel, R. A. Hoppe, & G. A. Milton (Eds.), *Social facilitation and imitative behavior* (pp. 91–110). Boston: Allyn & Bacon.

Csikszentmihalyi, M. (1975a). Play and intrinsic rewards. *Journal of Humanistic Psychology, 15,* 41–63.

Csikszentmihalyi, M. (1975b). *Beyond boredom and anxiety: The experience of games in work and play.* San Francisco: Jossey-Bass.

Dember, W. N. (1974). Motivation and the cognitive revolution. *American Psychologist, 29,* 161–168.

Easterbrook, J. A. (1959). The effect of emotion on cue utilization and the organization of behavior. *Psychological Review, 66,* 183–201.

Fenz, W. D. & Epstein, S. (1969). Stress in the air. *Psychology Today, 3,* 27–28, 58–59.

Goldfried, M. R. (Ed.). (1983). *Converging themes in psychotherapy.* New York: Springer.

Gould, D., Horn, T., & Spreeman, J. (1983). Sources of stress in junior elite wrestlers. *Journal of Sport Psychology, 5,* 159–171.

Gould, D., Weiss, M., & Weinberg, R. S. (1981). Psychological characteristics of successful and nonsuccessful Big Ten wrestlers. *Journal of Sport Psychology, 3,* 69–81.

Guidano, V. F. (1984). A constructivist outline of cognitive processes. In M. A. Reda & M. J. Mahoney (Eds.), *Cognitive psychotherapies: Recent developments in theory, research, and practice* (pp. 31–45). Cambridge, MA: Ballinger.

Guidano, V. F. (in press). *Selfhood processes and lifespan development.* New York: Guilford.

Harris, D. V. (1970). On the brink of catastrophe. *Quest, 13,* 33–40.

Hull, C. L. (1943). *Principles of behavior.* New York: Appleton-Century-Crofts.

Jerome, J. (1980). *The sweet spot in time.* New York: Summit.

Joyce Moniz, L. (1985). Epistemological therapy and constructivism. In M. J. Mahoney & A. Freeman (Eds.), *Cognition and psychotherapy* (pp. 143–179). New York: Plenum.

Kelly, G. A. (1955). *The psychology of personal constructs.* (2 vols) New York: W. W. Norton.

Landers, D. M. (1978). Motivation and performance; the role of arousal and attentional factors. In W. F. Straub (Ed.), *Sport psychology: An analysis of athletic behavior* (pp. 75–87). Ithaca, NY: Mouvement Publications.

Landers, D. M. (1980). The arousal-performance relationship revisited. *Research Quarterly for Exercise and Sport, 51,* 77–90.

Lazarus, R. S. (1982). Thoughts on the relations between emotion and cognition. *American Psychologist, 37,* 1019–1024.

Lazarus, R. S. (1984). On the primacy of cognition. *American Psychologist, 39,* 124–129.

Mahoney, M. J. (1974). *Cognition and behavior modification.* Cambridge, MA: Ballinger.

Mahoney, M. J. (1977). Reflections on the cognitive learning trend in psychotherapy. *American Psychologist, 32,* 5–13.

Mahoney, M. J. (1979). Cognitive skills and athletic performance. In P. C. Kendall & S. D. Hollon (Eds.), *Cognitive-behavioral interventions: Theory, research, and procedures* (pp. 423–443). New York: Academic Press.

Mahoney, M. J. (1984). Integrating cognition, affect, and action: A comment. *Cognitive Therapy and Research, 8,* 585–589.

Mahoney, M. J. (1985a). Psychotherapy and human change processes. In M. J. Mahoney & A. Freeman (Eds.), *Cognition and psychotherapy* (pp. 3–48). New York: Plenum.

Mahoney, M. J. (1985b). Academic clinical psychology: The quest for a richer harvest. In R. A. Kasschau, L. P. Rehm, & L. P. Ullmann (Eds.), *Psychology research, public policy and practice: Toward a productive partnership* (pp. 173–189). New York: Prager.

Mahoney, M. J. (in press). *Human change processes: Notes on the facilitation of personal development.* New York: Basic Books.

Mahoney, M. J. & Avener, M. (1977). Psychology of the elite athlete: An exploratory study. *Cognitive Therapy and Research, 1,* 135–141.

Mahoney, M. J., Avener, J., & Avener, M. (1983). Psychological aspects of competitive athletic performance. In L. Unestahl (Ed.), *The mental aspects of gymnastics* (pp. 54–66). Orebro, Sweden: Veje.

Martens, R. (1972). Trait and state anxiety. In W. P. Morgan (Ed.), *Ergogenic aids in muscular performance* (pp. 35–66). New York: Academic Press.

Martens, R. (1975). *Social psychology and physical activity.* New York: Harper & Row.

Martens, R. (1977). *Sport competition anxiety test.* Champaign, IL: Human Kinetics.

Martens, R. (Ed.). (1978). *Joy and sadness in children's sports.* Champaign, IL: Human Kinetics.

Maslow, A. (1971). *The farther reaches of human nature.* New York: Viking Press.

Meyers, A. W., Cooke, C. J., Cullen, J., & Liles, L. (1979). Psychological aspects of athletic performance: A replication across sports. *Cognitive Therapy and Research, 36,* 361–366.

Mischel, W. (1968). *Personality and assessment.* New York: Wiley.

Mischel, W. (1979). On the interface of cognition and personality: Beyond the person-situation debate. *American Psychologist, 34,* 740–754.

Morgan, W. P. (1985). Selected psychological factors limiting performance: A mental health model. In D. H. Clarke & H. M. Eckert (Eds.), *Limits of human performance* (pp. 70–80). Champaign, IL: Human Kinetics.

Morgan, W. P., & Pollock, M. L. (1977). Psychological characteristics of the elite distance runner. In P. Milvey (Ed.), *Annals of the New York Academy of Sciences* (pp. 382–403). New York: New York Academy of Sciences.

Nideffer, R. M. (1976). Test of attentional and interpersonal style. *Journal of Personality and Social Psychology, 34,* 394–404.

Ogilvie, B. C. (1968). Psychological consistencies within the personality of high level competitors. *Journal of the American Medical Association, 205,* 780–786.

Okwumabua, T. M., Meyers, A. W., & Schleser, R. (1983). Cognitive strategies and running performance: An exploratory study. *Cognitive Therapy and Research, 7,* 363–369.

Oxendine, J. B. (1970). Emotional arousal and motor performance. *Quest, 13,* 23–32.

Passer, M. W. (1984). Competitive trait anxiety in children and adolescents. In J. M. Silva & R. S. Weinberg (Eds.), *Psychological foundations of sport* (pp. 104–117). Champaign, IL: Human Kinetics.

Piaget, J. (1981). *Intelligence and affectivity: Their relationship during child development.* Palo Alto, CA: Annual Reviews.

Pierce, W. J. (1980). *Psychological perspective of youth sport participants and nonparticipants.* Unpublished doctoral dissertation, Virginia Polytechnic Institute & State University.

Privette, G. (1983). Peak experience, peak performance, and flow: A comparative analysis of positive human experiences. *Journal of Personality and Social Psychology, 45,* 1361–1368.

Ravizza, K. (1977). Peak experiences in sport. *Journal of Humanistic Psychology, 17,* 35–40.

Reda, M. A., & Mahoney, M. J. (Eds.). (1984). *Cognitive psychotherapies: Recent developments in theory, research, and practice.* Cambridge, MA: Ballinger.

Sarason, I. G. (1975). Anxiety and self-preoccupation. In I. G. Sarason & C. D. Spielberger (Eds.), *Stress and anxiety* (Vol 2) (pp. 689–722). New York: Wiley.

Scanlan, T. K. (1977). The effects of success-failure on the perception of threat in a competitive situation. *Research Quarterly, 48,* 144–153.

Shelton, T. O. & Mahoney, M. J. (1978). The content and effect of "psyching-up" strategies in weight lifters. *Cognitive Therapy and Research, 2,* 275–284.

Shriver, P. (1985). I'll tell you about tennis. *Sports Illustrated, 63,* 47–60.

Sonstroem, R. J. (1984). An overview of anxiety in sport. In J. M. Silva & R. S. Weinberg (Eds.), *Psychological foundations of sport* (pp. 104–117). Champaign, IL: Human Kinetics.

Spence, J. T., & Spence, K. W. (1966). The motivational components of manifest anxiety: Drive and drive stimuli. In C. D. Spielberger (Ed.), *Anxiety and behavior* (pp. 291–326). New York: Academic Press.

Spielberger, C. D. (Ed.). (1972). *Anxiety: Current trends in theory and research* (Vol. 1). New York: Academic.

Straub, W. F. & Williams, J. M. (Eds.). (1984). *Cognitive sport psychology.* Lansing, NY: Sport Science Associates.

Triplett, N. (1897). The dynamogenic factors in pacemaking and competition, *American Journal of Psychology, 9,* 507–533.

Wachtel, P. L. (1967). Conceptions of broad or narrow attention. *Psychological Bulletin, 68,* 417–429.

Wankel, L. (1984). Audience effects in sport. In J. M. Silva & R. S. Weinberg, (Eds.), *Psychological foundations in sport.* (pp. 293–314). Champaign, IL: Human Kinetics.

Weimer, W. B. (1977). A conceptual framework for cognitive psychology: Motor theories of the mind. In R. Shaw & J. Bransford (Eds.), *Perceiving, acting, and knowing* (pp. 267–311). Hillsdale, NJ: Erlbaum.

Weimer, W. B. (1982). Hayek's approach to the problems of complex phenomena: An introduction to the theoretical psychology of 'The Sensory Order.' In W. B. Weimer & D. S. Palermo (Eds.), *Cognition and the symbolic processes* (Vol. 2) (pp. 241–285). Hillsdale, NJ: Erlbaum.

Weinberg, R. S. (1984). Mental preparation strategies. In J. M. Silva & R. S. Weinberg (Eds.), *Psychological foundations of sport.* (pp. 145–156). Champaign, IL: Human Kinetics.

Weinberg, R. S., Gould, D., & Jackson, A. (1980). Cognition and motor performance: Effect of psyching-up strategies on three motor tasks. *Cognitive Therapy and Research, 4,* 239–245.

Wine, J. (1971). Test anxiety and direction of attention. *Psychological Bulletin, 76,* 92–104.

Zajonc, R. B. (1965). Social facilitation. *Science, 149,* 269–274.

Zajonc, R. B. (1980). Feeling and thinking: Preferences need no inferences. *American Psychologist, 35,* 151–175.

Zajonc, R. B. (1984). On the primacy of affect. *American Psychologist, 39,* 117–123.

7

Anxiety, Arousal, and Motor Performance: Theory, Research, and Applications

Robert Weinberg

INTRODUCTION

You get yourself ready and into the starting block as the starter shouts "take your mark." The finals of the Olympic trials for the 100 yard dash is about to begin. As you set yourself you feel that your heart is pounding hard, your muscles feel a little tight and your mouth feels a little dry. In a few short seconds you will know if the four years of hard work, dedication and practice was all worthwhile. This is your big moment and you are psychologically and physiologically ready but yet you feel a little anxious and scared. Will this anxiety you feel help or hinder your performance? The solution to this seemingly simple question has stimulated but yet perplexed sport psychology researchers. We all have probably experienced anxiety prior to a competitive performance whether it be shooting a foul shot with five seconds left and the score tied, serving in tennis with match point against you, attempting to kick the potential winning field goal in the last few seconds of a football game, or playing in front of your parents, for the first time. In fact a poll of over 400 wrestlers from 15–19 years of age, who were involved in 1981 national championship competition, found that these elite competitors characterized themselves as being anxious or worried in 66% of their matches (Gould, Horn & Spreeman, 1983). Anecdotally and intuitively it seems that sometimes these "pressure" situations bring out the best in people while sometimes it causes people to "choke" (perform poorly under pressure). Thus, the central question becomes what is the relationship between an individual's level of arousal and his or her subsequent performance and what variables mediate this relationship. Accordingly, the arousal motor relationship has been one of the most researched areas in sport psychology because its understanding is essential if we are to learn more about how to get individuals to reach their maximum levels of performance.

The remainder of this chapter will attempt to address and elucidate critical relationships between arousal and motor performance. To accomplish this task the paper will be organized as follows. First, some definitional distinctions will be made between arousal, state and trait anxiety as well as the multidimensional nature of arousal. This will be followed by a presentation of the various theories attempting to explain the anxiety-motor relationship including a critical look at the empirical evidence supporting or rejecting each one as well as methodological problems in testing the theories. A presentation of some alternate approaches examining the arousal-motor relationship will follow along with a look at how individual differences can mediate the relationship. Finally, some practical applications extrapolated from the review of the extant literature will be provided and future directions for research will be offered.

DEFINITIONS AND MEASUREMENT OF AROUSAL AND ANXIETY

Before the relationship between arousal and motor performance can be discussed it is important to distinguish between several terms and concepts associated with the study of arousal and anxiety. First, it is important to distinguish between arousal and anxiety since these two terms have been often used interchangeably in the literature. The early concept of arousal centered on the notion of energy mobilization during threatening situations, originally thought necessary for either defending oneself or fleeing the flight or fight mechanism (Cannon, 1929). This idea has since been refined by several prominent researchers (e.g., Berlyne, 1967; Hebb, 1955; Lacey, 1967; Malmo, 1959) but the most comprehensive conception was put forth by Duffy (1962). She views behavior as varying on two dimensions—direction and intensity. The direction of behavior is described as either approach or withdrawal behavior and this behavior may occur at many different degrees of intensity. Duffy views arousal as the intensity dimension of behavior and defines it as "the extent of release of potential energy, stored in the tissues of the organism, as this is shown in activity or response (1962, p. 17). Arousal can vary on a continuum from extremely low levels (e.g., sleep) to very high levels (extreme excitement). Thus, arousal refers to the entire continuum of a person's psychological activation.

However, the term anxiety, as generally employed in the psychological literature, usually is restricted to higher arousal states that produce feelings of discomfort or excessive concern and worry. In defining anxiety, an important conceptual distinction was made by Spielberger (1966), who distinguished between chronic (trait) and transitory (state) anxiety. He defined state anxiety as a transitory emotional state that varies in intensity and fluctuates over time." Trait anxiety refers to "relatively stable individual differences in anxiety proneness, that is, differences in the disposition to perceive a wide range of stimulus situations as dangerous and threatening and to respond to such threats with state anxiety reactions (Spielberger, 1972, p. 39). State-trait theory predicts that high trait-anxious individuals experience a greater number of situations as threatening and that they respond to these personal threats with state anxiety levels disproportionately higher than those of low trait-anxious individuals. Thus, an athlete's anxiety before or during an event will be determined by an interaction of their general level of anxiety (i.e., trait anxiety) and the specific situational constraints of the event (i.e., state anxiety). For example, both high and low trait-anxious individuals will probably exhibit higher levels of state anxiety when competing for the state championship than during a practice session. However, the high trait-anxious person probably will feel more threatened by the championship game than the low-anxious person and will react with higher levels of state anxiety. These differential reactions will have important implications for subsequent performance and will be discussed later in the chapter.

A final definition and measurement concern revolves around the multidimensional nature of arousal. Although arousal has long been considered a unidimensional concept, contemporary researchers (Borkovec, 1976; Davidson & Schwartz, 1976; Landers, 1980, Schwartz, Davidson, & Goleman, 1978) have argued that it is truly multidimensional in nature. Specifically, Borkovec (1976) argues that arousal can be defined by measurement of three response components including physiological, behavioral and cognitive. This conception is supported by physiological research (Lacey, 1967) which supports the existence of three separate but interacting response components. This notion becomes important when one attempts to analyze the arousal-performance relationship. That is, some of the inconsistent findings to be presented later in the chapter may be a measurement artifact resulting from taking a unidimensional approach rather than a multidimensional one. Furthermore, a multidimensional approach underscores the complexity of the arousal-performance relationship although such an approach is necessary if a comprehensive theory is to ever be developed. With these definitional and measurement considerations noted we will now take a close look at the arousal-performance relationship itself.

EXPLANATIONS FOR THE AROUSAL-PERFORMANCE RELATIONSHIP

Drive Theory

Drive theory was originally conceived by Hull (1943) but was later modified by Spence and Spence (1966) to explain the performance of complex skills. Simplistically stated, drive theory predicts that performance (P) is a multiplicative function of drive state (D) and habit strength, and thus $P = D \times H$. Drive was defined by Hull as a global, nonspecific energizer of all behavior which has been equated in the literature with physiological arousal since the latter is more amenable to scientific measurement. Habit refers to the dominance of correct and incorrect responses. According to the theory, increases in drive (arousal) enhances the probability of the dominant response being made. If the dominant response is correct (i.e., in the latter stages of skill acquisition) then increases in arousal will increase performance. However, when the dominant response is incorrect (i.e., during early skill acquisition) then increases in arousal will be detrimental to performance.

The traditional paradigm for testing drive theory has been to identify individuals who differ in emotional responsiveness (i.e., trait anxiety) and put them in a situation either with or without the presence of a stressor (e.g., shock). The latter category (no stressor) tested the chronic hypothesis of drive which stated that high trait-anxious subjects responded with greater drive (arousal) in all situations. Studies employing high and low trait-anxious subjects in the presence of a stressor tested the situational hypothesis reformulated by Spence and Spence (1966) which states that differences between high and low trait-anxious individuals would only occur when a stressor was present. This viewpoint is consistent with Spielberger's notion of state-trait anxiety which views trait anxiety as a personality disposition which predisposes a person to manifest higher levels of arousal only when confronted with stressful situations.

Martens (1971, 1974) has extensively reviewed the literature testing both the chronic and situational hypothesis with the drive theory framework. Specifically, in his review Martens found 28 studies testing the chronic hypothesis and 15 studies testing the situational hypothesis. Unfortunately, he concludes that the empirical evidence is equivocal for both hypotheses with about an equal number of studies supporting and rejecting each hypothesis.

These contradictory and ambiguous findings has led Martens (and most researchers) to conclude that drive theory does not provide an adequate explanation for the arousal-performance relationship. Furthermore, Martens argues that there exists an extremely serious problem when attempting to apply drive theory to motor behavior and complex motor skills. That is, it is extremely difficult to clearly determine the habit hierarchies (i.e., dominance of correct or incorrect responses) for the motor responses on complex motor tasks, thus making it virtually impossible to test the equation: Performance = Drive × Habit. For example, should walking on a treadmill be considered a novel task (dominant response incorrect) or well-learned (dominant response correct). Or take the example of a baseball player with a .300 batting average. Is his dominant response correct or incorrect? In most motor behavior studies the dominant response is considered incorrect as long as the learning curve has not reached asymptote and then after asymptote is reached the dominant response is considered correct. Since Martens argues that this assumption is crude at best he concludes that drive theory remains operationally non-functional for complex motor behavior.

Although most researchers have followed the lead of Martens, it should be noted that there is some disagreement with the above conclusions. In particular Landers (1980) cogently argues that it is indeed possible to determine the habit hierarchies for some motor tasks. For example, Hunt and Hillery (1973) employed motor mazes with known floor and ceiling effects so that subjects' probability of success/failure could be accurately measured and hence determine habit hierarchy. In addition, Carron (1976) used a choice reaction-time paradigm to develop habit hierarchies. Although these studies show mixed support for drive theory they do demonstrate that for some motor tasks habit strength can be operationally defined. However, the point remains that most real-life motor behavior such as tennis, soccer, basketball, gymnastics, etc. involve extremely complex motor skills that will be difficult if not impossible for which to measure habit hierarchy accurately. Thus, even if some laboratory tasks can be devised to assess habit hierarchy the practical utility in terms of complex motor skills would appear limited. This concurs with Bolles' (1967) conclusion that the worst failure of the drive concept continues to be that it does not help us explain behavior" (p. 329).

Inverted-U Hypothesis

We have seen that the equivocal results of drive theory did not support a linear increase in performance as arousal increased. The inverted-U hypothesis provides an alternative explanation for the arousal-performance relationship. Specifically, the inverted-U hypothesis predicts that performance would increase with increasing levels of arousal until some optimal point, whereupon further increases would cause a decrement in performance. Figure 1 shows the different predictions made by the two theories. This hypothesis has gained considerable support in the motor behavior area for a couple of reasons. First, it has a great deal of appeal on an intuitive level especially for coaches concerned that their athletes are not sufficiently "psyched-up" or that they are too "psyched-up." Second, the experimental evidence has generally supported the inverted-U hypothesis although there certainly have been some discrepant findings. I would like to focus on the experimental evidence including methodological problems in testing the inverted-U hypothesis.

Yerkes and Dodson (1908) were the first to show experimental support for the inverted-U hypothesis using mice as subjects. They found that an easily acquired habit, that is, one which does not demand difficult sense discriminations or complex association, may readily be formed under strong stimulation. Since this initial investigation, an abundant literature has accumulated testing the inverted-U hypothesis in both the general psychological and sport psychological literatures. Much of the early motor-performance evidence offered in support of the inverted-U hypothesis came from trait anxiety literature testing the drive theory hypothesis. Most of these studies, however, provided only an indirect test since instead of creating at least three distinct points along the arousal continuum these studies compared the performance of low and high trait-anxious subjects under two levels of arousal, assuming that at least three distinct points were created.

Several studies, however, have tested the inverted-U hypothesis by specifically varying three or more levels along the arousal continuum. For example, Matarazzo, Ulette and Saslow (1955), Singh (1968), Matarazzo and Matarazzo (1956), and Harrington (1965) have tested the inverted-U by varying three or more levels of trait anxiety. These studies resulted in equivocal findings but that may have been the result of trait anxiety not reflecting changes in arousal levels as discussed earlier, but instead a disposition to respond with greater arousal to certain situations.

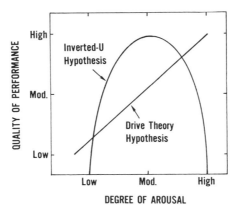

Figure 1 Drive theory and inverted-U hypothesis predictions concerning the arousal-performance relationship.

To provide a more appropriate test of the inverted-U hypothesis subjects with high, low and moderate levels of trait anxiety would be exposed to high, low and moderate levels of stress. Martens and Landers (1970) conducted such a study by assigning high, moderate and low trait-anxious junior high school boys to high, moderate and low levels of stress while performing on a motor tracking task. Physiological measures of heart rate and palmar sweating as well as questionnaire data confirmed the establishment of three levels of arousal. Results provided support for the inverted-U hypothesis in that moderate trait-anxious subjects performed significantly better than low and high trait-anxious subjects. In addition, subjects in the moderate stress group performed significantly better than subjects in the low and high stress groups.

A more recent study by Weinberg and Ragan (1978) also manipulated three levels of trait anxiety and stress. Their results produced a stress × trait anxiety interaction with high trait-anxious subjects performing best under low stress, whereas low trait-anxious subjects performed best under high stress. These results are consistent with inverted-U hypotheses predictions since both high and low trait-anxious subjects were performing best at moderate levels of arousal (i.e., high anxiety-low stress; low anxiety-high stress). Martens and Landers (1970), however, did not find this interaction using a similar experimental design. The inconsistency of these two studies might be explained by the fact that fear of shock coupled with ego-involving instructions was the stressor employed by Martens and Landers, whereas negative evaluation and ego-involving instructions were employed by Weinberg and Ragan. Studies by Katin (1965) and Hodges and Spielberger (1969) indicate threat of shock does not produce differential reactions differing in trait anxiety. Therefore, it is possible that Martens and Landers' failure to find a stress by trait anxiety interaction was due to the fact that shock, as a stressor, was not differentially perceived by subjects differing in trait anxiety. Despite this discrepancy, the overall findings of these two laboratory investigations are generally in support of the inverted-U hypothesis.

Some researchers have questioned laboratory tests of the inverted-U hypothesis arguing that it is very difficult to create high levels of arousal in the artificial environment of a laboratory and thus it is difficult to produce three distinct points along the arousal continuum. Furthermore, use of human subjects puts additional constraints on the type of manipulations employed by researchers. As a solution to this problem investigators have turned to field experiments in order to examine the external validity (generalizability) of the inverted-U hypothesis in competitive athletic situations. These field studies are more capable of eliciting the high levels of arousal needed to obtain three distinct points along the arousal continuum. Some examples of such studied will now be provided.

Lowe (1974) conducted such a field study in Little League baseball hitting. He compared the hitting performance of all players over the course of a season with the criticalness (stress) of the situation. The criticalness was assessed both within a game itself (i.e., situation criticality took into consideration the score of the game, the inning, how many outs, how many men on base when a batter went up to the plate) as well as each games relationship to other games (i.e., were the teams close to each other in the standings, how many games were left in the season, how close were the teams to first place). Situation criticality was corroborated by use of heart rates and other observational measures. Results indicated that Little Leaguers hit better when the situation criticality was moderate than when it was high or low which supported the inverted-U hypothesis.

Klavora (1978) tested the inverted-U hypothesis in a field setting by testing 145 high school basketball players competing for a city championship. Subjects completed the state-trait anxiety inventory just prior to each game. The performance of each player was then evaluated by the coaches (after the game) according to the athletic customary ability, to control for differences in playing ability. Five distinct points along the arousal continuum were thus achieved and performance results clearly supported the inverted-U hypothesis showing that the best performances occurred under moderate levels of state anxiety, average performances occurred under conditions of slight under or over-arousal and poor performances occurred under either very low or high levels of arousal.

A series of interesting studies conducted by Fenz and his colleagues (Fenz, 1975; Fenz & Epstein, 1967; Fenz & Jones, 1972) provide indirect support for the inverted-U hypothesis. They assessed heart rate and respiration rate periodically from the time parachute jumpers arrived at the airport until they were about to jump out of the plane. Results indicated that regardless of whether they were novice or experienced, the jumpers who consistently executed technically good jumps had increases in arousal as the time of the jump approached but then the last few minutes just prior to the jump they reduced their arousal to a more moderate level. In contrast, jumpers who consistently were rated as poor did not reduce their arousal level prior to the jump but rather arousal continued to increase right up to jump time. These findings have been consistently replicated and support the notion that moderate levels of arousal are better for performance than high levels. These series of studies are particularly appealing as they without question answer the criticism of laboratory studies in terms of not being able to produce high levels of arousal since parachute jumping is literally a "life or death" activity.

Although the evidence from field research is generally in support of the inverted-U hypothesis, the data is not unequivocal. For example, Giabrone (1973) replicated Lowe's study by investigating the effect of situation criticality on free throw shooting. Free throw shooting also had the advantage of maintaining constant difficulty level unlike Lowe's study which had to contend with different levels of task difficulty in terms of pitchers of varying abilities. Results both within and between players representing "Big Ten" college basketball teams indicated no relationship between arousal and free throw shooting.

Despite some exceptions as noted above, empirical studies have generally supported the notion of a curvilinear relationship between arousal and motor performance. However it should be noted that the inverted-U hypothesis provides no explanation as to what causes this relationship. Consequently, several researchers have argued that a much better understanding of what mechanisms produce this inverted-U relationship would eventually help practitioners attempting to manipulate arousal levels. Although several theories have been brought forth in an attempt to explain the inverted-U hypothesis the one motor behavior researchers tend to favor is known as attentional narrowing.

Attentional Narrowing

The research on attentional narrowing comes primarily from work in human factors and perception. The basic research methodology investigating attentional processes employs the dual-task or secondary task method which involves maintaining performance on a primary task while attempting to respond to a secondary task. This response to the secondary task is usually viewed as a stressor which can draw one's attention away from the primary task thus causing decrements in performance (Landers, 1980). In essence, increases in arousal can cause individuals to narrow their attentional focus to the central task while reducing their attention to the peripheral or secondary task. Several research studies lend support to this notion and Bacon (1974) summarizes the empirical evidence by stating that increases in arousal impairs performance through a loss of sensitivity to attend to the relevant stimuli in one's environment.

Probably the most highly recognized explanation of the relationship between arousal and attentional processes is Easterbrook's (1959) cue utilization hypothesis. Easterbrook argues that arousal progressively restricts the range of cues from the external environment. Viewed in terms of limited capacity models of attention, (e.g., Kahnenan, 1972) attentional capacity decreases as arousal increases. More specifically, increases in arousal create a source of distraction that competes for limited attentional capacity. This increase in arousal produced by external (e.g., shock) or internal (e.g., worry) stressors provides competing patterns of activation to those required by task performance (Hockey, 1979). Thus, the reduction in the range of cue utilization represents a change in the processing of environmental cues due to changes in arousal level (Dirkin & Hancock, 1983).

Implicit in Easterbrook's (1959) hypothesis is an inverted-U relationship between arousal and performance based on the attention to relevant or irrelevant cues in the environment. Basically, Easterbrook postulated that at low levels of arousal an individual has a broad perceptual range causing attentional discrimination to be poor. Consequently, either through low selectivity or lack of effort both task relevant and task irrelevant cues are attended to resulting in relatively poor performance. As arousal increases to a more moderate or optimal level, task irrelevant cues are eliminated and task relevant cues are selectively attended to. When the individual is attending only to task-relevant cues, then he or she is at the top of the inverted-U and maximum performance is the end result. However as arousal increases above this optimal level, task-relevant cues are not discarded causing further perceptual narrowing and performance decrements. This process continues until all task relevant cues are eliminated leaving only task-irrelevant cues putting the performer at the rock bottom of the inverted-U curve.

A practical example from the world of sport might help elucidate this principle. A basketball player shooting a free throw in a practice (i.e., low arousal) might be attending to irrelevant cues such as what other players are doing, who is in the stands besides the relevant cues of the rim and their form. During a real game (optimal arousal) however, the player may disregard those irrelevant cues and just focus on the relevant cues of shooting the ball in the basket since winning the game and performing well is important to him. At the championship game with his team behind by one point the player is fouled and has two shots to win the game with five seconds left (i.e., high arousal). In this case the player may get so worried and uptight that instead of paying attention to the task-relevant cues, these would be eliminated and task irrelevant cues (e.g., loud noise of the crowd) would be attended to. This type of behavior is more commonly known as "tunnel vision" in that attention is narrowed to a limited stimulus field at the expense of task-relevant cues. Another good example of "tunnel vision" would be a rookie quarterback who is brought into a close game for the first time with time running in the final quarter. On his first pass attempt he focuses only on the receiver and does not even see the linebacker who steps in front of the receiver to intercept the ball.

In summary, attentional narrowing as best expressed by Easterbrook's cue utilization hypothesis appears to provide the best explanation for the inverted-U relationship between arousal and motor performance. With this type of information, coaches can begin to work with athletes to attend to the proper cues in their specific performance environments which would put them at the top of the inverted-U curve performing up to their maximum.

Patterning of Neuromuscular Energy

An alternate way to approach the arousal-performance relationship was proposed by Weinberg and Hunt (1976). In our perusal of the literature on arousal and performance we felt that most researchers had focused on the end result of a movement or skill quantified into some performance measure. When so viewed, performance is task oriented with little carry over from task to task. However, an alternate way of looking at performance is through the process or quality of movement as seen through the patterning of neuromuscular energy. This approach is centrally concerned with how individuals organize and integrate their energies in the execution of motor skills. Each individual seems to exhibit a particular style of movement which represents the process of movement displayed by the individual. To better understand the end product of a movement it seems necessary to first understand the processes underlying the movement.

Understanding energy organization requires investigation of the most elementary organized neuromuscular process—the depolarization of muscle fibers that provide energy for shortening which can be measured by electromyography (EMG). There have been numerous studies investigating the relationship between arousal and motor performance using EMG (e.g., Bartoshuk, 1955; Rossi, 1959; Sidowski & Eason, 1960; Voor, Lloyd & Cole, 1969). In these studies EMG amplitude which measures the amount of energy released by muscle depolarization, has been used exclusively to evaluate the data. This variable alone does not provide much information about the quality of an individual's movement. To understand the patterning of neuromuscular energy, a more global approach to movement is necessary.

Along these lines, Weinberg and Hunt (1976) assessed the quality of movement by use of such EMG measures as anticipation, duration, and perseveration in addition to amplitude. These variables refer to the duration of electrical activity in the muscles before, during and after movement. In addition, sequential and simultaneous muscle contraction (cocontraction) were used as indices of motor patterning. In our first study we studied high and low-anxious subjects performing on a ball throwing accuracy test. Results indicated that after failure feedback (a stressor) low-anxious subjects performed significantly better than high-anxious subjects. Why did these differences occur? An explanation was provided by the EMG variables which indicated that high-anxious subject used significantly more energy before, during and after the throw than low-anxious subjects. In addition, low-anxious subjects displayed sequentical contraction of their muscles, whereas high-anxious subjects exhibited cocontraction. The movement pattern of the high-anxious subjects constituted a highly inefficient use of neuromuscular energy compared to that for low-anxious subjects and provides an explanation of performance differences between high and low-anxious subjects. In fact, 95% of all subjects were classified correctly as high or low-anxious (as initially determined by the Trait Anxiety Inventory) based on their patterning of neuromuscular energy.

In a second study (Weinberg, 1978), I attempted to replicate the previous findings as well as extend them by employing success as well as failure feedback. Performance results indicate that high-anxious subjects performed significantly better under success feedback (low stress) than failure feedback (high stress) whereas low-anxious subjects performed significantly better under failure feedback than success feedback. More importantly, analysis of the patterning of neuromuscular energy again predicted the performance results. Specifically, high-anxious subjects under success displayed more efficient quality of movement than under failure. Conversely, low-anxious subjects under failure exhibited more efficient quality of movement than under success. Thus, by assessing the process of movement we might gain a better understanding of the arousal-performance relationship instead of just describing it via the inverted-U hypothesis. Future research will need to be conducted to provide validity to such an approach.

FACTORS MEDIATING THE AROUSAL-PERFORMANCE RELATIONSHIP

Task Characteristics

One important factor mediating the arousal-performance relationship is the nature of the task. Fisk and Maddi (1961), argue that there is a wide range of arousal levels in which maximum performance can occur and that this range varies with the dimensions of the task. They further postulate that the more difficult the task combined with increasing energy requirement, the narrower the range for optimal performance. This seems plausible since it is well known how difficult it is to keep up one's optimal arousal at such sports as tennis, basketball and volleyball which require both precision and large expenditures of energy.

In dealing specifically with motor behavior, Oxendine (1970) developed a hierarchical classification of sports based on complexity and the degree of fine muscle control and judgement involved. He offered the following generalizations on the arousal-performance relationship:

1. A high level of arousal is essential for optimal performance in gross motor activities involving strength, endurance and speed.
2. A high level of arousal interferes with performance involving complex skills, fine muscle movement, coordination, steadiness and general concentration.

3. A slightly above-average level of arousal is preferable to a normal or subnormal arousal state for all motor tasks.

More specifically, Oxendine postulates that sports such as weight lifting, sprinting and football tackling and blocking would require high levels of arousal for maximum performance. Conversely, sports requiring fine muscle control such as golf, bowling, figure skating and field goal kicking would best be performed at low levels of arousal. (See Table 1) Although these observations appear to have face validity, does the empirical research investigating this issue support these contentions?

Along these lines, Weinberg and Genuchi (1980) attempted to test one of Oxendine's generalizations by investigating the relationship between competitive golf performance and anxiety in a field setting. Intercollegiate golfers completed a state anxiety questionnaire just prior to competition on three days of a tournament along with the Sport Competition Anxiety Test (SCAT) one hour before the start of a practice round. Results supported Oxendine's prediction in

Table 1 Optimal Arousal Level for Some Typical Sports Skills

Level of arousal	Sports skills
#5 (extremely excited)	football blocking and tackling performance on the Rogers' PFI test running (220 yards to 440 yards) sit up, push up, or bent arm hang test weight lifting
#4	running long jump running very short and long races shot putt swimming races wrestling and judo
#3	basketball skills boxing high jumping most gymnastic skills soccer skills
#2	baseball pitchers and batters fancy dives fencing football quarterback tennis
#1 (slight arousal)	archery and bowling basketball free throw field goal kicking golf putting and short irons skating figure 8's
0 (normal state)	

that high trait-anxious golfers (who also had the highest state anxiety scores) performed significantly poorer than low or moderate anxious golfers. Furthermore the best performance was by the low trait-anxious golfers (who also had the lowest state anxiety score). The moderate trait-anxious golfers performed between the low and high trait-anxious golfers. Since golf is a skill requiring precision, fine muscle coordination and concentration, it would be best performed at low levels of arousal which is just what we found.

This finding is not only intuitively appealing since most golfers attest to the detrimental effects of high levels of arousal but seems consistent with the attentional narrowing hypothesis discussed earlier. That is, high levels of arousal have typically been associated with shifts in attention to inappropriate or irrelevant cues increasing the chance of error. This narrowing of attention on irrelevant cues is particularly detrimental when tasks require total concentration combined with high degrees of precision and fine muscle coordination.

Although there is some empirical support for Oxendine's second hypothesis, Landers (1977) argues that there is little empirical evidence supporting the other two propositions. For example, Nideffer and York (1976) found that competitive swimmers performing a task seemingly involving speed experienced a decrement in performance under conditions of high physiological arousal. In other studies (Gutin, 1973; Levitt & Gutin, 1971) the fastest reaction times were associated with moderate as opposed to high levels of arousal. In a recent investigation (Gould, Weinberg & Jackson, 1980) one experiment found that performance on a leg-strength task was highest under high levels of arousal supporting Oxendine's contention, however, a second experiment produced no relationship between arousal and performance. Finally, Klavora (1975) investigated the possible differences of pre-competition emotional arousal of football players assigned to different positions. Oxendine would predict different optimal levels of arousal based on the different task requirements of the various positions in football (i.e., a lineman would need a higher arousal for optimal performance than a quarterback). However, results indicated no significant differences in optimal pre-competitive arousal level in football players who were playing different positions.

These equivocal findings might be at least partially an artifact of attempting to rank order motor skills on a continuum from those requiring only precision and accuracy to those requiring speed, strength and endurance. Oxendine (1970) proposed such a continuum in his original postulation but it is possible this approach may be overly simplistic. That is, such a classification system may not adequately account for such things as perceptual requirements of the task, task complexity, attentional demands, cognitive decision-making components, skill level, etc. just to name a few. In fact most sports usually require a combination of physical and psychological attributes for successful performance. For example, Oxendine lists speed events such as sprinting (running or swimming) as being performed best at high levels of arousal. However, most sprinters will tell you that if you are too aroused your muscles will tighten up thus hindering performance. Furthermore, to be successful at basketball requires speed and quickness on defense, precision and accuracy for shooting as well as strength and endurance for rebounding. So what level of arousal would be best if basketball players want to achieve maximum performance? To say that a moderate arousal would be best (as does Oxendine) since it combines both speed, endurance and precision would be taking an overly simplistic approach. Future research should more precisely categorize sports along different task dimensions before more accurate arousal-performance relationships across different tasks could be assessed.

Individual Differences

In addition to the type of sport skill, an athlete's individual makeup is also an important factor in determining optimal arousal levels. Since research suggests that high levels of arousal can contribute to distraction, perceptual narrowing, worry, errors in judgement as well as motoric inefficiency, the ability to learn how to control or regulate one's response to high arousal states should positively influence the quality of performance. One such personality factor which would appear to determine an individual's susceptibility to arousal-eliciting events is trait anxiety. On an intuitive basis some athletes seem to perform better under high pressure conditions whereas others seem to perform poorly (i.e., choke). For example, when faced with a stressful situation such as kicking the winning field goal in the last few seconds of a football championship game, one athlete who is high in competitive trait anxiety may become overaroused and "shank" the kick while a low competitive trait-anxious athlete may become aroused to an optimal level and successfully execute the field goal. There are two empirical studies which speak to the issue.

The first study was conducted by Klavora (1977) utilizing high school basketball players on 14 different teams. All subjects completed a trait anxiety inventory and then state anxiety was assessed just prior to 8–14 games, depending on when the player's team was eliminated from the tournament. Results indicated that both high and low trait-anxious subjects displayed inverted-U curves in terms of the relationship between arousal and performance. However, the interesting observation was that these curves were different for high and low trait-anxious athletes. That is, the low trait-anxious subjects' inverted-U was on the lower end of the arousal continuum (i.e., low state anxiety) whereas the inverted-U curve for high trait-anxious subjects was at the upper end of the arousal continuum (i.e., high state anxiety). Thus, athletes' optimal performances seem to occur in relation to their customary arousal levels rather than an absolute score on an anxiety test.

This notion of investigating an athlete's usual or customary arousal level when attempting to determine performance levels was further elucidated in a study by Sonstroem and Bernardo (1982) also using basketball players. They extended Klavora's study by investigating within subject variations in arousal across game rather than between subject difference. First, players were administered the SCAT and subsequently divided into high, moderate, or low competitive trait anxiety groups. State anxiety was then assessed before three different games. Arousal levels were defined as low, moderate, or high, based on the player's lowest, median and highest pregame state anxiety values across three games of basketball tournament. In essence, in testing the inverted-U hypothesis, a player's median state anxiety value across the three games was identified as her optimal (moderate) level of arousal and within subject analyses were conducted. Results indicated that low, moderate and high trait-anxious athletes all displayed inverted-U functions, with moderate arousal (as determined by their own state anxiety scores) producing the best performance in all cases. Thus, both of these studies supported the inverted-U hypothesis but point out that different people may exhibit this relationship relative to their own arousal states rather than some objective level of high or low arousal. A logical extension of this principle would suggest that arousing an entire team by a big pep talk may be beneficial for some people while detrimental for others depending on their customary level of arousal.

PRACTICAL APPLICATIONS

The preceding review has attempted to critically evaluate the theories and studies investigating the arousal-performance relationship. Although some of the research is equivocal and methodological problems, at times, have limited interpretation, there are several important points to be gleaned from the findings that should have important implications for the practitioners.

First, the preponderance of empirical evidence support an inverted-U relationship between arousal and skilled performance. In essence, this means that an athlete might perform below his or her maximal level due to underarousal or overarousal. The problem of underarousal impeding performance is probably not a widely spread one due to the place that sport competition occupies in our society as well as the nature of competition itself. For instance, most athletes have to continually deal with the pressures of winning, peer evaluation, coach and parent acceptance, spectators, game importance, etc. which in most cases will get an athlete sufficiently aroused (if not overaroused) for the competitive event. However, there are times when athletes might need to be aroused or psyched-up. This might occur if an athlete believes that he or she can easily defeat their opponent and thus might put forth a minimal effort or if the game is not a particularly important one over the course of a long season. Along these lines, my colleagues and I (Caudill & Weinberg, 1983a, 1983b; Gould, Weinberg & Jackson, 1981; Weinberg, Gould, & Jackson, 1980) have consistently found that "psyching-up was consistently better than not psyching up, particularly for performance involving predominately strength, speed and endurance. These studies were not performed under highly competitive or evaluative conditions and therefore psyching-up probably helped raise their arousal to more optimal levels. Thus, if a coach perceives that his or her athletes are not ready to play due to an emotional letdown, it would appear under these limited circumstances that raising one's arousal via psyching-up would be beneficial.

The problem that is probably more prevalent, however, is not psyching-up an athlete but rather psyching him or her out. In essence, athletes are usually aroused, excited and psyched-up for the big game and what they need to do is reduce this arousal to more optimal or moderate levels as suggested by the inverted-U hypothesis. In several surveys of major college football teams, for example, more than 40% of the athletes have reported experiencing enough anxiety before and during competition to interfere with their performance. In another survey, "too much anxiety" was the number one reason given by athletes for not performing up to their capacities. It becomes obvious from these surveys as well as anecdotal reports that excess levels of arousal are problematic in terms of performance. As mentioned earlier, all the pressures of winning that come from significant others in particular, as well as society in general, increase the importance of performing well and living up to high expectations. Add on to this things such as competing for college scholarships, making it as a professional, winning juniors tournaments, establishing national rankings, making the Olympic team etc. it is no wonder that athletes often become too uptight and perform below their level of ability.

So what can coaches, teachers and athletes do to alleviate or at least reduce the high levels of anxiety associated with sport competition? One direct way is through the use of relaxation techniques specifically designed to cope with anxiety. Along these lines, more and more coaches and athletes are beginning to realize the need to relax is critical to performance excellence under pressure situations and have begun to implement relaxation training into their practice sessions. It is beyond the scope of this paper to discuss these techniques in depth, but rather a brief description of several techniques will be provided.

Perhaps the most well known of the relaxation techniques is Jacobson's (1938) Progressive Relaxation. He proposed that muscular tension and anxiety are incompatible physiological states and that to relax, one must learn to distinguish between tension and relaxation. Therefore, his technique emphasizes teaching people to progressively tense and relax all major muscle groups in the body, thereby sensitizing them to proprioceptive feedback from the muscles. Drawing from the work of Jacobson (1938), Wolpe (1969) developed the technique of Systematic Desensitization. Although this technique involves progressive relaxation, it is different in that the individual is presented with a hierarchy of anxiety-producing stimuli. After mastering a given anxiety situation the individual attempts a more difficult one until the anxiety-producing situation is no longer threatening. For example, in tennis the hierarchy for players who double fault under pressure might include: (a) practice sessions, (b) a few minutes prior to competition, (c) serving the ball when way ahead, (d) serving the ball during a crucial game, (e) serving with set point against them.

A very popular and empirically sound program to cope with anxiety was developed by Meichenbaum (1977) and termed stress inoculation training. This is a cognitively based program which is broken up into three phases: (a) Educational Phase—This provides individuals with a conceptual framework for understanding the nature of their response to stressful events, (b) Rehearsal Phase—This provides individuals a variety of coping techniques such as developing positive coping statements to replace negative self-statements when a stressful situation is approaching, (c) Application Phase—Individuals are given an opportunity to practice their coping skills. Techniques such as imagery, modeling, behavioral rehearsal, role reversal, exposure to real stressors and in vivo graded homework assignments may be included. A more detailed description of stress inoculation training is provided by Meichenbaum (1974, 1975).

A second application gleaned from the empirical literature concerns the importance of individual differences. Specifically, it has been demonstrated that athletes vary greatly in their reactions to stressful situations. Although it appears that each athlete has an optimal level of arousal, that level can be different for different athletes. As Sonstroem and Bernardo demonstrated, each athlete's optimal arousal level was in relation to their own particular reactions to stressful competitive situation rather than some objective score on a test. For example, a score of 55 on Spielberger's state anxiety inventory may be real high for one athlete and cause impairments in performance, whereas the same score for another athlete may be moderate (compared to his usual anxiety state) thus producing optimal performance. In practical terms, this suggests that a big pep talk before the game might not be effective if it raises everybody's arousal. Rather, coaches need to carefully observe and communicate with each athlete to determine what is optimal for him or her in their quest for high quality performance.

A third implication concerns the nature of the task one is performing. In testing Oxendine's postulations, the empirical data support the fact that high levels of arousal are detrimental to sports requiring predominately fine muscle coordination, precision and accuracy. Athletes performing skills such as golf putting, field goal kicking, archery, foul shooting, etc. consistently refer to the potentially debilitating effects of high levels of anxiety. Since these skills require such fine muscle movements, any slight deviation from the correct movement will result in poor performance. It should be noted that in most of these types of skills there is some time passage between or before performances. In other words, the athlete has time to think about his or her performance and many times these thoughts are on irrelevant cues (e.g., The entire game rests on this field goal, I hope I don't strike out again, I hope I don't miss this putt). Why do you think most basketball coaches call time out before an opposing player is about to shoot a critical free throw? The reason is that the coach wants to give the athlete time to think about what an important shot he or she is about to take and hope that this will result in the focus of attention on inappropriate cues. Many times this results in a missed shot and the athlete is said to have "choked." In essence, the increased stress and pressure of the situation causes worry and focus of attention internally instead of externally on the relevant cues. Thus, coaches and athletes involved in sports requiring fine muscle coordination (and especially if there is time before each performance) should be prepared via some relaxation technique to cope with the inevitable high levels of anxiety that can debilitate performance. These relaxation and coping strategies, however, need to be well-practiced and well-learned before actually used in critical game situations.

FUTURE DIRECTIONS FOR RESEARCH

Psychophysiological Approach

One approach which may offer some important insights into the arousal performance relationship is psychophysiology. Psychophysiology has been defined as a body of knowledge concerned with the inference of psychological processes and emotional states from an examination of physiological measures (Sternbach, 1966). The instrumentation employed in psychophysiological research includes the electromyogram (EMG), the electrocardiogram (EKG), the electroencephalogram (EEG) and electrooculogram (EOG). It should be noted that just reporting multiple correlations between psychological and physiological measurements is not psychophysiology, although it has been interpreted as such by some physical educators and sport psychologists (Hatfield & Landers, 1983).

Psychophysiology is not a new approach to investigating the arousal-performance relationship having been previously employed primarily as manipulation checks for the creation of different levels of arousal. This would be important when testing the inverted-U hypothesis where the creation of three distinct levels of arousal is imperative. However, results have lacked consistent agreement between physiological and questionnaire measures of arousal as well as among the physiological measures of arousal themselves. Hatfield and Landers (1983) argue that these inconsistent results are due primarily to methodological problems. For example, most studies in the past have utilized only one physiological measure and averaged results across groups of subjects. This methodology has been employed despite the research of Duffy (1962, 1972), Lacey and Lacey (1958) and Lacey, Bateman and Van Lehn (1953) which has indicated that the individual should be used as the unit of analysis. In essence, intra-individual correlations should be used if researchers are to demonstrate that increases (or decreases) in arousal have indeed taken place (Hatfield & Landers, 1983). Furthermore, Duffy (1972) has argued that multiple measures of arousal should be employed to help overcome the low correlation among the autonomic measures of arousal. Finally, Landers and Hatfield note that even with the above techniques, other variables such as individual differences (i.e., an individual might display increased heart rate but decreased blood pressure to the same stressor) and task demands (i.e., different tasks elicit different autonomic responses) need to be taken into consideration.

Along these lines, a programmatic series of studies incorporating many of these suggestions has been conducted by Landers and his colleagues (Hatfield, Landers, Ray, Daniels, 1982; Landers, Christina Hatfield, Daniels & Doyle, 1980; Lewis, Daniels, Landers, Wilkinson & Hatfield, 1981), using competitive marksmen as subjects. For example, in one study, a variety of autonomic measures were assessed on an Olympic-caliber rifle shooter during the stress of a national competition. The athlete exhibited superior performance and was in fact leading the competition at the end of the second day but experienced a significant drop of 30 points on the final day. Psychophysiological parameters were continually recorded and results indicated that on the last day there was a distinct change in the placement of the shot within the cardiac cycle. That is, the control of his level of arousal on the last day faltered.

In another study (Landers, et al., 1980) different heart rates, breath holds and shot placements within the cardiac cycle were found for different individuals. In fact the best performance scores for each marksman were associated with these individual tendencies in arousal patterns. For example, one shooter may achieve his or her best scores with a breath held heart rate of 70 bpm whereas another shooter may achieve his or her best performance scores with a heart rate of 120–130. Additional studies conducted in the Soviet Union (Tretilova & Rodimiki, 1979) also demonstrated that different heart rates were associated with optimal performance for different marksmen. Of course, psychophysiology could be employed for a variety of areas within sport psychology. However, it would seem particularly relevant if programmatic, systematic psychophysiological research could be conducted in helping elucidate the arousal-performance relationship.

Process versus Outcome Research

Most previous research investigating the arousal-performance relationship examined the end result of some performances as a consequence of different arousal levels or conditions. In Martens' (1971) review performance was defined as "goal centered, purposeful, observable, behavior of a relatively short duration" (p. 153). When so viewed, performance is task-oriented with little carry over from task to task. Process research, on the other hand, continually assesses the relevant performance parameters during skill execution with the aim to gain a better understanding of the underlying causes of performance increments or decrements.

As discussed previously, Weinberg and Hunt (1976) and Weinberg (1978) used electromyographic assessments of motor patterning to pinpoint the performance breakdown of high-anxious subjects under high-stress conditions. This type of information helps explain what is actually happening to the athlete and thus would provide the coach or teacher with more knowledge to try and alleviate the problem. Some of the psychophysiological research just cited also employed a process approach to understanding how arousal and autonomic functioning can affect skilled performance. This type of research can serve the long term goal of providing explanations for the arousal-performance relationship rather than just describing it as does the inverted-U hypothesis.

SUMMARY AND CONCLUSIONS

The purpose of this paper was to critically review the arousal-performance relationship. To accomplish this task some definitions were first provided, different theories were then discussed along with the empirical data supporting or rejecting them, mediating variables were presented and finally practical applications and future directions for research were enumerated. As the reader has obviously realized, the arousal-performance relationship is one that has interested and intrigued both researchers and practitioners. This is due to the fact that it is such a critical relationship for those interested in achieving consistently high levels of performance. Unfortunately, it is a very complicated area to study and there are few easy answers to be gleaned from the empirical research. However, we have come a long way from some rather crude measurements of arousal and performance to more sophisticated psychophysiological monitoring systems which allow us to better quantify the construct of arousal as well as the underlying mechanisms that produce the final end product of performance. Coaches and athletes are also becoming more sophisticated in their training programs and monitoring of emotional states and researchers and practitioners are starting to get together and combine there respective expertise to solve the problems at hand. Hopefully, through increased technological capacities, methodological rigor, theoretical advances and mutual sharing by researchers and practitioners, a better understanding of the arousal-performance relationship will emerge.

REFERENCES

Bacon, S. J. (1974). Arousal and the range of cue utilization. *Journal of Experimental Psychology, 103*, 81–87.
Bartoshuk, A. K. (1955). Electromyographic gradients in goal-directed activity. *Canadian Journal of Psychology, 9*,. 21–28.
Berlyne, D. E. (1960). *Conflict, arousal, and curiosity.* New York: Harper & Row.
Bolles, R. C. (1967). *Theory of Motivation.* New York: Harper & Row.

Borkovec, T. D. (1976). Physiological and cognitive processes in the regulation of anxiety. In G. E. Schwartz & D. Shapiro (Eds.), Consciousness and self regulation: Advances in research (Vol. 1). New York: Plenum.

Cannon, W. B. (1928). The mechanism of emotional disturbance of bodily functions. *The New England Journal of Medicine, 198*, 877–884.

Carron, A. V. (1965). *Complex motor skill performance under conditions of externally-induced stress.* Unpublished master's thesis, University of Alberta.

Caudill, D., & Weinberg, R. S. (1983a). Psyching-up and track athletes: A preliminary investigation. Journal of Sport Psychology, 5, 231–235.

Caudill, D., & Weinberg, R. S. (1983b). The effects of varying the length of the psych-up interval on motor performance. *Journal of Sport Behavior, 6,* 86–91.

Davidson, R. J., & Schwartz, G. E. (1976). The psychology of relaxation and related states: A multi-process theory. In D. I. Mostofsky (Ed.), *Behavior control and modification of physiological activity.* Englewood Cliffs, N.J.: Prentice-Hall.

Dirkin, G. R. & Hancock, P. A. (1983). Attentional narrowing under stress. *Paper presented at North American Society for Sport Psychology and Physical Activity,* College Park, Maryland.

Duffy, E. (1962). *Activation and behavior.* New York: John Wiley & Sons, Inc.

Duffy, E. (1972). *Activation.* In H. S. Greenfield & R. A. Sternbach (Eds.), *Handbook of psychophysiology.* New York: Holt, Rinehart & Winston.

Easterbrook, J. A. (1959). The effect of emotion on cue utilization and the organization of behavior. *Psychological Review, 66,* 183–201.

Fenz, W. D. (1975). Strategies for coping with stress. In I. G. Sarason and C. D. Spielberger (Eds.), *Stress and anxiety* (Vol. 2). New York: Wiley.

Fenz, W. D. & Epstein, S. (1967). Changes in gradients of skin conductance, heart rate and respiration rate is a function of experience. Psychosomatic Medicine, 29, 33–51.

Fenz, W. D., & Jones, C. B. (1972). Individual differences in physiological arousal and performance in sport parachutists. *Psychosomatic Medicine, 34,* 1–8.

Fiske, D. W., & Maddi, S. R. (1961). *Functions of varied experience.* Homewood, Ill.: Dorsey Press.

Giambrone, C. P. (1973). *Effect of situation criticality on foul shooting.* Unpublished master's thesis, University of Illinois, Urbana.

Gould, D., Horn, T., & Spreeman, J. (1983). Perceived anxiety of elite junior wrestlers. *Journal of Sport Psychology, 5,* 58–71.

Gould, D., Weinberg, R. S., & Jackson, A. (1980). Effect of mental preparation strategies on a muscular endurance task. *Journal of Sport Psychology, 2,* 329–339.

Gutin, B. (1973). Exercise-induced activation and human performance. *Research Quarterly, 44,* 256–260.

Harrington, E. F. (1965). *Effect of manifest anxiety on performance of a gross motor skill.* Unpublished master's thesis, University of California, Berkeley.

Hatfield, B. D. (1982). *Central and autonomic nervous system activity during self-paced motor performance: A study of the activation construct in marksmen.* Unpublished doctoral dissertation, The Pennsylvania State University, University Park.

Hatfield, B., & Landers, D. M. (1983). Psychophysiology: A new direction for sport psychology. *Journal of Sport Psychology, 3,* 243–259.

Hatfield, B. D., Landers, D. M., Ray, W. J., & Daniels, F. S. (1982). An electroencephalographic study of elite rifle shooters. *The American Marksman, 7,* 6–8.

Hebb, D. O. (1955). Drives and the C.N.S. (Conceptual Nervous System). *Psychological Review, 62,* 243–254.

Hockey, R. (1979). Stress and the cognitive congruents of skilled performance. In V. Hamilton & D. M. Warburton (Eds.), *Human Stress and Cognition.* Englewood Cliffs, N.J.: Prentice-Hall.

Hodges, W. F., & Spielberger, C. D. (1969). Digit span: An indicant of trait or state anxiety? *Journal of Consulting and Clinical Psychology, 33,* 430–434.

Hull, C. L. (1943). *Principles of behavior.* New York: Appleton-Century Co.

Hunt, P. J., & Hillary, J. M. (1973). Social facilitation in a coaction setting: An examination of the effects over learning trails. *Journal of Experimental Social Psychology, 9,* 563–571.

Jacobson, E. (1938). *Progressive relaxation.* Chicago: University of Chicago Press.

Kahneman, D. (1973). *Attention and effort.* Englewood Cliffs, N.J.: Prentice-Hall.

Katin, E. S. (1965). Relationship between manifest anxiety and two indices of autonomic response to stress. *Journal of Personality and Social Psychology, 2,* 324–326.

Klavora, P. (1978). An attempt to derive inverted-U curves based on the relationship between anxiety and athletic performance. In D. M. Landers & R. W. Christina (Eds.), *Psychology of motor behavior and sport.*. Champaign, Ill.: Human Kinetics Publishers.

Lacey, J. I. (1967). Somatic response patterning and stress: Some revisions of activation theory. In M. H. Appley & R. Trunball (Eds.), *Psychological stress: Issues in research.* New York: Appleton-Century-Crofts.

Lacey, J. I., & Lacey, B. C. (1958). Verification and extension of the principle of autonomic response stereotype. *American Journal of Psychology, 71,*. 50–73.

Lacey, J. I., Bateman, D. E., & Van Lehn. (1953). Autonomic response specificity: An experimental study. *Psychosomatic Medicine, 15,* 9–21.

Landers, D. M. (1977). Motivation and performance: The role of arousal and attentional factors. In L. Geduilas & M. E. Kneer (Eds.), *Proceedings of the NCPESM/NAPECW National Conference.* Chicago: University of Chicago Circle, Office of Publication.

Landers, D. M. (1980). The arousal-performance relationship revisited. *Research Quarterly for Exercise and Sport, 51,* 77–90.

Landers, D. M., Christina, R. W., Hatfield, B. D., Daniels, F. S., & Doyle, L. A. (1980). Moving competitive shooting into the scientist's lab. *American Rifleman, 128,.* 36–37; 76–77.

Levitt, S., & Gutin, B. (1971). Multiple choice reaction time and movement time during physical exertion. Research Quarterly, 42, 405–410.

Lewis, D. A., Daniels, F. A., Landers, D. M., Wilkinson, M. O., & Hatfield, B. D. (1981). *Autonomic self-regulation and performance: A case study of an Olympic champion.* Paper presented at a meeting of the North American Society for Psychology of Sport and Physical Activity, Asilomar, CA.

Lowe, R. (1971). *Emotional arousal and Little League performance.* Unpublished doctoral dissertation, University of Illinois, Urbana.

Malmo, R. B. (1959). Activation: A neuropsychological dimension. *Psychological Review, 66,* 367–386.

Martens, R. (1971). Anxiety and motor behavior: A review. *Journal of Motor Behavior, 3,* 151–179.

Martens, R. & Landers, D. M. (1970). Motor performance under stress: A test of the inverted-U-hypothesis. *Journal of Personality and Social Psychology, 16,* 29–37.

Matarazzo, R. & Matarazzo, J. D. (1956). Anxiety level and pursuit motor performance. *Journal of Consulting Psychology, 20,* 70.

Matarazzo, J. D., Ulett, G. A., & Saslow, G. (1955). Human maze performance as a function of increasing levels of anxiety. *Journal of General Psychology, 53,* 79–95.

Meichenbaum, D. (1974). *Cognitive behavior modification.* Morristown, N.J.: General Learning Press.

Meichenbaum, D. A. (1975). A self-instructional approach to stress management: A proposal for stress inoculation training. In C. D. Spielberger & L. G. Sarason (Eds.), *Stress and anxiety* (Vol. 1). Washington, DC: Hemisphere.

Meichenbaum, D. (1977). *Cognitive behavior modification: An integrative approach.* New York: Plenum.

Nideffer, R. M., & York, T. J. (1978). The relationship between a measure of palmer sweat and swimming performance. *Journal of Applied Psychology, 61,* 376–378.

Oxendine, J. (1970). Emotional arousal and motor performance. *Quest, 13,* 23–30.

Rossi, A. M. (1959). An evaluation of the Manifest Anxiety Scale by the use of electromyography. *Journal of Experimental Psychology, 58,* 64–69.

Schwartz, G. E., Davidson, R. J., & Goleman, D. (1978). Patterning of cognitive and somatic processes in the self-regulation of anxiety: Effects of meditation versus exercise. *Psychosomatic Medicine, 40,* 321–328.

Sidowski, J. B., & Eason, P. G. (1960). Drive, verbal performance, and muscle action potential. *Journal of Experimental Psychology, 60,* 365–370.

Singh, W. P. (1968). Anxiety and sensory-motor learning. *Psychological Studies, 13,* 111–114.

Sonstroem, R. J., & Bernardo, P. (1981). Intra individual pregame state anxiety and basketball performance. A reexamination of the inverted-U curve. *Journal of Sport Psychology, 4,* 235–245.

Spence, J. T., & Spence, K. W. (1966). The motivational components of manifest anxiety: Drive and drive stimuli. In C. D. Spielberger (Ed.), *Anxiety and behavior.* New York: Academic Press.

Spielberger, C. D. (1966). Theory and research on anxiety. In C. D. Spielberger (Ed.), *Anxiety and behavior.* New York: Academic Press.

Spielberger, C. D. (1972). Anxiety as an emotional state. In C. D. Spielberger (Ed.), *Anxiety: Current trends in theory and research.* New York: Academic Press.

Sternbach, R. A. (1966). *Principles of psychophysiology.* New York: Academic Press.

Tretilova, T. A., & Rodimki, E. M. (1979). Investigation of the emotional state of rifle shooters. *International Sport Sciences, 1,* 745.

Voor, J. H., Lloyd, A. J., & Cole, R. J. (1969). The influence of competition on the efficiency of an isometric muscle contraction. *Journal of Motor Behavior, 1* 210–219.

Weinberg, R. S. (1978). The effects of success and failure on the patterning of neuromuscular energy. *Journal of Motor Behavior, 10,* 53–61.

Weinberg, R. S., & Genuchi, M. (1980). Relationship between competitive trait anxiety, state anxiety, and golf performance: A field study. *Journal of Sport Psychology, 2,* 148–154.

Weinberg, R. S., Gould, D., & Jackson, A. (1980). Cognitive and motor performance: Effect of psyching-up on three motor tasks. *Cognitive Therapy and Research, 4,* 239–245.

Weinberg, R. S., & Hunt, V. V. (1976). The interrelationships between anxiety, motor performance and electromyography. *Journal of Motor Behavior, 8,* 219–224.

Weinberg, R. S., & Ragan, J. (1978). Motor performance under three levels of stress and trait anxiety. *Journal of Motor Behavior, 10,* 169–176.

Wolpe, J. (1969). *The practice of behavior therapy.* New York: Pergamon.

Yerkes, R. M., & Dodson, J. D. (1908). The relation of strength of stimulus to rapidity of habit formation. *Journal of Comparative Neurology and Psychology, 18,* 459–482.

8

Anxiety, Attention, and Performance in Sports: Theoretical and Practical Considerations

Robert M. Nideffer

In 1976, I authored two publications that attempted to integrate research on the relationships between attentional processes, physiological arousal and performance, with observable behavior in complex performance situations (Nideffer, 1976a; Nideffer, 1976b). Those two publications were based on experiences and research that I had been involved in since 1960.

The first publication was a book titled *The Inner Athlete*. *The Inner Athlete* was written for both coaches and athletes, and in it an attempt was made to operationally define the attentional demands placed on athletes in a variety of competitive situations. It was emphasized that concentration on task relevant cues requires control over both the direction (external-internal) and width (broad-narrow) of attention. Integrating information from researchers like Easterbrook (1959), Wachtel (1967), Shakow (1962), and Cromwell (1968) and from practitioners of the martial arts like Tohei (1960), I described how increasing arousal could interfere with an individual's ability to control attention, to shift from one type of attentional focus to another.

The second publication appeared in the *Journal of Personality and Social Psychology* (Nideffer, 1976b). In this article a summary of the research that led to the development of a *Test of Attentional and Interpersonal Style* (TAIS), was presented. The TAIS had been designed to measure those attentional and interpersonal characteristics that laboratory research, clinical observations, and personal experience suggested were critical determinants of performance. It was to be the tool that operationalized my own theoretical notions about the relationship between attentional and interpersonal processes and would provide practical information that could be used to develop mental training programs.

Both *The Inner Athlete,* and the *Test of Attentional and Interpersonal Style* were well received. They appeared at an opportune time and generated considerable interest in the area of sport psychology. Unfortunately, neither of these two publications presented a clear articulation of the conceptual (theoretical) framework that led to the development of the TAIS.

Over the past ten years questions have been asked regarding the reliability, validity, and utility of the *Test of Attentional and Interpersonal Style* (Cox, 1985). Some of the questions have resulted from studies designed to test the validity of the TAIS. Other questions reflect a lack of understanding regarding the theory that the TAIS is based on. In the next few pages an attempt has been made to review these issues, and to describe some of the developments and changes that have occurred in my own thinking as it relates to the theory that underlies the *Test of Attentional and Interpersonal Style* (TAIS).

THEORY OF ATTENTIONAL AND INTERPERSONAL STYLE

Psychological theories are developed to improve our ability to *understand, predict,* and *control* behavior. Unfortunately, a great deal of the theorizing in psychology has been designed to explain abnormal and/or "irrational" behavior. Although many of these theories have provided us with a conceptual basis for understanding abnormal behavior, they have not contributed greatly to the ability to predict and/or control those pathological behaviors. A theory like Freud's might provide someone with an understanding of "underlying" dynamics, with an answer to their "whys" (why is the patient doing this), but it wouldn't make the patient's next observable behavior any more predictable.

When the Test of Attentional and Interpersonal Style was developed, my interest was in understanding, predicting, and controlling, "optimal" performance. I believed that the behavior of nonpsychotic individuals was predictable. Highly successful individuals are successful because they are better predictors of the behavior of people around them. There are those coaches, athletes, executives, teachers, etc., who seem to instinctively do and say the right thing at the right time. It is my contention that the difference between the type of disorganized behavior seen when an otherwise normal individual panics under stress (e.g., on an exam, in an emergency, when giving a speech) and the highly organized behavior of individuals who excel under pressure is due to differences in their control over arousal and over specific attentional processes.

Optimal Performance Requires Attention to Task Relevant Cues

The theory of attentional and interpersonal style postulates that for any individual to perform up to their potential, their attention must be focused on the most salient or task relevant cues.

FOUR DIFFERENT TYPES OF ATTENTION

Figure 1 presents the four different types of attention that an individual may be required to develop during the course of a performance. As may be seen in Figure 1, an individual's attentional focus can be described along two dimensions, width and direction. At any given moment in time, a person's attention can be

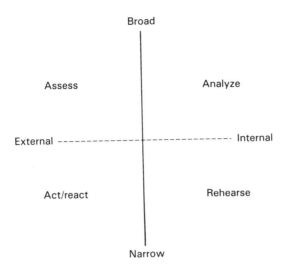

Figure 1   The four types of attention.

described by one of the four quadrants. A broad-external type of attention is required in order to rapidly assess environmental conditions. This particular attentional style is seen as highly developed in athletes who are good at "instinctively" reacting to competitive conditions. This type of attention is also required by complex sport situations that require an individual to be aware of a wide variety of cues in order to plan out a response (e.g., for a quarterback to be able to select an appropriate play).

A broad-internal type of concentration is required in order to analyze and plan. Once relevant external information is gathered, it must be held and then processed. The athlete recalls information about previous conditions from long term memory, and/or they may direct concentration towards immediate feelings (e.g., current level of muscle tension, feelings of self-confidence). All of this information is then used to develop an appropriate course of action, or to make a choice (e.g., which club to use for a particular golf shot).

Once a plan has been developed attention must shift again. An individual could develop a narrow-internal type of concentration if they wanted to systematically, mentally rehearse their planned performance. We can see this type of mental rehearsal in a variety of sports including golf, weight lifting, gymnastics, track and field events, etc.

Finally, a narrow-external type of attention is the kind of concentration required by those performance situations which demand a response from an individual. To return serve, the tennis player must have his/her attention fixed on the ball. If concentration is elsewhere (e.g., internally focused because they are planning how they will return or worried about missing), performance is likely to be less than optimal. You can't hit what you can't see.

Different Performance Situations Make Different Attentional Demands: Individuals Must Be Able to Shift Attention in Response to Changing Environmental Demands

Some situations make heavier demands than others for certain kinds of attention. For example, the job of coach requires greater analytical skills, than the job of sprinter.

Different Individuals Have Different Attentional Strengths or Preferred Styles

Just as there are physiological differences and intellectual differences between people, so too there are differences in attentional abilities. These differences may be due to several factors:

A. Alterations in biochemistry (e.g., hormonal imbalances, drug induced changes).

B. Genetic and/or hereditary differences (e.g., differences in information storage capacity or differences in perceptual acuity).

C. Learned differences, differences due to environmental factors and to exposure levels (e.g., the opportunity to practice certain skills).

Level of Arousal Affects an Individual's Ability to Shift Attention and to Meet the Attentional Demands of Performance Situations

Yerkes and Dodson (1908) conducted the basic research which suggested that an "inverted U" function best described the relationship between performance and physiological arousal. Performance is seen as less than optimal at very low and at very high levels of arousal. One of the reasons for this is that level of arousal affects an individual's willingness and/or ability to shift attention in response to changing task demands.

When arousal levels drop below "optimum," the motivation of the individual to concentrate on task relevant cues is not sufficient to cause them to want to maintain a task relevant focus. Under these conditions individuals allow their attention to wander, internally or externally, to stimuli which are of more interest. These internal and/or external distractors will slow an athlete's reaction time since the irrelevant cues must be broken away from prior to attending to the task.

When arousal levels get too high, several things begin to happen to attention. Research by people like Easterbrook (1959) indicates that selective attention and "effective cue utilization" is interfered with. Borrowing concepts from signal detection theory, it is as if increasing arousal results in an alteration of the signal to noise ratio. The higher the arousal the greater the noise (task irrelevant input) and the more difficult it is to identify and attend to the signal (Cox, 1985).

From an applied perspective we can hypothesize that a couple of very specific things happen to an individual's attentional abilities as arousal increases. According to Hullian Drive Theory, the individual will rely more heavily on those skills or habits that are most highly developed. This suggests that individuals will become more dependent upon their preferred attentional style, whether this is the best way to respond or not. Thus, the analytical athlete will become more analytical as pressure increases. Errors will begin to occur if the performance situation requires a different type of attentional focus.

If arousal continues to rise and the noise in the system gets very high (e.g., heart rate and respiration rate are elevated), then panic may set in and the individual will lose all control over attention. They will no longer "rely on their attentional strength," they will be unable to filter out any irrelevant stimuli, or to stay focused. Their attention will be captured by the most demanding stimuli at the moment (e.g., their own heart rate, a negative thought, a scream from the sidelines, etc.). At this point, the individual's body and/or the environment is controlling their mind, rather than vice-versa.

Attentional Abilities Can Be Conceptualized as Existing Along a State-Trait Continuum

As has already been mentioned, there are differences between individuals with respect to the upper limits of any attentional skill. Some more gifted individuals have greater analytical skills and processing capacities than others. Still others seem to have been born with greater sensitivity to environmental cues. It is quite likely that some of the differences we see in terms of individuals' tolerances for stress has to do with absolute differences in abilities. Those individuals who "feel the pressure," yet continue to perform effectively, probably have more of the attentional abilities that a given performance situation requires, than individuals who feel the pressure and fail to perform.

Independent of the upper limits of a person's attentional skills, however, is the extent to which those skills appear to be trait like (operative across situations, independent of task relevance), vs. state like (changing as a function of changing situational demands). There are behavioral examples of individuals who seem to be completely dominated by a particular attentional style. The "absent minded" professor who is so much in his or her head that he/she is unaware of what is going on in the world. The con artist who reacts quickly and instinctively to immediate conditions without any apparent thought about the future or the consequences of his/her action. These two examples lie at the extreme trait end of the attentional continuum, and by statistical definition, represent only a small segment of the general population. If we ask ourselves why a particular attentional style might dominate an individual we can come up with several reasons. In the case of very extreme examples, however, it is quite likely that the capacity for a particular type of attending is so highly developed relative to other abilities (because of biological factors as well as environmental factors) that shifting from one type of attention to another, even under optimal conditions, is extremely difficult. If that person stays in performance situations which make use of their particular attentional skills they will appear well adjusted. Move them into a situation that requires attentional shifting and/or a different type of attending, however, and they will be unable to make the adjustment.

Fortunately, relatively few people are at the extreme trait end of an attentional continuum. Just as most highly intelligent individuals have a fairly good balance between their verbal skills and their performance skills, so too most of us have fairly well balanced attentional skills. Even so, there will be "relative" strengths and weaknesses, or attentional preferences. For example, your analytical skills may be a little closer to the trait end of the continuum than your assessment skills (broad-external). It is this slight imbalance in skills that can make our behavior under pressure (when arousal increases) more predictable. The closer an attentional ability is to the trait end of the continuum, the greater the "habit strength" in Hull's terms. Under optimal conditions of arousal attentional skills are affected by situational factors (especially for the well balanced individual). Under increasing arousal preferred attentional styles begin to dominate and take on trait characteristics.

Arousal Can Be Controlled by Controlling What You Attend To

I have already mentioned that concentration is affected by arousal. To use the title of a Joseph Heller book, the *Catch 22* in this, is that the reverse is also true. Over the years we all develop conditioned emotional responses to a wide variety of stimuli. Certain events act as triggers to increase the flow of adrenaline, increase muscle tension, and to generate a variety of negative thoughts or self-doubts. In a similar fashion there are other events and/or thoughts that act as triggers to calm us down, to get our attention back on the task at hand. If you can learn what those triggers are, you can gain control over arousal by controlling what you attend to. Good method actors do this when they cry on cue.

PROCESS VS. OUTCOME CUES

A general, yet very helpful way of classifying stimuli (external and internal) in a performance situation is on the basis of whether it is process oriented, or outcome oriented. Outcome oriented cues would be those internal and external stimuli that are directly related to the process of performing. A thought that focuses your attention on execution or strategy would be a process cue. The ball coming at you would be a process cue. These are stimuli that trigger very complex, yet automatic motor responses. Quite often, these cues are emotionally neutral. As an athlete gets caught up in process cues, and in the process of performing, arousal automatically adjusts to a more optimal level.

Outcome oriented cues are those thoughts and stimuli that serve to remind you of the consequences of various outcomes. Thoughts about the importance of an event are examples of outcome cues. A scoreboard showing you are behind in a competition with only three seconds left is an outcome cue. Quite often outcome cues are emotional triggers, acting to increase arousal.

In sport, both process and outcome cues have a very critical role. Attention to outcome cues prior to a practice session can help get arousal high enough to keep an athlete involved. Individuals motivate themselves to make the sacrifices they need to make, by reminding themselves of the importance of outcome. Once arousal is elevated, however, and once performance has begun attention should be directed to process cues. During performance, outcome cues are often distractors. Learning to shift from process to outcome cues as a means of maintaining an appropriate level of arousal is a worthwhile goal for any athlete (Nideffer, 1986).

In addition to the four attentional abilities already mentioned, there are several personal and/or interpersonal characteristics that seem to be operative in most performance situations. Like the attentional characteristics these interpersonal styles can be conceptualized as existing along a state-trait continuum.

A. The stronger a particular style (e.g., the need to assume control), the more trans-situational (trait like) the behavior, and the more likely the behavior will control the individual rather than vice-versa, especially under pressure.

B. Mismatches between the demands of performance situations and an individuals dominate attentional and interpersonal characteristics generate arousal because they act to trigger ambiguity, often result in performance errors, and sensitize the individual to negative outcome cues.

Psychologists have been measuring personality traits, needs and interpersonal behaviors for years. Different investigators have chosen to emphasize different characteristics. With respect to the interpersonal styles measured by the TAIS, the choice was a subjective, introspective, intuitive one. I made observations of my own behavior and the behavior of others in a variety of performance situations, and then asked myself what variables seemed to be operative across situations. I am using operative in two senses here. Operative in the sense that for most individuals, these characteristics do seem more trait like than state like. Operative in the sense that control over these particular characteristics is a key factor in most performance situations.

The characteristics that are measured by the TAIS include the following:

A. Need to be in control in interpersonal situations: High scorers describe themselves as being in control, and as desiring control. Extreme low scorers avoid a leadership role and are much less anxious when they don't have to assume responsibility.

B. Level of self-confidence: High scorers feel good about themselves and have an optimistic outlook.

C. Physical orientation. High scorers are or have been physically competitive.

D. Speed of decision making: High scorers make decisions more slowly, having a tendency to ruminate and worry seeming to sacrifice speed for the sake of accuracy. Low scorers make decisions much more quickly and prefer to sacrifice accuracy for the sake of speed.

E. Extrovertedness: High scorers enjoy being with other people and tend to assume more of a leadership role in social situations.

F. Introvertedness: High scorers enjoy time alone with their thoughts. They have a need for personal space and privacy.

G. Intellectual expression: High scorers express their thoughts and ideas, they take more control in group discussions.

H. Negative affect expression: High scorers are willing to set limits, to confront and challenge others, to express their anger verbally and physically.

I. Positive affect expression: High scorers are willing to express support and positive feelings to others, both verbally and physically.

TAIS PROFILE ANALYSIS

To illustrate the relationship between the theory just presented and the practical application of that theory through the use of the TAIS, let me give a couple of examples of how test information might be used. Consider first the case of a golfer. This individual's greatest attentional strength (preferred style) is their ability to assess situations (broad-external). They score high on the TAIS scale measuring need for control, they make decisions quickly, and they score high on the scale measuring expression of anger. Remember, extreme scores on these scales indicate that they are higher in "habit strength."

Our theory would suggest that arousal will increase for the golfer to the extent there is a mismatch between his attentional and interpersonal style and the performance situation. If for example, he is playing behind a group of very slow golfers, he is out of control (of the pace of play) and cannot move as quickly as he would like. Under these conditions, he is likely to experience an increase in arousal. With increasing arousal, his preferred styles will become even more dominate. Feelings of anger and frustration will increase and it is likely that associated with these will be increases in muscle tension or "bracing." Generally speaking, increasing arousal results in physiological changes as well as attentional changes. Heart-rate, respiration-rate, skin conductance, and blood pressure often increase, along with increases in muscle tension. Bracing as the general increase in muscle tension is referred to, can directly interfere with fine motor coordination and timing. The golfer tightens up in neck and shoulders and his swing is interfered with. If the tension causes him to straighten up, he will top the ball. More often than not it will result in his trying to muscle the ball, losing considerable distance.

The golfer's anger and frustration will not only affect his swing, but it will interfere with concentration and decision making. In spite of the fact that he has time (while waiting) to plan his shot, he is unlikely to take advantage of that time. He will be concentrating on his own frustration until it is time for his shot. Then, his need to move quickly will take over. He will assess the situation he is in, but he is likely to fail to adequately analyze and plan. He won't take time to reduce his own anger, to monitor and compensate for his internal tension increases. Instead, he will step up to the ball and "blast it."

As a second example, consider the case of a quarterback who is very capable of assessing (reading and reacting instinctively) the situation, but scores low in terms of analytical ability (broad-internal), and intellectual expressiveness. In addition, the individual has a very low score on the interpersonal control scale, and on the scale measuring expression of negative affect. Our theory would predict that when the coach calls the plays from the bench (the coach is the leader), this individual should function relatively well. If the coach expects the quarterback to be a "field general" and/or a team leader both on and off the field, there will be attentional and interpersonal mismatches. Arousal will be high, and performance will be impaired. Decision making will be interfered with because the individual will not "think," he will react too quickly. Execution will be interfered with because of the associated changes in muscle tension described earlier.

APPLICATION OF THE THEORY

The application of the theory is relatively straightforward.

A. You assess the demands of the performance situation along the attentional and interpersonal dimensions just described.

B. You assess the individual's abilities to meet the demands of the performance situation through use of the TAIS, and/or through history and behavioral observations.

C. You look for attentional and interpersonal mismatches to:

1) Anticipate those particular aspects of a situation that are more and/or less likely to be stressful.

2) Anticipate how the individual is likely to respond attentionally and interpersonally under pressure. Does that increase or decrease the mismatch?

3) Determine what personal (e.g., attentional), interpersonal (e.g., ability to communicate intellectual thoughts), and/or situational changes must occur to improve the match between the individual and the performance situation.

TAIS VALIDITY AND RELIABILITY

There are two articles that provide a detailed description of the development and validation of the TAIS (Nideffer, 1976b; Nideffer & Pratt, 1982). A very brief summary of early research concluded the following: "Research efforts indicate the test has good test-retest reliability as well as some construct and predictive validity. An advantage of the TAIS relative to other psychological measures is that its test profile describes particular attentional and interpersonal characteristics. These characteristics are operationally definable and permit prediction of performance over a variety of life situations (Nideffer, 1976b)."

Although the TAIS has been shown to have some good reliability and predictive and construct validity, a great deal of the variance in performance situations still remains unaccounted for. Over the past ten years several investigators have raised some questions about the utility and validity of the TAIS as a predictor of performance. Concern has been expressed about: (1) The extent to which the test measures the four attentional abilities; (2) whether the test measures an individual's ability to shift attention from one style to another; (3) the size of the interscale correlations and the fact that most factor analytic studies of the TAIS subscales identify 5 to 6 factors rather than 17; (4) the extent to which situation specific attentional measures will provide better predictors of performance than the more general TAIS measures.

When the TAIS was constructed, behaviorally oriented attentional items were written that were expected to reflect an individual's ability to develop the four different attentional focuses (broad-external, broad-internal, narrow-internal, narrow-external). Unfortunately, item analyses procedures on the original sample failed to support the separation of a narrow-external focus of attention from a narrow-internal one. Individuals who indicated that they were capable of narrowing their concentration, seemed to be able to focus either externally or internally. As a result of the item analyses procedures the items from the two scales were combined into a single scale (NAR) which reflected effective narrowing of attention.

Conceptually, it still makes sense to think of (and to attempt to assess) the attentional demands of performance situations with respect to all four of the identified attentional dimensions. It also makes sense to attempt to independently assess an individual's ability to develop a narrow-internal focus and a narrow-external focus.

With respect to the issue regarding whether or not the TAIS provides a measure of an individual's ability to shift attention in response to changing situational demands, it does. Since there is not a scale on the test labeled "shifting" some authors have incorrectly concluded that the test does not measure this ability.

In fact, there are three scales on the instrument that provide an indication of an individual's ability to shift (OET, OIT, RED). The OET scale contains items which indicate performance errors are occurring because a person has failed to shift from a broad-external focus to some other type of attention. Thus, these individuals are "overloaded" by external cues and unable to narrow and/or to attend to relevant internal cues. The OIT scale provides an indication of the failure to shift from a broad-internal focus. High scores indicate the person is overloaded by internal information and unable to narrow and/or to attend to relevant external cues. Finally, high scores on the RED scale indicate that the person is not shifting back and forth from an internal to an external focus (or vice versa) when needed. Their attention has narrowed, but narrowed so much that they are not aware of all the task relevant cues. They have become so focused on an external or an internal cue, that they fail to shift.

Several studies have factor analyzed the 17 TAIS subscales and as a result have identified six factors or clusterings of TAIS scales that account for approximately 85 percent of the variance in scores, independent of subject's gender, culture, or occupation. The six factors have been labeled: (1) attentionally effective; (2) overloaded; (3) extroverted; (4) performance anxiety; (5) angry-impulsive; and (6) physically oriented (Nideffer & Pratt, 1982). Some investigators have suggested that the failure to identify 17 independent factors that reflect the 17 TAIS subscales means that the hypothesized attentional and/or interpersonal abilities either do not exist, or are not measured by the instrument.

The median interscale correlation coefficient for the TAIS is .27, this is considerably below the median interscale correlation coefficients for tests like the Minnesota Multiphasic Personality Inventory, and the Wechsler Adult Intelligence Scale (.55). Typically, factor analytical studies of these two instruments result in the identification of from two to three stable factors. The fact that there is considerable overlap between scales, however, does not prevent an instrument from being quite useful in clinical and applied settings for identifying very important individual differences (Dahlstrom, Welsh, & Dahlstrom, 1975; Wechsler, 1955).

To expect different human characteristics (physical, mental, emotional, perceptual, etc.) to be statistically independent is naive. It is true that attitudes and/or response styles can act to artificially inflate the correlations across measures. For example, individuals who are feeling good about their own life at the moment, are likely to rate everything a little more optimistically. It is also true, however, that very real relationships exist across characteristics, characteristics that need to be thought of in independent ways in spite of the correlations.

There is little doubt for example that height and weight are correlated. It is important, however, to be able to think about and apply these two characteristics as if they were separate dimensions. From a clinical standpoint, we may talk about problems associated with height, independent of a person's weight and vice-versa. Likewise, we may treat the verbal and performance skills measured by instruments such as the WAIS, and the SVIB and the assessment skills (ability to read the environment) and analytical skills measured by the TAIS as conceptually independent, in spite of some statistical overlap. From a practical standpoint, the degree to which these abilities are or are not correlated for a given individual becomes very important. Everyone deviates from the "statistical mean" in one way or another. Assessment is a process by which we determine how individuals deviate, and what that deviation means in relation to performance.

SPORT SPECIFIC MEASURES OF ATTENTIONAL STYLES

There has been a great deal of criticism of the validity and reliability of self-report measures. Investigators have been particularly critical of those tests that are more "general" and less situation specific in their orientation. It has been argued by some that general traits or response styles don't exist. Human personality characteristics, needs and/or cognitive styles may be highly situation specific. It has been suggested that it is the situational specificity of human behavior that reduces the validity of self-report tests.

Several investigators have attempted to develop sport specific measures of the attentional abilities measured by the TAIS (Etzel, 1979; Van Schoyck & Grasha, 1981). In sports like tennis, basketball, soccer, and shooting, researchers have developed sport specific translations of each of the seventy five attentional items on the TAIS.

Although some investigators (Van Schoyck & Grasha, 1981) have reported greater validity for sport specific measures, the amount of variance accounted for by these measures is less than might be expected. It is possible that the attentional constructs we are trying to measure can't account for as much of the variance as the theory might suggest. It is also possible that we have reasonable constructs, but are not doing a good job of measuring.

MEASUREMENT PROBLEMS IN APPLIED RESEARCH

There are a number of measurement problems that individuals conducting research in applied situations must begin to overcome if they hope to develop and/or establish the validity of psychological tests. Zero order correlation coefficients are no guarantee that an instrument cannot be a valid measure of what it was designed to measure. To obtain reliable information from respondents, applied researchers must be concerned with factors like subjects' willingness and ability to cooperate. In addition, the researcher must be able to assess and/or control response set and response style influences.

Let me give you a hypothetical example. Let's assume that as a researcher who has developed a test of attentional and interpersonal style, I manage to convince the right people that I should be allowed to collect test data on the U.S. divers at their Olympic trials. My reasons for wanting the information are fairly obvious, I have a captive population of the best divers in the world. What I don't have, however, is a lot of control over the situation.

Competing in the Olympic trials is for most athletes the realization of a dream. Their goal is to make the Olympic team, and to hopefully win a gold medal. They have a job to do at the trials and they are under a great deal of pressure. Everything they have been training for is on the line. Individual athletes come to the trials with some team-mates (if they are good enough) and their coach. Usually, the athlete's coach is an outsider (e.g., unaware of my role as a researcher), and neither the coach nor the athlete have had anything to say about my involvement. Mistrust is high because everyone is competing for the same spots on the team.

A meeting is called of all the athletes and a large number of issues are discussed. Most of these are highly relevant, including things like who the judges will be, how forms must be filled out, what will happen after the team is selected, etc. In the middle of the meeting I am introduced and given five minutes to "make my pitch." During that time I am expected to get the cooperation of the athletes for my research, to avoid creating any problems for people involved, and to maintain tight experimental controls.

I tell the athletes that I have developed a test that I hope will prove useful in the future for helping athletes perform better under pressure. I ask for their cooperation, telling them participation is voluntary and that the test results are confidential. I tell them that they are a highly select group and will help me establish normative data to compare other athletes with in the future. If I am lucky, the organizers of the training camp have set aside a specific time (e.g., 30 minutes right after the meeting) for the athletes to take the test. I also tell the athletes that I will provide those who participate with some feedback about their own scores in relationship to the group as a whole. Just for the sake of specificity, let's assume the meeting has taken place at eight in the evening, after a long day of working out and after dinner. The athletes have listened to people for an hour, it is now nine and the tests are passed out. My goal in testing the athletes, is to see if my test will be able to predict which of the thirty individuals in the room will make it into the finals. Since all of the divers will be scored it is relatively easy to try and use some type of regression analysis to predict the divers' total score in both the preliminaries and finals. Statistically, I have two problems that are very difficult to overcome.

1. With only thirty subjects in my sample, I can have very little faith in the results of any regression analysis. If I follow the rule of thumb of 10 subjects per variable, I must limit myself to using only three of seventeen TAIS scales, or to using some weighted combination of scores (e.g., factor scores). Even if I do that, there are not enough subjects to replicate the study. Since twelve divers will make it into the finals, I may try and conduct some type of between groups analyses comparing those who make it into the final with those who don't. Unfortunately, this type of analysis won't provide me with as much information as a regression analysis might.

2. Because I have a highly select group (These are the top 30 divers out of a country with over two hundred million people), any correlations between test scores and performance are likely to be dramatically attenuated. Everyone in the sample is at the very top of the performance distribution, thus there is little dispersion of scores. Not only will there be little dispersion of diving scores, but to the extent that the attentional characteristics are indeed related to performance, there will be little dispersion in these scores as well! Small wonder the correlations I see are "moderate" at best.

In addition to the statistical problems that I will run into there are several situational and interpersonal factors that will affect the accuracy of the diver's responses to the test. Let me describe how some of the divers will respond to the testing situation and you will begin to get a feeling for these problems.

1. The first diver to receive the test is the youngest diver in camp at fifteen years of age. He is extremely talented physically, but has not been at all interested in school. He is much more immature than the other divers and is maintaining a "macho" I can do anything front. This individual has never really stopped to analyze himself and/or the competition. He will not admit that he doesn't understand many of the test items he guesses at answers. In general his attitude is "when in doubt, I must be the best." Looking at his scores they seem obviously inflated, relative to some of the other more experienced divers.

2. A second diver is a veteran of two previous Olympic trials. It has been a long day and he is tired. He cooperated with some research efforts in previous years and never learned anything from them. He believes that the research has nothing to do with team selection and believes that it really is voluntary. He walks out, refusing to take the test.

3. A third diver seems to lack self-confidence. He is somewhat introverted and doesn't trust anyone. He doesn't believe me, and he is afraid of what the test might show. He is afraid to walk out, not sure how that will affect how he is seen. He doesn't really believe that participation is voluntary. Some of his own interpersonal characteristics, and situational factors combine to cause him to fake good. As he reads each item, he simply asks himself what type of response will look good and he responds that way.

4. A fourth diver who happens to be the best diver in camp and a sure bet to make the Olympic team, has had a bad (for him!) practice. He got distracted once and ruined a dive. In this individual's mind that is something that should never happen! He demands perfection. His relative failure on the day (situational factor) along with his drive for perfection (personal factor) combine to result in excessively self-critical responses to test items. When asked if he becomes distracted by external events, he answers "all the time," even though it actually happens very rarely. As a result, he looks much worse on the test than we might expect.

5. The fifth diver is a very controlled, cautious individual. He has been taught from a very early age that no matter how good you are, you need to maintain some humility. A value system has been beaten into him and as a result he has developed a response style (a way of behaving across situations) that tends to minimize his own accomplishments, and to elevate others. Inwardly he is actually quite confident, but he has learned to "walk softly and carry a big stick."

I could continue with other examples, but the point is that there are a large number of factors which dramatically influence subjects' responses. The applied researcher must be sensitive to and attempt to control: 1) ignorance on the part of the respondent; 2) motivation and willingness to cooperate; 3) response sets (more transient situational influences); 4) response styles (trans-situational attitudes or beliefs that affect responses). These factors are very difficult to control under the conditions that most applied researchers are expected to work within.

To a certain extent, the movement to more situation specific measure represents an attempt to control many of these factors. Using the diving example, the more sport specific the questions, the more likely the diver is to be able to relate to (understand and have observed) the test item. Even then, however, issues of translation do occur. As mentioned, many athletes do not spend a great deal of time analyzing performance. Once an event is over, it's over and they don't ask themselves why they performed the way they did. As a result, their ability to reliably tell you what they were thinking and/or feeling at a particular point in time is not very good. To provide reasonably accurate feedback, these individuals must first be taught to make more accurate observations.

Some of the negative attitudes and lack of cooperation can be overcome by more situation specific measures, and/or by instructions that help the athlete see the relevance of the research to them. This means having the time to sell the person on why they should cooperate, and it means being able to provide them with useful feedback.

Response sets (e.g., an excessively negative attitude because of a bad day) can be controlled by providing the individual's taking the test with "anchor points" against which they should judge their own behavior. For example, I might ask divers to rate themselves on each item, on a ten point scale. I tell them that the "average" diver at the Olympic Trials will give himself a six on this ten point scale. This helps me insure that the athlete is comparing himself to the "average elite diver," not to the number one diver in the world, not to perfection, and not to someone who has never been on a diving board.

Response style influences can also be overcome by providing anchors for ratings and by forcing the individual to overcome their own tendency to either be ultra conservative, or to "let it all hang out."

Table 1 presents the correlations between the coach's ratings of 15 members of the Mission Viejo Diving Teams' performance, and their scores on the TAIS. The 15 members of the team that were tested were all "elite" divers and included U.S., World, and Olympic champions. The coach was rating each individual's performance over an entire year on a ten point scale. The coach was instructed to rate the divers so that the "average" elite diver would receive a six on the ten point scale and the worlds best diver would receive a nine or a ten.

The fifteen Mission Viejo divers that were tested, took the TAIS under two different response set conditions. The first time they took the test they were given a fairly standard set of instructions. They were told that the research was being conducted to see if the TAIS would be useful in predicting diving performance and for developing training programs. They were asked to answer all of the questions on the test.

Once the divers completed the test for the first time, they were given another answer sheet and asked to fill it out again. This time, they were asked to "in their

Table 1 Correlations between the Test of
Attentional and Interpersonal
Style and Coach's Rating of
Diving Performance

TAIS scale	Standard instructions	Elite instructions
BET	-.12	.11
OET	-.50	-.63*
BIT	-.04	.02
OIT	.00	-.43
NAR	.37	.64**
RED	-.35	-.26
INFP	-.20	-.03
BCON	-.61*	-.88**
CON	.03	.03
SES	.06	.31
P/O	-.19	.18
OBS	-.26	-.14
EXT	-.38	-.24
INT	.62*	.45
IEX	-.39	-.22
NAE	-.13	-.34
PAE	-.36	-.29

*p < .05.
**p < .01.

own mind," attempt to translate each question so that it related specifically to diving. Since they were to answer each question by indicating the frequency with which it described their behavior (e.g., Never, Rarely, Sometimes, Frequently, All the Time), they were given an "anchor point." The divers were told that the "average elite diver" would answer "sometimes" to each of the questions.

It should be obvious that the problem of attenuated correlations mentioned earlier would exist with this small sample of divers. As it happened, Mission Viejo had the finest concentration of divers in the world, thus performance differences across divers were minimal. The problem of trust and cooperation, however, was dramatically reduced in this sample. These divers had been working together for over a year. The researcher had also been working with the team members for over a year. There were no suspicions on the part of the divers that these results would be used against them in any way. In fact, they believed that results of testing might be useful in developing mental training programs.

The "elite instructional set" was designed to help control response set and response style problems. In effect, that particular set was turning a more general measure of attentional and interpersonal style into a diving specific measure. To enhance the likelihood that individuals would think of their abilities in relation to the other divers, they were told how the "average elite diver" would answer.

As may be seen in Table 1, there were some significant relationships between the coach's ratings of performance, and the divers' TAIS scores. As we might have expected, these relationships were stronger under the elite instructional set. What Table 1 indicates, is that the better the diver, the more capable they are of narrowing attention (NAR), of avoiding external distractions (OET), and of sticking to the rules and controlling their behavior (BCON). In addition, there was a significant relationship between the introversion score and diving ability (INT) under the more general response set.

The results just presented are consistent with what we might expect to find when testing world class individuals. The correlations are probably attenuated, yet we still find evidence of the type of skills and controls required to perform at this level as a diver. Results also suggest that some of the concerns about response set, response style, trust, and cooperation can be controlled under certain circumstances. Even here, however, control was not complete.

Under the general instructional set, the scores of one of the world champion divers looked to be completely out of line. This individual's level of self-esteem was low, they indicated that they were not attentionally effective, that in fact they made more mistakes than the "average" diver, that they were overloaded and distracted. Looking at their scores under the general response set, they certainly seemed to be unhappy with their performance and with life in general.

When the coach discussed his ratings of divers he prefaced his comments about the world champion by saying "you will probably be surprised at the rating I gave X." "I gave X a six on your ten point scale, because I rated performance for this diver in relation to what I feel the individual is capable of and should be doing." Both coach and athlete were unhappy with the performance over the year (even though the individual was world champion). In spite of my instructions to the coach to rate world champions higher, he had deviated from them.

Under the more diving specific response set (elite set), this individual's scores looked like those of a world champion. Thus, if I had wanted to predict performance the elite set would have been much more accurate than the more general response set. On the other hand, if I wanted to understand how the diver was feeling and I wanted to be able to understand attitude and motivation, I would have learned a great deal more from the general response set.

WHY ARE YOU TESTING?

All of the controls that have been mentioned, make sense under one particular set of circumstances. If your goal in testing is to predict behavior across individuals, then you must do everything you can to make sure the person answering questions can provide you with accurate behavioral information. In most selection and screening situations, the bottom line is actual performance "on the day."

In a great many situations, the goal behind testing isn't necessarily predicting the outcome of a particular performance situation. Instead, the goal behind testing is to increase understanding of what causes an individual to behave a certain way. When we talk about "teambuilding" in sports situations, we are talking about providing the individual members of a team with greater understanding of their own behavior and the behavior of critical others. How are they affected by increasing pressure (e.g., what does this do to their ability to control attentional processes), what effect will changes in their behavior have on others.

A very good example of the ongoing use of test information as a part of a team building process can be found in "Born to Win," by John Bertrand (1985). John

Bertrand was the captain of Australia II, the boat which captured the Americas' Cup. In the book, Bertrand devotes an entire chapter to the psychological preparation of the crew and discusses in detail how he used test information to improve his ability to relate to, and motivate his men.

The more situation specific your instruments, and the more you control for an individual's response style and/or response set, the more information you are likely to lose about the person's attitudes toward themselves, toward their performance, and toward life in general. In the case of our world champion diver, it was much more important (from a motivational standpoint) for the coach to know how the individual was feeling in general, than it was under sport specific conditions. It was the person's general feelings that permeated the practice affecting relationships to the coach and other team members. To be a better motivator, the coach had to respond to the diver's feelings, not to their objective level of performance.

SUMMARY

The field of applied sport psychology is growing at a very rapid pace. The 1984 Olympics served as a showcase for the application of psychology to sport. One of the dangers that professionals face in attempting to respond to the interest being shown by the general public is to begin attempting to apply psychological techniques in the absence of sound psychological theory (Nideffer, 1981; Nideffer, 1985). Both the Test of Attentional and Interpersonal Style and the theory relating attentional and interpersonal processes to performance, which underlies the test, were introduced in 1976, in an attempt to begin to bridge the gap between research and practice.

There can be little doubt that conceptually the TAIS has had considerable impact on the thinking of both researchers and practitioners in the sport psychology area (Salmela, 1981; Cox, 1985). The Coaching Association of Canada is so convinced of the importance of coaches understanding the types of attentional processes required in performance situations, that this information plays a major role in the National Coaches Certification Program (Coaching Association of Canada, 1981). Use of the TAIS as a tool for assessing concentration skills and for designing performance enhancement programs is widespread in sport, in spite of the limited predictive validity that has been demonstrated to date. There appears to be a rather large gap between the faith and confidence many applied sport psychologists place in the applicability and utility of the TAIS and related theory, and the faith or lack of it, that the researcher has.

Working in an applied setting like sports creates very special challenges for researcher and practitioner alike. Researchers must begin to gain greater control over the issues of subject ignorance, response set, and response style. Until this occurs, we are not likely to see a convergence between the thinking of the researcher and the thinking of the practitioner. In addition to subject problems, researchers need to give a great deal more thought to what it is they are trying to evaluate. The question of the validity of a test, is not, or should not be, a general question. Instead, the question should be, "valid for what?"

The TAIS was designed to be used as a tool to identify performance relevant attentional and interpersonal strengths and weaknesses. Ideally, a person's scores on the test would provide us with information about the frequency, intensity, and duration of a variety of performance problems (e.g., How often does the person get distracted by some task irrelevant stimulus? How compelling is the distraction? How long does the distraction last?).

In point of fact, in applied settings tests end up being used in several different ways. At times, they are used as a part of a selection and/or screening process. When tests are used in this fashion, they must allow for valid "between subject" comparisons. This means that the absolute elevation of a person's scores in relation to a norm group or to other individual's being tested is critical. Valid between subject comparisons requires two things: (1) the ability to rate ones' self in relation to others; (2) the willingness to make that rating.

Most of the time, subjects in situations where selection and screening decisions are being made, are not motivated to answer in a completely honest fashion. If they want to be selected, they are motivated to exaggerate what they perceive will be seen as strengths, and to minimize weaknesses. This response set will dramatically affect the absolute elevation of test scores.

Even if an individual is willing to attempt to honestly evaluate their own abilities, their answers to test items will still be affected by situational factors, more general response styles (e.g., conservatism), and their past experience or lack of it. The establishment of validity for a test as a part of a selection and screening process will depend upon the ability of the examiner to control all of the conditions that affect the absolute elevation of test scores.

Tests are also used as training tools and for counseling purposes. Under these conditions, it is easier to control the tendency of individuals to fake good. More often than not, individuals are motivated to take the test because they see it as "in their own best interest." This is not to say that factors like response styles and response sets won't affect the scores, they will. The absolute elevation of an individual's scores, however, is far less important in a training situation, than in a selection and screening situation.

If your interest is in developing a concentration training program for an athlete, you need only know what that individual's own attentional strengths and weaknesses are. You can think of frequency of a problem in absolute terms (e.g., how many times does the problem occur in one month). You can also think of a problem in terms of relative frequency or type of error (e.g., how often does an athlete get distracted by his/her own thoughts vs. by something his/her opponent does.). If an individual is motivated to be as honest as they can on a test, the relative position of their attentional and interpersonal scales to each other, will remain in spite of most response set and response style influences. Thus, you will know the type of mistake that they are most likely to make,even if you don't know the frequency with which that particular mistake will be made.

All of this means that it is possible for a test to lack the type of predictive validity we usually look for in selection and screening situations (between subject predictions), and still have good within subject predictive validity. To evaluate the use of a test as a tool for the development of mental training programs, you would want to see if it identifies within subject strengths and weaknesses.

Future research on the TAIS should be designed to look for within subject changes. In addition, researchers need to begin reporting the types of efforts that they are making to reduce the impact of uncontrolled responses sets and response styles. Without knowing the conditions of test administration in detail and without knowing something about the level of trust and the effectiveness of communication in the testing situation, it is impossible to replicate and/or evaluate the research.

In the past some investigators have attempted to look at the attentional constructs in isolation. Research is much more likely to be productive if attentional constructs are examined on a within subject basis, and in the context of the other personal and interpersonal characteristics. To design studies that systematically manipulate arousal along a dimension predicted by TAIS scores (e.g., to divide subjects into groups on the basis of extreme scores on the need for control scale or on the intellectual expressiveness scale), and to then see if the test predicts the type of attentional disturbances an individual will experience.

My own clinical intuition tells me that a great deal is to be gained by using a more general instrument like the TAIS, than by using highly situation specific tests. This is especially true when that instrument is used as part of a counseling process by a professional who has been trained in the appropriate use of psychological tests. On the other hand, from an educational perspective, a great deal can be said about the use of situation specific measure.

If the theoretical constructs that have been expressed in this paper have any validity, then teaching others to use these constructs as windows for viewing their particular worlds (e.g., coaching, business, diving), should improve their ability to understand, predict, and control behavior. To this end I have been experimenting with several versions of an 18 item inventory that has been called the Inventory of Concentration and Communication Skills (ICCS).

The different versions of the ICCS are designed to teach individuals to be able to observe and identify the attentional and interpersonal characteristics that are measured by the TAIS, as they relate to a specific performance situation. A coach for example could use a sport specific ICCS to identify and rate an athlete's attentional and interpersonal skills within a particular performance situation. Early attempts at establishing the inter-rater reliability of these inventories have been quite promising (reliability coefficients average around .7). Hopefully, these types of instruments will prove useful for providing coaches and others with the type of structure they need to recognize and develop those mental and interpersonal skills that are performance relevant, as well as the technical and tactical skills that they currently focus on.

REFERENCES

Bertrand, J. (1985). *Born to Win*. New York: Bantam Books.

Coaching Association of Canada. (1981). *National Coaching Certification Program: Coaching Theory III*. Ottawa, Coaching Association of Canada.

Cox, R. H. (1985). *Sport Psychology Concepts and Applications*. Dubuque, Iowa: William C. Brown.

Cromwell, R. L. (1968). Stimulus redundancy and schizophrenia. *Journal of Nervous and Mental Disease, 146*, 360–375.

Dahlstrom, G. W., Welsh, G. S., & Dahlstrom, L. E. (1975). *An MMPI Handbook Vol. II*. Minneapolis: University of Minnesota Press.

Easterbrook, J. A. (1959). The effect of emotion on cue utilization and the organization of behavior. *Psychological Review, 66*, 183–201.

Etzel, E. F. (1979). Validation of a conceptual model characterizing attention among international rifle shooters. *Journal of Sport Psychology, 1*, 281–290.

Nideffer, R. M. (1976a). *The Inner Athlete*. New York: T. Y. Crowell.

Nideffer, R. M. (1976b). Test of Attentional and Interpersonal Style. *Journal of Personality and Social Psychology, 34*, 3, 394–404.

Nideffer, R. M. (1981). *The Ethics and Practice of Applied Sport Psychology.* Ithaca, N.Y.: Mouvement Publications.
Nideffer, R. M. & Pratt, R. (1982). A Review of the Test of Attentional and Interpersonal Style. *Enhanced Performance Associates Quarterly Report.* San Diego: Enhanced Performance Associates.
Nideffer, R. M. (1985). Current concerns in sport psychology. In J. M. Silva & R. S. Weinberg, (Eds.),*Psychological Foundations of Sport.* Champaign, Ill.: Human Kinetics.
Nideffer, R. M. (1986). *An Athletes' Guide to Mental Training.* Champaign, Ill.: Human Kinetics.
Salmela, J. (1981). *The World Sport Psychology Source Book.* Ithaca, N.Y.: Mouvement Publications.
Shakow, D. (1962). Segmental set. *Archives of General Psychiatry, 6,* 1–17.
Tohei, K. (1960). *Aikido The Art of Self Defense.* Tokyo, Rikugei Publishing House.
Van Schoyck, S. R., & Grasha,A. F. (1981). Attentional style variations and athletic ability: The advantages of the sport specific test. *Journal of Sport Psychology, 3, 149–165.*
Wachtel, P. (1967). Conceptions of broad and narrow attention. *Psychological Bulletin, 68,* 417–429.
Wechsler, D. (1955). *Manual for the Wechsler Adult Intelligence Scale.* New York: The Psychological Corporation.
Yerkes, R. M., & Dodson, J. D. (1980). The relationship of strength of stimulus to rapidity of habit formation. *Comparative Neurology and Psychology, 18,* 459–482.

9

Anxiety, Arousal, and Sport Performance: An Application of Reversal Theory

John H. Kerr

INTRODUCTION

Scientific principles are being applied increasingly to the study of sport. Physiologists now have a clearer understanding of the physical fitness requirements of sports events. Accordingly, the content and scheduling of training sessions, rest requirements and food intake are more systematically controlled than before. Also, technological advances have resulted in video tape recorders being used in conjunction with computer systems. This development has allowed biomechanics specialists and sports coaches to analyze and refine the techniques required in sports events in a more sophisticated and detailed manner. With the improvements in technique and physiological preparation, differences in sports performance are often finite. Consequently there has been a concentration of interest on the psychological factors affecting performance. The study of anxiety in sport has been a particular focus of this interest, which has recently taken on greater significance.

Whereas in the scientific areas of physiology and biomechanics, factors affecting performance may be relatively constant, psychology must attempt to cope with human behavior and its intrinsic inconsistencies. In the sporting context, where individuals are often subject to stress, the situation may be further complicated. Patmore (1979) in her book *Playing on Their Nerves* underlines the immensity of the problem:

> *Sport is not like a novel or a play, with the ending already decided. It is alive and dynamic. Anything can happen, really anything at all. Human beings under pressure are wonderfully unpredictable; their nature is a puzzle to us all, and psychology has only scratched the surface. When human beings are placed in an area, and their hopes and fears exposed in front of thousands of observers, they are likely to do extraordinary things. (p. 9)*

One theory from psychology which grapples with the complexities of human behavior is the newly evolving theory of psychological reversals (Smith & Apter, 1975; Apter, 1982). The theory is based on the inconsistencies associated with human behavior pinpointed above. Although essentially concerned with motivation, more specifically the individual's experience of motivation, it also relates to human emotions and human cognition.

It should be made clear from the beginning that reversal theory is conceptually different from optimal arousal theory with its basis in the inverted-U hypothesis (Yerkes & Dodson, 1908). Optimal arousal theory (Hebb, 1955) continues to be used by sports psychologists (e.g., Klavora, 1979; Rushall, 1979 and Landers, 1980), for much of their theoretical analysis at one level, and as the foundation for practical advice offered to sports coaches and sports performers at another. This is to say the least surprising! One only has to review some of the critiques that have emerged from psychologists working in other areas and those more concerned with the applied area of sport, to realize that there are profound inadequacies associated with several facets of the theory.

Conjecture might lead to the suggestion that the continued use of optimal arousal theory may be due to the unavailability of a sufficiently viable alternative approach. The purpose of this chapter is to present an alternative theoretical view and point out how it differs radically from some of the basic assumptions of optimal arousal theory. In order to clarify some of the criticisms referred to above and to assist in the comparison of the optimal arousal theory approach with the reversal theory approach, a review of these criticisms seems appropriate.

LIMITATIONS OF OPTIMAL AROUSAL THEORY

Optimal arousal theory proposes a close relationship between a subject's level of activation or arousal and level of performance. As shown in Fig. 1, the level of performance continues to increase with increases in arousal up to a certain point, beyond which any further increases in arousal produce a decrement in performance. This point, at the apex of the inverted-U shaped curve, is considered to be the point of "optimal arousal" at which performance is at a peak. Much of the writing on motivation which incorporates the optimal view suggests that if arousal levels are too high or too low then, in order to maximize performance, arousal must be increased or decreased to some "intermediate" level. As such, optimal arousal theory is homeostatic in nature in that the subject's behavior is aimed at maintaining arousal at a single preferred level. Tied in with this is the idea that this point of optimal arousal also reflects the greatest degree of positive "hedonic tone" or felt pleasure. Consequently, if arousal levels deviate from the preferred level, either up or down, then the subject's experience becomes less pleasant and, in the particular direction of continued increases in arousal, results in feelings of anxiety.

Some authors (e.g., Fiske & Maddi, 1961) have argued that the preferred level of optimal arousal may vary with the particular point in the sleep-waking cycle at which a subject finds himself, or with the type of task being performed. This latter idea dates back to the early work of Yerkes and Dodson (1908), often quoted in the sports psychology literature, which related task complexity to the optimum level of motivation.

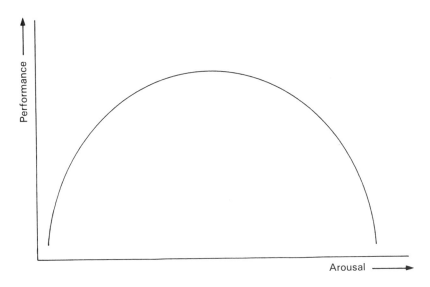

Figure 1   Hypothesized relationship between arousal and performance according to optimal arousal theory.

Criticism of the optimal arousal approach is directed at several different facets of the theory. For instance, Welford (1976) has highlighted some of the limitations:

> *While the model seems accurate as far as it goes, it does not advance our understanding very much. Where, for instance does the optimal point come? Why does it seem to differ from one task to another? Does performance beyond the optimal point merely revert to what it was before the optimum was reached, or are the imperfections different above and below the optimum. (p. 131).*

The results of experimental studies supporting the theory are brought under the spotlight by Baddeley (1972):

> *One of its major weaknesses as a theory is its ability to account for almost any result so long as the exact location on the U-curve is not specified in advance. (p. 542).*

Also Martens (1972), who himself carried out empirical studies on the inverted-U hypothesis (Martens & Landers, 1970), pointed out that:

> *With respect to the inverted-U hypothesis, many, if not most, believe that this relationship is firmly established. The evidence reviewed for various levels of trait anxiety, induced muscular tension, and psychological stress showed no clear support for this relationship for motor responses. . . . (p. 61).*

These views were re-emphasized by Cooke (1981, 1982) almost ten years later in her study "A critical appraisal of the Yerkes-Dodson Law" where she wrote:

> *The inverted-U-curve can be shown to be just as much an artefact of the statistical analysis as of the experimental design. (p. 43)*

A detailed examination of some of the psychophysiological experimental studies which apparently provided supportive findings for the inverted-U relationship was undertaken by Naatanen (1973). In this critical review of the activation-performance relationship he points to specific features of experimental designs which could have caused the decrement in the subjects' performance observed by the experimenters as arousal levels continued to be increased.

From a different point of view, the homeostatic nature of this theoretical approach is also under attack. Murgatroyd (1985a, p. 3) has listed a number of established psychologists who are at odds with the basic premise of the homeostatic construct. This list includes Maslow (1954), Bühler (1959) and Frankl (1969), along with Harlow (1953) and Allport (1960). Each one has rejected the homeostatic model as a satisfactory explanation of motivation.

Perhaps one of the simplest, or rather more easily understood, queries about optimal arousal theory is provided by Apter (1982, p. 86). He identifies four nouns, common in everyday speech, which are reflections of pleasant, unpleasant, and high and low arousal, questioning the ability of optimal arousal theory to distinguish between them. These four nouns: anxiety, excitement, boredom and relaxation, provide particular problems for optimal arousal theorists because of their single optimal state and homeostatic formulations. The possibility of low or high arousal being experienced as pleasant by individuals under certain circumstances is not easily encompassed within this approach. Some attempts at explanation (e.g., Hebb, 1955) have suggested that excitement is a reflection of moderately high arousal whilst very high arousal is reflected in feelings of anxiety. This explanation is, however, not very satisfactory because, following this argument, one would always have to go through feelings of excitement before becoming anxious. Similar reasoning applies to relaxation and boredom at the other end of the arousal continuum. Clearly this is at odds with human experience.

Some readers may feel that this review of the criticisms put forward by various authors about optimal arousal theory is rather one-sided or perhaps unbalanced. If this is the case, and they wish to consider some of the evidence "for" the case of optimal arousal theory, especially with respect to sport, then Landers (1978 and 1980) has provided reviews. Landers (1978, p. 78) seems to be in a little doubt about its value, stating, "There are probably few situations in sport where a slightly above average or high level of arousal is best for optimal performance." Nevertheless, it seems difficult to share his confidence in the light of the substantive criticisms noted above.

Finally, because of its single optimal state and homeostatic basis, optimal arousal theory gives little attention to the possibility of high levels of experienced pleasure at the extreme ends of the arousal dimension. Many types of risk-taking behavior in dangerous sports, such as parachuting, mountaineering and motor-racing (Apter, 1982; Kerr, 1983 and Kerr, 1984), involve extremely high levels of arousal and are experienced as pleasurable by the participants.

REVERSAL THEORY AND AROUSAL

Perhaps a good point of entry into the concepts and hypotheses encapsulated within reversal theory is to focus on the four nouns, anxiety, excitement, boredom

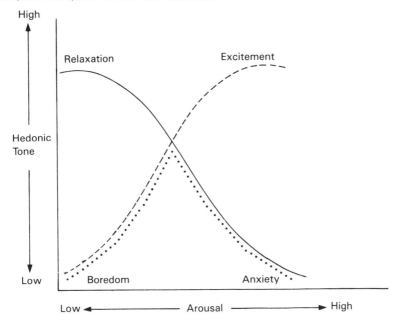

Figure 2 Relationship between arousal and hedonic tone for the telic state (solid line) and the paratelic state (broken line). The dotted line indicates the single curve of optimal arousal theory. (Adapted from Apter, 1982)

and relaxation, identified earlier. Rather than trying to fit these four nouns into a hypothetical U-shaped relationship, reversal theory suggests that the relationship, when we consider felt arousal and hedonic tone, takes the form of an X shape (see Fig. 2). Here, high levels of arousal can be interpreted by the individual in two ways which, according to reversal theory, can be experienced as feelings of anxiety or feelings of excitement. Similarly, low levels of arousal can also be interpreted in two different ways and are then experienced by the individual as relaxation or boredom.

A degree of support for these ideas has come from experimental research work. Apter (1976) himself carried out a study, the results of which were not consistent with optimal arousal theory, showing that very high and very low arousal can be associated with positive affective tone. Heide and Borkovec (1983) have shown that relaxation can be tension producing for certain subjects, whilst Apter and Svebak (in press) have argued that for some people the inability to experience excitement and accompanying high arousal can in fact be stressful. Svebak and Stoyva (1980) state:

> . . . there is clearly a great deal of human behavior oriented to the pursuit of high arousal and where high arousal is perceived as positive and pleasurable. Examples abound: consider sports such as ski-jumping, sky diving, hang-gliding, rock-climbing, surfing, diving and bull-fighting, hot-rodding and many others. In fact much of what we do in our leisure time is directed to the attainment of high arousal. One thinks of drama, the reading of detective mysteries, and going to parties. . . (p. 440)

Elsewhere, Kerr (1985) has also put forward the case that high arousal experienced during participation in sports is expected and often anticipated with relish.

Given that high or low levels of arousal can be interpreted in two different ways, what is it that causes the individual to experience feelings of boredom rather than, say, relaxation in any particular situation at any one time?

CONCEPT OF METAMOTIVATIONAL STATES

A fundamental building block of reversal theory which helps in the understanding of how arousal is interpreted is the notion of metamotivational states. These are hypothesized as alternative states in which the individual can experience different motives at a given moment in time. They do not reflect a range of behavior along a continuum, some point on which an individual might be placed, but rather should be thought of as distinctly opposite states. A person may find himself in one of these states for just a few seconds or for longer periods of time, depending on the conditions prevailing at that time. Changes from one of the pair to the other are, of course, possible and are thought to take place often. In the theory, these changes are called "reversals" and provide the origin of the theory's title. They are considered possible because of the bistable nature of the system which comprises the opposite pairs of metamotivational states. Different from a homeostatic system with a single preferred state (e.g., inverted-U), bistable systems are considered to have two alternative preferred states, either of which exhibits a degree of stability. This second building block of reversal theory, the bistability exhibited between pairs of metamotivational states, is important for the understanding of human motivation. Bistable systems are common enough in areas such as engineering and biology. In chemistry, good examples of bistable systems are found in so-called reversible reactions. Most people who have studied chemistry, even at an elementary level, will be familiar with these chemical reactions which can be made, under suitable conditions, to proceed in either direction. For example, passing steam over red hot iron produces iron oxide and hydrogen. However, if hydrogen is passed over red hot iron oxide, the reverse takes place and steam is produced. In this case, both the iron and the iron oxide exist as alternative stable states.

Bistable systems from chemistry or other sciences are relatively easy to understand, but how do these reversal theory concepts—metamotivational states, bistability and reversals—relate to human behavior? A number of these pairs of metamotivational states have been identified by the theory and given labels. For instance, the X shaped relationship in Fig. 2 represents the interpretation of high and low arousal while individuals are in the "telic" or "paratelic" states. The three other recognized pairs include the negativistic-conformist, sympathy-mastery and allocentric-autocentric states. However, it is the telic-paratelic pair which is most relevant with respect to the arousal and, in particular, anxiety aspects of human behavior.

In the telic state (telic from the Greek "telos" meaning goal) individuals are usually serious minded, planning oriented and generally attempt to avoid arousal. By contrast, in the paratelic state the individual is spontaneous, playful and oriented towards the present, preferring immediate pleasure and high arousal.

Table 1 Contrasting characteristics of the telic and paratelic states (from Apter, 1982, p. 52)

	Telic	Paratelic
Mean-ends dimension	Essential goals	No essential goals
	Imposed goals	Freely chosen goals
	Unavoidable goals	Avoidable goals
	Reactive	Proactive
	Goal-oriented	Process-oriented
	Attempts to complete activities	Attempts to prolong activity
Time dimension	Future-oriented	Present-oriented
	'Points beyond itself'	'Sufficient unto itself'
	Planned	Spontaneous
	Pleasure of goal anticipation	Pleasure of immediate sensation
	High significance preferred	Low significance preferred
Intensity dimension	Low intensity preferred	High intensity preferred
	Synergies avoided	Synergies sought
	Generally realistic	Make-believe prevalent
	Low arousal preferred	High arousal preferred

Apter (1982) has listed the contrasting characteristics of the telic and paratelic states along three dimensions, shown in Table 1. Clearly then, for the individual in the *paratelic* state, high arousal is preferred and experienced as pleasant feelings of excitement. Conversely, low arousal is unpleasant and characterized by feelings of boredom. In the *telic* state, the same arousal conditions produce different experiences. Feelings of anxiety are the outcome of the unpleasant high arousal and feelings of relaxation are associated with low levels of arousal. Changes in the experienced sensations of the individual from, say, excitement to anxiety would accompany any reversal from paratelic to telic state, if high arousal conditions were operative. Similarly, under low arousal conditions reversal from telic to paratelic states would be reflected in the switch from experienced relaxation to experienced boredom. It should be remembered that at any one time only one member of the telic-paratelic pair, together with one of each of the other metamotivational pairs, is operative. Consequently, only one preferred level of a variable, in this case arousal, is operative at a given moment.

PSYCHOLOGICAL REVERSALS—AN ILLUSTRATION

Consider for a moment the activity of running or jogging. During the last eight to ten years a huge explosion in the numbers of people engaging in this activity has taken place. Why is it that so many people should be attracted to the running craze?

Motives for engaging in this type of activity will vary with the individual and the experience attached to this motivation will be exhibited in different ways. For some runners the activity will be performed in a telic state of mind. The dedicated athlete runner will be concerned with times, the distance covered and the speed of running; it is a goal-oriented, serious business. The purposefulness, determination and commitment towards completing the task provide pleasure, as does the planning of training and anticipation of some future race or competition.

For the coronary heart patient embarking on a rehabilitation program, the running is also a telic oriented behavior. The goal in this case is the restoration of a satisfactory level of health. The process has to be carefully planned, with each small improvement in distance or time, each minor goal contributing to the overall goal of improved health. Here the jogging or running is merely the means to the end.

Running whilst in the paratelic state is a complete contrast. Times, distances and speed become much less relevant; the runner is participating for the enjoyment of running. The feeling of the sun or rain on the face, the pleasure of running in the park or perhaps the city in the early morning, provides the joy of immediate sensation. Intense experiences brought on by the movement of muscles and limbs and the kinaesthetic awareness associated with the sweating, hard-breathing activity are the kind which are relished in the paratelic state. This is why running can provide such a welcome relief from the pressures of work which, by its very nature, often has a telic orientation.

In this case running provides the opportunity to switch to the paratelic state and pleasant feelings are obtained from the immediate situation and especially the bodily sensations associated with it. It is, of course, highly likely that for any particular individual several reversals will take place during the course of a run. Research work carried out by Walters, Apter and Svebak (1982) showed that during the course of a normal working day frequent reversals took place. Variations in frequency were found between individuals and from day to day.

In reversal theory, reversals from one metamotivational state to another are thought to be triggered by three classes of inducing agents. Although they are considered to interact in a facilitative or inhibitive manner, for convenience here they are described separately. The first of these has to do with contingent events; something about the individual or the environment changes, initiating a reversal. Secondly, it is possible for frustration to build up and cause a reversal where the needs of an individual are not being met in one metamotivational state. Thirdly, the longer an individual remains in any one state, the greater are the chances that satiation effects will induce a reversal.

The voluntary control of reversals, according to the theory, is not possible; the process is thought to be an involuntary one. Nevertheless, it is possible for individuals to place themselves in an environment where a reversal is likely to take place. For instance, going to the theatre or cinema or as a spectator to large sports events is likely to induce the paratelic state, in the same way that arriving at the office or workplace or going to church is liable to invoke the telic metamotivational state. Returning to the example of running, it is relatively easy to recognize a number of situations during the activity where reversals could take place.

A runner initially in the paratelic state and enjoying the immediate pleasures of running may trip and fall, or twist an ankle as a rough piece of ground is traversed. This is an obvious example of a contingent event which might induce a reversal to the telic state. Or this same runner may encounter another runner further ahead on the route and decide to try and catch the leading runner. Due to this change in the environment a reversal has been triggered from the paratelic to the telic metamotivational state. From being concerned only with immediate sensations, the runner has now set the goal of catching the runner in front. Running speed now becomes important and the distance between the two runners is evaluated as the runner's activity becomes oriented towards reaching the goal of overtaking the other runner. Once this goal is achieved, a further reversal to the paratelic state may take place with the runner happy to continue with running for its own sake.

For long distance or marathon athletes running is a serious business; the concern is with improving 'personal best' times, breaking records or time barriers. Training is carefully planned with a specific race, time target or goal in mind. These athletes become expert at monitoring their progress as they run; they can tell if the pace is too slow or too fast; running speed is measured against the time taken to complete a certain part of the race. Clearly for these athletes running would normally be undertaken in the telic state. Interestingly, many of these athletes report 'flow' or altered states of consciousness during races. Mike Spino, a former long distance athlete from the United States, describes this type of experience, which for him occurred during a six mile run in 1967:

> My mind was crystal clear. . . . I felt like a skeleton flying. . . all perfectly natural . . . time lost all semblance of meaning, distance, time, motion were all one . . . sound barely touched my consciousness . . . pouring feeling . . . a perfect expression of my own art form. (Scott, 1971, p. 244–5 see also Kerr, 1985, p. 97)

This is an example of telic-paratelic reversal because, according to Apter (1982, p. 65), "flow experiences would appear to be one form of paratelic experience." Thus, it would seem that even for the serious long distance runner for whom running is likely to be a telic-oriented activity, reversals to the paratelic state are possible and are sometimes experienced by the individual as an altered state of consciousness.

The example of running was used here to try and focus on some concepts of reversal theory. By attempting to draw out some of the motives individuals have for running and analyzing their behavior, the intention was to show the relevance of reversal theory for interpreting real-life situations. Some caution is required however, because as Apter (1982) pointed out, reversal theory:

> . . . does not assume that there is a single one-to-one correspondence between given mental states and a given piece of behaviour, such that for a given individual the same behaviour is always accompanied by the same significant mental states' or, between individuals, that similar behaviour is associated with similar mental states. (p. 5)

Consequently there is a certain danger in assigning telic and paratelic labels to particular aspects of behavior. Ultimately the subjective experience of the individual and the manner in which motives within this experience are structured, interpreted and organized is the most important consideration.

FLOW OR ALTERED STATES OF CONSCIOUSNESS

Returning briefly to the notion of altered states of consciousness, a good deal of support for these flow states or altered states of consciousness has come from the writings of Csikszentmihalyi (1975). He has found from people engaged in a wide range of activities, including composers writing music, surgeons in the operating theatre, rock climbers and games players, that these experiences are relatively common. Expounding on the nature of flow states, Csikszentmihalyi points out that they require no goals or external rewards but that the process itself is intrinsically rewarding. Individuals report that their concentration is concerned with a limited stimulus field; they can easily cope with the demands for action and often temporarily forget themselves and their identity. Perhaps the feelings associated with flow states are best understood by examining two quotations from Csikszentmihalyi's (1975) book. The first is a dancer describing her feelings during a good performance:

> *Your concentration is very complete. Your mind isn't wandering, you are not thinking of something else; you are totally involved in what you are doing. Your body feels good. You are not aware of any stiffness. Your body is awake all over. No area where you feel blocked or stiff. Your energy is flowing very smoothly. You feel relaxed, comfortable and energetic. (p. 39)*

The second is a rock climber:

> *The mystique of rock climbing is climbing; like the justification of poetry is writing; you don't conquer anything except things in yourself. . . . The act of writing justifies poetry. Climbing is the same: recognizing that you are a flow. The purpose of the flow is to keep on flowing, not looking for a peak or utopia but staying in the flow. It is not a moving up but continuous flowing: you move up only to keep the flow going. (p. 47)*

Although the discussion here is brief, from the descriptions of Csikszentmihalyi and the individuals he quotes the characteristics of the flow state are similar to the characteristics of an individual's likely behavior in the paratelic state. The important point arising is that flow experiences are a particular type of paratelic experience and that they occur when the individual is participating in an exciting activity with accompanying high arousal and feelings of pleasure. Sports performers and others do not report experiencing flow states when subject to feelings of anxiety and, according to the arguments of reversal theory, flow experiences are not concomitant with the telic metamotivational state.

TELIC/PARATELIC DOMINANCE

In order to decide which metamotivational state an individual is in at any one time, a measuring instrument is required. Remember, caution was expressed with respect to assuming that a particular piece of behavior would be associated with a particular metamotivational state. A psychometric instrument known as the Telic Dominance Scale has been developed by Murgatroyd et al. (1978). This scale is designed to provide an insight into the phenomenological world of a person.

It is thought that individuals have a preference for one or other of the pair of metamotivational states. In this case focusing on the telic-paratelic pair, individuals are said to be telic dominant or paratelic dominant. The term 'dominance' used here is not directly comparable with the concept of a 'trait', nor can the Telic Dominance Scale be regarded as a trait type instrument like, for instance, the Eysenck Personality Inventory (1969). However, it should still be possible to regard it as a personality characteristic. In reversal theory, the Telic Dominance Scale is not concerned with consistencies of personality and action, but is a rather more complex concept. Put succinctly, dominance is concerned with "the ways in which the person predominantly experiences his or her phenomenological field" (Murgatroyd, 1985b, p. 21). Dominance is the predisposition to be in one state or the other over time and does not necessarily relate to the amount of time actually spent in that state. This is clearly different to the traditional concept of traits where a person designated as an extrovert would be expected to be extroverted all the time. Here, unlike the trait approach, it is possible for the person to be in the opposite state of mind, even though it is not preferred. For example, the normally paratelic dominant person may find that a lengthy period of revision prior to exams will mean that he or she must spend long periods of time in the telic state in order to pursue the goal oriented activity of exam revision. A 'state' version of this scale does exist and provides a quick and useful method of identifying which particular metamotivational state is operative at any one time (Svebak & Murgatroyd, 1985).

AROUSAL REDUCTION—OTHER POSSIBILITIES FOR INTERVENTION

There is no lack of evidence from clinical psychology that high arousal conditions are not desirable. Its concern with anxiety control has led to the use of techniques aimed at arousal reduction. This idea has been readily received by sports psychologists and is being advocated for use with sports performers (e.g., Unestahl, 1982; Weiss and Tschan, 1983 and Zaichkowsky, 1982).

It appears that the intention here is that athletes who incorporate programs involving biofeedback, progressive relaxation, self hypnosis or autogenic training will be better able to control their level of arousal towards some optimum whilst performing in sports competition. Clearly these notions are founded on optimal arousal theory and are not compatible with the approach of reversal theory. This position, however, warrants further examination.

Consider the typical person who seeks psychological or psychiatric help and is recommended some type of self-regulatory arousal reduction therapy. Svebak and Stoyva (1980) have described typical characteristics of someone seeking biofeedback training:

> He (or she) betrays many signs of excessive arousal: he may complain of tension and muscle cramping, inability to relax, difficulties in falling asleep. He may fidget, crack his knuckles and so forth. He may report that he feels out of control. And he may indicate that when he is startled, or made anxious, he requires a long time to settle down again. (p. 440)

The authors go on to say that, given these types of symptoms, the use of biofeedback or some other related therapy for arousal reduction seems appropriate enough. On the other hand Budzynski, Stoyva and Peffer (1980), for example, have discussed the problems associated with relaxation training and the fact that not all subjects are able to achieve a state of low arousal. It must also be said that very few of the considerable number of top sports performers encountered by this author could be described in the above manner.

From the reversal theory perspective, arousal reduction techniques will certainly not always be appropriate. For individuals under the influence of the telic system, then, high arousal is experienced as anxiety and one option is certainly to reduce levels of arousal by the methods described above. This is consistent with a good deal of the work carried out in clinical psychology. For the individual under the influence of the paratelic system, however, the attempt to cultivate low arousal by the above methods would only result in feelings of boredom and not relaxation. In this case an attempt at arousal reduction would be inappropriate. In fact the opposite, an attempt to increase arousal up to high levels, is what is required. Biofeedback and the other self-regulatory techniques are generally thought of in terms of arousal reduction; they could however conceivably be used to deliberately increase arousal just as effectively (Svebak & Stoyva, 1980).

Apart from attempting to affect the arousal level of an individual, it is possible to adopt another, completely different course of action (see Fig. 3). If a reversal from one metamotivational state to another could be initiated, this would result in individuals reinterpreting levels of felt arousal. This would mean that a switch from the telic state, where high arousal is experienced as anxiety, to the paratelic state, where high arousal is experienced as excitement, could completely alter hedonic tone in relation to this arousal. The unpleasant feelings associated with anxiety would become pleasant. Conversely, switches from paratelic to telic would also result, at the lower end of the arousal dimension, in a reinterpretation of boredom as relaxation. Apart from using 'state' type scales, it could be possible for sports psychologists or even coaches to be trained to recognize that a particular metamotivational state was operative. If it was not the most appropriate state at that time then a change could be initiated. Even though reversals are thought to be involuntary, as mentioned earlier (p. 11), it may be possible for an individual to, for example, alter his environment or utilize a cognitive restructuring or imaging strategy, triggering a reversal. Although the resultant effects may be rapid, the reversal is still technically involuntary. What is more likely, psychotherapeutic intervention techniques could produce a reinterpretation of high arousal through a reversal. The use of therapeutic

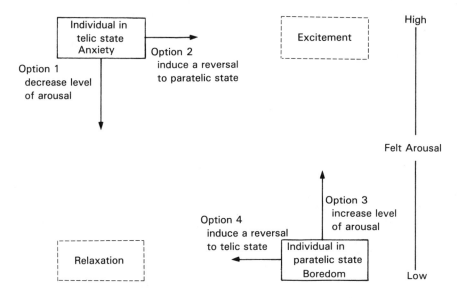

Figure 3   Possible options affecting felt arousal.

intervention techniques in this fashion is currently being explored (e.g., Murgatroyd & Apter, 1986). Emerging from this work are developments which, once established, would appear to have implications for future work in sports psychology.

Although not with reversal theory in mind, some discussion about intervention techniques is already conspicuous in the sports psychology literature. Rushall (1982) has discussed 'on site' intervention at the competition venue and Heyman (1984) has provided a more general review. Certain cognitive behavior intervention procedures carried out by an 'educated' coach or sports psychologist might prove effective.

In summary, as Svebak and Stoyva (1980) point out, there are four possible strategies with respect to pathological arousal levels:

1. Lowering unpleasant *high* arousal (e.g., progressive relaxation).
2. Causing a reinterpretation of unpleasant *high* arousal (metamotivational reversal).
3. Increasing unpleasant *low* arousal (e.g., innovative biofeedback techniques).
4. Causing a reinterpretation of unpleasant *low* arousal (metamotivational reversal).

Thus, according to reversal theory, there are three other intervention possibilities in addition to the well-established arousal reduction techniques.

CONCLUSION

It takes time for any new theory to become established. In just ten years, reversal theory has made considerable progress from its beginnings in 1975. It is also true to say that as a theory it is still developing and a rapidly accumulating body of knowledge is growing around it. Like most other general theories of psychology, in time the hypotheses, concepts and ideas are used in the applied context. The purpose of this chapter has been to draw the attention of sports psychologists, and indeed others working in sport, to this new theoretical approach to motivation and, more specifically, to anxiety.

Reversal theory has, in the view of the present writer, an enormous potential for psychology in general; it really would be a pity if sports psychologists failed to recognize and take advantage of this potential.

SUMMARY

Here an attempt has been made to highlight some of the advantages of reversal theory. It provides a particular challenge to optimal arousal theory, and especially that theory's inability to cope with the differences between everyday notions of anxiety and excitement, and relaxation and boredom. Perhaps one of reversal theory's most attractive features is its admission right from the start that human behavior is intrinsically inconsistent.

It has not been possible here to come to grips with all the important aspects of the theory. A comprehensive coverage of the theory is provided by Apter (1982); applications in a number of areas can be found in Apter, Fontana and Murgatroyd (1985) and a review of research on reversal theory in Apter (1984).

REFERENCES

Allport, G. W. (1960). *Personality and social encounter.* Boston: Beacon Press.

Apter, M. J. (1976). Some data inconsistent with the optimal arousal theory of motivation. *Perceptual and Motor Skills, 43,* 1209–1210.

Apter, M. J. (1982). *The experience of motivation: The theory of psychological reversals.* London: Academic Press.

Apter, M. J. (1984). Reversal theory and personality: A review. *Journal of Research in Personality, 18,* 265–288.

Apter, M. J., Fontana, D., & Murgatroyd, S. (1985). *Reversal theory: Applications and developments.* Cardiff, Wales: University College Cardiff Press.

Apter, M. J., & Svebak, S. (in press). Stress from the reversal theory perspective. In C. D. Spielberger & J. Strelau (Eds.), *Stress and anxiety* (Vol. 12). Washington, D.C.: Hemisphere.

Baddeley, A. D. (1972). Selective attention and performance in dangerous environments. *British Journal of Psychology, 63,* 4, 537–546.

Budzinski, T. H., Stoyva, J. M., & Peffer, K. E. (1980). Biofeedback techniques in psychosomatic disorders. In A. Goldstein & E. Foa (Eds.), *Handbook of behavioral interventions. A clinical guide.* New York: Wiley.

Bühler, C. (1959). Theoretical observations about life's basic tendencies. *American Journal of Psychotherapy, 13,* 561–581.

Cooke, L. E. (1981). *A critical appraisal of the Yerkes-Dodson Law.* Unpublished Ph.D. thesis. University of Leeds, England.

Cooke, L. E. (1982). *Stress and anxiety in sport.* Sports Council Research Project. Sheffield England: Sheffield City Polytechnic.

Csikszentmihalyi, M. (1975). *Beyond boredom and anxiety: The experience of play in work and games.* San Francisco: Jossey-Bass.

Eysenck, H. J., & Eysenck, S. B. J. (1969). *Personality structure and measurement.* London: Routledge and Kegan Paul.

Fiske, D. W., & Maddi, S. R. (1961). A conceptual framework. In D. W. Fiske & S. R. Maddi (Eds.), *Functions of varied experience* (pp. 11–56). Illinois: Dorsey, Homewood.

Frankl, V. E. (1969). *The will to meaning: Foundations and applications of logotherapy.* New York: Plume.

Harlow, M. F. (1953). Motivation as a factor in the acquisition of new responses. In M. R. Jones (Ed.), *Current theory and research in motivation: A symposium.* (pp. 24–29). Lincoln, Nebraska: University of Nebraska Press.

Hebb, D. O. (1955). Drives and the C.N.S. (Conceptual Nervous System). *Psychological Review, 62,* 243–254.

Heide, F. J., & Borkovec, T. D. (1983). Relaxation and induced anxiety—paradoxical anxiety enhancement due to relaxation training. *Journal of Consulting and Clinical Psychology, 51,* 171–182.

Heyman, S. R. (1984). Cognitive and interventions: Theories applications and cautions. In W. F. Straub & J. M. Williams (Eds.), *Cognitive sport psychology* (pp. 289–303). Lansing, New York: Sports Science Associates.

Kerr, J. H. (1983). *Is high arousal really so undesirable.* Paper presented at the Sport and Science Conference. British Society of Sports Psychology. Liverpool University. Liverpool, England. Sept. 15–17.

Kerr, J. H. (1984). *Understanding the exhilaration of speed sports.* Paper presented at and published in the proceedings of International Congress on Sports Medical Aspects of Speed Sports. Groningen, Holland. 27–29 Sept.

Kerr, J. H. (1985). A new perspective for sports psychology. In M. J. Apter, D. Fontana, & S. Murgatroyd (Eds.), *Reversal theory: Applications and developments* (pp. 89–102). Cardiff, Wales: University College Cardiff Press.

Klavora, P. (1979). Customary arousal for peak athletic performance. In P. Klavora & J. V. Daniel (Eds.), *Coach, athlete and the sport psychologist* (pp. 155–169). Toronto, Canada: Publications Division, School of Physical and Health Education, University of Toronto.

Landers, D. M. (1978). Motivation and performance: The role of arousal and attentional factors. In W. Straub (Ed.), *Sport psychology an analysis of athlete behavior* (pp. 74–85). New York: Mouvement Publications.

Landers, D. M. (1980). The arousal-performance relationship revisited. *Research Quarterly for Exercise and Sport, 51,* 77–80.

Martens, R., & Landers, D. M. (1970). Motor performance under stress. A test of the inverted-U hypothesis. *Journal of Personality and Social Psychology,* XVI, 1–29.

Martens, R. (1972). Trait and state anxiety. In W. P. Morgan (Ed.), *Ergogenic aids and muscular performance* (pp. 35–66). New York: Academic Press.

Maslow, A. H. (1954). *Motivation and personality.* New York: Harper and Row.

Murgatroyd, S., Rushton, C., Apter, M. J., & Ray, C. (1978). The development of the telic dominance scale. *Journal of Personality Assessment, 42,* 519–528.

Murgatroyd, S. (1985a). Introduction to reversal theory. In M. J. Apter, D. Fontana, & S. Murgatroyd (Eds.), *Reversal theory: Applications and developments* (pp. 1–19). Cardiff, Wales: University College Cardiff Press.

Murgatroyd, S. (1985b). The nature of telic dominance. In M. J. Apter, D. Fontana, & S. Murgatroyd (Eds.), *Reversal theory: Applications and developments* (pp. 20–41). Cardiff, Wales: University College Cardiff Press.

Murgatroyd, S., & Apter, M. J. (1986). A structural phenomenological approach to eclectic psychotherapy. In J. Norcross (Ed.), *Handbook of eclectic psychotherapy.* New York: Bruner/Mazel.

Naatanen, R. (1973). The inverted-U relationship between activation and performance: A critical review. In S. Kornblum (Ed.), *Attention and performance* (pp. 155–174). London: Academic Press.

Patmore, A. (1979). *Playing on their nerves. The sport experiment.* London: Stanley Paul.

Rushall, B. S. (1979). *Psyching in sport.* London: Pelham Books.

Rushall, B. S. (1982). On-site psychological preparation for athletes. In T. Orlick, J. Partington, & J. H. Salmela (Eds.), *Mental training for coaches and athletes* (pp.140–149). Ottawa, Canada: Sport in Perspective Inc. and Coaching Association of Canada.

Scott, J. (1971). *The athletic revolution.* New York: Free Press Collier-Macmillan.

Smith, K. C. P., & Apter, M. J. (1975). *A theory of psychological reversals.* Chippenham, England: Picton Press.

Svebak, S., & Stoyva, J. (1980). High arousal can be pleasant and exciting. The theory of psychological reversals. *Biofeedback and Self-Regulation, 5*(4), 439–444.

Svebak, S., & Murgatroyd, S. (1985). Metamotivational dominance: A multimethod validation of reversal theory constructs. *Journal of Personality and Social Psychology, 48,* 1, 107–116.

Unestahl, L. E. (1982). *Inner mental training.* Salt Lake City, Utah: Veje Publishing.

Walters, J., Apter, M. J., & Svebak, S. (1982). Colour preference, arousal and the theory of psychological reversals. *Motivation and Emotion, 6*(3), 193–215.

Weiss, M. R., & Tschan, M. (1983). Emotional stress in competitive sport: Courses and solutions. In G. Schilling & K. Herren (Eds.), *Excellence and emotional states in sport. Proceedings of the VIth FEPSAC Congress* (Vol. 1, pp. 209–214). Magglingen, Switzerland: Eidgenössischen Turn- und Sportschule.

Welford, A. T. (1976). *Skilled performance.* Brighton, England: Scott Foresman and Company.

Yerkes, R. M., & Dodson, J. D. (1908). The relation of strength of stimulus to rapidity of habit formation. *Journal of Comparative Neurology of Psychology,* XVIII(4), 459–482.

Zaichkowsky, L. D. (1982). Biofeedback for self-regulation of stress. In L. Zaichkowsky & W. Sime (Eds.), *Stress management in sport* (pp. 55–64). Reston, VA: AAHPERD.

10

Emotions in Sports

Erwin Hahn

This chapter provides a brief overview of emotions in sports. The psychological background and concepts of emotions in sport psychology are described and recent literature in research on emotions in sports are reported. The role of emotions in sport practice and sport psychological research in the following areas is discussed: Elite sports, youth sports, school sports, leisure time sports, and rehabilitative sports.

EMOTIONS IN ELITE SPORTS

"Emotions are stressors and disturbers of performance. In elite sports, they should not be of any relevance." From this perspective, coaches are responsible for the development of performance and competitive skills and emotions play a subordinate role. Since emotions are not trainable and, therefore, not predictable, they may be neglected by the coach.

In training and competition, emotions are generally not taken into account by the coach. They belong to the individual peculiarities of an athlete. In cases where emotions have a positive influence on performance, coaches use these successes to enhance training. In cases where emotions have a negative influence, a coach may reproach the athlete for having these interfering qualities.

Performance is considered to be the result of input provided by the coach, whereas emotions are the personal problem of the athlete. For this reason, emotional control is only very rarely dealt with in practice. Where this is done, it is in the form of an individual coaching during competition. The following interviews with Olympic coaches are examples of coaches attitudes:

After the 1968 Olympic Games at Mexico City a national coach said: "For the female athlete in gymnastics we had to create a special kind of anxiety." And she got the gold medal.

After the 1984 Olympic Games at Los Angeles a national coach said: "Our athlete had written information in his pocket of what to do, and a teammate gave to him the same information. But in the overfloating feelings of happiness to be very close to the strongest opponent, he underrated the importance of this information and made the wrong decision, choosing the wrong equipment, the wrong pole." And he only got the silver medal.

Top level sport and coaching philosophy neglect the existence of emotions. Training is strongly cognitive and mentally oriented. Input-output learning is emphasized: Emotions are considered obstructive, and subsumed under the black box of learning. However, "emotional training" is sometimes included in tactical training such as the learning of aggressive behavior in several team sports, oppression of the opponent, and foul play with a view to win.

In pre-competition states, coaches like to stress the technomotor level and to play down the emotional situation. With the aid of affirmative and general appeals ("Now play very well," "everything will go splendidly") coaches like to calm themselves down.

In this way, sport psychological intervention is oriented to a clinical approach; the coaches have done their best, but the athletes do not work very well. There exist personal disturbances which need psycho-correction and therapy. Ogilvie and Tutko (1966) state that the philosophy of coaches does not touch the "problem athlete."

Emotions such as fun, sensation seeking, sympathy, love, empathy etc. are welcomed qualities, whereas problematic emotions such as pain, tediousness, worry, anger, jealousy, anxiety, blame etc. are feared.

For emotions are diffuse, not very precise and irritating in some way it is impossible to train them. Therefore, coaches do not take care of them.

EMOTIONS IN YOUTH SPORTS

In talent selection and promotion there is a tendency towards transferring the top-level training to training in youth sports.

Duty and sense of duty, responsibility for training, team spirit, cognitive orientation and concentrative skills are developed at the expense of personal emotions.

Pressure is applied to introduce strong performance behavior, organized by prospective plans for the sport career, which take only into account the perspectives in sport skill development. High rates of drop outs are the consequence since the athletes are unable to bring the different needs into agreement.

In some cases, we can get the impression that not the most talented come to the top, but those who are in a better position to suppress personal emotions.

In top-level sports, athletes can permit themselves to show affects and emotions since, at this stage, they have learned to suppress emotions if necessary and to show them if expected.

EMOTIONS IN SCHOOL SPORTS

Objectives of school sports are to introduce physical activity into life as a factor of social, physical and mental health.

Therefore, sport lessons can be regarded as a joyful and nonmental experience. The pupils' emotions have an initiating function for play and learning.

The underlying idea is that both talented children and children with limited motor abilities get an opportunity to experience fun, cooperation, learning, and personal success. The affective goal setting and social learning have to be of great relevance.

In some cases, school sport is perverting into mere success orientation without regarding the emotions of average and handicapped children. To be able to create a positive atmosphere for long-time and lifetime participation in sport, it is necessary to satisfy the needs of all participants.

All this must be reflected in school curricula. If we want health of the whole society and psychological health of every individual child, we have to take emotions into account.

EMOTIONS IN LEISURE TIME SPORTS

Participation in leisure time sports is voluntary. Everyone can choose a sport according to his needs and interests. Fun and social contacts are basic components.

The holiday like situation of people often induces initiatives to learn motor skills in new fields without pressure to learn and without social supervision by the environment.

Sport equipment industry has reacted very strongly and, in cooperation with the mass media and the sports organizations, attempts are made to use the area of leisure time sports as a means to introduce the ideals of health, beauty, youth etc.

The only prerequisite is to practice leisure time sports regularly in conformity with the physical capacities and not with situational moods. The emotional impetus is reduced for physical purposes. Some kind of leisure performance is created by displacing emotional qualities. Fun as duty is the end of the original engagement.

Animation instead of performance, cooperation instead of competition, variety instead of unidimensional sport must be the motto.

EMOTIONS IN REHABILITATIVE SPORT SITUATIONS

In rehabilitation and therapy we need the personal emotions to introduce physical activity and sports to disabled and convalescent persons.

The experience to be in a better position to manage personal problems, to master oneself and to get a new self-confidence must be the determining aspects of sport therapy. The focus is the idea of self-realization and not the performance status.

EMOTIONS IN THE CONTEXT OF SPORTS

Emotions are a prerequisite for sport engagement. They are human needs, based upon the will to master the own world by way of assimilation and accommodation (Piaget). The need of locomotion and movement are the early expressions. In creating own interests and values, emotions are key stimuli for practicing sport.

The philosophy of education and training, however, is to neglect emotions and to favor mental skills. Good teachers and coaches can combine emotional impact and mental development.

Good teachers and good coaches are in a position to see both the requirements of the curricula and the necessity of personal emotions.

The organization of outstanding performance—even in sports—does not take care of the affective basis of the persons involved. There are strong relations to the theory of "sport as reproduction of work" (Güldenpfennig et al., 1972, 1974). Working and training capacities are only related to progress, productivity, profitability and economy. The only questions that count are whether the athlete works or not, whether success is realized or not and whether social and national prestige is attained or not.

But the psychological aspect—and this is also confirmed by successful coaches—operates with the control of emotions in sport situations. Action theory (Hackfort, 1983; Nitsch, 1975, 1981, 1985; Nitsch & Hackfort, 1981, 1984) can develop the fundamental basis i.e., the ability to calculate the relevance of all factors relating to top performances—also the emotions.

RESEARCH OF EMOTIONS IN PSYCHOLOGY

In the beginning, the investigation of emotions was one of the most important fields of scientific psychology (James, 1884; Wundt, 1911; Cannon, 1927; Krüger, 1928; Lersch, 1962). These early phases did also include the discussion of sport psychological questions (Klemm, 1938).

Then the topics changed and research increasingly focused on cognitive factors of personality structure; the relevance of intellectual and motivational dominance was evident.

Affective and also emotional behavior is described as a non-effective and a relatively uncontrollable situational strategy for common life. The private area of human behavior is no topic for an investigation it is rather a case for psychotherapy, behavioral therapy, or clinical psychology. In this way, investigations on emotional aspects are reduced to a minimum.

The variety of human emotions and their very different consequences for behavior are one of the problems of the scientific research.

Emotions are reactions resulting from the evaluation and estimation of a specific situation or a series of situations; they are the timbres of motivation, anticipation, and action.

These emotions are conscious only to a very limited extent. In the majority of cases, they act and react subcortically and influence "unconsciously" the decisions for action.

Emotions often are in contradiction to cognitive and mental involvement and disturb the "normal" way of action. For this reason, they are described as irrational, disturbing, and less calculable.

Schlosberg's (1954) model of emotions distinguishes three independent dimensions of emotions:

- mood: agreeable/disagreeable
- inclination/refusal
- activation: small/high

After the estimation of a specific situation, it is important (unimportant), useful (threatening) or favorable (unfavorable) to react in a definite way.

According to Lazarus (see Lazarus & Averill, 1972), the permanent analysis of positive and negative elements in a definite situation is the trigger for action realization. This step by step analysis entails a change of consciousness immediately after the helplessness during a competition. The value system will be changed and the action be re-estimated and newly defined.

Schachter and Singer (1962) are describing the genesis of emotions in a three step development. The experiences of previous situations create a specific physiological level of arousal. Being confronted with specific anticipational marks of the situation, the emotions regulate the energetic input for action. Without the cognitive and perspective strategies emotions sometimes organize actions in a non goal oriented way. In such a case, the outputs of emotional experiences and expressions go from regression to aggression, good temper to violence, love to hate, cooperation to destruction, social acceptance to deprivation, fun to stress.

In concrete situations, however, we do not know whether cognitive reflections lead to emotions or whether the emotions are the prerequisite for cognitive decisions.

Therefore, in most of the theories, emotions are described as being diffuse, unprecise and irrational. They are discussed within the framework of other constructs such as motivation, stress and arousal.

In general psychology, emotions are described as personal qualities which have to be taken into account. Emotion control is only relevant for clinical psychology, including analysis, prognostics and therapy for the individual.

There are only a few application systems to control emotions with a view to achieve a better way of life.

CONCEPT OF EMOTIONS IN SPORT PSYCHOLOGY

When looking at the text books for sport psychology, we find the same tendencies as in general psychology. In the first books, we find many indications for emotions in sport activities.

Rudik (1958), for instance, is describing emotional characteristics in different sport activities, especially the feelings of the athletes (feeling of the water in swimming, feeling for the ball in team sports etc.) and the peculiarities of emotional processes in sport activities.

Puni (1961) tries to discuss psychological problems before the start and during the competition as emotional processes which result from the level of arousal. He also introduces the psychological effects of success and failure into sport psychology.

Sport science develops in two directions: Goal oriented sports are oriented towards training and competition. From school to elite sport emotions play a subordinate role; they are described in training purposes and psychological preparation as motivation training, arousal conditions or stress management. Emotions can support performance, but in some cases, it might also be necessary to reduce them in order to avoid disturbances.

Leisure-oriented sports are to develop positive emotions for well being, psychohygienics and modern way of life.

If we study the proceedings of the International (ISSP; 1965–1985) and the European (FEPSAC; 1969–1983) Society of Sport Psychology, we can see the tendencies in the research of emotions.

In 1965 (Antonelli), we find a lot of emotions' research in sport, but it is not very essential and without theoretical basic concept.

The cognitive theory of sport is displacing the application of emotional research. Only in the fields of leisure-time sports, play in early childhood, sport in rehabilitation, and sport with disabled we find some recent research.

A close theory of negative emotions is developed and adapted to sport. On the occasion of the 1978 Munich Symposium of sport psychology, there was a profound discussion between the two positions of anxiety theory (Spielberger) and sport (ISSP and FEPSAC Managing Councils). The theory of aggression is also introduced into sport.

After a long period (1978–1985) of description of anxiety and aggression in sport, recent research activities do also include the control of these emotions.

The action theory of Nitsch and Hackfort (1984) resulted in great progress with respect to investigations of emotions and their control. In the state of anticipation of actions the athlete is calculating the risks, costs and effects of his action. Not only negative and restrictive emotions border the performance level; positive emotions can also develop successful plans for realization. In the realization, positive emotions can also create a supporting and performance-oriented atmosphere.

At least in the interpretation of the action the result is topic of subjective evaluation and estimation.

Scientific research was mostly oriented to negative and diminishing factors of performance and competition. Anxiety, anger and aggression are described as limiting factors.

In 1983, after editing a reader on "Anxiety in sports" (Apitzsch), the European Congress of FEPSAC at Magglingen/Switzerland was entitled "Excellence and emotional states in sport" (Schilling & Herren, 1985). In 1986, the annual conference of the Spielberger group, at Visegrad, was entitled "Stress and Emotion" and the 1988 European Congress of Sport Psychology, at Bad Blankenburg/German Democratic Republic will follow this new direction of FEPSAC work with the topic "Unity of cognition, emotion and motivation in the regulation of sport activities."

After the period of the development of cognitive and mental skills and the description of limiting emotional factors such as anxiety and aggression, sport psychology now tries to find a complex theory of psychoregulation where all components of performance abilities and skills are represented, brought into relevant relation to each other, and can be controlled for optimal realization in competition.

Also in competitive situations, cognitive, motivational and affective elements are represented in consciousness. According to the situation, the conscious state can vary between emotional overfloating and strong concentration. Emotional control can bring the consciousness into the necessary balance (Hahn, 1984).

This required balance must be taken care of, not only with respect to the negative and blocking emotions, but also with respect to the supporting and positive ones.

Analysis and control is needed, but this purpose must realize important research, also in the field of positive emotions and their consequences.

EMOTIONS IN SPORT: ANALYSIS OF LITERATURE AND CURRENT RESEARCH

In the early phases, the concept of sport psychology also included the emotions, and created a clear relationship between cognition, emotion, arousal and performance.

The reasons why sport psychology focusses on other topics are to be found in general psychology and sport science. Emotions have always been subordinated to other subjects; only negative emotional behavior such as anxiety, aggression, anger etc. are an exception.

Seen from the scientific perspective, sport does, at present, only consider negative emotions. As a consequence, sport science introduced into practice and into society that "sport is negative."

When looking at this, a dialectical position become obvious. If the objective of sport is performance (up to peak performance), it is described with negative emotions and emotion control; if the objective is physical activity, positive emotions such as well-being are also developed. Depending on the objectives, school sport has to take account of both directions of emotional approach.

The analysis of research was carried out by using the European project documentation (1980), the German documentation (1984, 1985), and the documentation of literature based upon the pool of the Federal Institute of Sport Science in Cologne.

Investigations in aggression and anxiety reached an international standard, but they are excluded from this survey. Only publications after 1975 are taken into consideration. There are only very few theoretical monographs; they concentrate on the theories of emotion and try to introduce new aspects for research (Landers, 1980; Vallerand, 1983; Hackfort, 1985; Nitsch, 1985; Schellenberger, 1986; Kuhl, 1986).

In the field of top-level sport we have a number of books dealing with the pre-competitive preparation and the effects of success and failure (Butt, 1977; Nideffer, 1976; Tutko & Tosi, 1976; Kunath, 1975; Unestahl, 1983; Rudolph & Kunath, 1974; Allawy, 1978; Antonelli & Salvini, 1978; Janbroers, 1977; Orlick, 1980; Rushall, 1979; Salmela, 1980; Thomas, 1978; Gabler a.o., 1979; Glencross, 1978; Matsuda, 1979; Vanek, 1980; Straub, 1978). They analyze topics such as psychological preparation, emotional control, psycho-regulation, anticipation, stress reduction, desensibilization, effective coaching, emotional disturbances during competition, valuation of winning and losing, success and failure.

Special subjects of psychological research in this field are: self-regulation of emotional states during the period of competitions (Cernikova, 1972, 1980; Genova, 1983; Olszewska, 1981), the interdependence of cognitive, emotional and motor behavior (Abolin, 1976, 1981; Gasowski, 1976, 1977; Kunath, 1978; Schellenberger, 1986; Tschernikova, 1974), emotion and arousal (Anshel, 1985; Kuhl, 1986), psychological preparation, emotional control and the influences on competition (Falar, 1978; Gamal, 1981; Galkin, 1984; Hosek, 1977; Jurov, 1979; Jindrova, 1977; Kauss, 1978, 1980; Kolomejcev, 1983; Kopysov, 1981, 1983; Lesley, 1980; Levik, 1982; Loehr, 1985; Madievskij, 1976; Matsuda, 1977; Murphy, 1978; Nekrason, 1983; Popescu, 1975; Razumov, 1978; Salmela, 1977; Singer, 1980, 1982; Sopov, 1983; Tolocek, 1981; Wolkov, 1977), stress factors and stress management (Krone, 1986; Long, 1980; Machac, 1977, 1979; Sigaev, 1983; Smith, 1979; Surkina, 1981), the mastering of success and failure (Allmer, 1978; Iso Ahola, 1976; McAuley, 1983; Rosenblum, 1979; Ryann, 1981; Willimczyk, 1985), and problems in competitive youth sports (Kaminski, 1979; Martens, 1978; Stevenson, 1982).

Contents of essays elaborated in the field of sensibility vary between satisfaction and aspects of happiness by sport (Abe, 1983; Best, 1976; Carpinter, 1983; Carter, 1976; Kew, 1981; Tiwald, 1974, 1976).

The relevance of the affective area for the behavior of coaches is described in a number of investigations (Hotz, 1980; Stützle, 1983; Thiel, 1983; Woodford, 1979).

The ambivalent role of school sport in the development of emotional and social learning is a topic of international relevance (Allmer, 1984; Bernsdorff, 1981; Cheffers, 1976; Dodds, 1976; Geblewicz, 1977; Goslina, 1982; Harter, 1981; Ilg, 1976; Kneer, 1976; Marsh, 1984; Melograno, 1974; Santangelo, 1965; Schwantes, 1982, 1983; Simons, 1984; Snyder, 1982).

The emotional experience in leisure time sport is related to well-being, emotional health and fun (Abele-Brehm, 1984; Ewing, 1982, 1984; Koenig, 1982; Lipsky, 1981; Nelson, 1976; Snyder, 1982).

Environmental and social factors involved in improving and teaching emotional behavior are in the center of research carried out with respect to children; body image and body concept are important fields of work (Anderson, 1982; Belaief, 1977; Bennet, 1975; Blouin, 1981; Frostig, 1980; Harris, 1978; Larson, 1976).

Also in the areas of women's sport (Allison, 1984; Berger, 1981) and sport for older people (Birkmeier, 1979; Pirani, 1984) emotional aspects begin to be included in research activities.

Only in the filed of psychological preparation and stress management for elite athletes there is a small basis for agreement as to the purposes of psycho-regulation.

In all the other fields, theories and measurements differ so much from each other that an empirical comparison and correlation is not realistic.

SUMMARY AND CONCLUSION

Research activities on emotions in sport concentrated on investigations of so-called negative emotions and there are many analyses of the negative effects of these emotions.

Identical loads and also identical external conditions of sport, arousal, performance and competition result in very different emotional states. In the individual behavior of the athletes, we can recognize optimal stimulation or greatest disturbances.

The emotional stress of definite loadings is modified by the time of realization and the environmental conditions.

The same training purposes may also lead to very different emotional states. In a learning process, we have to create a positive climate and confidence with a view to realize a positive learning involvement for training. Fun and success in sport are only two aspects of the final objective: the performance.

Given this background information, it is necessary to carry out investigations on positive emotions in sport. Investigations of this kind should concentrate

- on the description of positive emotions in the different areas of sport and their consequences for training, performance, and competition
- on the area of observable positive emotional behavior and its relevance
- on the psychology of coaches to find transferable methods to create a positive emotional climate
- on psychophysiological research to study the changes in the nervous system during positive emotions

The action theory by Nitsch and Hackfort (1981, 1984), is a good theoretical basis for such research activities.

The European Society of Sport Psychology (FEPSAC) will support research in this area and made this topic a priority subject.

REFERENCES

Cannon, W. B. (1927). The James-Lange theory of emotions. *American Journal of Psychology, 39,* 106–124.

Güldenpfennig, J., Jensen, J., & Pfister, R. (1972). *Sport im Spätkapitalismus.* Frandfurt/M.: Rowohlt.

Güldenpfennig, J., Volpert, W., & Weinberg, P. (1974). *Sensumotorisches Lernen und Sport als Reproduktion der Arbeitskraft.* Köln: Pahl-Rugenstein.

Hackfort, D. (1983). *Theorie und Diagnostik sportbezogener Ängstlichkeit.* Univeröff Diss. DSHS Köln.

Hahn, E. (1984). Psychohygiene als Aufgabe der Sportpsychologie für wichtige Wettkämpfe. In H. Rieder (Ed.), *Sportpsychology International.* Köln: bps.

James, W. (1884). What is emotion. *Mind, 9,* 188–205.

Klemm, O. (1938). Zwölf Leitsatze zu einer Psychologie der Leibesübungen. *Neue psychologische Studien, 9,* 81–91.

Krüger, R. (1928). *Das Wesen der Gefühle.* Leipzig: Akademische Verlagsanstalt.

Lazarus, R.S., & Averill, J. R. (1972). Emotion and cognition. In C. D. Spielberger (Ed.), *Anxiety: Current trends in theory and research* (Vol. II). Washington: Hemisphere.

Lersch, P. (1962). *Aufbau der Person.* München: Barth.

Nitsch, J. R. (1975). Sportliches Handeln als Handlungsmodell. *Sportwissenschaft, 5,* 39–55.

Nitsch, J. R. (1981). Stresstheoretische Modellvorstellungen. In J.R. Nitsch (Ed.), *Stress.* Bern: Huber.

Nitsch, J. R. (1985). Emotionen und Handlungsregulationen. In G. Schilling & K. Herren (Eds.), *Excellence and emotional states in sport.* Magglingen: ETS.

Ogilvie, B. C., & Tutko, T. A. (1980). *Problem athletes and how to handle them.* London: Pelham.

Puni, A. Z. (1961). *Abriss der Sportpsychologie.* Berlin, DDR: Sportverlag.

Rudik, P. A. (1958). *Psychologie.* Berlin, DDR: Sportverlag.

Schachter, S., & Singer, J. E. (1962). Cognitive, social and physiological determinants of emotional state. *Psychological Review, 69,* 379–399.

A comprehensive bibliography is available from the author.

Schilling, G., & Herren, K. (Eds.) (1985). *Excellence and emotional states in sport.* Magglingen: ETS.

Schlosberg, H. S. (1954). Three dimensions of emotion. *Psychological Review, 61,* 81–88.

Wundt, W. (1911). *Grundriβ der Psychologie.* Leipzig: Engelmann.

III

ANXIETY CONTROL
IN SPORTS

11

Health, Anxiety, and Physical Exercise

William P. Morgan and Kathleen A. Ellickson

OVERVIEW

This chapter is comprised of three independent sections dealing with health, anxiety and physical exercise. Sport psychologists have historically focused on the relationship between anxiety and performance in sport settings, and this is understandable when one considers the brief history of sport psychology. However, as this young field has grown and developed, there has been an increasing concern with the converse question; that is, the influence of physical exercise on anxiety. Both approaches are concerned with exercise and anxiety, but the research and applications tend to be quite different. The former approach has a *performance* focus, and it is associated with *antecedent* research paradigms and interventions, whereas the latter involves *health,* and it is characterized by *consequent* designs and evaluations. Another trend in this area involves both health and performance, but it is not restricted to competitive sports or exercise for health reasons. This emerging area involves health, safety, and performance of individuals involved in stressful occupations and high-risk recreational activities. Recent examples of sport psychology research in this latter area will be reviewed in the final section.

ANXIETY AND PERFORMANCE

The relationship between arousal and sport performance has been analyzed from a number of perspectives in recent years. Enhancing athletic performance through the monitoring and manipulation of pre-competitive and competitive anxiety has been a focus of coaches, athletes and researchers in the exercise and sport sciences. Various technologies have been developed to increase and decrease sport related arousal levels in an effort to help athletes control the physiological and psychological symptoms associated with anxiety states. There have been five theoretical orientations used in the exercise and sport sciences which have dealt with arousal level in competitive athletes, and these approaches will be reviewed in the following sections.

Drive Theory

The earliest point of view was derived from drive theory (Hull, 1943). Drive theory predicts that performance increases with elevations in arousal. In other words, a direct relationship is thought to exist between arousal level and performance, and maximal performance is dependent upon high levels of arousal. This theory serves as the basis for most "psyching" procedures employed by coaches and sport psychologists, but it does not appear to have been supported by a single study in the sport psychology literature (Martens, 1970).

Research by Hammer (1968) involving 2,300 high school and junior college athletes who participated in ten different sports refutes drive theory. No differences on anxiety, as measured by the Taylor Manifest Anxiety Scale, were found between successful athletes, unsuccessful athletes, and nonathletes. According to Hammer (1968) drive theory predicts that the "successful" athletes should have demonstrated high anxiety levels, while "unsuccessful" athletes should have been characterized by low arousal levels. In a related study involving 103 wrestlers and football players, Hammer (1967) reported there were no differences in anxiety scores between high and low achieving athletes and nonathletes.

In a study involving college wrestlers, Morgan and Hammer (1974) made several observations that refuted traditional models of sport anxiety. Anxiety levels of wrestlers (1) were evaluated during the pre-season, (2) following weigh-in at a state tournament, (3) one hour prior to competition, and (4) 15 to 30 minutes following the tournament. First of all, each team participating in the tournament demonstrated an increase in anxiety one hour before competition. In other words, there were no significant differences on pre-competitive anxiety levels between teams which finished first, second, third, and fourth in the tournament. Second, "high anxious" and "low anxious" athletes were compared, and there was no significant difference in the performance of the two groups; that is, success was not associated with level of anxiety.

Inverted-U Theory

The second theoretical orientation used in the exercise and sport sciences to account for arousal level in competitive athletes is based on the Yerkes-Dodson Law, and this law is also known as the Inverted-U Theory (Yerkes & Dodson, 1908). According to this theory, as arousal level increases, there is an increase in performance, up to a certain point, and arousal beyond this point results in a performance decrement. Landers (1980) has reviewed the research evidence in the sport sciences both supporting and refuting this hypothesis, and he has agreed with Mahoney and Avener (1977) who concluded that:

> *Individual differences in susceptibility to arousal have been frequently observed. These results suggest that absolute levels of arousal may be less important than patterns of arousal change and the methods used by athletes to cope with precompetitive anxiety. If this is true, absolute levels of arousal may not necessarily be a determinant of performance (p. 94).*

Table 1 Summary of Research Evidence Supporting the Inverted-U
Theory, Application Targets, and Presence or Absence of
Ecological Validity

Basis of research evidence	Application target	Ecological validity
Learning	Performance	Absent
Non-athletes	Athletes (elite)	Absent
Novice performer	Skilled performers	Absent
Simple motor skills	Complex motor skills	Absent
Controlled laboratory setting	Dynamic sport arena	Absent

There are several reasons why the Inverted-U Theory has been popular. First, it is presented in many motor learning and sport psychology texts as a matter of fact, and there is limited motor *learning* evidence in support of this theory. However, there is an enormous difference between learning and performing a task. There are many reasons why the limited motor learning research should not be generalized to applications in sport settings, and these reasons are summarized in Table 1.

Threshold Theory

The third theoretical orientation involves a related explanation based on the concept of a threshold or paradoxical distance effect (Morgan, 1972). This view is similar to the inverted-U concept in specifying that increases in arousal lead to increases in performance up to a specific point, and then once a given threshold is reached there is a sudden decrease in performance. This view differs from the Inverted-U Theory, however, in maintaining that once the threshold is reached a rapid reversal in performance results. In other words, rather than a range of arousal for optimal performance, this orientation views the most effective arousal level as representing a discrete point. This view has been derived from work involving ergogenic aids in which various substances (e.g., drugs) have been observed to facilitate muscular capacity up to a certain point, but then quickly lose their effectiveness at a given dosage (Morgan, 1972). There does not, however, appear to be any research evidence supporting this theoretical orientation.

Quiescence Theory

The fourth theoretical orientation, and the one currently in vogue, is based upon the concept that quiescence enhances performance. This model represents the antithesis of drive theory, and it specifies that performance increases as arousal decreases. Rather than "psyching up" athletes, this approach relies on relaxation procedures in an effort to reduce the arousal level of athletes prior to competition. There is an absence of compelling evidence in support of this view, and there is considerable anecdotal evidence and theoretical rationale that argues against it. Also, there now exists a number of empirical studies which refute this hypothesis (Hanin, 1980).

Optimal Arousal Theory

The fifth point of view is based on the work of Hanin (1980), and it suggests that each individual has an arousal zone of optimal function (ZOF). Hanin's (1980) proposal of a ZOF maintains that performance efficiency is best when the individual's level of arousal falls within this zone. Many contemporary sport psychologists have ignored or simply dismissed Hanin's ZOF concept on the basis of redundancy; that is, it has been erroneously viewed as a reiteration of the inverted-U theory. The two theories are· quite different, however, since ZOF theory *does not* argue that a *moderate level* of arousal is superior to low or high levels. Indeed, the ZOF theory posited by Hanin predicts that some individuals will have their best performances when highly aroused, others when deeply relaxed, and others when moderately aroused. In other words, there is not an optimal level of arousal for a given task (e.g., free throw shooting), but rather, low, moderate, or high arousal may be the most effective for a given basketball player shooting free throws.

Hanin's empirical evidence for this theory is based upon retrospective and prospective simulations using the State-Trait Anxiety Inventory (STAI) developed by Spielberger (1972). In this work the athlete's recall and prediction of state anxiety prior to competition has been contrasted with actual ratings in the same settings. The correlations between retrospective evaluations and actual evaluations obtained 1–2 hours before competition average approximately .75. In other words, athletes were asked several weeks after the competition how they had felt 1–2 hours before the event. The retrospective measurement, on the STAI, was compared with the STAI score they had actually achieved prior to competition. Hanin's work empirically demonstrates that athletes are able to accurately recall their pre-competitive anxiety. Furthermore, prospective data obtained by correlating predicted pre-competitive levels of state anxiety (STAI) with actual anxiety levels 1–2 hours prior to competition were also significant.

Hanin (1980) also found that recall of pre-competitive anxiety prior to a stressful gymnastics event (beam) was more accurate than for less stressful events (floor exercise). The correlation between actual state anxiety and retrospective recall was .89 for the beam, whereas the correlation between actual state anxiety and retrospective recall was .74 for floor exercise.

One implication of this theory is that since state anxiety is highly variable in athletes, the challenge is one of helping each individual athlete reach his or her optimal level of "useful anxiety" (Hanin, 1980). According to this theory, the task is not to increase or decrease arousal level in groups of athletes, but rather the challenge is to focus on each individual's optimum anxiety level prior to competition and help him or her reach that zone in a consistent manner.

The "zone" referred to by Hanin (1980), on the average, varies between plus or minus four points of the individual's most efficient state anxiety level as measured by the STAI. Assume, for example, that pre-competition anxiety levels are available for a 5,000 meter runner on 25 occasions. Also, assume that the runner's state anxiety was 60 prior to his or her personal best (PB). This runner's ZOF would then be operationalized as 56–64 on the STAI (i.e., 60 ± 4). With 25 performances to examine, it would be quite easy to determine whether or not the individual's ZOF actually falls between 56 and 64 on the STAI measure of state anxiety. Hanin (1980) empirically established the most efficient level of anxiety by testing athletes over many competitive trials and thereby demonstrating the validity of the zone of optimal functioning in actual athletic conditions. Empirically, Hanin found a correlation of .74 between the successfulness of the athlete's performance and the degree to which he or she achieved their optimal arousal zone three days before competition. Athletes were less successful in competition when state anxiety, measured three days before competition, was higher or lower than the optimal zone. Hanin (1980) also found that male and female athletes, as one would expect, did not differ on resting levels of state or trait anxiety as measured by the STAI, nor did they differ in pre-competitive settings.

There is actually a great deal of indirect support for Hanin's theory in the sport psychology literature. It has been shown, for example, that winning and losing performances of college wrestlers competing in a dual meet, as well as tournament competition, was not associated with pre-competition state anxiety levels (Morgan, 1970; Morgan & Hammer, 1974). Also, the generalizability of Hanin's results has recently been extended to include English speaking athletes in the United States (Raglin & Morgan, 1988). These investigators evaluated the state anxiety of college swimmers under resting or base-line conditions, and these swimmers were asked to complete the state anxiety inventory a second time estimating how they thought they would feel one hour prior to a very difficult dual meet scheduled for the following day. These swimmers were then tested one hour prior to the scheduled meet. The meet was very difficult and the outcome was decided in the final milliseconds of the final event—an emotionally charged relay. The swimmers studied in this investigation won the meet by three points, and the overall results are summarized in Figure 1.

The swimmers predicted that they would experience a significant increase in state anxiety when tested one hour prior to the forthcoming competition, and the actual state anxiety just prior to the competition was significantly elevated (P < .01) over the base-line level. A repeated measures ANOVA revealed that the prospective and actual ratings of state anxiety did not differ, but both values were

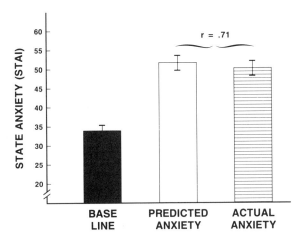

Figure 1 Prospective and actual ratings of state anxiety in swimmers prior to competition.

significantly above the base-line. The correlation between the prospective and actual ratings was significant (r = .71, P < .01), and these overall results are in close agreement with the report by Hanin (1980) involving Soviet athletes. Also, there was no relationship between anxiety and performance ratings provided by the coach. These findings certainly argue in support of the international perspective advanced in this volume. That is, an English scale, the STAI, was translated for use in Russian research, and the results of the research were replicated with English speaking athletes. This finding offers compelling support for the cross-cultural validity of the STAI, Spielberger (1972). The results also argue against the use of relaxation procedures for the purpose of enhancing performance. Indeed, had the team under investigation in this case been relaxed, they might not have "upset" their superior opponents!

Further support for the efficacy of Hanin's model is provided by a series of recent investigations involving elite distance runners (Morgan & Bradley, 1985; Morgan & O'Connor, 1986; Morgan, O'Connor, Sparling & Pate, 1987). In this research, elite distance runners were asked to recall how they felt just prior to competition in their primary event. They were asked to recall how they felt as they moved "to-the-line" for the start. These elite runners completed a Body Awareness Scale (Morgan, Raglin & Wang, in preparation) that focuses on somatic, as opposed to psychic symptoms, and the scale was completed under three conditions of simulated recall. These retrospective instructional sets were:

1. How you usually feel just prior to competition.
2. How you felt just prior to the best performance (BP) of your career.
3. How you felt just prior to the worst performance of your career.

This research indicated that male and female runners did not differ on somatic arousal at base-line, or prior to competition. All *groups* of runners competing at distances ranging from 1500m to 42.2km, were characterized by *significant elevations* in pre-competition arousal under the best, worst and usual conditions. However, some runners had *no change* in arousal prior to competition, while others typically experienced *large increases* in arousal. This research with elite distance runners demonstrated that the use of relaxation procedures, or "psyching" techniques, prior to competition would theoretically impair performance for a substantial number of runners. These results support Hanin's ZOF theory, and they emphasize the necessity of employing systematic monitoring with individual athletes in order to empirically establish the individual's ZOF. This theory, and the research evidence that has accumulated, supports the view that performance *is not* correlated with arousal. It is not correlated in a positive, negative, or curvilinear manner. In other words, ZOF theory offers an attractive, alternative theory of arousal and performance that is heuristic and novel in that it emphasizes individual differences.

There is one additional reason to argue against the carte blanche or laissez faire application of relaxation procedures for athletes in pre-competition settings, and this additional consideration extends to the popular use of relaxation training in general with athletes. It is now well documented that "relaxation induced anxiety" (RIA) and panic attacks occur in some individuals when they are taught traditional methods of progressive muscular relaxation (Heide & Borkovec, 1984;

Smith, 1975). Therefore, in addition to performance decrements, the indiscriminate use of relaxation procedures can also produce distress in some individuals.

PHYSICAL EXERCISE AND ANXIETY

This section includes an overview of research dealing with the tranquilizer effect of exercise. This review will be restricted to the short-term or acute effects of exercise since there has been very little research on the long-term effects of exercise. A comprehensive treatment of exercise and mental health appears in a recent edited volume, and this work includes reference to anxiety, the focus of this section, as well as additional topics such as depression, self-esteem and schizophrenia (Morgan & Goldston, 1987).

Individuals who engage in habitual physical activity report that exercise makes them "feel good," and the sensation of feeling good following a vigorous exercise bout undoubtedly explains why many people exercise on a regular basis (Morgan, 1984). It is not clear, however, whether the exercise *per se* causes the improved affect reported by exercisers, or whether the distraction from various stressors afforded by exercise represents the crucial factor (Raglin & Morgan, 1985). Furthermore, it is known that approximately 50% of those sedentary individuals who adopt an exercise program return to their sedentary lifestyles within several months (Dishman, 1987; Martin & Dubbert, 1985; Ward & Morgan, 1984). It is not known why individuals discontinue exercise programs, but it is possible that the improved affect reported by habitual exercisers does not occur in those individuals who become exercise recidivists. At any rate, it is important to recognize that research involving tension reduction following exercise may suffer from attenuation due to the use of exercise adherents in most of the published research to date.

In addition to the potential problem of attenuation, there is also limited evidence that some individuals experience panic attacks following exercise. It is unlikely that individuals of this type would volunteer for exercise experiments. The lactate hypothesis of exercise-induced anxiety (EIA) has become institutionalized within psychiatry, and the research in exercise science that refutes EIA has been based entirely on physically active individuals (Morgan, 1979; Raglin & Morgan, 1985). Therefore, the research findings discussed in this section are not necessarily generalizable to anxious, sedentary individuals, and exercise interventions with such individuals should be employed with caution.

Research Designs

Repeated measures designs have been employed in most of the published studies involving the influence of exercise on state anxiety. The typical design has consisted of administering the state anxiety scale (Spielberger, 1972) to subjects under resting conditions, and then again following exercise of varying intensity and duration. Most of this research has been carried out in the walking or running modes; duration has usually ranged from 20 to 40 minutes; and the intensity has varied from 40% to 80% of maximal aerobic power in most of these studies.

In some cases the 4-item state anxiety scale (Spielberger, 1972) has been administered to test subjects, and this scale has been found to be particularly effective where a need exists to evaluate state anxiety *during,* or *immediately* following vigorous exercise (Morgan, Horstman, Cymerman, & Stokes, 1980). Most of the studies have included an assessment of state anxiety 5 to 10 minutes following exercise. In one investigation, however, state anxiety was assessed systematically across the subsequent 24-hour period, and in a second case for three hours following exercise (Raglin & Morgan, 1985).

Representative Findings

In one of the first investigations 40 adult males completed the state anxiety scale (Spielberger, 1972) before, immediately following, and 20–30 minutes following aerobic running performed at approximately 60% of maximum for a period of 45 minutes (Morgan, 1979). State anxiety was observed to increase immediately following exercise, but a substantial and significant decrease (P < .001) below the pre-test level was noted at 20–30 minutes post-exercise. This particular finding has been consistently replicated in a series of studies (Morgan *et al.,* 1980; Raglin & Morgan, 1985). In other words, state anxiety is elevated immediately following vigorous exercise, but it decreases significantly within a short period of time.

In a later experiment Morgan et al. (1980) administered the modified 4-item scale to subjects throughout an exercise bout performed on a treadmill at 80% of maximal aerobic power (MAP). On one day they walked at this relative exercise intensity until they could no longer continue, and on a subsequent day they ran to exhaustion at 6 mph, and a grade that would require 80% MAP. The duration of the exercise averaged 23 minutes and 24 minutes for the running and walking trials respectively. This exercise resulted in an increase in blood lactate from a resting level of 10mg% to a post-exercise value of 90mg%; a fourfold increase in plasma epinephrine; a seven-fold increase in plasma norepinephrine; and the peak heart rate during exercise averaged 190 beats per minute. State anxiety increased in a linear manner during the first half of the exercise sessions, reached a plateau, and then remained stable for the remainder of the exercise bout. These results are summarized in Figure 2.

In other words, the exercise stressor provoked a significant increase in cardiovascular and biochemical indices of stress, and these physiological changes were accompanied by increases in state anxiety. This psychobiochemical response was classified as *eustress* rather than *stress* because it was followed by a sudden decrease in state anxiety during the post-exercise recovery period. Recent research has shown that lower exercise intensities are not associated with a significant decrease in state anxiety, and this recent work supports the concept that a threshold must be reached in order for tension reduction to occur (Farrell, Gustafson, Garthwaite, Kalkhoff, Cowley, & Morgan, 1987).

The characteristic increase in state anxiety following intense exercise can be modified. It is known that perception of threat governs the extent to which a given stressor will be perceived as stressful. In an effort to evaluate the extent to which perception of threat influences state anxiety, an experiment was conducted in which 18 adult males were randomly assigned to either a control, placebo, or meditation group. All of the subjects exercised at 80% of MAP to a point of

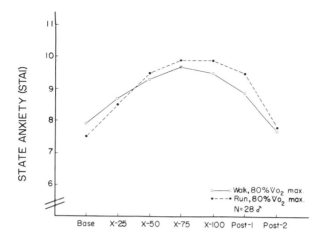

Figure 2 State anxiety before, during, and following vigorous exercise performed in the walking and running modes.

self-imposed exhaustion. The subjects in the control group performed exercise in the same manner as subjects in the previous experiment (Figure 2). The subjects in the placebo group received a lactose capsule, and they were told that the substance contained in the capsule would prevent the fatigue and discomfort experienced when performing the exercise during a previous trial. The third group received similar suggestions, but they were taught a simple form of meditation in place of the placebo. The subjects in the three groups completed the 4-item state anxiety scale before, at the conclusion, and following exercise. The results are summarized in Figure 3.

The control group experienced a significant increase in state anxiety with exercise, and this was followed by a sudden decrease in state anxiety during recovery. This is a typical or customary response, and one that is consistently observed with exercise intensity in this range (i.e., 80% MAP). Both the placebo and meditation treatments were observed to be effective in that state anxiety did not increase in either case. Thwarting of the anxiety response may not be desirable from a health standpoint, and it is likely that paying attention (i.e., associating) to increases in state anxiety probably plays a protective role. At any rate, the results reinforce the view that stress is a *process* consisting of a stressor, perception of threat, and state anxiety responses (Spielberger, 1987).

Causality and Comparative Efficacy

It has been estimated that a large proportion of patients examined by general practitioners and internists suffer from conditions that involve an inability to cope with various stressors. It has also been reported that 10 to 30 percent of the patients seen by physicians suffer from anxiety neurosis (Morgan & Goldston, 1987). It is also noteworthy that a recent survey of 1,750 primary care physicians revealed that 60% prescribed exercise for the treatment of anxiety (Ryan, 1983). An important question that has not been adequately addressed involves the issue of whether or not it is the exercise itself that is responsible for the observed

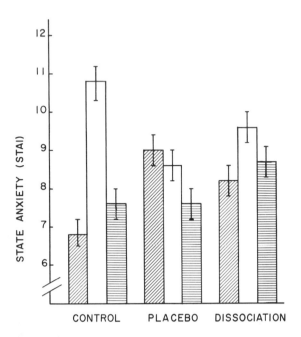

Figure 3 Influence of a placebo (lactose capsule) and
meditation on exercise-induced elevations in state anxiety.

tension reduction. The tacit assumption has been that tension reduction follows
exercise and, therefore, exercise reduces anxiety, but there is little evidence to
support such a view. If exercise were shown to actually reduce anxiety, its efficacy
in comparison with traditional therapies would also require attention.

It has been shown that simply sitting in a quiet room is just as effective as
transcendental mediation (TM) in reducing stress indices (e.g., epinephrine,
norepinephrine, lactate). Also, Hughes (1984) has reported that resting in a quiet
room is just as effective in reducing various stress indices as various forms of
meditation and muscular relaxation. In an effort to quantify the comparative
efficacy of exercise, Bahrke and Morgan (1978) randomly assigned 75 adult males
to an exercise, meditation, or control (placebo) condition. The subjects in the
exercise group walked on a motor-driven treadmill at 70% of MAP. The subjects
in the meditation group were taught a simple meditation strategy (Benson, 1975),
and the subjects in the control group rested quietly in a sound-filtered room. All
groups performed the various treatments for 20 minutes, and heart rate was
monitored throughout for all groups. Oxygen uptake and skin temperature was
also monitored in the non-exercise groups. All subjects completed the state
anxiety scale (STAI) before and following the various treatments, and the results
are summarized in Figure 4.

All three groups experienced significant decreases in state anxiety, but the
three groups did not differ. In other words, resting quietly in a sound filtered
room was just as effective in reducing anxiety as vigorous exercise or meditation.
While the exercise group had a significantly higher post-treatment heart rate than
did the meditation and control groups, the latter groups did not differ on heart

rate, oxygen uptake or skin temperature. These results led Bahrke & Morgan (1978) to hypothesize that "distraction" from the stressors in one's life, or "time out" from the cares and worries of the day represented the crucial anti-anxiety ingredient in these somewhat diverse treatments.

There is now additional research supporting the view that exercise is no more effective than resting in a sound controlled environment in its ability to reduce anxiety or blood pressure (Raglin & Morgan, 1985). It appears, however, that the anti-anxiety effect of exercise persists for a greater period of time than does the tension reduction observed following quiet rest (Raglin & Morgan, 1987). In other words, it appears that exercise and quiet rest differ *qualitatively* but not *quantitatively*.

Mechanisms

The proposal that the anxiolytic effects of exercise are produced by "distraction" or "time out" rather than the exercise *per se,* does not offer an explanatory mechanism to explain the action. It has been proposed by a number of authors that exercise-induced euphoria occurs as a result of changes in brain neurotransmitter levels (e.g., norepinephrine) and peptides (e.g., beta endorphin), but these mechanistic explanations are largely hypothetical (Morgan, 1985). The norepinephrine hypothesis is derived almost entirely from small animal research, and the beta endorphin hypothesis has recently been challenged. Farrell et al. (1987), for example, have shown that anxiety is reduced following exercise even if production of beta-endorphin is blocked by means of naltrexone, an opiate antagonist.

Summary

There is an extensive literature demonstrating that active, physically fit individuals experience a reduction in state anxiety following vigorous physical exercise. These effects occur in persons with high trait anxiety, as well as those who fall within the normal range, and these effects have been found to be

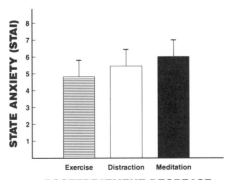

Figure 4 Decreases in state anxiety following exercise, meditation, and quiet rest in a sound filtered room.

independent of age and gender. It appears that the anxiolytic effects of exercise last for approximately 2–3 hours, whereas passive interventions such as meditation and quiet rest have less persistent effects. The mechanisms responsible for exercise-induced tension reduction have not been identified, and research involving the question of "why" anxiety is reduced after exercise needs to be undertaken.

TRAIT ANXIETY AND PANIC BEHAVIOR

There is both a sound theoretical rationale and empirical evidence supporting the view that individuals scoring high on trait anxiety, as measured by the STAI (Spielberger, 1972), are predisposed to have high state anxiety responses when exposed to various stressors. This prediction has been tested under conditions of vigorous exercise in both laboratory and field settings involving the use of self-contained breathing apparatus of the type worn by firefighters (e.g., SCBA) and commercial as well as recreational divers (SCUBA). It has been recognized for many years that certain individuals experience respiratory distress when exercising and wearing respirators (Morgan, 1983a), and it has been hypothesized that respiratory distress is governed in part by various psychological states and traits (Morgan, 1983b).

Respirator Research

It is recognized that heavy physical exercise often leads to hyperventilation, and this is regarded as a normal physiological response to heavy exercise. It is also known that the hyperventilation syndrome is characterized by selected psychological traits (Morgan, 1983c). Irrespective of the reasons why hyperventilation occurs, however, individuals with disturbed ventilatory patterns are placed at considerable risk if this occurs in concert with other stressors. This point is lucidly illustrated in a narrative provided by the auxiliary operator at Reactor Number 11 of Three Mile Island (TMI) following the highly publicized accident that took place at TMI.

> I had to get up to the second level to open my valve, but the elevator was broken. I should have walked, but I started running. I started hyperventilating. My instinct was to rip off my mask, but I knew the air was heavy with particulates. I said a prayer. I had to gather my wits. I saw I was sweating and breathing heavy. I made myself walk to the valve. I opened it. Then I walked toward the door. My air pack's two-minute warning bell was tingling. I burst through the door, kicking it open. I ripped the mask off and put on another. Usually we've got personnel to help us—but not that day.

There are many problems associated with the wearing of self-contained breathing apparatus (SCBA) of the type worn by the operator in the TMI incident, and these have been described by Morgan (1983a). The tanks are heavy and somewhat cumbersome, the mask creates facial pressure, vision is restricted, verbal communication is impaired, and there is added resistance to breathing which becomes more significant as the exercise intensity increases. These problems are created by the very support system which permits survival, and this person-respirator interface represents a classic person-machine problem. There have been reports of firefighters found after a fire in an unconscious state, or perhaps dead, and their mask is off. Subsequent testing demonstrates that the breathing valve is operational, and the tank may have an air supply. The operator at TMI described above mentions that his instinct was to rip his mask off, and it has been reported that some individuals have done this when stressed (Morgan, 1983a).

Hyperventilation is associated with various symptoms such as visual clouding and complete loss of vision; tingling sensations in the extremities; muscle spasms, tetany, and convulsions; rapid heart rate and palpitations; and in some cases unconsciousness (Morgan, 1983c). These symptoms stimulate sympatho-adreno-medullary functioning, elevations in state anxiety, and increased symptoms leading to additional endocrine activity and more anxiety. In the case of the TMI operator it is noteworthy that he considered removing his mask, realized the air was heavy with particulates, decided he had to "gather his wits," paid attention to his breathing, and did not remove his mask even though the egress bell rang which meant that his tank's air supply fell below two minutes. The *stress process* has been conceptualized by Spielberger (1972, 1987) as a complex psychobiologic process consisting of a stressor, perception of threat, and state anxiety response. The perception of threat is governed by various factors such as past experience, appraisal, cognitive strategies, and of course, trait anxiety.

In an effort to evaluate the extent to which trait anxiety influences respiratory distress in individuals wearing self-contained breathing apparatus (SCBA), a series of experiments were carried out by Morgan and Raven (1985) and Wilson, Morgan and Raven (1986). In this research 45 subjects completed the State-Trait Anxiety Inventory (STAI) (Spielberger, 1972) prior to exercising at light, moderate, and heavy loads on a treadmill while wearing a SCBA. The respirator was a full-face mask (ultravue) type, and it had an inspiratory resistance of 85mm H_2O at 85 liters/minute air flow, and the expiratory resistance was 25mm H_2O at 85 liters/minute air flow. This respirator was similar to the one used by the TMI operator described in the earlier narrative. The stressor, therefore, consisted of the combined effects of the SCBA and the progressively increasing work loads. Perception of respiratory distress was quantified by means of a 7-point psychophysical category scale (Morgan, et al., 1985), and the results are summarized in Figure 5. The ratings of breathing discomfort increased significantly in a linear manner with progressive increases in exercise intensity. Also, the perception of breathing discomfort was significantly higher under the SCBA condition at each work load.

The reason for terminating exercise was recorded by an investigator who was unaware of the subject's trait anxiety score. If a subject reported that he/she was not getting enough air, or could not breathe, and had a rating in the 5 to 7 range on the dyspnea scale, the individual was classified as having respiratory distress. If the primary reason for terminating exercise was general or leg fatigue, for example, the limiting factor was classified as non-respiratory.

Since the perception of threat following exposure to a stressor is governed in part by an individual's *trait* anxiety (Spielberger, 1987), it was hypothesized that individuals scoring one standard deviation above the sample mean on *trait* anxiety would experience respiratory distress. The investigator who employed trait anxiety scores for use in predicting respiratory distress had no involvement with the treadmill test. In other words, the investigators who made the classifications

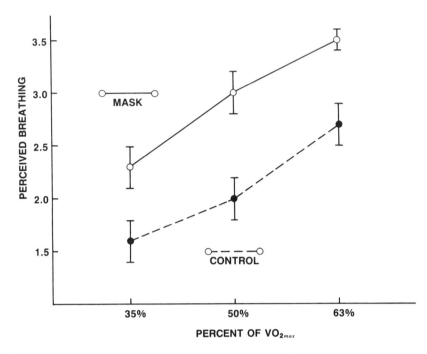

Figure 5   Perception of breathing during exercise performed at 35%, 50%, and 64% of
$\dot{V}O_2$ max under controlled conditions and while wearing a mask (SCBA).

and predictions were blinded to one another's data until the experiment was completed. They were separated in space by approximately 4,000 km, and the two data sets were exchanged in sealed envelopes at the conclusion of the investigation.

It was predicted that individuals with trait anxiety scores of 39 or higher would experience respiratory distress, and this cut-off point was chosen on the basis that a score of 39 fell one standard deviation above the sample mean. It was predicted that five subjects with trait anxiety scores ranging from 39 to 63 (mean = 57.2) would experience respiratory distress and 4 of the 5 did. In other words, there was one *false positive*. Furthermore, an individual scoring 27 also experienced respiratory distress, and this subject was the only *false negative*. In other words, 5 of the 6 subjects who experienced distress were identified a priori yielding a hit rate of 83%, and 38 of the 39 (97%) individuals who did not experience respiratory distress were correctly predicted. These results offer additional support for the efficacy of the STAI (Spielberger, 1972) in general, and *trait* anxiety in particular, in predicting the response to a given stressor. There has been a longstanding debate in the field of sport psychology concerning the utility of traits (Morgan, 1980) in predicting behavior in exercise and sport settings. The present findings offer additional support for the pro-trait argument. Indeed, two of the trait anxious subjects in these experiments ripped their masks off because they were "suffocating!" Trait anxiety clearly plays a significant mediating role in the stress process associated with respirator (SCBA) use.

SCUBA Research

The research involving industrial respirators (SCBA) has been extended to include the self-contained underwater breathing apparatus (SCUBA), and the initial pilot studies indicate that a remarkable similarity exists with respect to SCBA and SCUBA usage. First of all, it is noteworthy that approximately one half of the diving fatalities are not explainable on the basis of equipment, environmental, or medical factors. There has been a tendency for workers in this field to attribute these "unexplained" fatalities in SCUBA divers to psychological factors (Morgan, 1986). It is believed, for example, that divers sometimes experience panic, and these panic attacks lead to various types of diving accidents. The proceedings of an international workshop dealing with the unconscious diver reveals that respiratory control and various psychological factors have been implicated in diving accidents (Lanphier, 1982). Furthermore, the use of respirators, on land and underwater, are characterized by many of the same problems. The major difference is that most users of SCUBA are recreational sport divers, whereas most individuals who use SCBA do so as an occupational necessity. There, of course, are commercial and military divers, but the proportion is small when contrasted with the millions of recreational SCUBA divers worldwide.

Results of a national survey involving trained SCUBA divers has revealed that 54% experienced panic or near-panic behavior on one or more occasions while diving (Morgan, 1986). Therefore, it is reasonable to regard SCUBA diving as a high risk sport, and it is important to recognize that panic behavior was not restricted to beginning or novice divers in this study. In other words, perception of threat was mediated by factors other than diving experience. One explanation, of course, would be that panic behavior in divers would be governed in part by *trait* anxiety.

Recent research at the University of Wisconsin supports the view that *trait* anxiety is effective in predicting panic behavior. In this research, students have been evaluated with the STAI at the beginning of a semester, and the instructor has recorded incidents of panic behavior during the course (Morgan, Lanphier & Raglin, 1987). Classifications of panic behavior, and predictions of panic, have been carried out in a blind setting. The findings have been reasonably consistent across several semesters, and the results will be combined for discussion purposes.

The instructor classified 8 of 42 students as having panic or near-panic behavior on two or more occasions during the course of a given semester's instruction. Using a cut-off point of 39 or above on the *trait* scale of the STAI (Spielberger, 1972), it was predicted *a priori* that 5 of the 8 would experience panic attacks during the course of the semester. Thirty-two individuals did not experience panic behavior according to the instructor's ratings, and each of these individuals were correctly classified on the basis of *trait* anxiety which fell below the cut-off point. In other words, 88% (37 of 42) of the predictions were correct, and this finding demonstrates that individuals who possess elevated trait anxiety are more likely to experience panic behavior when confronted with various stressors inherent in SCUBA diving.

Summary

The research in this section indicates that it is possible to identify those individuals who are likely to experience respiratory distress and panic while exercising and wearing respirators on land (SCBA) or underwater (SCUBA). The overall accuracy has been observed to vary from 88% (SCUBA) to 93% (SCBA), and the predictions have been based solely on *trait* anxiety. This empirical evidence offers strong support for the conceptual model of stress and anxiety proposed by Spielberger (1966, 1987). The data also lend additional support to the view that selected psychological traits are effective in predicting behavior in exercise and sport settings (Morgan, 1980). In view of the observation that it is possible to identify individuals who are at risk from the standpoint of health and safety when exercising and wearing respirators, it appears that two intervention strategies might be adopted. First, individuals judged to be at risk could be counseled out of occupational and recreational activities requiring the use of respirators. Second, it might be possible to teach high-risk individuals how to cope with various stressors once they are encountered. This latter approach is already taken in most training programs, but the simulations are approached in a generic manner with little or no attention to important individual differences such as *trait* anxiety. Furthermore, training simulations are limited because of ethical constraints; that is, human test subjects cannot be exposed to "real" risk.

SUMMARY

The material reviewed in this chapter has been concerned with the interaction of anxiety, health, exercise and performance in sports. From a performance standpoint it is concluded that Hanin's theory of arousal and performance possesses the most compelling theoretical rationale, empirical basis, and potential for application. In terms of the interaction between vigorous exercise and state anxiety in non-sport settings, it is apparent that exercise of a moderate intensity is associated with consistent decreases in anxiety. The actual mechanism(s) responsible for this anxiolytic effect remain to be elucidated in future research and the once popular beta-endorphin hypothesis no longer seems viable. The pervasive effectiveness of Spielberger's conceptualization of stress as a complex psychobiologic process is demonstrated in the concluding section involving trait anxiety, exercise, and respirator wear. This research involving trait anxiety has implications for the millions of individuals worldwide who are engaged in recreational, industrial, and military activities involving vigorous exercise and respirator wear.

REFERENCES

Bahrke, M. S., & W. P. Morgan. (1978). Anxiety reduction following exercise and meditation. *Cognitive Therapy and Research, 2,* 323–333.

Benson, H. (1975). *The relaxation response.* New York: William Morrow and Company.

Dishman, R. K. (1987). Exercise adherence and habitual physical activity. In W. P. Morgan & S. E. Goldston (Eds.), *Exercise and Mental Health.* Washington, DC: Hemisphere.

Farrell, P. A., A. B. Gustafson, T. L. Garthwaite, R. K. Kalkhoff, A. W. Cowley, & W. P. Morgan. (1986). Influence of endogenous opioids on the response of selected hormones to exercise in humans. *Journal of Applied Physiology, 61,* 1051–1057.

Hammer, W. H. (1967). A comparison of differences in manifest anxiety in university athletes and nonathletes. *Journal of Sports Medicine and Physical Fitness, 7,* 31–34.

Hammer, W. H. (1968). Anxiety and sport performance. In G. S. Kenyon (Ed.), *Contemporary Psychology of Sport.* Chicago: Athletic Institute.

Hanin, Y. L. (1980). A study of anxiety in sports. In W. F. Straub (Ed.), *Sport Psychology: An Analysis of Athlete Behavior.* Ithaca, NY: Mouvement Publications.

Heide, F. J., & Borkovec, T. D. (1984). Relaxation-induced anxiety: Mechanisms and theoretical implications. *Behavior Research Therapy, 22,* 1–12.

Hull, C. L. (1943). *Principles of Behavior.* New York: Appleton-Century-Crofts.

Landers, D. M. (1980). The arousal-performance relationship revisited. *Research Quarterly, 51,* 77–90.

Lanphier, E. H. (Ed.) (1982). *The Unconscious Diver: Respiratory Control and Other Contributing Factors.* Bethesda, MD: Undersea Medical Society, Inc.

Mahoney, M. J., & M. Avener. (1977). Psychology of the elite athlete. *Cognitive Therapy and Research, 1,* 135–145.

Martens, R. (1970). Trait and state anxiety. In W. P. Morgan (Ed.), *Ergogenic Aids and Muscular Performance,* New York: Academic Press.

Martin & Dubbert. (1985). Adherence to exercise. In R. L. Terjung (Ed.), *Exercise and Sport Sciences Review,* New York: McMillan.

Morgan, W. P. (1970). Pre-match anxiety in a group of college students. *International Journal of Sport Psychology, 1,* 7–13.

Morgan, W. P. (1972). Sport psychology. In R. N. Singer (Ed.), *The Psychomotor Domain.* Philadelphia: Lea & Febiger.

Morgan, W. P. (1979). Anxiety reduction following acute physical activity. *Psychiatric Annals, 9,* 36–45.

Morgan, W. P. (1980). The trait psychology controversy. *Research Quarterly in Exercise and Sport, 51,* 50–76.

Morgan, W. P. (1983a). Psychological problems associated with the wearing of industrial respirators: A review. *American Industrial Hygiene Association Journal, 44,* 671–676.

Morgan, W. P. (1983b). Psychometric correlates of respiration: A review. *American Industrial Hygiene Association Journal, 44,* 677–684.

Morgan, W. P. (1983c). Hyperventilation syndrome: A review. *American Industrial Hygiene Association Journal, 44,* 685–689.

Morgan, W. P. (1984). Physical activity and mental health. In H. J. Montoye and H. M. Eckert (Eds.), *Exercise and Health.* Champaign, IL: Human Kinetics.

Morgan, W. P. (1985). Selected psychological factors limiting performance. A mental health model. In H. M. Eckert and D. H. Clarke (Eds.), *The Limits of Human Performance.* Champaign, IL: Human Kinetics.

Morgan, W. P. (1986). Psychological characteristics of the female diver. In W. P. Fife (Ed.), *Special Concerns of Women in Diving.* Bethesda, MD: Undersea Society, Inc.

Morgan, W. P., & P. Bradley. (1985). Psychological characteristics of the elite distance runner-1. Technical Report. Colorado Springs, CO: United States Olympic Training Center.

Morgan, W. P., & S. E. Goldston. (1987) (Eds.), *Exercise and Mental Health.* Washington, DC: Hemisphere.

Morgan, W. P., & W. H. Hammer. (1974). Influence of competitive wrestling upon state anxiety. *Medicine and Science in Sports, 8,* 58–61.

Morgan, W. P., D. H. Horstman, A. Cymerman, & J. Stokes. (1980). Exercise as a relaxation technique. *Primary Cardiology, 6,* 48–57.

Morgan, W. P., E. H. Lanphier, & J. S. Raglin. (1986). Psychologic characterization of scuba divers. Annual Report, Seagrant Institute, Madison, WI.

Morgan, W. P., & P. J. O'Connor. (1986). Psychological characteristics of the elite distance runner-2. Technical Report, United States Olympic Training Center, Colorado Springs, CO.

Morgan, W. P., P. J. O'Connor, P. B. Sparling, & R. R. Pate. (1987). Psychologic characterization of the elite female distance runner. *International Journal of Sports Medicine, 8,* 124–131.

Morgan, W. P., & P. Raven. (1985). Prediction of distress for individuals wearing industrial respirators. *American Industrial Hygiene Association Journal, 46,* 363–368.

Morgan, W. P., J. S. Raglin, & Y. Wang. (1986). Validation of a body awareness scale for use in pre-competition settings, (In preparation).

Raglin, J. S., & W. P. Morgan. (1985). Influence of vigorous exercise on mood state. *Behavior Therapy, 8,* 179–183.

Raglin, J. S., & W. P. Morgan. (1987). Influence of exercise and quiet rest on anxiety and blood pressure. *Medicine and Science in Sports and Exercise, 19,* 456–463.

Raglin, J. S., & W. P. Morgan (1988). Predicted and actual levels of pre-competition anxiety in swimmers. *Journal of Swimming Research, 4,* 5–7.

Ryan, A. J. (1983). Exercise in medicine. *The Physician and Sportsmedicine, 11,* 10.

Smith, J. C. (1975). Meditation as psychotherapy: A review of the literature. *Psychological Bulletin, 82,* 558–564.

Spielberger, C. D. (1966). *Anxiety and Behavior.* New York: Academic Press.

Spielberger, C. D. (Ed.) (1972). *Anxiety: Current Trends in Theory and Research* (Vol. 1), New York: Academic Press.

Spielberger, C. D. (1987). Stress, emotions, and health. In W. P. Morgan & S. E. Goldston (Eds.), *Exercise and Mental Health.* Washington, DC: Hemisphere.

Ward, A., & W. P. Morgan. (1984). Adherence patterns of healthy men and women enrolled in an adult exercise program. *Journal of Cardiac Rehabilitation, 4,* 143–152.

Wilson, J. W., W. P. Morgan, & P. B. Raven (1986). Psychophysiological screening for respirator wear. *Journal of the International Society of Respiratory Protection, 4,* 34–61.

Yerkes, R. M., & J. D. Dodson. (1980). The relation of strength of stimulus to rapidity of habit formation. *Journal of Comparative Neurological Psychology, 18,* 459–482.

12

Athletic Stress and Burnout: Conceptual Models and Intervention Strategies

Ronald E. Smith

The competitive athletic setting can be a highly demanding one from both a physical and a psychological perspective, and one which is therefore capable of eliciting high levels of stress in participants. From youth settings to the professional level, athletes must cope with the pressures of intense competition. For some athletes, athletic competition is a challenging and enjoyable activity, while others find the competitive setting to be a threatening and aversive situation.

High levels of athletic stress can have a wide range of negative consequences. Stress can undermine enjoyment and performance, and high levels of life stress can significantly increase the likelihood of injury (Cryan & Alles, 1983; Passer & Seese, 1983). It is therefore not surprising that sport has served as a valuable naturalistic setting for the study of antecedents and consequences of stress and for the development of intervention strategies designed to reduce its negative cognitive, affective, and behavioral effects.

In recent years, the term burnout has also begun to appear with increasing frequency in athletics. Coaches at all levels have begun to discuss the dangers of burnout in their profession. Elite athletes have dropped out of sports at the peak of their careers, maintaining that they are "burned out" and that participation has become too aversive for them to continue. Concern about the large number of athletes who drop out of sports during the adolescent years has been fueled by speculation that years of inappropriately intense competitive pressures during childhood may cause some youngsters to burn out and abandon sport participation (Martens, 1978; Orlick & Botterill, 1975). Burnout among athletic trainers and team physicians has also been addressed (Gieck, Brown, & Shank, 1982).

Burnout is typically viewed as a response to stress, and several investigators have noted the desirability of relating burnout to the theoretical and research literature on stress and coping (Jones, 1981; Shinn, Rosario, Morch, & Chestnut, 1984; Smith, 1986). The present discussion incorporates the phenomena of athletic stress and burnout within a common conceptual framework and describes a number of intervention strategies that are directed toward specific components of the theoretical model.

PARALLEL MODELS OF STRESS AND BURNOUT

Both stress and burnout result from interactions among situational factors, cognitive events, physiological responses, and coping behaviors. In discussing the relationship between stress and burnout, we shall see that there are important parallel interactions among these four sets of factors.

The term "stress" is typically used in two different but related ways. The first usage refers to situations that tax the physical and/or psychological capabilities of the individual. The focus here is on the balance between the demands of the situation and the personal and environmental resources available to the person. Situations are likely to be labeled as "stressors" when the demands test or exceed the resources of the person. The second use of the term relates to the individual's response to the situation. Used in this manner, stress refers to the cognitive, affective, and behavioral response pattern that occurs in response to situational demands. Clearly, these two uses of the term are not synonymous, since people may vary considerably in how "stressful" they find the same situation.

A conceptual model showing the dynamics of and relationships between stress and burnout is presented in Figure 1. The stress model shown in the upper portion encompasses relationships among situational factors, cognitive appraisal of various aspects of the transaction between the person and the situation, physiological responses, and behavioral responses. Each of these components is, in turn, influenced by motivational and personality variables.

The first component of the model, the situation, involves interactions between environmental demands and personal and environmental resources. Stress results from an imbalance between demands and resources. Demands can be external, as when an athlete confronts a strong opponent in an important contest, or they can have an internal origin in the form of desired goals, personal standards of behavior relating to values or commitments, or unconscious motives and conflicts. When demands are not met, costs in the form of anxiety, guilt, anger, and self-derogation may occur.

Typically, we think of stress as occurring in situations where demands exceed resources ("overload"). However, stress can also result when resources greatly exceed demands, or when the person is not challenged to use his or her resources. Feelings of stagnation and boredom are common responses to this state of affairs, and a condition of "underload" can also take its toll.

Although people often view their emotions as direct responses to situations, in most instances situations exert their effects through the intervening influence of thought (Lazarus, 1982; Smith & Ellsworth, 1985). Through their own thought processes, people create the psychological reality to which they respond. Cognitive appraisal processes play a central role in understanding stress because the nature and intensity of emotional responses are a function of at least four

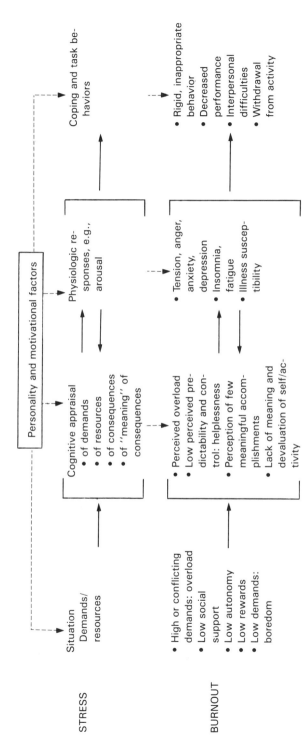

Figure 1 Conceptual model showing the parallel relationships assumed to exist among situational, cognitive, physiologic, and behavioral components of stress and burnout. Individual differences in motivation and personality are assumed to influence all of the components. (Smith, 1986)

different appraisal elements: appraisal of the demands; appraisal of the resources available to deal with them; appraisal of the nature and likelihood of potential consequences if the demands are not met; and the personal meaning of those consequences for the person. The meanings attached to the consequences derive from the person's belief system. Smith (1985) has discussed how excessive or inappropriate stress responses can result from errors in any of these appraisal elements. For example, an athlete with low self-confidence or self-efficacy may misappraise the balance between demands and resources so that failure seems imminent. Likewise, appraisal errors may occur in relation to the subjective likelihood and/or valence of the potential consequences, as when an athlete anticipates that the worst is *certain* to happen. Finally, personal belief systems and internalized standards influence the ultimate meaning of the situation for the athlete. For example, an athlete who believes that his or her self-worth depends on success will attach a different meaning to athletic outcomes than will an athlete who can divorce self-worth from success or failure. Many people appear to be victimized by irrational beliefs concerning the meaning and importance of success and social approval, and such beliefs predispose them to inappropriate stress reactions (Ellis, 1962; Rohsenow & Smith, 1982).

When appraisal indicates the threat of harm or danger, physiological arousal occurs as part of the mobilization of resources to deal with the situation. Arousal, in turn, provides feedback concerning the intensity of the emotion being experienced, thereby contributing to the process of appraisal and reappraisal (Lazarus, 1966; Schachter, 1966).

The fourth component of the model consists of the output behaviors that constitute the person's attempt to cope with the situation. These include task-oriented, social, and other classes of coping behaviors that are affected by the demands of the situation, cognitive appraisal processes, and whatever physiological responses occur.

Each of these four components can be affected by motivational and personality factors. Motivational and personality variables can be viewed as predispositions to seek out certain situations and goals and to perceive, think, and respond emotionally and behaviorally in certain ways. Personality probably has its strongest effects at the level of cognitive appraisal. Indeed, most of the personality variables that are the focus of psychological research (e.g., self-concept, locus of control, repression-sensitization) are basically cognitive appraisal styles.

Burnout is a reaction to chronic stress (Cherniss, 1980; Freudenberger, 1980). The burnout syndrome also has physical, mental, and behavioral components, and its development represents complex interactions between environmental and personal characteristics. Its most notable feature is a psychological, emotional, and at times a physical withdrawal from a formerly pursued and enjoyable activity. In contrast to withdrawal based on a change in interests, an incompatible preferred alternative, or a value reorientation, burnout results from an increase in stress-induced costs (Smith, 1986). The lower portion of Figure 1 presents the burnout syndrome within a parallel cognitive-affective framework. Within this framework, burnout represents the manifestations or consequences of the situational, cognitive, physiological, and behavioral components of stress.

At the situational level, a number of factors have been shown to contribute to burnout (Beehr & Newman, 1978; Berkeley Planning Associates, 1977; Pines &

Aronson, 1981; Shinn, et al., 1984). Though generally assessed in work environments, these factors can readily be extrapolated to the athletic environment as well. Studies of young athletes indicate that such factors as difficulties with coaches and interpersonal difficulties with peers (low social support), high competitive demands, time and energy demands, insufficient skills, and boredom can be sources of athletic stress (Gould, 1983; Gould, Feltz, Horn, & Weiss, 1982; Orlick & Botterill, 1975). In young adults, regimentation and lack of personal autonomy can be a major reason for dropping out of sports (Jones & Williamson, 1979; Meggyssey, 1970). Similarly, lack of autonomy created by autocratic coaches and low solidarity and social support are among the factors that have been associated with dropout in high school athletes (Robinson & Carron, 1982). All of these factors are capable of increasing the demands and costs of athletic participation for athletes, and these factors may also relate in a direct manner to the stresses experienced by other members of the athletic community, such as coaches, administrators, and trainers. On the other hand, low levels of success and accomplishment can reduce the reward value of participation (Gould et al., 1982).

Imbalance between demands and resources over a long period of time can give rise to a number of cognitions that have been identified in burnout victims. Cognitive appraisal of demands, resources, and consequences results in perceived overload. In most cases of burnout, the person feels overmatched against the demands of the situation, although boredom experienced when resources greatly exceed demands can also be involved. There is often a perception of low accomplishment (Maslach & Jackson, 1981; Caccese & Mayerberg, 1984) which, if extended over a sufficient period of time, results in low perceived control over the situation. A state of learned helplessness can result which undermines still further the person's motivation and ability to cope (Seligman, 1975). Perhaps the most pernicious aspect of learned helplessness is a loss in ability to discriminate between those aspects of the situation that are under control and those that are not. Eventually, the person may conclude that nothing can be changed. A final cognitive characteristic of burnout is a loss of meaningfulness concerning what one is doing and a subsequent devaluation of the activity (Freudenberger, 1980; Pines & Aronson, 1981). We would expect burned out athletes, coaches, trainers, and administrators to begin to question the value and significance of their efforts and to begin to perceive their situation as an aversive treadmill.

At the physiological level, chronic stress produces tension, fatigue, and irritability. Victims of burnout begin to feel emotionally depleted and have difficulty experiencing positive emotions. Sleep-related disorders, increased susceptibility to physical illness, and lethargy tend to occur (Freudenberger, 1980). As in the case of stress, the model assumes a reciprocal relationship between the cognitive and physiological components. That is, the physiological responses are largely elicited by the kinds of appraisals the person makes, but these bodily responses are also part of a feedback loop that affects appraisal and reappraisal. Thus, bodily sensations of arousal, fatigue, or illness serve to prompt and reinforce appraisals of overload, helplessness, and so on. At the physical and emotional levels, the term burnout aptly captures the subjective experience of those who suffer from it; it conveys the image of energy dampened, the fire of enthusiasm extinguished.

The behavioral consequences of burnout involve a decreased level of efficiency and a psychological if not physical withdrawal from the activity. A commonly noted response to stress is rigidity in behavior. The person appears to get into a behavioral rut that does not permit the degree of flexibility needed for effective coping, task performance, or interpersonal functioning. As a result of this rigidity, the person's behavior may become inappropriate and may be the source of interpersonal difficulties as well as lowered task efficiency. Another possible response to excessive stress is behavioral disorganization. Whether rigidity or disorganization occurs, the result frequently is alienation of others and a further reduction in the amount of social support available to the person. The erosion of social support serves to remove important buffers against the stressful demands of the situation and to decrease an important environmental resource.

As in the case of stress, certain individual difference variables increase the risk of burnout by influencing the balance between rewards and costs. To this point, researchers have been more concerned with situational factors than with individual difference variables predictive of increased burnout potential (Perlman & Hartman, 1982). On theoretical grounds, such factors as low frustration tolerance, an external locus of control, unrealistic performance standards, poor social and problem-solving skills, fear of failure and/or disapproval, high trait anxiety, the Type A behavior pattern, and depressive tendencies have been suggested as potential moderator variables (Smith, 1986).

Conceptualizing stress and burnout within a common framework has the advantage of clarifying the parallel processes that seem to comprise these related phenomena. Moreover, it is possible to relate the theoretical and empirical literature on stress and coping to burnout and, indeed, to view burnout as a particular type of stress response. In a practical vein, this also implies that principles of prevention and amelioration that have been applied in the area of stress might have applicability to burnout as well. With this in mind, we now consider intervention strategies.

INTERVENTION STRATEGIES

The parallel models of stress and burnout discussed above suggest a variety of intervention strategies. In a general sense, any of the model's components may be a target for intervention. Since stress and burnout involve transactions between the person and the situation, intervention may be directed at the situational, cognitive, physiological, or behavioral components, as well as at the broader level of the personality and motivational variables that are assumed to influence the four basic components. It is important to recognize, however, that the model is a reciprocally interactive and recursive one, so that measures taken to modify any one of the components will almost certainly affect other components as well.

The broadest level at which intervention might be directed is that of personality (including motivation). Severe personality disorders are likely to create vulnerability to stress in athletic situations as well as in many others. While some athletes have sufficiently severe personal problems to warrant professional treatment, other less expensive and time-consuming approaches are sufficient to alleviate the vast majority of athletic stress problems encountered by the sport psychologist. Moreover, focussed intervention strategies, particularly those that affect cognitive processes, can have a generalized effect on more global personality processes.

At the situational level, changes in certain features of the athletic environment can dramatically alter its capacity to generate stress. These may involve the reduction of demands, the increasing of resources, or both. For example, environmental demands can be reduced by matching competitors on such variables as size, physical maturation, and ability. Likewise, programs may be designed to differ in degree of competitive intensity, allowing participants to choose the program most attractive to them. Another approach to change at the situational level involves modification of the sport itself. For example, the height of the basketball goal can be lowered for elementary school children, or a smaller ball can be used (Henry, 1979). This decreases performance demands on young children and increases their chances for success and enjoyment.

Among the most important of environmental resources is the availability of social support. Substantial empirical evidence indicates that social support acts as an important buffer against stressors, and that low social support or a loss of support constitutes a significant stressor in its own right (Heller & Swindle, 1983; Sarason & Sarason, 1985). Parents, coaches, and teammates are important potential sources of social support for athletes, and intervention programs which increase the amount and/or quality of support can help tip the balance of the demands/resources scale in a positive direction. These may take the form of training programs or resource materials that give parents and coaches behavioral guidelines for creating a more positive environment for young athletes (e.g., Smith, Smoll, & Curtis, 1979; Smith, Smoll, & N. Smith, 1988). Team-building programs can increase team cohesion and the amount of social support available from teammates (Nideffer, 1981).

Environmental changes can also be produced by changes occurring within the behavioral component of the model. Clearly, behavior is influenced by the environment, but the environment is also influenced and sometimes transformed by behavioral changes. For example, acquisition of various types of skills by the athlete can increase personal resources and reduce demands. Training which increases sport skills can make athletic demands easier to cope with, and increased social skills can help athletes develop a more positive social environment and increase the quality of social support received from coaches and teammates.

Stress can also be reduced at the level of physiological arousal. Arousal-control skills such as muscle relaxation and meditation can be highly effective in preventing excessive arousal from interfering with performance.

Finally, intervention strategies can be directed at modifying the cognitive behaviors of athletes. This is in many ways the key component in the model, since most of the interventions directed at other model components ultimately are mediated by and/or exert their effects on the appraisal processes. Even if the situation cannot be changed, athletes can be trained to discover, challenge, and change the appraisal elements that are, in actuality, generating their stress responses. As noted previously, these cognitions are frequently based on implicit irrational beliefs relating to the "horribleness" of failure or the disapproval of others (Smith, 1980). Worrying and dwelling upon the seemingly catastrophic consequences of failure dominates the thought patterns of many high-stress athletes. Such cognitions also interfere with deployment of attention to the task at hand and with productive planning, thus resulting in lowered performance. From the perspective of the cognitive-affective model, the "mentally tough" athlete is one who is able to keep arousal within a range that optimizes performance and who is able to direct attentional and other cognitive processes to successful completion of the task at hand under adverse environmental conditions.

The model of burnout presented in Figure 1 suggests foci for intervention that parallel those discussed in relation to stress. Assuming that the situational factors listed in Figure 1 are found to contribute to athletic burnout, a variety of approaches that affect the balance between demands and resources might be indicated. On the demand side, some degree of stress is endemic to the sport setting. But additional and unnecessary sources of stress can be created by coaches, parents, and peers. Programs directed at modifying problematic coaching and parent behaviors and at helping coaches to structure practices and game experiences in ways that are more rewarding to athletes could be effective. Training methods that result in feelings of accomplishment and the prevention of tedium and boredom should help to enhance the reward/cost equation.

On the resource side, both individual and situational resources can be enhanced. The learning of athletic, social, and problem-solving skills can positively alter the demands/resources balance. At the situational level, the availability of social support has been shown to be an important buffer against burnout (Shinn et al., 1984).Programs designed to increase social support, such as coach training, team building, and social skills and communication training, team building, and social skills and communication training, could have significant promise in reducing athletic burnout.

Research has generally suggested that individual coping strategies are either unrelated or positively related to burnout (Pearlin & Schooler, 1978; Pines & Aronson, 1981; Shinn et al., 1984). This may be due to the fact that many of the strategies examined in these studies were attempts to cope with stress and burnout through avoidance of feelings and the work situation. The present model of burnout would predict that coping skills directed at modifying cognitions that produce maladaptive emotional responses and at controlling somatic arousal could help to reduce burnout. Such skills could also help to counteract the learned helplessness that seems to be a core factor in the burnout syndrome. Rosenbaum and Ben-Ari (1985) have found that subjects who report having self-control skills are more resistant to experimental conditions designed to produce learned helplessness.

To illustrate how intervention programs may be directed at either the situational level or at increasing personal resources, two different programs will be described. The first is designed to increase social support and decrease stress by training coaches to relate more effectively to their athletes. The second program is designed to increase stress coping skills in athletes.

Coach Effectiveness Training: A Situational Approach

It goes without saying that coaches occupy a central and critical role in the athletic setting. The nature of the relationship between athlete and coach is widely acknowledged as a primary determinant of the ways in which children are ultimately affected by their participation in organized athletic programs, and this influence extends to all levels of athletic competition. The manner in which coaches structure the athletic situation, the goal priorities they establish explicitly and implicitly, and the ways in which they relate to their players can markedly influence how athletes appraise the situation and the amount of stress they experience.

The interpersonal climate that coaches create can vary considerably in the amount of social support that is available to serve as a potential buffer against the stresses of athletic competition. It follows, then, that one possible intervention approach is to assist coaches in creating a less stressful and more supportive team atmosphere.

The vast majority of athletes have their first athletic experiences in youth sport programs staffed by volunteer coaches. While many of these coaches are fairly well versed in the technical aspects of the sport, they rarely have had any formal training in creating a positive psychological environment for their players. Moreover, through the mass media, these coaches are frequently exposed to college or professional coaches who model aggressive behaviors and a "winning is everything" philosophy that is highly inappropriate to a recreational and skill development context. The vast majority of youth coaches are committed to providing a positive experience for their players, however, and our experience has shown that coaches are responsive to attempts to provide them with information and behavioral guidelines. One such program, known as Coach Effectiveness Training, was developed for Little League Baseball.

Regardless of its nature, an intervention program is most likely to be successful if it has an empirical foundation. Accordingly, our project was carried out in two phases. In the first phase, research was done to establish empirical relationships between specific coaching behaviors and players' attitudes toward their coach, their teammates, the sport, and themselves. This research was guided by an information-processing model of coach-player relationships in which the impact of coaching behaviors is affected by the player's perceptions, evaluations, and recall of the behaviors. Thus, if we wish to understand how coaching behaviors affect players' reactions, we need to take into account the mediating processes that occur in the player. From a methodological perspective, we need to measure the actual coaching behaviors, the players' perception and recall of these behaviors, and the resulting evaluative reactions of the players.

To measure coaching behaviors, a behavioral assessment system was devised to permit the direct observation and recording of overt behaviors during practices and games. Using a 12-category coding system (the categories being reinforcement, nonreinforcement, mistake-contingent encouragement, mistake-contingent technical instruction, punishment, punitive technical instruction, ignoring mistakes, maintaining discipline, general encouragement, general technical instruction, organizational behaviors, and game-irrelevant communication), trained observers coded the naturalistic behaviors of 51 Little League Baseball coaches. These coaches were observed during a total of 202 complete games, resulting in the coding of more than 57,000 discrete behaviors. A behavioral profile was generated for each coach based on a mean of 1,122 behaviors.

At the conclusions of the season, 542 players ranging in age from 8 to 15 were interviewed in their homes to obtain measures of their perception and recall of their coach's behavior and their personal reaction to the coach, teammates, and other aspects of their sport experience. Empirical relationships between observed coaching behaviors, players' perception and recall of such behaviors, and player attitudes (Smith, Smoll, & Curtis, 1978) formed the basis for a series of behavioral guidelines for coaches.

The guidelines are based primarily on (a) a conception of success or "winning" based on giving maximum effort, and (b) coaching techniques based on principles of positive control rather than aversive control. An important goal of the guidelines is to increase the level of social support within the team and to increase the desire of athletes to learn and to give maximum effort while reducing fear of failure. The importance of reinforcement, encouragement, and sound technical instruction is emphasized, while aversive control procedures based on punishment and criticism are discouraged because they help foster fear of failure. If coaches demand of their athletes only that they give maximum effort, and if they reinforce effort rather than focusing only on outcome, players can learn to set similar standards for themselves. Players have complete control over effort and only incomplete control over outcome, and it is well established that lack of perceived control is an important aspect of stress responses (e.g., Folkman, 1984). As far as winning is concerned, it is emphasized that if athletes are well-trained, give maximum effort, and have positive achievement motivation rather than performance-disrupting fear of failure, winning will take care of itself within the limits of their ability. Moreover, athletes are more likely to develop their athletic potential and less likely to burn out in a supportive and enjoyable sport environment than in a stressful and nonsupportive one.

In the second phase of our project, we developed, implemented, and evaluated the coach training program. Thirty-one Little League Baseball coaches were randomly assigned to an experimental (training) group or to a no-treatment control group. The two groups were matched as closely as possible on the behavioral and player attitude measures obtained the preceding year. The experimental group was given a preseason training program of approximately three hours duration. The behavioral guidelines were presented both verbally and in written materials given to the coaches. The didactic presentation was supplemented by a modeling component in which the trainers demonstrated how to apply the principles effectively. In addition, coaches were given copies of their behavioral profiles, and specific self-monitoring procedures were introduced to increase their self-awareness of their behavior patterns, since the data from the first phase of the project indicated a striking lack of self-awareness on the part of most coaches.

The effects of the Coach Effectiveness Training program were assessed by essentially repeating the Phase 1 procedures. Coaches in both groups were observed four times during the course of the season by trained observers who were blind to the experimental procedure, and behavioral profiles were again generated for each coach. At the end of the season, 325 players who had played for the coaches were interviewed to obtain player measures.

The results of the program evaluation were very encouraging. On both behavioral and player perception measures, the trained coaches differed from the controls in a manner consistent with the behavioral guidelines. They gave more reinforcement in response to good effort and performance and responded to mistakes with more encouragement and technical instruction and with fewer punitive responses. These behavioral differences were reflected in their players' attitudes as well, despite the fact that the average won-lost percentages of the two groups of coaches did not differ. Trained coaches were better liked and rated as better teachers, and players on their teams liked one another more and enjoyed their sport experience more. These results seemingly reflect the more socially supportive environment created by the trained coaches. Moreover, children who played for the trained coaches exhibited a significant increase in self-esteem as compared with scores obtained a year earlier, while those who played for the untrained coaches showed no significant change. Finally, children who were low in self-esteem exhibited the strongest differences in evaluative responses toward the trained as opposed to the untrained coaches. This was also encouraging, because it is the low esteem player who is most in need of a positive athletic experience. Such children seem to respond very positively to supportive coaches, and they exhibit an increase in their feelings of self-worth (Smith, Smoll, & Curtis, 1979).

It thus appears that coaches can be trained in a cost-effective manner to relate more effectively to athletes and to create a more supportive athletic environment. Adaptations of the original program have been offered to coaches at all competitive levels, including professional sports. As of early 1986, more than 5,000 coaches and managers had taken part in the training program. A companion sport orientation program for parents based on the same general principles has also been developed. Both programs are situational interventions designed to reduce stress and increase social support from significant others in the athletic environment.

Increasing Coping Skills: Cognitive-Affective Stress Management Training

A second approach to reducing stress is directed at the athlete. Coping with stress is a complex process, and a variety of coping skills may prove effective in preventing or reducing stress responses. There are likely to be both individual and situational determinants of how effective a given coping skill will be. It therefore follows that a training program should teach a variety of coping skills. It should also provide the opportunity not only for skill acquisition, but also for rehearsal of the coping skills. One such program is cognitive-affective stress management training (Smith, 1980; Smith & Ascough, 1985). This program has been successfully applied to a variety of populations, including test anxious college students (Smith & Nye, in press), problem drinkers (Rohsenow, Smith, & Johnson, 1985), medical students (Holtzworth-Munroe, Munroe, & Smith, 1985), and athletes (Crocker, Alderman, & Smith, in press; Smith, 1984; Ziegler, Klinzing, & Williamson, 1982).

Although it differs in important respects from other coping skills programs, such as stress inoculation training (Meichenbaum, 1977) and anxiety management training (Suinn & Richardson, 1971), the cognitive-affective program also represents an attempt to combine a number of effective clinical techniques into an educational program for self-regulation of emotional responses. These include cognitive restructuring, self-instructional training, somatic and cognitive relaxation skills for arousal control, and the induced affect technique for skill rehearsal under affective arousal. Athletes have proven to be an ideal target population for the program because they are able to acquire a number of the coping skills (e.g., muscle relaxation) somewhat more quickly than other populations. Moreover, they are typically exposed to the stressful athletic situations frequently enough to permit careful monitoring of their progress, and behavioral performance measures of unquestioned ecological validity are readily available for assessment and research purposes.

The training package can be administered in either an individual or group format, and a trainer's manual is available (Smith & Rohsenow, 1986). For descriptive purposes, the program as administered on an individual basis may be divided into five partially overlapping phases: (a) pretraining assessment, (b) training rationale, (c) skill acquisition, (d) skill rehearsal, and (e) posttraining evaluation. When administered on a group basis, the preliminary assessment phase is less extensive unless research data are being collected.

Pretraining Assessment

When the program is administered to individual athletes, several sessions may be devoted to assessing the nature of their stress responses, the circumstances under which they occur, the manner in which performance is affected, and the coping responses that are currently being used. This phase is also directed at assessing the athlete's cognitive and behavioral strengths and deficits so that the program can be tailored to the individual's specific needs. For example, the focus of training for an athlete who already has fairly good relaxation skills but has little control over self-defeating thought processes will tend to be focused on developing cognitive skills. On the other hand, a primary focus on the development of relaxation and self-instructional skills may be the preferred approach for a chronically tense child athlete.

A variety of assessment techniques can be employed during this phase, including careful interviewing, administration of questionnaires and rating scales, and self-monitoring by the athlete. For example, we frequently employ a 100-point "tension thermometer" which can be completed in seconds and obtain "readings" from the athlete at various times before and during competition. Athletes can also be asked to monitor the frequency with which certain kinds of thoughts occur before, during, and after competition. Measures like the Irrational Beliefs Test (Jones, 1968) can also be useful in targeting specific self-defeating ideas for cognitive restructuring.

Training Rationale

In any behavior change program, initial conceptualization of the problem is of crucial importance in obtaining compliance and commitment to the program. The conceptualization should be shared by the athlete and the trainer, it should be understandable and plausible, and if should have clear intervention implications.

We have found it fairly easy to ensure that subjects arrive at our basic conceptual model of stress (or burnout) simply by asking them to describe a recent stressful incident. This description should contain situational, cognitive, physiological, and behavioral components, and these can usually be elicited by followup questions if they are not mentioned spontaneously (e.g., "What kinds of thoughts went through your mind?"). Labeling these elements and the relationships among them provides an entree to the conceptual model and its intervention components. An overview of the training program is then presented in relation to the athletes' specific needs. This procedure provides a credible rationale and conceptual framework for the subject.

Two important points are emphasized during the conceptualization phase and throughout training. One is that the program is not psychotherapy, but an educational program in self-control of emotion. We emphasize that the components of "mental toughness" (a quality highly valued by athletes) are specific skills that can be learned in the same way that other sport skills are learned. The second point emphasized is that the results of the program will be a function of how much commitment the athlete shows to acquiring the skills. Our goal here is to place the locus of responsibility on the athlete so that positive changes are attributed to the athlete rather than to the trainer. This should enhance both self-efficacy and the durability of change, and it is consistent with the *self*-regulation orientation of the program.

Skill Acquisition

The end-product of the cognitive-affective program is the development of an "integrated coping response" having somatic and cognitive components. The skill acquisition phase thus consists of the learning of cognitive and somatic relaxation skills and the development of cognitive coping responses through cognitive restructuring and/or self-instructional training.

The acquisition of relaxation skills is faster and easier for most subject than are the cognitive modification procedures. For this reason, we begin with training in somatic and cognitive relaxation skills. Relaxation skills are useful in controlling the physiological arousal component of the stress response so that the athlete can prevent an increase in arousal beyond the optimal arousal level for performance of the task at hand.

Somatic relaxation training is carried out using an abbreviated version of Jacobson's (1938) progressive muscle relaxation technique. Although some of the training is done by the trainer, most of it is accomplished through daily practice by the athlete in the form of homework assignments. As training proceeds, increasingly larger body units are combined until the entire body is being relaxed as a unit. Special emphasis is placed on the use of deep breathing to facilitate relaxation. The mental command, "Relax," is repeatedly paired with the exhalation phase of the breathing cycle and with voluntary relaxation so that in time, the command becomes an eliciting cue for inducing relaxation (Lazarus, 1972) and, eventually, part of the integrated coping response. The somatic relaxation skill provides a coping response that can quickly be utilized within stressful situations without interfering with ongoing task-oriented behavior.

Cognitive relaxation is learned by means of Benson's (1976) meditation technique. Meditation cannot readily be used as a coping skill in stressful situations, as somatic relaxation can, but it can be extremely useful as a means of dealing with pre-event anxiety, conserving energy, and combatting worry and other dysfunctional thought processes. Many athletes who have sleep problems find this a helpful technique in conjunction with somatic relaxation.

Training in cognitive coping skills begins with a didactic description of the manner in which emotional responses are elicited by ideas, images, and self-statements. Because such thought patterns are well-practiced and automatized, subjects often have limited awareness of the appraisal elements that underlie their dysfunctional emotional responses. To facilitate identification of stress-inducing cognitions and development of adaptive self-statements, subjects are given written materials to read as well as daily homework forms on which they list a situation that they found upsetting, the emotion they experienced, what they must have told themselves about the situation in order to have upset themselves, and what they might have told themselves instead that would have prevented or minimized their upset. This cognitive restructuring procedure is designed to help subjects to identify, rationally evaluate, and replace any dysfunctional and irrational ideas that underlie their maladaptive emotional responses.

The most common sources of maladaptive stress in athletes are fears of failure and fears of disapproval. For many of them, athletic success has been their major source of recognition and self-esteem, so that feelings of self-worth are closely linked to the adequacy with which they perform. Successful cognitive restructuring of these fears usually involves separating self-worth from successful outcome and focusing on maximum effort (e.g., "All I can do is give 100%. No one can do more."). Written materials on identifying and challenging irrational beliefs, discussions with the trainer, and the homework assignments form the basis for an "anti-stress log" on which subjects list their irrational self-statements and an "anti-stress" substitute for each. The latter form the basis for later practice and rehearsal.

In self-instructional training, the focus is on helping athletes develop and use specific task-relevant self-commands that direct attention and enhance performance of the task at hand. Examples of such commands are: "Don't get shook up. Just think about what you have to do." "Take a deep breath and relax." "Pay complete attention to what you need to focus on. Block everything else out." Athletes who are not psychologically-minded enough to profit from extensive cognitive restructuring can profit a great deal from self-instructional training alone. In most cases, however, both cognitive restructuring and self-instructional training are employed. In this respect, the cognitive-effective program differs from Suinn and Richardson's (1971) anxiety management training, which does not involve these cognitive interventions. Meichenbaum's (1977) stress inoculation training, on the other hand, shares the cognitive-somatic training emphasis, but emphasizes self-instructional training.

Skill Rehearsal

Stress coping skills are no different than any other kind of skill. In order to be most effective, they must be rehearsed and practiced under conditions that approximate the real-life situations in which they will eventually be employed. In the cognitive-affective program, a variant of a psychotherapeutic procedure known as induced affect (Sipprelle, 1967; Smith & Ascough, 1985) is used to generate high levels of emotional arousal which are then controlled by the subject by employing the coping skills learned in the preceding phase of the program. Induced affect is designed to allow rehearsal of coping responses in the presence of two kinds of cues: (a) imaginal representations of external cues which tend to elicit stress, and (b) internal cues resulting from emotional arousal. While the external cues are fairly specific to certain situations, the internal cues are probably common to differing emotional responses which may occur across a variety of situations. Practice in dealing with the latter class of cues should help to maximize the generalization of the coping skills across a wide variety of stressful situations (Goldfried, 1971; Suinn & Richardson, 1971). The theoretical and research literature pertaining to the induced affect technique is summarized in Smith and Ascough (1985).

The induced affect technique is not employed until the trainer is certain that the athlete has learned the coping skills well enough to ensure success in controlling the level of arousal that is generated. During initial use of the technique, arousal is kept at a moderate level and is increased as the athlete demonstrates control. During skill rehearsal, the athlete is asked to imagine as vividly as possible a stressful situation (for example, getting ready to shoot a free throw in a critical situation). He is then asked to turn his attention down inside and focus on the feeling that the situation elicits, and it is suggested that as he focuses on it, the feeling will begin to grow and to become stronger and stronger. The suggestions continue as the subject begins to respond with increased emotional arousal, and indications of arousal are verbally reinforced and encouraged by the trainer. At intervals during the induce affect, the trainer asks the subject what kinds of thoughts are occurring, and this information is used to elaborate upon the arousal. It also provides information (often previously unreported by the subject) concerning the cognitions that accompany (and, it is hypothesized, mediate) the arousal.

When the appropriate level of arousal is obtained, the subject is instructed to "turn it off" with his coping responses. Initially, relaxation alone is used as the active coping skill. Later, self-statements from the subject's "anti-stress log" are used to reduce arousal. Finally, the cognitive and somatic coping responses are combined into the "integrated coping response," which ties both the self-statements and the relaxation response into the natural breathing cycle (see Figure 2). As the subject inhales, he emits a stress-reducing or task-oriented self-statement. At the peak of inhalation, he says the words "So" or "And," and as he exhales, he gives the self-instruction, "Relax" while inducing muscular relaxation. (Recall that during relaxation training, exhalation, the mental command to relax, and voluntary relaxation were repeatedly associated with one another to facilitate cue-controlled relaxation.) The integrated coping response may be modified as appropriate and employed repeatedly in the stressful situation without disrupting ongoing behavior.

The theoretical basis for the use of induced affect as a rehearsal technique departs radically from that underlying Meichenbaum's stress inoculation approach; it is more consistent with the rationale for anxiety management training (Suinn & Richardson, 1971). As its name implies, Meichenbaum's procedure is on immunizing the individual to large stresses by "learning to cope with small, manageable units of stress" (1977, p. 149). In the cognitive-affective program, the emphasis is quite the opposite in that the subject practices using the coping skills to reduce levels of affective arousal that are as high as or higher than those elicited by *in vivo* stressors. The ability of athletes to control this high level of arousal with their coping skills results in significant increases in self-efficacy (Nye, 1979). The question of which approach is more efficacious awaits further research. Two comparative studies (Smith & Nye, in press; Ziegler et al., 1982) have found the techniques to be approximately equal in effectiveness, but both studies involved group administration of the programs, which typically result in appreciably lower levels of arousal during induced affect.

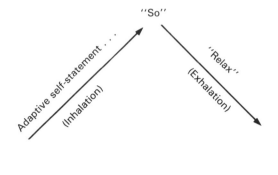

e.g., "It's not that big a thing . . . so . . . relax."

"I may not like this, but I can definitely stand it . . . so . . . relax."

"I need to concentrate, not to make myself uptight . . . so . . . relax."

"I'm in control . . . so . . . relax."

Figure 2 Schematic representation of the integrated coping response that is learned in the cognitive-affective stress management program. The coping self-statements used during the inhalation phase may be products of either cognitive restructuring or self-instructional training. (Smith, 1980)

Posttraining Evaluation

A variety of measures can be used to assess the effectiveness of the intervention. These include self-monitoring of emotional states and cognitive events by the athlete, performance measures that might be expected to improve with stress reduction, and standardized psychological test scores. All of these classes of measures have shown positive changes in the research studies of the cognitive-affective program cited above, and they can also be employed in a single-subject design when individual athletes are trained. Comprehensive evaluation of outcome with individual athletes can be extremely valuable not only for scientific purposes, but also in planning and supplementing the program with other psychological skill programs such as goal-setting and mental rehearsal.

Although the cognitive-affective program has yet to be applied in an empirical study of burnout intervention, the parallel model of burnout presented in Figure 1 suggests its potential utility in counteracting some of the dysfunctional cognitive and physiological events that are part of burnout. To the extent that maladaptive emotional responses such as anxiety, anger, and depression are involved, these can be readily approached from a coping skills perspective. However, the burnout literature cited earlier suggests that individually-oriented intervention programs are most likely to be successful if they are part of a more comprehensive intervention package which also involves situational interventions to reduce excessive demands and enhance social support.

CONCLUSION

Anxiety has been and will continue to be one of the major focal areas of research, theory development, and intervention. Sport is an unusually rich naturalistic laboratory for the study of a wide range of psychological phenomena, and it offers a multitude of opportunities for the researcher and clinician who is interested in anxiety. Intervention studies hold considerable promise not only for increasing the range of techniques available to enhance the enjoyment and performance of participants, but also for helping to elucidate the mechanisms that underlie anxiety reduction and the situational and individual difference variables that predict favorable outcomes.

SUMMARY

Parallel conceptual models of athletic stress and burnout were presented and implications for intervention strategies were discussed. Based on a person × situation interactional perspective, the cognitive-affective models specify interactions among situational factors, cognitive appraisal processes, physiological events, and behavioral responses, and they suggest a variety of intervention strategies that may be utilized to reduce stress and burnout. Two specific intervention programs were then described. The first is a situational intervention program designed to decrease stress and increase social support by training coaches to relate more effectively to athletes. The second program is a coping skills program directed at the individual which permits athletes to learn and to rehearse under affective arousal an integrated stress coping response having cognitive and somatic elements.

REFERENCES

Beehr, T. A., & Newman, J. E. (1978). Job stress, employee health, and organizational effectiveness: A facet analysis, model, and literature review. *Personnel Psychology, 31,* 665–699.

Berkeley Planning Associates. (1977). *Evaluation of child abuse and neglect demonstration projects 1974–1977: Vol 9. Project management and worker burnout: Final report.* Springfield, VA: National Technical Information Service. (NCHSR 78–72)

Benson, H. (1976). *The relaxation response.* New York: Avon.

Caccese, T. M., & Mayerberg, C. K. (1984). Gender differences in perceived burnout of college coaches. *Journal of Sport Psychology, 6,* 279–288.

Cherniss, C. (1980). *Staff burnout: Job stress in the human services.* Beverley Hills, CA: Sage.

Crocker, P. R. E., Alderman, R. B., & Smith, F. M. R. (in press). Cognitive-affective stress management training with high performance youth volleyball players: Effects on affect, cognition, and performance. *Journal of Sport and Exercise Psychology.*

Cryan, P. D., & Alles, W. F. (1983). The relationship between stress and college football injuries. *Journal of Sports Medicine, 23,* 52–58.

Ellis, A. (1962). *Reason and emotion in psychotherapy.* Secaucus, NJ: Lyle Stuart.

Folkman, S. (1984). Personal control and stress and coping processes: A theoretical analysis. *Journal of Personality and Social Psychology, 46,* 839–852.

Freudenberger, H. J. (1980). *Burnout.* New York: Doubleday.

Gieck, J., Brown, R. S., & Shank, R. H. (1982). The burnout syndrome among athletic trainers. *Athletic Training,* August, 36–41.

Goldfried, M. R. (1971). Systematic desensitization as training in self-control. *Journal of Consulting and Clinical Psychology, 37,* 228–234.

Gould, D. (1983). Future directions in youth sports participation research. In L. Wankel & R. Wilberg (Eds.), *Psychology of sport and motor behavior: Research and practice.* Edmonton: University of Alberta Faculty of Physical Education and Recreation.

Gould, D., Feltz, D., Horn, T., & Weiss, M. (1982). Reasons for attrition in competitive youth swimming. *Journal of Sport Behavior, 5,* 155–165.

Heller, K., & Swindle, R. W. (1983). Social networks, perceived social support, and coping with stress. In R. D. Felner, L. A. Jason, J. N. Moritsugu, & S. S. Farber (Eds.), *Preventive psychology: Theory, research, and practice.* Elmsford, NY: Pergamon.

Henry, G. M. (1979). Should the basket be lowered for young participants? *Journal of Physical Education and Recreation, 50,* 66–67.

Holtzworth-Munroe, A., Munroe, M. S., & Smith, R. E. (1985). Effects of a stress management training program on first- and second-year medical students. *Journal of Medical Education, 60,* 417–419.

Jacobson, E. (1938). *Progressive relaxation* (2nd ed.). Chicago: University of Chicago Press.

Jones, J. M., & Williamson, S. A. (1979). Athletic Profile Inventory: Assessment of athletes' attitudes and values. In J. H. Goldstein (Ed.), *Sports, games, and play: Social and psychological viewpoints* (pp. 157–188). Hillsdale, NJ: Erlbaum. ✦

Jones, J. W. (Ed.) (1981). *The burnout syndrome.* Park Ridge, IL: London House Management Press.

Jones, R. G. (1968). *A factored measure of Ellis' irrational belief system, with personality and maladjustment correlates.* Unpublished doctoral dissertation, Texas Technical College.

Lazarus, A. (1972). *Behavior therapy and beyond.* New York: McGraw-Hill.

Lazarus, R. S. (1966). *Psychological stress and the coping process.* New York: McGraw-Hill.

Lazarus, R. S. (1982). Thoughts on the relation between emotion and cognition. *American Psychologist, 37,*. 1019–1024.

Martens, R. (Ed.) (1978). *Joy and sadness in children's sports.* Champaign, IL: Human Kinetics.

Maslach, C., & Jackson, S. E. (1981). The measurement of experienced burnout. *Journal of Occupational Behavior, 2,* 99–113.

Meggyssey, D. (1970). *Out of their league.* Berkeley, CA: Ramparts Press.

Meichenbaum, D. (1977). *Cognitive-behavior modification.* New York: Plenum.

Nideffer, R. M. (1981). *The ethics and practice of applied sport psychology.* Ithaca, NY: Mouvement Press.

Orlick, T. D., & Botterill, C. (1975). *Every kid can win.* Chicago: Nelson-Hall.

Passer, M. W., & Seese, M. D. (1983). Life stress and athletic injury: Examination of positive versus negative events and three moderator variables. *Journal of Human Stress, 9,* 11–16.

Pearlin, L. I., & Schooler, C. (1978). The structure of coping. *Journal of Health and Social Behavior, 19,* 2–21.

Perlman, B., & Hartman, E. A. (1982). Burnout: Summary and future research. *Human Relations, 35,* 283–305.

Pines, A. M., & Aronson, E. (1981). *Burnout: From tedium to personal growth.* New York: Free Press.

Robinson, T. T., & Carron, A. V. (1982). Personal and situational factors associated with dropping out versus maintaining participation in competitive sport. *Journal of Sport Psychology, 4,* 364–372.

Rohsenow, D. J., & Smith, R. E. (1982). Irrational beliefs as predictors of negative affective states. *Motivation and Emotion, 6,* 299–314.

Rohsenow, D. J., Smith, R. E., & Johnson, S. (1985). Stress management training as a prevention program for heavy social drinkers: Cognitions, affect, drinking, and individual differences. *Addictive Behaviors, 10,* 45–54.

Rosenbaum, M., & Ben-Ari, K. (1985). Learned helplessness and learned resourcefulness: Effects of noncontingent success and failure on individuals differing in self-control skills. *Journal of Personality and Social Psychology, 48,* 198–215.

Sarason, I. G., & Sarason, B. R. (Eds.) (1985). *Social support: Theory, research, and application.* Boston: Nijhoff.

Schachter, S. (1966). The interaction of cognitive and physiological determinants of emotional state. In C. D. Spielberger (Ed.), *Anxiety and behavior* (pp. 193–224). New York: Academic Press.

Seligman, M. E. P. (1975). *Helplessness: On depression, development, and death.* San Francisco: Freeman.

Shinn, M., Rosario, M., Morch, H., & Chestnut, D. E. (1984). Coping with job stress and burnout in the human services. *Journal of Personality and Social Psychology, 46,* 864–876.

Sipprelle, C. N. (1967). Induced anxiety. *Psychotherapy: Theory, Research, and Practice, 4,* 36–40.

Smith, C. A., & Ellsworth, P. C. (1985). Patterns of cognitive appraisal in emotion. *Journal of Personality and Social Psychology, 48,* 813–838.

Smith, R. E. (1980). Development of an integrated coping response through cognitive-affective stress management training. In I. G. Sarason & C. D. Spielberger (Eds.), *Stress and anxiety* (Vol. 7). (pp. 265–280). Washington, DC: Hemisphere.

Smith, R.E., & Nye, S. L. (in press). A comparison of induced affect and covert rehearsed in the acquisition of stress management coping skills. *Journal of Counseling Psychology.*

Smith, R. E. (1984). Theoretical and treatment approaches to anxiety reduction. In J. M. Silva & R. S. Weinberg (Eds.), *Psychological foundations of sport* (pp. 157–170). Champaign, IL: Human Kinetics.

Smith, R. E. (1985). A component analysis of athletic stress. In M. Weiss & D. Gould (Eds.), *Competitive sports for children and youths: Proceedings of the Olympic Scientific Congress* (pp. 107–112). Champaign, IL: Human Kinetics.

Smith, R. E. (1986). Toward a cognitive-affective model of athletic burnout. *Journal of Sport Psychology, 8,* 00–00.

Smith, R. E., & Ascough, J. C. (1985). Induced affect in stress management training. In S. Burchfield (Ed.), *Stress: Psychological and physiological interactions. Washington, DC: Hemisphere.*

Smith, R. E., & Nye, S. L. (in press). A comparison of induced affect and covert rehearsal in the acquisition of stress management coping skills. *Journal of Counseling Psychology*

Smith, R. E., & Rohsenow, D. J. (1986). *Cognitive-affective stress management training: A training manual.* Delphi, IN: Center for Induced Affect.

Smith, R. E., Smoll, F. L., & Curtis, B. (1978). Coaching behaviors in Little League Baseball. In F. L.Smoll & R. E. Smith (Eds.), *Psychological Perspectives in Youth Sports* (pp. 174–201). Washington, DC: Hemisphere.

Smith, R. E., Smoll, F. L., & Curtis, B. (1979). Coach Effectiveness Training: A cognitive-behavioral approach to enhancing relationship skills in youth sport coaches. *Journal of Sport Psychology, 1,* 59–75.

Smith, R. E., Smoll, F. L., & Smith, N. J. (1988). *Parents complete guide to youth sports.* Reston, VA: American Alliance.

Suinn, R. M., & Richardson, F. (1971). Anxiety management training: A nonspecific behavior therapy program for anxiety control. *Behavior Therapy, 2,* 498–510.

Ziegler, S. G., Klinzing, J., & Williamson, K. (1982). The effects of two stress management training programs on cardiorespiratory efficiency. *Journal of Sport Psychology, 4,* 280–289.

13

Behavioral Intervention for Stress Management in Sports

Richard M. Suinn

The study of anxiety has represented an important part of clinical psychology, leading to scholarly efforts on assessment, on theoretical concepts, and on intervention strategies (Barlow & Wolfe, 1981; Kutash, Schlesinger, et al., 1980; Tuma & Maser, 1985). Behavioral approaches have demonstrated particular value in such efforts to measure, to understand, and to modify anxiety states (Barlow, 1981; Borkovec, Wilkinson, Folensbee, & Lerman, 1983; Deffenbacher & Suinn, in press; Suinn, 1982a, in press a; Turner, 1984; Williams & Spitzer, 1984). In a similar way, principles and techniques derived from behavioral psychology have been influential in sports applications (Suinn, 1979, 1985, in press b, c). This chapter will analyze sport performance from a behavioral perspective, discuss stress and anxiety, and present some examples of stress management interventions used with athletes.

ATHLETIC PERFORMANCE: BEHAVIORAL ANALYSIS

One way of conceptualizing athletic performance is to view performance as a complex set of responses—cognitive, emotional, and motoric, which have been shaped through learning experiences. Among sports competitors, the most important outcome is reflected in performance under competitive conditions. In essence, performance during practice sessions, no matter how perfect, is still considered only a subgoal. In this sense, athletic performance is similar to other performing arts, including theater, dance, music, and public speaking, whereby the primary goal is to display one's skills during the actual play, recital, concert, or public appearance.

Such final performances may be analyzed as influenced by several component elements: the strength of correct athletic responses, the presence of interfering incorrect responses, and the athlete's level of transfer of responses from the practice environment to the competitive environment (Suinn, 1980a; in press d). The level of potential skill and the pace of acquisition of such skill are influenced by factors such as the athlete's genetic competencies, past exposure to sports training and performing (which promotes "learning to learn" athletic skills), and the quality of coaching, training programs, nutritional planning, etc. To the degree that performance may be disrupted, then other variables may restrict the level of actual achievement at any single time, such as seen in the negative impact of jet lag, temporary health problems, or general life stress.

Of major relevance to this chapter are the three components of correct responses, incorrect responses, and transferability of skills. Correct athletic responses involve those that make up the primary positive aspects of the sport: the motor skill itself, preparatory-arousal responses, cognitive or cue-instructional responses, and attentional/concentration responses. Incorrect athletic responses involve interfering motor habits, inappropriate arousal or conditioned emotionality, and negative cognitions. The transferability of responses from practice settings to competitive settings is a function of the nature of the practice and its similarity to game stimulus conditions. A few comments will elaborate on these three components.

Regarding the correct athletic responses, a high level of performance reflects a well developed motor skill itself. In other words, the athlete will have learned the proper neuromuscular responses, sometimes identified as "proper technique," such as the arm rotation that maximizes the force of a karate blow, or the appropriate timing that defines the diving or gymnastic routine. Another type of correct response involves the preparatory-arousal sequence, i.e., the achievement of the athlete's optimal level of activation (Suinn, 1982b). Such activation may be stimulated physically through stretching and warm-ups, or mentally through "psyching up" strategies. In addition, the athlete's motivational, drive state, or goal setting phase may be involved. Cue-instructional responses include such cognitive responses as game strategies or thought stimuli associated with triggering complex motor responses. In the latter case, the self-instruction of "be loose and dynamic" may precipitate not only a muscular event, but also effort, a certain style, and an emotional level, all in the same instant. Finally, attentional/concentration responses are those which focus the neuromuscular and sensory-perceptual states to a narrowed set of cues and an equally narrowed set of responses related to the special demands of the competition.

Regarding the incorrect athletic responses, these are important in that their presence impairs the effective appearance of the correct responses. For instance, if the athlete has not extinguished a tendency to flinch, then accurate shooting would be impaired. Similarly, if the athlete's arousal level is too low, then the motor performance may be diminished in intensity or preciseness. With an inappropriately high arousal, motor coordination can be affected and concentration disrupted. In conditioned emotionality, the athlete experiences negative emotions under specific cue conditions, e.g., when confronting an opponent who has always proven better, or in facing the next team while mired in a losing season. Instead of negative emotions, negative cognitions may prevent performance. One correlate of negative thoughts is low self-efficacy ("I'm not good enough"). Recent data on athletics has confirmed that efficacy was indeed predictive of athletic performance on a new athletic task during early learning trials (actual experience is more important on later trials) (Feltz & Mugno, 1983; McAuley, 1985).

Regarding transfer, it is important that skills displayed under practice conditions generalize to competition conditions. One principle regarding generalization is that such transfer is enhanced to the degree that the practice conditions are similar to game conditions. There are a variety of ways in which practice can differ from competition: practice "opponents" are not real opponents (but only sparring partners); environmental conditions are dissimilar (nothing can duplicate the noise level of basketball's Paley Pavilion, or football's Texas Stadium with a home town crowd). Research has also demonstrated that transfer is affected by training variables such as the use of immediate versus summary feedback, and the reliance upon grouped training versus alternating training methods (Schmidt, in press).

From the above behavioral analysis, stress and anxiety can be better placed in context. During practice or training, when motor skills are being acquired, stress may interfere with the proper learning of the correct motor skills. Following acquisition and prior to performance on competition day, the presence of anxiety may be experienced as excessively high arousal (being "hyper"), or as an "out-of-body" sensation. During performance, anxiety states can lead to loss of smooth motor coordination, can disrupt concentration and attentional focus, and may precipitate negative cognitions. In addition, frequent appearance of stress responses during competition can lead to anxiety being a conditioned emotional response to competition cues, leading to sleep disturbances, excessive precompetition worry, and impaired performance. Finally, to the degree that the competitive environment is by nature a stress-related one, stress coping skills deserve attention as a routine part of an athlete's training.

STRESS AND ANXIETY: BEHAVIORAL ANALYSIS

I have elaborated upon a behavioral model of stress and anxiety elsewhere (Suinn, in press a), and will summarize this conceptualization here. The term *stress* will be used to refer to a state that is experienced as anxiety or tension prompted by the presence of certain factors. The cue conditions that precipitate such stress shall be labeled as *stressors,* while *anxiety* or *stress responses* shall mean those characteristics which, when present, lead to the inference of the existence of stress. Stress results from the interaction between stressor variables (such as unfair judging, poor field or course conditions, being behind in game score, biased crowd participation) and person variables (such as personal sensitivities, tendency to appraise conditions as threatening, poor coping skills, perception of control, history of success).

The presence of stress can be inferred through any or all of three basic response domains: the affective-autonomic, the somatic-behavioral, or the cognitive (Deffenbacher & Suinn, in press; Suinn & Deffenbacher, 1980). For a given athlete, stress responses may appear in different patterns, including the dominance of symptoms in one domain and not the others (Barlow, Mavissakalian, & Michelson, 1982; Lang, 1971; Malloy, Fairbank, & Keane, 1983; Mavissakalian, Michelson, Greenwald, Kornblith, & Greenwald, 1983; Ost, Jerremalm, & Hoihansson, 1981). Where the affective-autonomic domain is involved, the stress responses may include heightened autonomic arousal, distress, and psychophysiologic symptoms. Where the somatic-behavioral domain is involved, symptoms will include muscular tightness and motor coordination decrements. Where the cognitive domain is involved, responses will show as negative thoughts, uncontrolled cognitions, disruptions of attention or concentration, or hypervigilance. Such stress reactions have direct relevance for athletic performance. In the presence of affective-autonomic reactions, the athlete may experience hyper-arousal and excessively burn off energy, or may have stomach cramps or loose bowels, or be unable to sleep or rest. Where somatic-behavioral reactions are present, the athlete may lose fluidity and flexibility, with resulting danger of injury. With interferences with coordination, accuracy and power can be restricted. Where cognitive reactions are present, attention may be inappropriately focused on nonessentials or distractibility may be precipitated. Cognitions may take the form of worrisome ruminations about outcomes ("I won't last long enough to finish the race"), personal evaluations ("I don't feel I trained hard enough"), or on apprehensive anticipations ("What if . . . I get behind early . . ."). Such cognitions can interfere with the athletic task at hand.

In addition to the recognition of the three domains, it is helpful to identify external and internal stressors. External stressors include such circumstances as the appearance of a particular opponent, or unexpected weather or course or field conditions, or seeing someone else's score posted, or simply the sight of the starting gate. A bad call by a referee, or entering the home court or home field of an opponent, are also examples of external stressors. Internal stressors include thoughts, or appraisals, or perceptions. Examples of internal stressors include: being aware of physiological signs of fatigue; or *interpreting* a bodily response as fatigue and concluding that this means the race or game or fight is lost; or even continuous wondering if fatigue will set in before the event is complete. The next section will present some examples of stress management for athletes, with particular attention to circumstances where the stressors are external, where they are internal, and where the stress responses are autonomic-physiological, somatic-behavioral, or cognitive.

STRESS MANAGEMENT

External Stressors

Stress management to control external stressors can take several forms: removal of the external cues, extinction of the conditioned emotional response to those cues, or conditioning new responses to such cues. Since continued attention to stress cues maintains stress, then removal of such cues is a step toward reduction of the stress. For some athletes, seeing other competitors perform arouses tension and anxiety. Preventing such observations would therefore be one way of at least delaying the onset of the anxiety. Thus, one world class fencer would always sit with a towel over his head, to prevent seeing the other competitors and to enable focusing instead on other matters (Suinn, 1976). Pentathlon team members bring books or read slogans on their pistol cases instead of watching the judges scoring their targets. I train Alpine skiers to actively concentrate on nearby trees ("Look for the tree with the thickest branches") or on the clouds ("Count the number of animals formed by clouds"). This approach at least temporarily prevents stress cues from taking hold, and reduces the tendency of stress to build up due to accumulated exposure.

A second approach involves the actual extinction of the anxiety response-external cue relationship. Where external stressors are specifically identified as involving stable cues, desensitization can help. Desensitization is a behavior therapy, whereby relaxation responses are used in counterconditioning the anxiety (Wolpe, 1969). I have applied this approach in working with a recreational skier who suffered severe agony in a ski accident. Her injury was so severe that any cues associated with skiing would precipitate flashback responses and emotionality. Desensitization was successfully used to eliminate the problem.

A third approach conditions new responses or changes the meaning of the initial stressor. Prior to the 1980 Summer Olympics to be held in Moscow, Russia, athletes and coaches were concerned about the extreme nationalism and the negative feelings which could be activated by the sights and sounds of the Russian stadium. A classical conditioning program was developed, whereby the sight of red (as in the Russian flag) was paired with feelings of competency and readiness to perform at peak levels. Since these Summer Games were cancelled for U.S. athletes, the training was not completed. On the other hand, a similar approach was successfully used with members of a university women's volleyball team, in preparation for a series with the UCLA basketball team. Here, the perception was that the UCLA team members were unusually talented, strong, tall, etc. An imagery-rehearsal method, visual motor behavior rehearsal (VMBR) (Suinn, 1984), was used to have the women more accurately judge the UCLA team: what do they really look like in "real life," stripped of their reputation.

Internal Stressors

Since internal stressors also include negative thoughts, examples of cognitive approaches will also be covered in a later section. One illustration of an internal stressor is the awareness of fatigue or of errors and their consequences. The sequence involves attending to the early signs of fatigue, followed by worry and tension, which leads to muscle tightness and motor interference via cramps. In behaviorist terms, the fatigue signals act as cues, which can serve as stimuli for stress responses, or as will be shown later, as cues for adaptive behaviors. With errors, the sequence involves the committing of a performance error, evaluating this negatively, inappropriate thoughts or emotions being precipitated, and finally, having performance disrupted.

Research has shown that the presence of errors or the onset of fatigue cues need not always be associated with a stress sequence. Mahoney and Avener (1977) discovered that successful Olympic gymnasts differed from less successful ones in terms of their responses following the onset of an error. The successful athletes used the error as information to plan the next sequence of moves; the unsuccessful athletes were emotionally reactive or ruminative about the error. Morgan (1984), in his studies on marathoners, concluded that an 'associational' style was preferable in effective running. In the associational style, the runner continuously monitors his/her physical state, using the bodily signals as data for making adjustments in running, to maintain a steady state. Morgan refers to this as a "pay as you go" method for expending energy while achieving pace. Poor runners ignore their physical signals, and instead run harder earlier to achieve a fast pace, but then wear down, and eventually lack energy to complete the race; these are the "buy now, pay later" runners. Thus, in both the gymnast and marathoner studies, error or bodily signals can serve either as triggers for further stress or as signals for adapting.

An approach to such types of internal stressors would aim at changing the signals from stress prompters to information for coping. In this way the stress management actually involves prevention. If the internal stressor involves bodily cues, then the athlete should be trained by coaches, or informed by exercise physiologists, of the meaning of these signals, and to separate those which signify danger from those which can be handled. Suinn, Morton, and Brammell (1979) trained cross-country runners to identify early signs of fatigue, then to cue-off a relaxed style of running, using a combination of relaxation training, visual motor behavior rehearsal, and thought-cueing. Data on oxygen consumption during treadmill testing confirmed that the athletes could alter their styles and that this led to reduction in oxygen utilization, signifying more efficient physiological efficiency. With respect to errors, I have included error-correction preparation in work with athletes. For instance, skiers would rehearse the skill of immediately recovering from an error, and of refocusing on the next sequence of correct responses, during VMBR training.

Autonomic-Physiological Stress Responses

As cited earlier, an athlete's stress response may involve the autonomic-physiological domain. In this circumstance, the appearance of stressors seems to be experienced as increased heart rate, higher respiration, and other symptoms of excessive arousal. Although relaxation training alone may not be sufficient to eliminate such stress, one technique appears to have value as an arousal/activation control procedure. Anxiety Management Training (AMT) (Suinn, 1983) involves training a person in the direct use of relaxation under conditions of arousal, including anxiety arousal, anger arousal, or other impulsive activation. Using visualization of, for instance, a stress situation, the athlete permits the situation to precipitate the physiological arousal. Relaxation is then initiated to reduce the heart rate, respiration, etc. Unlike desensitization, AMT is applicable to cases whereby the stressors are multiple or vaguely defined. Recent modifications of AMT also make it applicable where cognitions are part of the stress triggers (Hutchings, Denney, Basgall, & Houston, 1980).

One illustration of the use of AMT for multiple stressors is its application with the U.S. Modern Pentathlon Team. In the Modern Pentathlon, athletes compete in five events: shooting, running, swimming, riding, and fencing. Since the events are highly different from one another, stress management training would be extremely lengthy were such training to target each of the events separately. AMT was used with one pentathlete who experienced stress reactions in pistol shooting, fencing, and horseback riding. Following an abbreviated training, the athlete developed sufficient AMT skills as to win against an international field, including a former bronze medalist.

In a procedure quite similar to AMT, Ziegler et al. (1982) trained runners in stress management, on the premise that stress reduces cardiovascular and respiratory efficiency. In effect, they assumed that stress involved the autonomic-physiological domain, creating physiological inefficiency, and increasing oxygen consumption. Similar to Suinn, et al. (1979), treadmill testing confirmed the significant improvement in physiological measures following stress management.

Somatic-Behavioral Responses

Stress responses may also include the somatic-behavioral domain, and show up in neuromuscular tightness, motor coordination dysfluencies, restless and random activity, or constricted movements. Free movements may be lost, and error-patterns may be repeated. In some cases, these responses may actually reflect excessive autonomic-physiological arousal or cognitive stressors. However, where the stress responses are limited to only the somatic-behavioral domain, then certain stress management procedures can be appropriate.

If the stress appears as tightness and rigidity, then simple relaxation or breathing exercises may be useful, including the Jacobsen deep muscle technique (Jacobsen, 1938; Suinn, 1980b). Where the anxiety appears as uncoordinated, restless activity, the recommendation could be for the athlete to engage in motor behaviors oppositional to these, such as more deliberate and slow-paced walking, less rapid speech, or slow-motion arm movements. By this method, more controlled neuromuscular feedback signals will be transmitted internally. In some cases, an athlete lacks the sensitivity to know when muscles are relaxing. In such instances, I have paired up athletes, with one person putting his/her hands on the shoulders of the other. Sensing this weight, the athlete preparing to relax, can then monitor shoulder muscle relaxation by feeling the shoulders lower under the combined weight and relaxation exercise.

Occasionally the athlete's stress response involves motor constriction, whereby free range of movements seems lost. With one wrestler, this appeared in his grabbing and holding on, rather than fluidly using different throws or holds. To counter this tendency to freeze, I had him begin each match with broad, exaggerated, wide-ranging motions in order to cue off freer movements.

Cognitive Stress Responses

Cognitive stress responses involve thoughts that are either themselves consequences of a stressor, or may act as stressors to precipitate other stress responses. These thoughts may be disruptive cognitions, worrisome ruminations, poor self-efficacy statements, or helpless-oriented thoughts such as a sense of not being in control. Athletes who can benefit from cognitive stress management techniques are those whose thought processes dominate as stress responses and whose thought symptoms remain even when the autonomic-physiological, and somatic-behavioral stress responses are eliminated. Not all of the various cognitive stress management techniques are equally helpful to a specific athlete. Their value depends upon the fit of the techniques to the normal coping style of the athlete; an athlete who tends to rely upon restructuring as a problem-solving style, for instance, is much more likely to be able to apply such a strategy to anxiety management. In addition to restructuring, other cognitive techniques include self-talk, attentional refocusing, and efforts relating to discriminative control.

Cognitive restructuring has long been a common approach to thought management (Ellis, 1962; Goldfried, Decenteceo, & Weinberg, 1974; Meichenbaum, in press). This approach confronts the irrationality of the athlete's thoughts and requires restructuring them to match reality. An Olympic fencer often hurried her warm-up time due to officials delaying her ability to get to the fencing strip on time. Her prior reaction was to think, "I'm holding everyone up, they're mad at me, I shouldn't take any more time." Without a decent warm-up, she also would feel, "I'm not really ready to fence . . . I haven't even warmed up, I can't possibly perform well . . . oh, well let's get it over with." In working with her, I had observed her rapid ability to eliminate inappropriate feelings, including anxiety, through new insights or through changing her perceptions. Hence, restructuring was utilized, whereby she was required to re-evaluate the circumstances for delays, her own rights as a competitor, and the rationality of her rushing her warm-up. Her thoughts now altered to, "I have as much right to warming-up; they kept me waiting too, so now they can wait a little for me; if I'm taking up too much time, it's the judge's obligation to tell me and not my responsibility . . . " In stress associated with being in a slump, restructuring has also proven of value. Athletes in slumps typically randomly try out different technique changes in hopes of pulling out of the slump . . . and soon conclude that "nothing works." One approach I have relied upon is to have the athlete change a single part of his/her technique, systematically testing this change several times. Even if this does not lead to performance improvement, the athlete is still encouraged to understand that "at least we've made progress in ruling this area out," as opposed to feeling that nothing whatsoever had been gained.

Self-talk involves the use of self-instruction to cue off adaptive behaviors and to replace interfering useless thoughts. Negative self-talk generally involves ambiguous, urging, but directionless self-instructions, such as, "pay attention and concentrate, dummy." A major problem is the inability of the athlete to know what instructions are appropriate since the athlete may not know what is going wrong. Training programs that rely upon behavioral analyses and charting can provide the precision that is lacking (Desiderato & Miller, 1979; Komaki & Barnett, 1977; Locke & Latham, 1985; Ziegler, 1978). By systematic behavioral analysis, an athlete can not only detect what errors are occurring, but what corrective action is needed; by doing such analysis and making such corrections, the source of the stress can be removed. For example, a tennis player may be frustrated by his/her unforced errors. Charting may point out that such errors are related to approach shots that are down-the-line, where there is less court space. A self-instructional correction might therefore be, "Here's an approach shot, just stroke it across court." This combination of behavioral analysis and self-talk/self-instruction can replace negative thoughts, and attending stress responses.

Attentional refocusing was cited earlier as a means for coping with external stressors. In this approach, the athlete stops attending to stress stimuli (such as staring at the starting area), and instead attends to a non-stress stimulus (such as the cloud formation). This method has applications as well to negative thoughts. One member of the U.S. National Cross-Country Ski Team kept thinking, "I'm not smooth on hill climbing, hills are always a problem." As a consequence, when she approached a hill, she exerted extra effort, would lose her rhythm, ski poorly, and confirm her worst fears. Prior to the next race, I instructed her to instead search for the tallest tree on each hill she approached. This not only refocused her attention on new thoughts, thereby displacing the negative ones, but also raised her head higher and freed up her breathing passageways. This performance helped her earn a third place finish, making up for an extremely poor initial run.

Work surrounding discriminative training can also help in thought management. Brokovec conceptualizes maladaptive worry as due to poor discriminative control (Borkovec, Wilkinson, Folensbee, & Lerman, 1983). He says that the initial stimulus causing worry responses generalizes to other irrelevant stimuli; hence the original stimulus control is weakened. Instead a wide variety of other stimuli now precipitate worry. As treatment, therefore, he recommends that individuals set a time and a specific place to engage in worrying behaviors. This leads to worry responses becoming reattached to a specific stimulus, thereby creating new discriminative stimulus control, and limiting worry behaviors to such stimulus circumstances. One application of this general concept is my recommendation to athletes who worry to distinguish between those worries that have adaptive consequences and those which are maladaptive. Adaptive worrying triggers off behaviors which are useful, such as checking equipment to insure that everything is properly prepared. For maladaptive worries, the athlete is either to isolate them mentally (picture these thoughts as being placed in a compartment in your mind, where you now shut the door on them until the race is over), or eliminate them from attention (picture these thoughts as running through your head, straight through your head, and out . . . and gone).

FINAL COMMENTS

Stress management may be considered for two reasons: to remove obstacles to learning or performance, or to enhance the subjective satisfaction of athletic activities by removing distress. In the former, stress management training is provided because the presence of stress inhibits learning or blocks optimal performance. The value of stress management in this circumstance is obvious. In the latter, learning and performance may not be at all affected by the anxiety. In fact, there is reason to believe that all athletes might experience some stress prior to competition (Gould, Horn, & Spreeman, 1983; Mahoney & Avener, 1977; Meyers, Cooke, Cullen, & Liles, 1979). The distress may not have a role in affecting performance, but may be a detractor in that it prevents emotional satisfaction. Thus, stress management skills can help an athlete *feel* better, even though he/she does not *perform* better.

In considering stress for athletes, assessment is important. From the stimulus end, it should be recognized that the conditions which produce stress may be very specific. Although there may be some value to considering a general trait of anxiousness, the trend in sports anxiety assessment is for a more sport-specific orientation (Suinn, in press c). This is similar to the measurement of trait anxiety as contrasted with state anxiety, or of general anxiety versus mathematics anxiety. From the response end, it has been previously stated that different athletes may exhibit stress through different domains: autonomic-physiological, somatic-behavioral, or cognitive. It is my contention that: (1) different "individual stress profiles" exist; (2) moreover that different stress *sequences* also exist — with one athlete reacting to an external stressor first with negative thoughts, which in turn prompt autonomic-physiological and somatic behavioral symptoms . . . while another athlete may respond first with autonomic-physiological stress responses, which in turn precipitate cognitive or somatic-behavioral symptoms, and (3) the stress management techniques with most benefit will be those which are individually matched to these individual differences and to the existing coping styles and/or skills of the athlete.

The acquisition and application of stress management techniques by an athlete should be viewed in the context of skill acquisition, akin to motor skill acquisition and performance. Stress management skills do not appear suddenly overnight but require training and practice; nor do they appear with instant success during competition without a prior history of application in this context. *Knowledge* of stress management is no guarantee of the skilled *application* of such activities. Athletes should view stress management training as training similar to weight lifting. In addition, it is important to consider stress management as self-control training. The eventual goal is the ability of the competitor to initiate stress management through his/her own skills, and to not have to rely upon the presence of the psychologist. In essence, the optimal is represented by many sports events at the Olympic Games: the athlete is entirely self-reliant, without benefit of even a coach (who is restricted from the competition floor in many Olympic events).

Finally, the analysis of performance must be broad-based, before it is concluded that stress management is required. As mentioned earlier, in some cases, anxiety may be present in an athlete but without any effects directly on performance. In some instances, stress may actually be part of the excitement and attractiveness of the sport for a competitor, such as in high risk sports. And in some cases, what may appear to be a poor performance because of stress may actually be attributable to other sources, which must always be considered in any analysis. Specifically, intense autonomic arousal may be related to physical illness, sleep irregularities may be caused by oxygen deficit at altitude, muscular tightness may be associated with the need for orthopedic adjustments, mental slumps and depression may be caused by overtraining, poor concentration may be connected with deficits in attentional skills, and hyperactivity and nervousness may be a function of allergies.

In sum, stress management can be an important contributor to either the performance of an athlete, or to the satisfaction experienced by an athlete. Proper assessment of the individual circumstances facing the athlete or experienced by the athlete is critical to program planning for stress. Such assessment needs to encompass not only the stress characteristics of the athlete in question, but also the ruling out of other non-stress factors which might contribute to the issue being confronted. Various stress management approaches are available with varying degrees of research or case history validation. A proper match and training in such approaches can enhance athletic endeavors for athletes of all levels.

SUMMARY

This chapter covers stress management for athletes, and began with a brief behavioral conceptualization of athletic performance and analysis of stress.

Examples of external and internal stressors were offered, as well as of stress responses from autonomic-physiological, somatic-behavioral, and cognitive domains. Further discussed are specific types of stress management approaches used with athletes, and associated with external versus internal sources of stress, and with the three stress response domains. Finally, some general observations and comments regarding stress management assessment and training were provided.

REFERENCES

Barlow, D. (Ed.) (1981). *Behavioral assessment of adult disorder.* New York: Guilford.

Barlow, D., Mavissakalian, M., & Michelson, L. (1982). Patterns of psychophysiological change in the treatment of agoraphobia. *Behaviour Research and Therapy, 20,D 347–356.*

Barlow, D., & Wolfe, B. (1981). Behavioral approaches to anxiety disorders: A report on the NIMH-SUNY research conference. *Journal of Consulting and Clinical Psychology, 49,* 448–454.

Borkovec, T., Wilkinson, L., Folensbee, R., & Lerman, C. (1983). Stimulus control applications to the treatment of worry. *Behaviour Research and Therapy, 21,* 247–251.

Deffenbacher, J., & Suinn, R. (in press). Concepts and treatment of the generalized anxiety syndrome. In L. Ascher & L. Michelson (Eds.), *International handbook of assessment and treatment of anxiety disorders.* New York: Guilford Press.

Desiderato, O., & Miller, I. (1979). Improving tennis performance by cognitive behavior modification techniques. *The Behavior Therapist, 2*(4), 19.

Ellis, A. (1962). *Reason and emotion in psychotherapy.* New York: Stuart.

Feltz, D., & Mugno, D. (1983). A replication of the path analysis of the causal elements in Bandura's theory of self-efficacy and the influence of autonomic perception. *Journal of Sport Psychology, 5,* 263–277.

Goldfried, M., Decenteceo, E., & Weinberg, L. (1974). Systematic rational restructuring as a self-control technique. *Behavior Therapy, 5,* 247–254.

Gould, D., Horn, T., & Spreeman, J. (1983). Competitive anxiety in junior elite wrestlers. *Journal of Sport Psychology, 5,* 58–71.

Hutchings, D., Denney, D., Basgall, J., & Houston, B. (1980). Anxiety management and applied relaxation in reducing general anxiety. *Behaviour Research and Therapy, 18,* 181–190.

Jacobsen, E. (1938). *Progressive relaxation.* Chicago: University of Chicago Press.

Komaki, J., & Barnett, F. (1977). A behavioral approach to coaching football: Improving the play execution of the offensive backfield on a youth football team. *Journal of Applied Behavior Analysis, 10,* 657–664.

Kutash, I., Schlesinger, L., et al. (Eds.) (1980). *Handbook on stress and anxiety.* San Francisco: Jossey Bass.

Lang, P. (1971). The application of psychophysiological methods to the study of psychotherapy and behavior change. In A. Bergin, & A. Garfield (Eds.), *Handbook of psychotherapy and behavior change.* New York: Wiley.

Locke, E., & Latham, G. (1985). The application of goal setting to sports. *Journal of Sport Psychology, 7,* 205–222.

Mahoney, M., & Avener, M. (1977). Psychology and the elite athlete: An exploratory study. *Cognitive Therapy and Research, 1,* 135–141.

Malloy, P., Fairbank, J., & Keane, T. (1983). Validation of a multimethod assessment of posttraumatic stress disorders in Vietnam veterans. *Journal of Consulting and Clinical Psychology, 51,* 488–494.

Mavissakalian, M., Michelson, L., Greenwald, D., Kornblith, S., & Greenwald, M. (1983). Cognitive-behavioral treatment of agoraphobia: Paradoxical intention vs self-statement training. *Behaviour Research and Therapy, 21,* 75–86.

McAuley, E. (1985). Modeling and self-efficacy: A test of Bandura's model. *Journal of Sport Psychology, 7,* 283–295.

Meichenbaum, D. (in press). *Stress inoculation training.* New York: Pergamon Press.

Meyers, A., Cooke, C., Cullen, J., & Liles, L. (1979). Psychological aspects of athletic competitors: A replication across sports. *Cognitive Therapy and Research, 3,* 361–366.

Morgan, W. (1984). Mind over matter. In W. Straub & J. Williams (Eds.), *Cognitive sport psychology.* Lansing, NY: Sport Science Associates.

Ost, L., Jerremalm, A., & Hoihansson, J. (1981). Individual response patterns and the effects of different behavioural methods in the treatment of social phobia. *Behaviour Research and Therapy, 19,* 1–16.

Schmidt, R. (in press). Motor learning: Theoretical aspects. In J. Skinner, et al. (Eds.), *Future directions in exercise/sport research.* Champaign, IL: Human Kinetics.

Suinn, R. (1976). Body thinking for Olympic champs. *Psychology Today, 36.*

Suinn, R. (1979). Behavioral applications to psychology to U.S. world class competitors. In P. Klavora (Ed.), *Coach, athlete, and the sport psychologist.* Toronto: University of Toronto Press.

Suinn, R. (1980a). Psychology and sports performance: Principles and applications. In R. Suinn (Ed.), *Psychology in sports: Methods and applications.* Minneapolis: Burgess Publishing.

Suinn, R. (1980b). Muscle relaxation exercise. In R. Suinn (Ed.), *Psychology in sports: Methods and applications.* Minneapolis: Burgess Publishing.

Suinn, R. (1982a). The treatment of generalized anxiety disorder. In S. Turner (Ed.), *The behavioral treatment of anxiety.* New York: Plenum.

Suinn, R. (1982b, March). A holistic approach to peak performance. Invited Address, 15th Annual Sports Medicine and Conditioning Seminar, Seattle, WA.

Suinn, R. (1983). *Manual: Anxiety measurement training (AMT).* Fort Collins, CO: Rocky Mountain Behavioral Sciences Institute, (revised).

Suinn, R. (1984). Visual motor behavior rehearsal: The basic technique. *Scandinavian Journal of Behaviour Therapy, 13,* 131–142.

Suinn, R. (1985). *The seven steps to peak performance. Manual for mental training for athletes.* Fort Collins, CO: Colorado State University, Department of Psychology.

Suinn, R. (in press a). Stress management by behavioral methods. In J. Nospitz & D. Coddington (Eds.), *The adjustment disorders.* Washington, DC: American Psychiatric Association Task Force on Treatment of Psychiatric Disorders.

Suinn, R. (in press b). Psychological approaches to performance enhancement. In M. Asken & J. May (Eds.), *Sports psychology: The psychological health of the athlete.* New York: Spectrum.

Suinn, R. (in press c). Future directions in sport psychology research: Applied aspects. In J. Skinner et al. (Eds.), *Future directions in exercise/sport research.* Champaign, IL: Human Kinetics.

Suinn, R. (in press d). Behavioral approaches to stress management. In M. Asken & J. May (Eds.), *Sports psychology: The psychological health of the athlete.* New York: Spectrum.

Suinn, R., & Deffenbacher, J. (1980). Behavioral intervention methods for stress and anxiety. In I. Kutash, & L. Schlesinger (Eds.), *Handbook on stress and anxiety.* San Francisco: Jossey-Bass.

Suinn, R., Morton, M., & Brammell, H. (1979). Psychological and mental training to increase efficiency in endurance athletes. *Final Report to U.S. Olympic Women's Athletics Developmental Subcommittee.*

Tuma, A., & Maser, J. (Eds.) (1985). *Anxiety and the anxiety disorders.* Hillsdale, NJ: Erlbaum.

Turner, S. (Ed.) (1984). *Behavioral theories and treatment of anxiety.* New York: Plenum.

Williams, J., & Spitzer, R. (Eds.) (1984). *Psychotherapy research: Where are we and where should we go?* New York: Guilford Press.

Wolpe, J. (1969). *The practice of behavior therapy.* New York: Pergamon Press.

Ziegler, S. (1978). *The effects of feedback and social reinforcement on coaching behavior.* Unpublished doctoral dissertation, West Virginia University.

Ziegler, S., Klinzing, J., & Williamson, K. (1982). The effects of two stress management training programs on cardio-respiratory efficiency. *Journal of Sport Psychology, 4,* 280–289.

14

Fructification of Anxiety and Its Autoregulative Control in Sports

Milos Machac and Helena Machacova

"Reason" receives, processes and stores information, sets targets and programs, is able to be sober and to have foresight. Only in linkage with emotions which as against the distant goal emphasize the present or the near future, emotions which can be shortsighted and biased, has reason any chance to bear significant influence upon human behavior. Emotiogenic stimuli represent the "key" towards arousing the powerful energetic resources of man.

A healthy man looks at future danger as though he were looking through the optics of a "reversed telescope." In other words in our evaluations of the significance of future negative phenomena we are exaggerated optimists. By comparison in the evaluation of positive future events we are more realistic.

From the fact that we mostly incline to take an optimistic view of distant danger it follows that the motivating effect of such danger is not adequate to the reality. We very often squeeze out from our conscious or suppress information which is unfavorable for us. Thus, for instance, the smoker does not take into consideration the significantly higher probability of cancer incidence, a big eater does not acknowledge the generally known hazards of such behavior for the cardiovascular system, etc.

As soon as the danger is close at hand we are surprised at the pressing urgency of the onset of emotionally negative tensions (anxiety, concern, fear) which goes hand in hand with aversive tendencies in behavior. The trainer should know the time distance between the onset in his trainee of the first symptoms of unrest, nervousness, sleep disorders, anxiety and the important contest in order to be able, with the help of a psychologist, to curb increased pre-start tension. *Premature and excessively increased activation level will exhaust the athlete and will cause disorders of psychic and motor coordination.* Individuals will differ immensely. The differences will depend on the personality qualities of the contestants, the importance of the contest, the aspirations of the athlete and his estimate of the qualities of his rivals in the given contest; the time limit of emotional involvement towards a certain critical event may therefore be expressed in minutes, days and months. Intraindividually these time units are usually identical.

In sports competition the contest situation is usually arranged such that the athlete is driven to achievement both by the desire to win and by the fear of defeat—this is because no one is assured of victory and there is always only one winner, all others must taste the bitter fruit of defeat.

No matter how enticing is the participation of the athlete in a big contest it also arouses anxiety and the inclination to evade possible frustration, disappointment from failure. At greater time distance the tendency to "participate" is usually more explicit and more unambiguous than later when doubts and pre-start anxiety begin to strengthen.

ADAPTATION AND MALADAPTATION ROLE
OF ANXIETY IN SPORTS

Under certain circumstances anxiety has adaptational significance, under other circumstances it leads to behavioral destruction. In the former instance anxiety may become the warning signal against danger. Stronger anxiety may become more dangerous than the danger it warns against.

Intensive training also assumes an *increased activation level* (emotionally vegetative arousal). This is easier to achieve by emotionally negative stimulation. It has been proven experimentally that *aversive stimuli* (i.e., stimuli arousing fear and anger) have *greater influence on the nonspecific activation system of the organism than emotionally positive stimuli.* Action alertness provoked by an aversive stimulus situation is primarily available for reactions of the aversive, defensive type. A frightened organism is energetically prepared, programmed and oriented for fleeing, not for e.g. observing the beauty of the nature. Nevertheless under certain conditions the possibilities of sublimation remain preserved. Sublimation means that developmentally higher and more complex activities use for the implementation of their program energetic resources which were initially available for more primitive activities.

For a healthy person mild anxiety and fear are factors which increase total activity, work motivation. Anxiety is a state which arouses in us the endeavor to do something for strengthening or restoring our emotional balance, for strengthening the feeling of security, self-consciousness and the positive emotional sphere.

A person without anxiety is usually spared the stress of many situations, his life is calmer. *The fact that he is not the bearer of anxiety means, however, that he also does not bear any challenge for activity which follows from anxiety.* When "everything is O.K." we are not concerned or worried about the future, there is no need for training activity, for effort to improve achievement which stabilizes the athlete emotionally and gives him self-consciousness. *Anxiety* may thus become an important "drive" which *supplies positive training motivation from emotionally negative energetic resources.*

An athlete who is satisfied, calm, happy and complacent usually has poor prerequisites for systematic and hard training and for improved achievement.

Some athletes try to overcome this handicap intuitively by the deliberate implantation of fear or feelings of insecurity and thus to force themselves to indulge in activities which they have no desire to do. Self-indulgence may more effectively be suppressed using the aversive mechanism. Athletes and students describe the procedure as the *"technique of the fear relay."*

Autostimulation by fear is useful for those activities which are not attractive, where long stretches of preparatory work alternate with short stretches of control. Many students who are aware of the danger of a leisurely attitude try to evoke in advance the unpleasant situation which could arise if they failed an exam, the consequences of such failure in the family, the loss of prestige with friends, etc.

The stimulation effect of more distant danger on everyday work may be provided by the plan of staged preparation. The subject matter of the whole semester may be divided into weekly or daily "portions" whose regular "consumption" is to provide the trainee with greater security that the task will be fulfilled within the given time limit. This will also secure the adequate decrease of unpleasant tension. The training plan and "logbook" should fulfill the same function for the athlete. *Deliberate anticipation of endangerment is thus put into the service of motivation for systematic work.*

In top training full of hard work and sacrifice the athlete must continuously convince himself that it is worthwhile, that sports achievement and the social value of a peak sports performance will of set investments in form of various injuries and diseases resulting from the premature wear of the organism. The outcomes are strengthened psychic bonds and linkages between the athlete and society which is often represented by the sports public.

Psychic bonds or relations are the effect of man's socialization, his social integration. They keep us in rapport with certain phenomena, especially with phenomena of social nature. Psychic bonds make man dependent on attitudes and other norms of the relevant social group.

Psychosocial linkages are the soil from which grow diligence and conscientiousness. *A performance in a "big contest" is not, however, a mere reproduction of what had previously been diligently trained* and perfectly mastered. The special psychosocial context in which the performance of the athlete takes place turn it into a phenomenon of novel psychological quality (the feeling of special responsibility, random moments linked with the possibility of winning or losing "everything," the tendency of loss of self-assuredness and the fear of the destruction of achievement caused by anxiety).

The pre-start situation is characterized by highly *eruptive emotionality* and increased vegetative irritability which often makes it difficult for the athlete to maintain anxiety at a level at which it may still be engaged to serve to attain the desired performance. Another psychophysiological characteristic of fear and anxiety is the tendency to aversive behavior (the inclination to evasion, to escape). The interference of defensive and desirable activities and excessive activation are the causes of distraction, discoordinated convulsive and cumbersome movements. The very awareness of the onset of any of the symptoms of anxiety will lead to the anticipation of other indicators and to the worsening of the psychic state and performance. Behavior influenced by emotions may be controlled by reason but *fear and especially anxiety have the prerequisites to refuse to obey reason* (relative autonomy of the emotionally vegetative sphere).

The stability of performance and emotions may to a considerable extent be increased by drill, by the automation of the respective skills and aptitudes in conditions which model demanding contest situations. A perfectly consolidated stereotype is more resistant to stress than a newly trained stereotype.

Great dependence on the result of the contest, responsibility, worry about the result, concern about possible failure—in fact all that has helped motivate training should in the prestart stage retreat into the background in order to be replaced by positive emotional turning, a feeling of security, the ability to keep track of what is going on lightness, spontaneity, flexibility, for the athlete to enjoy the contest. These feelings should only be mildly "spiced" with anxiety.

In brief we should *"unnerve" the athlete in training and to calm him down before start.* Unnerving is a matter of strengthening psychosocial linkages, calming down is the effect of the weakening of these linkages. This is in direct contradiction to the spontaneous inclination of the athlete on the basis of natural adaptation mechanisms.

One of the tasks of long term preparation for peak performance is *to turn anxiety into a helper for overcoming training drudgery and to find a suitable harness to tame it in prestart situations* when it can easily become an unpredictable and destructive factor.

Today there exists a wide range of psychological mainly relaxation-based procedures which are used to this effect. *Relaxation is the counterpart of tension, excitement and anxiety, prestart stage fright and stress.* A person who is relaxed is in a state that is psychophysiologically contrary to all states which are characterized by psychic and physiological tension, i.e., all states which are desirable in the pre-start situation and which are described as readiness for action, combat readiness, etc. With the nearing start the athlete must not be completely calm. The warm-up exercises serve to start and warm up the organism. The prestart situation colors the emotional reaction of the athlete with anxiety which must be individually optimal. It should not cause a decline in performance but should stimulate it. The experience of such anxiety need not have the exclusive character of emotionally negative tension. What we often get is an emotionally ambivalent situation, with anxiety alternating with pleasant pre-start excitement.

ARTIFICIAL PSYCHOLOGICAL INTERVENTION IN THE CURRENT PSYCHOPHYSIOLOGICAL STATE OF THE ATHLETE

The prestart situation is characterized by increased activation level which is among others manifested by the tendency "to do something," to deal with, for example, the rival's and one's own weaknesses and advantages, to be concerned with matters whose importance at the given moment is questionable and to deal with matters which at the given moment cannot be changed. Anxious and distracted thoughts beat off rest and sleep. A vicious circle is formed from which "sane reason" does not find a way out.

Similar spontaneously originating dysfunctions in the emotionally vegetative sphere may be overcome or prevented by artificial regulative intervention into psychophysiological states. The artificial character of these interventions is given by the fact that contrary to "sane reason" they do not approach the emotional vegetative sphere via the cognitive sphere.

People find it very difficult to become accustomed to the idea that the content of worry and anxiety may in the given case be insignificant. They have the natural inclination to resolve difficulties with regard to their content. They find it difficult to believe that the emotional state may be changed "without any reason," that is, without any change in existing reality. *In natural life situations the dependence of emotions on cognition and cognition on reality is a matter of course.* For the psychologist this, however, is an impassable approach: he cannot change reality nor make it significantly more acceptable by sophistication. The psychologist's effort to form a less painful or less disagreeable interpretation of the actual state of affairs is usually not very effective.

On the other hand psychological procedures which evade the cognitive sphere have reached considerable successes in manipulation of actual emotionally vegetative states. *Direct (non-content resp. non-cognitive) control of emotionally vegetative states relatively independent of the external situation and of its cognitive processing has evident advantages.* By being extricated from the content of cognitively-practical interactions the autoregulative intervention becomes the matter of *a "closed system" relatively independent of the immediate constellation of external influences.* For this reason we have defined psychological autoregulation as a deliberate, non-content intervention in the dynamics of psychophysiological events extricated from the context of the practical interaction of the subject and his environment (Machac, 1976).

Present autoregulative methods have a basically autorelaxation character. They are based on isometric or dynamic exercises (yoga, Marishchuk's relaxation training, or Elsa Gindler's concentration-relaxation exercises). The skeleton of Schultz' autogenic training and its numerous modifications is formed by autosuggestive formulas and ideas linked with them.

Autorelaxation methods have two basic *shortcomings:* their effect is *short lived* and there do not exist objective criteria for assessing the quality of training. If we do not have objective information on the course of the training we cannot predict the subsequent effect and we cannot correct errors made by the trainee.

Without objective criteria for assessing the quality of training the success or failure of the autoregulative intervention becomes more or less a question of the subjective impression of the trainee. We know from experience that some trainees assess their autoregulative "achievements" too optimistically others are careful and reticent. It often happens that the trainee will do something that in no way resembles the required relaxation operations.

With regard to the duration of the subsequent effect and with regard to the objective evaluation of its course as well as with a view to other questions relating to the character of induced changes in the psychophysiological state and improving performance autogenic training (AT) and other autorelaxation methods differ significantly from the autoregulative method which we have termed *RAM, the Relaxation-Activation Method.* We have been using the method for some time now. It represents an artificial way of deliberately influencing the dynamics of the emotionally vegetative process using psychologically noncognitive means.

TRAINING THE RELAXATION–ACTIVATION
METHOD (RAM)

Some 800 trainees have already undergone RAM training, of them one third were athletes. Information on the character of RAM and its effect were first published in the early 1960s (Machac, 1962, 1964a, b).[1]

RAM training is carried out in home conditions and takes 3–5 months. It starts with 2 to 3 trainings a week always lasting 30 mins. Later on there are 1–2 trainings a week. After the end of the training course the trainees always engage in RAM when they want to tune their current psychic state (especially to get rid of anxiety), to improve their mental and physical performance, to prepare for the solution of demanding tasks, to speed up the regeneration of work dispositions, etc.

Training is carried out according to instructions which the trainees receive at approximately one month intervals either individually or in groups. Consultations are linked with the laboratory control of home training. We also use various object aids of feedback character and films. The trainees receive complex instructions in form of written "Instructions for RAM Training."

It is usually impossible to provide a sufficiently instructive verbal description for training RAM. Nor can we learn to ski or ride a bicycle only by diligently reading instructions. The emotional sphere is especially unsuitable for verbal communication. We are speaking about something which can be neither seen nor touched. Nevertheless, some individuals have mastered RAM training by merely studying the cited handbook.

This short communication does not provide us with the opportunity to describe the instructions for training and precludes also the use of required laboratory controls.

Thanks to autogenic training, ideas concerning relaxation have been considerably broadened, even if often in a distorted manner. There exists a sum of personal experience on the basis of which ideas concerning the relaxation components of RAM can be constructed. Greater difficulties are connected with the training of activation phases. Some experience with activation can be created for instance with the aid of Bakon's (so-called siderical) pendulum, based on attempts to swing the pendulum by imagining this movement and then gradually suppressing the idea of the swinging of the pendulum, while maintaining tension which is empty of content, not occupied by any program.

RAM consists of relaxation and activation phases (Rph and Aph). The relaxation phase prepares for the activation phase. One Rph and one subsequent Aph form one regulation cycle. The whole training usually consists of three cycles. The first two cycles are a preparation for *the most important, third cycle.* Badly performed last Rph and Aph devalues the preceding autoregulative work.

Every Rph takes roughly 5–10 mins, the Aph will take in the order of 10–30 secs. Relaxation operations calm and dissolve tension. Aph is characterized by a rapid increase of tension and excitement. Figure 1 shows the dynamics of the fluctuations of tension and relaxation during one autoregulative training. The curve informs the beginner of the desirable dynamics of the feeling of tension and

---

[1]An English language monograph devoted to the given subject was published under the title "Harmonizing of mental states and performance" (Machac, 1976). It also contains extensive references.

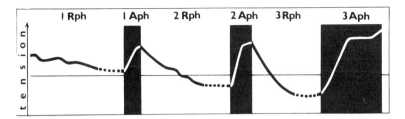

Figure 1 Instruction curve of course of relaxation activation training with regard to the dynamics of relaxation and tension. Rph—relaxation phase, Aph—activation phase. The middle parts of relaxation phases have for technical reasons been deleted. Curves depicting neurovegetative manifestations of activation changes (GSR, blood pressure, heart beat) have similar shape (see Machac, 1964 b, 1976).

relaxation during training. As we shall see later its shape agrees with the shape of curves which represent activation fluctuations of some vegetative parameters during autoregulative interventions. The diagram shows that the difference between maximum relaxation and maximum activation increases. This is the *"activation system pendulum."* The last Aph is longest and strongest.

As against excitement which we experience in natural situations Aph excitement is free of any ideas, that is, it is non-cognitive (non-content) and is accompanied by muscle relaxation. (In laboratory controls a quiescent EMG) Aph does not tolerate muscle straining. In this it differs from normal (reactive) activation. During Aph EEG retains the quiescent alpha rhythm. (However, there is a significant average 0.9 secs acceleration of this rhythm).

The duration of training is not determined by time. It is determined by the quality of prescribed operations and the fulfillment of the set targets. Thus, for instance, muscle relaxation is subjectively manifested by emotional equanimity, an increased psychic distance towards negative and positive influences, the slackening tension of skeletal muscles, etc.

This is followed by *psychic relaxation* by which the process of relaxation culminates. Its aim is the temporary clearance of psychic linkages with the outer world and the discontinuation of ideation and imagination processes. The weakening of the exteroception component of the consciousness is accomplished by the strengthening of the somatic component (proprioception and interoception). The global feeling of the "physical existence" without any further relations becomes the sole content of the conscious. An important subjective indicator of the completion of psychic relaxation and thereby of the entire Rph, apart from the attenuation of cognitive processes is the removal of remnants of anxiety and thereby the strengthened feeling of well-being and security.

This psychic state is very fickle. We are not able to completely eliminate the influx of associations. We have to respond patiently to every revitalization of the cognitive sphere by maneuvering, such as will result in the return of "cognitive calm." Several seconds suffice and the trainee may proceed to the activation phase.

In other autoregulative methods the "clearance" role is played by concentrating consciousness on a certain part of the body or on a word or image (autogenic training, yoga, zen exercises). It is possible to persist in such a state for a lengthy period of time. Concentration of the attention on some object contradicts RAM. In this method we are not merely concerned with "curbing" these associations but with temporarily discontinuing all relations generally, including the relationship of the subject to the observed object. The discontinuation of psychic linkages allows to achieve a better "sealing of the system."

More recent investigations have shown that the function of the vegetative nervous system may be conditioned not only by classical methods but that *instrumental learning* (operant conditioning) may also be applied when technical conditions have been created for such procedure (e.g., the technique of biological feedback). In our experiments with psychological autoregulation we proved that deliberate noncontent manipulation of the psychophysiological system in the sense of relaxation and activation is manifested by the whole complex of corresponding vegetative changes (RAM vegetative pattern).

Influencing vegetative function was, however, not the primary aim of our research. We investigated the problem of objective indicators of changes taking place during autoregulative intervention and their possible use for distinguishing good and bad autoregulative training. *The knowledge of the "vegetative pattern" of the good relaxation activation intervention (RAI) allows us to reveal the errors of trainees,* to eliminate them and to compare the effect of bad and good training.

Psychic states represent an area in which the responses of many subjects must be taken with reservations. Most people do not wish to discuss their psychic states, and if so only in very general outline. The vagueness and external undepictability of psychic states very often catathymally distorts the subject's statement on the actual state (influenced by desires, concern, the effort to conform to what the subject believes is expected of him, etc.).

We have therefore attempted to develop a set of objective indicators which would allow us to control and evaluate the course of RAI more reliably.

FORMULAS OF "VEGETATIVE" BEHAVIOR DURING AND AFTER THE RELAXATION ACTIVATION INTERVENTION (RAI)

All experiments which we shall describe were conducted with subjects who had already undergone RAI training. All of them were asked to do home training during the experiment.

The only difference between home training and the experiment consisted in that in the experiment the trainees were asked to signalize the beginning and end of each individual phase by pressing foot microswitch. All of them trained in a dark soundproof room. They lay in a supine position with closed eyes. No stimuli were given during the experiments.

Changes in *galvanic skin resistance (GSR)* were monitored in 24 trainees in 66 exercises,in 172 attempts to pass from relaxation phase (Rph) to activation phase (Aph). We also monitored the respiration curve. In all subjects the activation phase was manifested as a rapid and very intensive drop in electric skin resistance. The average drop in electric skin resistance was 40.66% of preactivation level.

In relaxation phases on the other hand resistance increased and usually reached maximum immediately before the onset of Aph (see Fig. 2).

A comparison of the subjective evaluation of the quality of the course of Rph and Aph within the same relaxation activation intervention (RAI) with

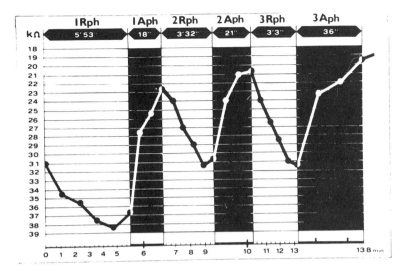

Figure 2 Dynamics of the course of mean changes of electric skin resistance during RAM. During activation phases Aph the skin resistance of all trainees drops rapidly (mean drop in % of preactivation level $\bar{x}$ = 40.66%, standard deviation SD = 16.95, N = 169). During relaxation phases resistance increases and spontaneous fluctuations decrease. The intervals on the time axis are 20 secs. The graphic representation of data on the duration of relaxation phases are condensed four fold in time for technical reasons. (The same applies for Figs. 3 and 4). Averaged are individual curves of 24 trainings, usually three Aph and Rph cycles each. (See also Machac, 1964 b, 1976).

parameters of the electric skin resistance curve indicated their possible use for objective control of training and guidance of trainees. It was found that a stronger feeling of tension during Aph within the same session correlates significantly with minimum electric skin resistance (measured in percentage of preactivation level).

Decline of the number of spontaneous GSR deviations (the so-called unrest index) and explicit trend towards higher GSR values correlate with the growth of the feeling of relaxation.

The actual absolute level of electric skin resistance is on the other hand irrelevant from the point of view of relaxation.

Changes in systolic arterial blood pressure, during RAI were monitored in 18 subjects with normal blood pressure in 115 experiments (see Fig. 3).

Rph was manifested by rapid and towards the end by milder decline while Aph was manifested by an intensive rise in blood pressure, on the average by 26.7 torrs. *Changes in heart rate* during RAI were analyzed in 14 trainees in 38 sessions, usually after three cycles of Rph and Aph. (There was a total of 112 transitions from Rph to Aph.) Next to ECG we also recorded the EEG and EMG (electromyogram) and the EDG (electrodermogram—skin electric activity record.)

It was found that heart beat in Rph and Aph differed significantly. Rph was manifested by a mild drop in heart beat, the onset of activation phases was manifested by a rapid increase in heart beat and their final stage by a rapid

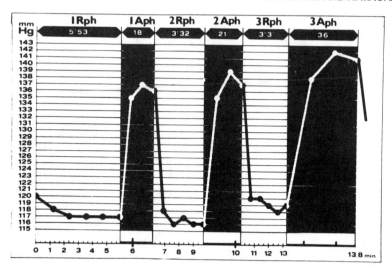

Figure 3 Dynamics of the mean changes of systolic blood pressure during RAI. During the activation phase blood pressure rapidly increases and after the end of RAI it returns to preactivation values, initially at a quick rate, slower towards the end. Blood pressure decreases during Rph but not explicitly. Means activation fluctuation $\bar{x}$ = 26.7 mm Hg (SD = 10.8, N = 115). We averaged 18 individual curves. (See also Machac, 1976).

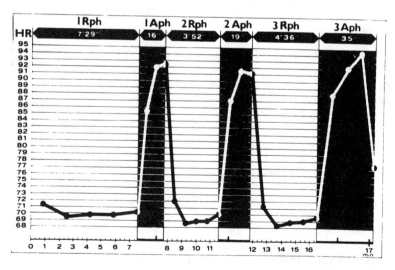

Figure 4 Dynamics of the course of heart rate through the duration of RAI. The activation phase is characterized by a rapid increase of heart beat. After the end of the phase heart rate quickly decreases to values which are somewhat lower than initial values. Mean heart rate increase $\bar{x}$ = 22 beats/min (SD = 14.6, N = 112). We averaged 38 curves usually of three Rph + Aph cycles each). (See also Machac & Morávek, 1965).

deceleration of heart rate. The mean increase of heart beat during activation phases was 22.00 beats per min. (see Fig. 4).

In the initial five seconds of every Aph and Rph the heart beat accelerates on the average by 14–16 beats/min.

Heart beat variations take place in parallel with variations of systolic blood pressure and skin galvanic reactions. The subjectively "best" Aph in comparison with the "worst" Aph (within the same session) manifest higher acceleration of heart beat.

In RAI heart rate, blood pressure, GSR etc. variations are a component of deliberately conducted psychophysiological changes and in this sense they are under volitional control.

The study of relations between changes in the individual autonomous channels, for example, in emotions, did not lead authors to unambiguous conclusions. This most frequently concerned GSR, heart rate, blood pressure and skin temperature. Small or insignificant correlations were found. This led to the hypothesis of the individual specificity of autonomous reactions (Lacey et al., 1953) under which he understands that the individual responds by maximum activation of a certain psychological function independently of the type of stressor.

The *electrodermogram (recording electric skin potentials)* in 14 subjects who conducted a total of 100 attempts at passing from Rph to Aph showed that during Rph electric skin activity decreases, to rise enormously during Aph. During the activation phase we found in 83% of all cases a generalization of skin potentials also on EEG leads, respectively on ECG (see Fig. 5).

Pupillary dilatation is a generally known indicator of excitement and psychic tension. Here we are concerned with the so-called orientation reflex.

The transition from Rph to Aph was always accompanied by pupillary dilatation (mean value 1.02 mm) even under strong recording light.

RAI emotional effects are a feeling of recuperation following psychic load, the elimination of negative emotional tension (anxiety, fear) and the removal of the feeling of inner discomfort and the accelerated regeneration of work dispositions. The most explicit autoregulative results were achieved in a dysphoric mood.

After every measuring of physiological changes which occurred in the course of autoregulative interventions in the laboratory the trainees described their impressions of the given exercise, but also their recent home experiences with RAM. This usually concerned objective, as well as subjective observations concerning various recurrent life situations which make it possible to discover the subsequent turning effect of RAM. The protocols in which trainees among others freely record changes in mood and reactions after RAM intervention also contain a large amount of this type of information.

On the basis of material on the subsequent effects of RAI collected over a period of several years we constructed a questionnaire (56 items) which 16 trainees filled in two and 24 hours after RAI. Using cluster analysis of the matrix of intercorrelations between items we ascertained three groups of questions which we designated "performance," "relations" (social interaction), and "state" (general life feeling, mood). The cluster "performance" or "efficiency" is characterized for instance by the following items: Readiness for activity, mental efficiency, physical efficiency, recalling capacity, concentration, voluntary striving, yielding to failure. The cluster "relations" is characterized by the following items:

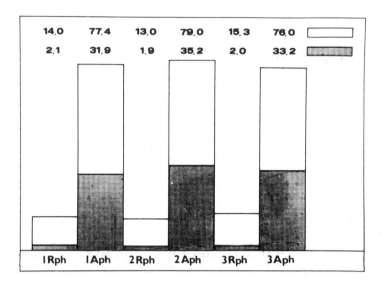

| 14.0 | 77.4 | 13.0 | 79.0 | 15.3 | 76.0 | ☐ |
| 2.1 | 31.9 | 1.9 | 35.2 | 2.0 | 33.2 | ▦ |

| 1 Rph | 1 Aph | 2 Rph | 2 Aph | 3 Rph | 3 Aph |

Figure 5 Level of electric skin activity (electric potentials of the skin) during RAI. The dark areas show values of skin potentials generalized in EEG and EMG, quantification is planimetric.

Feeling of self-confidence, feeling of subjection, inferiority, dislike for social contact, state-shyness, sense of dependence, decisiveness. The cluster "states" is characterized by the items: Tendency to anxiety, form (good-bad), irritability, feeling of calmness, feeling of disagreeable inner strain.

In all three clusters of items we found statistically significant positive RAI effect in the first and second presentations of the questionnaire. Each of these factors significantly correlates with the group of items which represents "the central effect" of RAI. It represents the following items: desire for action, self-consciousness, determination, a pleasant feeling of excessive energy, the feeling of a full life. The tuning effect of RAI on the central cluster of items may briefly be characterized as the *anxiolytical effect.*

In our observation of the subsequent effect of RAI we did not feel it sufficed to investigate the subjective impression of trainees. We asked ourselves the question *whether the long-term subjective subsequent effect is also manifested by persisting vegetative changes.* The sympatico-tropic character of RAI, namely of Aph, showed that it would first of all be necessary to study changes in the *level of catecholamines* in autoregulative intervention. These hormones are permanently present in small quantities in the blood and psychic states their level changes. The suitability of indicating psychic load and changes in psychic states by the amount of secerned catecholamines was proved especially by Levi (1963) and others.

The *level of noradrenaline* in the urine showed no statistically significant change after RAI. Monitoring *adrenaline* in the urine over 20–24 hours after RAI showed that the given method has long-term stimulation effect on the secretion of this hormone which is considered to be the indicator of changes in activation level (see Fig. 6). This fact corresponds with the statements made by trainees on *the persistence of subsequent changes in the emotional sphere.*

CHANGES IN PERFORMANCE

Changes in performance were first of all assessed on the basis of questionnaire data reflecting the experience of subjects using RAM for the fulfillment of working tasks. The trainees stated that their working or sports condition had improved after RAI, that their mobility and speed had increased, their resistance to load had grown and that their thinking, invention and concentration had improved. The existence of such changes was confirmed by experimental laboratory trials. These were model situations suitable for monitoring the psychomotor tempo, concentration, suitable for measuring tolerance to so-called secondary loading, performance under conditions of frustration, time stress and in a situation of the electric shock, expectancy etc. (Machac, 1976).

RAM was practically tested during several peak contests in a wide range of sports disciplines, (Czechoslovakian championships, the European track and field championships, and the 1980 Olympic Games). The objective of our work was the realization of the performance potential of the athlete in stressogenic

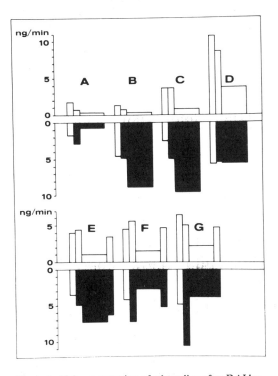

Figure 6 Urinary excretion of adrenaline after RAI by individual subjects (N = 7). The urine was taken in time intervals of 11–15, 15–19, 19–11 hrs and in three subjects 11–15 hrs. The respective 4 or 16 hour intervals are shown in the histogram. The columns above the abscissa give data for the first day (control), columns under the abscissa give values for the second day (experimental). Dark columns show secretion after RAI (See also Machac & Benes, 1969).

situations. In the given context we consider it adequate to mention the 1980 Olympic Games: We started training with 40 athletes roughly one year before the Games. We acquainted their coaches with the substance and meaning of psychological preparation in a letter. The letters were sent to coaches of measurable sports. The participation of athletes was voluntary for those who had been entered by their coaches and for those who decided to take part themselves. The main criterion for participation given to coaches was the difficulty to perform in important contests. Among those who applied for participation there was a large number of those who were not prospective nominees to the Olympic team or whose coaches believed that they had no such prospects ("let the psychologists give them a try" was what they thought). It should be added that this category included two athletes who later won Olympic medals.

Most of the athletes who applied for participation *suffered from excessive or premature prestart stress.* Of those who underwent RAM 14 were nominated to the Olympic team, i.e., approximately 7% of the Olympic team. Four sportsmen could not cope with prestart training, one athlete was injured in the contest and one woman athlete arrived in Moscow so late that RAI was out of the question. We thus had eight athletes who were psychologically properly prepared for start and who gained 18 Olympic points, 2.2 points per every psychologically prepared athlete. On the other hand the other athletes (control group), gained on the average 0.64 points i.e., 3.4 times less.[2]

The main practical problem of the psychological preparation of athletes for a "big contest" is *inconsistent "self-assuredness"* or the leisurely optimism of athletes and their coaches at a time when they should have already started psychological training. Important events which are six months or one year distant are often beyond the horizon of the sphere of their emotional involvement. Most athletes apply for training so late that the time left for mastering and practically testing RAM in preliminary contests is not sufficient.

This situation is to a certain extent influenced by the fact that our public believes that "care of the psyche" is something for weaklings and psychology is sometimes mistaken for psychiatry.

The second important problem on which depends the success of psychological prestart preparations is its *objective control* not only at the time of psychoregulative training but also before start, that is, several hours to one day before start.

The ability to reliably conduct autoregulative training weakens before the start of a big contest. This is related to strong emotionally negative tension. Systematic monitoring of a group of representatives before the Olympic Games showed that weeks or days before a contest athletes are drawn into the emotional vortex of expectation of the contest situation. Long before the contest restless sleep, disorders of digestion, etc., but especially a disturbed ability to relax grow slowly while shortly before start all symptoms of unrest rapidly increase.

Athletes usually have the tendency to dissimulate difficulties. (Participation in the contest is inevitable and it is therefore necessary to extricate oneself from ideas of failure). In such a situation the athlete is less critical and sober in the

---

[2]This is an unofficial assessment, where a 1st position (gold medal) = 7 points, a 2nd position (silver medal) = 5 points, and a third position (bronze medal) = 4 points, a 4th position = 3 points, a 5th position = 2 points and a 6th position = 1 point.

evaluation of his psychic preparedness for performance. If the athlete is left to himself he mostly returns to old patterns of prestart emotional dynamics. It is a though he had forgotten that there is a novel and practically proven instrument for tuning the desirable prestart state. As far as he does conduct RAI he will be satisfied with low quality intervention and will not attempt corrective training.

The psychologist equipped with the respective recording apparatus and experience is able to preempt these tendencies. We proceed from the assumption that in the milieu of a big contest the athlete is continuously exposed to stressogenic influences; as a result emotional equilibrium developed by autoregulative training "disintegrates" somewhat sooner than under normal life conditions. Therefore several days before start the quiescent state should be strengthened by repeated psychoregulation, for example, training every three days. The last training must be situated in time in such a manner as to allow substitute training in case of failure. Some athletes had to repeat training several times before we could state that the quality of training was really good. This would not have been possible without RAI instrument control.

PROBLEM OF OBJECTIVE INDICATORS
OF RAI QUALITY

A certain minimum sufficient for objective control of RAI is the recording of the respiration curve, electric skin resistance and heart rate. *Electric skin resistance* with other indicators of activation changes has the advantage of very sensitively depicting minor spontaneous fluctuations of the activation level but is also well suited for measuring robust activation changes.

After each RAI an interview is conducted with the trainee in which he is asked to evaluate the training, to compare it with RAI conducted at home, to say which Rph was best, which worst, what were the hindrances. (The same for the individual Aph). The trainees link their ideas of the quality of the intervention with subjective feelings during training and with experiences with subsequent effects. We then see to it that their subjective feelings, experiences and performances following RAI are linked with the respective parameters of recorded curves. The notion of *"training quality"* is thus the result of long-term comparison of introspective data with performance experiences and with experimental data. Some trainees with longer autoregulative practice after a number of feedback "RAM experience-GSR curve" confrontations acquire the ability to find shortcomings in their autoregulative performance by independent readings of experiment records.

RAI quality must therefore be evaluated both with regard to activation-relaxation and with regard to the pleasure-displeasure dimension. For the trainee the direct indicator of training quality is the emotional experience aspect of RAI.

In autoregulation experiments feelings on the tension-relaxation scale are consistent with fluctuations in the electric skin resistance. In compliance with the theoretical concept of activation we consider *electric skin resistance to be the objective indicator of psychophysiological tension. Practically applicable objective correlates of pleasure or displeasure are not always available. We therefore have to seek indirect ways of depiction.*

In the pleasure-displeasure dimension the psychologist depends on the response of the trainee, he can, of course, confront it with the trainee's behavior and with certain activation parameters which may be considered *as indirect indicators of the pleasure coloring of RAI.*

In the final stage of relaxation the trainee is to experience the feelings of security and well-being, totally free of all remnants of anxiety. We know from experience that Aph started at an inappropriate moment, for example, when relaxation is disturbed by mild anxiety, does not proceed smoothly, has a "stepwise" character, is linked with the feeling of "inner friction," sometimes has emotionally negative coloring, is usually weak and does not have the desirable subsequent tuning effect.

Another indirect indicator of RAI quality is its duration. We know that quality RAI may be carried out within approximately 10–40 mins. Quality performance of all operations is not possible within a shorter period of time and longer persistence in supine position often gives rise to physical discomfort.

The distance between the lowest activation point on the curve at the end of each Rph and the respective Aph is to increase gradually (in the following cycles). The activation system is to be set into "pendulum motion" such that the last activation should be the strongest. Should we allow a strong Aph already in the initial cycle we shall have to expect difficulties with the following Rph. Deep relaxation is the condition of strong and quality activation.

We have also found that athletes who master RAI are not able to perform quality RAI when they have been subjected to excessive training. Activation phases lack explosiveness, GSR fluctuations are slow, not explicit, in some instances they do not differ from relaxation phases and yet trainees have the subjective feeling that they have invested great effort in the Aph stage and consider the RAI they have conducted to have been "good." Length rest will suffice to remove such a state.

In women GSR changes similarly during RAI as a consequence of premenstrual tension. The GSR curve in relaxation phases in such cases does not have any clear tendency towards higher values of skin resistance and is manifested by minor permanent restlessness. The Aph curve does not significantly differ from the Rph curve.

We have ascertained empirically that a *prognostically good RAI* is such during whose performance (1) the sequence of prescribed psychological operations has been observed, (2) the demands have been met on the emotional tuning of key intervention moments and (3) demands set by the instruction curve on the objective dynamics of relaxation activation fluctuations during training, namely demands on the GSR parameters of the last Rph and Aph have been met.

Intensity of the last Aph is considered acceptable when it reaches 40% cutting down of skin resistance while observing all other requirements on the performance of RAI. Absolute intensity of activation is in itself not decisive. Outstanding, mostly young trainees, achieve a reduction of skin resistance of up to 70–80% as compared with that recorded before the start of Aph.

As a whole RAI has a sympaticotropic effect which persists for 20–30 hours or longer. It is remarkable that the change in psychic state which follows RAI cannot be described as increased tension. In some individuals we have, however, immediately after RAI observed tension and restlessness persisting for approximately half an hour and similar to manifestations of inner "overpressure" which reminds the effect of psychostimulating drugs. In some we observed uncontrolled laughter and other manifestations of euphoria. These were, however, exceptions. Most subjects behaved calmly after RAI with manifest signs of improved mood. *The post-RAI state may roughly be described as a state of emotionally positive calm which easily and according to need alternates with a positively tuned work tension, resistant to load effects.*

RAM strengthens the stability of the positive emotional sphere thereby increasing man's resistance to stress and shortening the duration of his stress reaction in time. Increased resistance to stress after RAI corresponds with our recent endocrinological findings: In seven subjects we found significantly increased saliva cortisol levels (morning samples) after RAI. This state persisted for three days in which the analyses were made.

Contrary to the general ergotropic character of changes in activation phases certain parameters (such as muscle relaxation, the absence of arousal in EEG) pertain to the reference framework of relaxation. Despite increased activation readiness and the increased level of adrenaline in the blood over night the trainees find it easier to go to sleep and their sleep is deeper and more wholesome.

We conceive the relaxation-activation intervention as a psychogenic type of eustress which contrary to the course of distress quickly passes into emotionally positive calm with the possibility of readily mobilizing the necessary forces and abilities in any situation which should require it.

A certain tension which is linked with eustress is probably the cause of the unexpectedly long duration of the RAM tuning effect. Mere relaxation induced by autogenic training is much more labile.

SUMMARY AND CONCLUSIONS

Autoregulative methods have a common objective, namely to help provide man exposed to psychically demanding situations with a feeling of psychophysiological harmony, equilibrium, to free him of negative affective states, especially anxiety, ill-humor and a feeling of fatigue which threaten his vital energy, achievement and sometimes his health. This goal may be achieved by incorporating the emotionally vegetative aspect of the psychophysiological activity in the sphere of intentional regulation.

Tuning of the actual psychophysiological state is achieved primarily by "natural" means of external conditions are favorable for such methods, a good vital basis, correct rules which guide our behavior, enough time, a good life pattern, conditions for sports activities or for other adequate physical effort.

Autoregulative methods should not be substitutes for natural ways of restoring one's working capacity. They are to help man, in form of "concentrated" artificial rest, to restore his emotionally vegetative homeostasis, whose continuous maintenance is a problem for an ever increasing number of inhabitants of industrially advanced countries.

Autoregulation must not absorb too much time or psychic capacity and must not be based on ideological foundations whose acceptance means cognitive maladjustment. In our concept autoregulation must help present man to fulfill all his functions in the conditions of present day life. The ivory castle and the creation "of one's own world" are out of the question.

Autoregulative means widely exceed the framework of the possibilities of "natural" homeostatic mechanisms and compensation activities acquired in everyday life. The index of "natural" and "naive" homeostatic mechanisms are often no longer adequate for coping with present complex and demanding life situations. In the future artificial autoregulative means will have to be applied. This is as yet a somewhat unusual idea.

Current psychophysiological knowledge, however, justify the claim that even in the emotional sphere randomness may be restricted and deliberate intervention expanded. Man has the possibility to regulate his own psychophysiological states, relatively independently of the constellation of external influences.

The first steps which have to date been made in the field of autoregulation research show that their mental hygiene and theoretical contribution to the complex solution of man's relationship with his environment is immense.

RAM has a non-specific tuning effect on the actual psychophysiological state of man. The method has successfully been applied to people of different professions (students, athletes, artists, scientists, technicians and other creative workers). The nonspecific character of its effect is borne out by the fact that it has successfully been used in the therapy of certain psychosomatoses, for example, its normotonic effects in primary hypertonics in surprising. In this respect our work is only in its initial stage.

Our experiences with peak athletes training for the "big contest" have shown that long-term relaxation-activation autoregulative training is an effective means for increasing the reliability of performance, limiting random unfavorable psychogenic effects and removing discrepancies between potential and actual performance. An athlete who is properly psychologically prepared need not fear psychological failure. We know means for effectively controlling the psychic, that is, psychophysiological condition. It is evident that it costs a lot of effort.

Signals causing fear and anxiety are always connected with activities which are of an overt or covert defensive, dodging or fleeing nature. Defensive behavioral trends interfere with the behavior required in a situation of highly demanding sports performance.

For a healthy person mild anxiety and fear are factors which provide energy and increase general activity. However, excessive anxiety can lead to a total destruction of behavior. It has been experimentally proven that impulses which cause fear and anger have a greater influence on the brain nonspecific activation system than impulses which are emotionally positive. High emotional eruptiveness and increased irritability are typical for pre-start situations. A sportsman who is "emotionally labile" or one who is too dependent on success can thus easily find himself in a chaotic emotional vortex of uncertainty and fear which can, to a certain extent, exhaust his powers even before the game or race has started. Hyperactivity or premature activity are the most typical psychoregulatory problem of top sportsmen when a competition is approaching. An activation optimum can be achieved by maintaining the ability to rest, saving one's strength, and also the ability to implement one's performance potential at the right moment.

Spontaneously developed dysfunctions in emotional and vegetative reactions can be prevented with the aid of artificial psycho-regulatory interventions. Under natural conditions emotions depend upon cognition and cognition on reality and/or its interpretation in a person's mind.

Autoregulative (non-cognitive) approaches, however, control emotional and vegetative states directly through psychological manipulations with psychophysiological states. This procedure is relatively independent on the external situation and its interpretation. Psychological autoregulation thus represents an intentional, direct intervention into the dynamics of psycho-physiological activities. This is a relatively closed system, which is temporarily removed from the context of subject-environment interaction.

The majority of autoregulation methods are of an essentially auto-relaxation type (Schultz' autogenous training is typical). Approximately 25 years we have been using the Relaxation Activation Method (RAM), which has specific advantages in comparison to autogenous training and other autorelaxation methods:

1. The course of a good quality training period is typically reflected in the dynamic changes of some vegetative functions (pulse frequency, blood pressure, the electrical skin resistance, skin potentials, EEG and others).

2. Objective recordings of important parameters concerning the course of an exercise period provide feedback information for RAM learning, as well as data for prediction of subsequent effects. In unsuccessful interventions there is the possibility of reparation, if the subsequent performance is considered important enough.

3. The tuning effect of RAM lasts for a substantially longer time than that of other self regulation methods.

4. RAM intervention is composed of relaxation and activation stages which alternate. The relaxation stages prepare for the activation stages. The RAM effect is not simple autorelaxation.

5. RAM strengthens the stability of the emotionally positive sphere, improves mental and physical performance, increases resistance to stress and improves the regeneration of work abilities.

6. RAM causes sympaticotropic changes (and/or activation changes), which last from 20–30 hours to 3–4 days. This is confirmed by increased adrenaline levels in urine and increased cortisol levels in saliva.

7. We assume that RAM is a method for the psychogenous evoking of eustress, which in contrast to distress, rapidly changes into an emotionally positive state of calmness. When the situation requires it, this state can readily lead to a mobilization of the required strength and abilities.

REFERENCES

Lacey, J. J., Bateman, D. E.,& Van Lehn, R. (1953). Autonomic response specificity: An experimental study. *Psychosomatic Medicine, 15.*

Levi, L. (1963). The urinary excretion of adrenaline and noradrenaline during experimentally induced emotional stress in clinically different groups. *Acta Psychotherapeutica et psychosomatica, 11,* 218–227.

Machac, M. (1962). Predstartovni stavy a moznosti jejich autoregulacniho zvladnuti. (Pre-start states and the possibility of their autoregulation control). *Teorie a praxe telesne vychovy (Theory and Practice of Physical Education), 11,* 10.

Machac, M. (1964a). Skin galvanic manifestations of the relaxation activation autoregulative intervention. *Ceskoslovenska Psychologie (Czechoslovak Psychology), 8*(1), 1–15.

Machac, M. (1964b). The relaxation activation autoregulative intervention. (Method of training and psychological characteristics). *Ceskoslovenska Psychologie (Czechoslovak Psychology, 8*(2), 97–112.

Machac, M. (1976). *Harmonizing of mental state and performance.* Praha: Univerzita Karlova.

Machac, M., & Benes, V. (1969). Effect of relaxation activation autoregulative method of shift of catecholamines in the urine. *Activitas Nervosa Superior, 11*(1), 46–53.

Machac,M., & Moravek, M. (1965). Fluctuations of heart rate during relaxation and activation phases of psychological autoregulative intervention. *Ceskoslovenska Psychologie (Czechoslovak Psychology) 9*(4), 381–394.

15

Biofeedback-Assisted Self-Regulation for Stress Management in Sports

Leonard D. Zaichkowsky and C. Zvi Fuchs

Biofeedback as an area of inquiry and application is a rather recent development, first appearing in the literature in the 1960s. Since that time, psychologists, physicians and other health professionals have conducted extensive research on the topic. Research and application of biofeedback technology in the motor skills area is predictably of a more recent vintage with the first paper appearing only ten years ago (Zaichkowsky, 1975). Our purpose in writing this paper is to briefly discuss the concept of biofeedback, then critically review studies which investigated the relationship between biofeedback and motor skill learning and performance.

WHAT IS BIOFEEDBACK?

At the core of biofeedback is the principle of feedback, a concept psychologists, motor behavior researchers and practitioners have researched and applied for decades. The feedback provided the individual is however rather unique in that it is feedback about biological processes, processes the individual is not normally aware of or able to voluntarily control.

In order to provide one with meaningful, precise and rapid biological feedback three methodological elements are needed. First, some type of instrumentation (usually electronic) through the use of sensing devices and transducers allows for more or less immediate measurement of biological functions. Second, information about this process is amplified by the instrument and "fed-back" to the individual. In other words, the individual is provided with "feedback" about some "biological" process' thus the term *biofeedback*. Third, there is usually some effort on the part of the experimenter (therapist) and subject to utilize the feedback for purposes of helping the subject gain voluntary control over a particular biological process. Such efforts usually take the form of some combination of verbal instructions in the use of cognitive strategies that facilitate gaining voluntary control, verbal instructions to make the feedback display change in the desired direction, or the presentation or removal of reinforcers contingent upon changes in the feedback display.

Following is a description of the major biological systems for which "biofeedback" devices have been developed and employed for dealing with a variety of clinical disorders:

1. *Muscle feedback* (EMG) detects activity of muscle and has principally been used for relaxation training, desensitization, tension headaches, and muscle rehabilitation.

2. *Thermal feedback* detects peripheral skin temperature and has been demonstrated to be useful for relaxation training, migraine headaches and vasoconstrictive disorders.

3. *Electrodermal biofeedback* (EDR) is a term which refers to feedback obtained from electrical activity at various skin sites. Presently there is a proliferation of terms and general lack of consensus regarding the measurement of electrodermal activity. The numerous specific measures include: galvanic skin response (GSR), skin conductance response (SCR), skin resistance response (SRR), skin conductance level (SCL), skin resistance level (SRL), and skin potential response (SPR). Electrodermal feedback has been used to teach relaxation and as an adjunct in therapy (e.g., systematic desensitization).

4. *Cardiovascular biofeedback,* using a variety of relatively simple sensors (e.g., electronic, mechanical, plethysmographic), has been utilized by researchers and clinicians to provide feedback about heart rate and blood flow. Studies have shown that subjects can decrease and increase heart rate voluntarily. Presently heart rate biofeedback is being researched for the treatment of cardiac arrhythmias.

5. *Electroencephalographic feedback* (EEG) measures brain wave activity. Has been used for relaxation training but has been found inefficient compared to EMG and thermal feedback. Also used in treating seizures.

As pointed out at the outset of this paper, research and application of biofeedback technology in the field of sport and exercise science is a recent event. A review of the literature has enabled us to produce two major categories of research and application. Although somewhat artificial because of their interacting, overlapping nature, we have chosen to label these categories the control of *psychological stress,* and the control of *physiological stress.* It should be pointed out that the "psychological" studies tended to emphasize the reduction of muscle tension, which may or may not have been associated with competitive stress or anxiety, or were designed to teach cognitive control over muscle activity, and in some cases autonomic activity—a kind of "athlete fine-tuning." The studies we labeled as "physiological" were primarily concerned with using biofeedback to increase performance by reducing cardiovascular and respiratory stress, induce specific muscle relaxation in order to improve flexibility, reduce muscle pain and soreness after workout, and increase the strength of healthy muscles.

CONTROL OF PSYCHOLOGICAL STRESS

To date a substantial number of studies have been reported where biofeedback (primarily EMG) was used to reduce stress/tension in order to improve motor performance. Three of these studies used the stabilimeter as a laboratory measure of performance (Blais & Orlick, 1977; French, 1978, 1980; Teague, 1976). Another study (Pinel & Schultz, 1978), used measures of hand steadiness and grip strength. The remaining studies used the sports skills of archery (Bennett & Hall, 1979), synchronized swimming (Wenz & Strong, 1980), basketball and American football (DeWitt, 1980), gymnastics (Dorsey, 1976; Goodspeed, 1983; Tsukomoto, 1979), and rhythmic gymnastics (Peper & Schmid, 1983).

The majority of the above studies reported successful outcomes following EMG biofeedback intervention. For instance, DeWitt (1980), French (1978, 1980) and Pinel & Schultz (1978) all reported that high levels of muscle tension disrupted performance, but when subjects used EMG biofeedback they were able to reduce muscle tension and improve performance. The three studies which used gymnasts as subjects reported mixed results. Tsukomoto (1979) found no difference between groups who learned to relax with biofeedback and groups that did not. In our work at Boston University, Dorsey (1976) found that anxious gymnasts trained with EMG biofeedback performed better than control subjects on four out of six events under moderate and high conditions of stress. Further, the gymnasts reported that biofeedback helped them to better control stress and enhanced their performance.

More recently Goodspeed (1983) extended upon the Dorsey work using nine female gymnasts at a Division I university as subjects. Goodspeed studied the effects of a comprehensive self-regulation training program which included electrodermal (GSR) and temperature biofeedback, on state anxiety and performance. The gymnasts were able to demonstrate temperature self-regulation and significantly improved performance over the previous year. Although it was not possible to attribute causality to the "treatment," the gymnasts perceived the treatment program as being significant in their overall improvement.

Peper and Schmid (1983) applied similar biofeedback training to members of the U.S. Rhythmic Gymnastics team. The two year program included home practice and training camp instruction in progressive relaxation, autogenic training, imagery rehearsal, arousal and energy awareness, EMG, temperature and electrodermal biofeedback training. Most of the team members demonstrated voluntary control over peripheral temperature, EMG activity, heart rate and skin conductance. Additionally the athletes reported the program to be highly beneficial in integrating the mental skills into their workouts, using relaxation to re-energize, controlling their arousal states, and most importantly enhancing their gymnastic performance.

The recent research of Daniels and Landers (1981) is an excellent example of creative biofeedback being applied to help athletes improve performance. In this innovative study, elite rifle shooters were given auditory feedback about their heart rate and respiration rate during shooting and were asked to coordinate the motor act of firing with specific heart rate and respiration rate patterns. Subjects trained using this feedback improved in both performance and performance consistency from pre-training to post-training, whereas a verbal instruction group showed little or no change. The authors concluded that biofeedback training is a useful tool for enhancing shooting performance and recommended its use in other sports where psychophysiological measures could be monitored.

In summary it can be said that the majority of studies which employed a form of biological feedback primarily to control "psychological" stressors demonstrated positive outcomes. That is not to say that these studies were classically conducted or without methodological flaws. These methodological shortcomings will be discussed in the closing section of this paper.

CONTROL OF PHYSIOLOGICAL STRESS

Biofeedback training has also been used to decrease or increase levels of physical stress in healthy persons in order to improve athletic performance. We were able to trace sixteen studies directly concerned with the manipulation of the cardiovascular and/or muscular systems during exercise, as well as several studies that used biofeedback in conjunction with other relaxation techniques.

Cardiovascular Control

In this section we find it important to review the pioneering and very little known work of two unpublished papers in the field of heart rate control during exercise stress. The first to show significant control of heart rate prior to and during low intensity work loads on a bicycle ergometer was Mize (1970). These reductions, however, were not significant during higher intensities. In another study, LeFevers (1971) showed that biofeedback training for heart rate lowering during rest can be transferred to the exercise situation on a treadmill, even during high intensity stress levels (160–180 bpm).

The first published study on heart rate regulation was conducted by Goldstein, Ross and Brady (1977). This served as a milestone publication for it provided biofeedback procedures and experimental design. The experimental group that received 25 sessions of beat-to-beat heart rate and criterion feedback during performance on a treadmill (2.5 mph, 6 degree grade), showed significantly lower mean heart rates (-12 bpm), systolic blood pressure (-17 mmHg) and rate pressure product (-28%) than the control group. These results were maintained as long as 5 weeks after the cessation of training. On the other hand, the control group which did not show any significant changes during the experiment, failed to change even when they received biofeedback training later.

Replication of the Goldstein et al. study by Perski and Engel (1980) using a bicycle ergometer also showed a substantial reduction (-20%) in heart rate for the biofeedback trained group in comparison to the control group, but no significant change in systolic pressure. In contrast to the Goldstein study, substantial reductions in heart rate for the control group were obtained after they received biofeedback training.

Very recently Lo and Johnston published two studies which examined the effects of two kinds of feedback on bicycle ergometer performance. They used interbeat interval feedback (a correlate of heart rate), pulse transit time feedback (a correlate of systolic blood pressure), and their product (which correlates very highly with the more conventional rate pressure product). In the first study, Lo and Johnston (1984a) found that both biofeedback conditions were superior to verbal instructions in decreasing sympathetic arousal during mild intensity cycling (4 kg. 29–31 rpm). These reductions, however, were limited to the practice sessions and were not transferred to a non-biofeedback condition. In the second study (Lo & Johnston, 1984b) these researchers found that the product feedback of interbeat interval and pulse transit time was more effective in decreasing the cardiovascular effects of the previous aerobic regime, than relaxation training or cycling alone.

Decreases in heart rate and oxygen consumption for biofeedback trained subjects during calibrated submaximal work (40% and 70% of maximal work load) were also reported by Cohen and Knowlton (1981). Their findings, however, were limited to practice sessions only. It is interesting to note that the findings obtained by Cohen and Knowlton were a result of short-term EMG frontalis biofeedback. These findings suggest a carry-over or transfer effect, that is, transfer of voluntary muscle training to the control of autonomic functions. On the other hand, in a study using a similar design, Kirkcaldy and Christen (1981) did not find any transfer from frontalis EMG biofeedback to either central or autonomic nervous system activity.

The ability to control heart rate while executing anaerobic exercise has also been explored. Carrol and Rhys-Davies (1979) examined the relationship between isometric and isotonic contractions of the forearm flexors on heart rate acceleration learning. They found that during 2/3 of maximal voluntary contraction (MVC), biofeedback trained subjects produced greater heart rate increases than subjects who received instructions alone. Some indications for the ability to learn heart rate acceleration during 20% of MVC of the forearm muscles can also be found in Magnusson's (1976) work. Clemens and Shattock (1979) also found that bi-directional learning (increase/decrease) of heart rate control was possible during performance of static exercises, with the hand dynamometer, while using 0%, 10%, 30%, and 50% of MVC.

Self-regulation, of the cardiovascular and respiratory systems, was also demonstrated successfully in healthy non-athletes during exercise (Powers, 1981) and in trained male cross country runners during a submaximal treadmill run (Ziegler, Klinzing, & Williamson, 1982). These findings, however, were a result of a combined regime of biofeedback and other relaxation techniques, therefore making it difficult to single out the contribution of biofeedback to the rather impressive results. The evidence for the ability of healthy adults to learn to control their cardiovascular and respiratory systems, during performance of a variety of submaximal exercise regimes is quite convincing. It remains now to pursue this line of research with top athletes, who are performing at near maximal capacity. It will be interesting to determine whether BFT can help these athletes to improve their performance; or whether a ceiling effect precludes significant improvement. It should be remembered however, that an athlete operating on a lower heart rate and oxygen consumption can, in the long run, be expected to work more efficiently.

Flexibility Control

Another physiological parameter that has been investigated is the use of biofeedback for purposes of improving flexibility in gymnasts and track athletes. In a two stage study, Wilson and Bird (1981) divided 10 gymnasts into 2 groups. The control group practiced self relaxation while the biofeedback group received EMG feedback from their hip extensors. At the end of 9 sessions both groups significantly improved their hip flexion, but the biofeedback group improved more quickly across trials. In the second stage of their study, 15 female gymnasts were divided into 3 groups: control (no treatment), modified progressive relaxation, and EMG hip extensors feedback plus relaxation. Results showed that all 3 groups improved their hip flexion, with no one group superior to the others in any of the parameters that were studied.

In a similar study with 30 athletes, Cummings and Wilson (1981) studied the effects of specific EMG feedback from the hip extensors in comparison to modified progressive relaxation and an active regimen of flexibility exercises. All 3 methods improved the athlete's hip flexibility after 8 sessions. However, when the athletes were instructed to stop any hip flexibility training for 2 weeks, only the relaxation and EMG biofeedback groups maintained their near maximal flexibility level.

The limited number of "biofeedback flexibility" studies makes it difficult to draw any conclusions. It seems, however, that EMG flexibility training of specific muscles can facilitate the development of flexibility.

Pain Control

EMG biofeedback has also been used in an effort to determine its effects on muscle soreness, which is usually felt in the untrained muscles after initial exercise exposure. McGlynn, Laughlin and Filios (1979) trained 20 subjects in eccentric leg press (60% MVC) until they had to stop exercising because of unbearable pain. The subjects were divided into a control group and a group which received EMG biofeedback from their quadriceps 6, 25, 30, 49 and 54 hours after they stopped their workout. Both groups rated their mean pain level immediately after termination of their workout and 24, 48 and 72 hours post exercise. At the same times, EMG measurements (without feedback) of the quadriceps muscle were taken for both groups. Results showed that only the biofeedback trained group recorded significant reductions in the perceived mean pain level along all measurements. EMG mean levels, however, were not significantly different for either group. Nevertheless, the finding, that specific EMG feedback significantly reduces muscle pain but not EMG muscle tension, is in direct opposition to previous findings by the same researchers (McGlynn, Laughlin, & Rowe, 1979) who found biofeedback training of the biceps muscle significantly reduced mean EMG levels but not muscle pain.

The conflicting findings in the area of EMG biofeedback and the control of post exercise pain are difficult to explain. We know, however, that the perceived level of pain is probably one of the most limiting factors in training and competition. We also know that in the area of rehabilitation biofeedback is a very effective method for managing chronic pain (Basmajian, 1979). It seems therefore that more research is needed in order to draw definite conclusions about the role of biofeedback in the management of post exercise pain.

Strength Training

Improvement of muscle strength and function with EMG biofeedback in neurologic and paretic patients is a well documented phenomenon (Basmajian, 1979). The practical implications of the previous findings for healthy subjects, were shown only recently by Middaugh, Miller, and Filios (1982).* Their results showed that active abduction of the abductor hallucis was enhanced by EMG biofeedback from surface electrodes that were placed over the muscle. The significantly greater EMG activity that was exhibited by the subjects during the feedback trials reflects an increase in motor unit recruitment and probably an increase in muscle strength.

The issue of changes in muscle strength due to EMG biofeedback training was recently addressed by Lucca and Recchiuti (1983). The subjects in their study were 30 healthy young females who were divided equally into 3 groups. The experimental group performed isometric contractions of the knee extensors while receiving EMG feedback from surface electrodes that were placed over the belly of the rectus femoris muscle. The second group performed isometric contractions of the same muscle group, but without feedback, while the third group (control) did not exercise. After a 19 day program the biofeedback trained group showed significantly greater gains in average time peak torque when compared to the group who exercised only.

It seems that the mechanism underlying the strength increases in healthy muscles, due to specific EMG biofeedback training, can be explained psychologically by greater awareness and knowledge of results inherent in the biofeedback procedure and neurophysiologically by the increase of firing rates of active motor units and/or recruitment of new unactive motor units. The interested reader, in the theoretical and possible practical implications of EMG biofeedback in exercise programs, skill learning and motor performance, is referred to Wolf's (1980) excellent paper and to our recent paper (Zaichkowsky & Fuchs, 1986).

CONCLUSIONS

While it is natural to have conflicting and confusing findings during the initial stages of any scientific investigation, this review of literature indicates that:

1. Biofeedback training alone or in conjunction with other self-control methods can be an extremely useful way for teaching performers to self regulate their psychophysiological stress responses and thus improve performance.

---

*These researchers designed a study which they hoped would permit them to better understand the learning mechanisms involved in neuromuscular rehabilitation. Middaugh et al. used the left abductor hallicus muscle for study since this muscle is infrequently used and thus poorly developed even in healthy persons. Thus the use of normal subjects and not patients seemed to be justified.

2. Control of cardiovascular and respiratory functions during submaximal work loads can be achieved via biofeedback training, in order to improve exercise tolerance and work efficiency.

3. EMG biofeedback training for flexibility and reduction of muscle soreness has received little research attention to date; however, available data suggests possible positive application.

4. Strength training of specific healthy muscles by EMG biofeedback training seems to be promising but more research is needed.

It should be remembered that the preceding conclusions are based on findings obtained from studies that usually used healthy exercising adults as subjects and only rarely did these studies use top level athletes, performing at near maximal capacity. Therefore, the implications of these findings for highly trained athletes should be evaluated cautiously and await further research.

By and large the studies dealing with sport and biofeedback which we reviewed were not exemplary models of research methodology. In some instances the shortcomings were a result of problems associated with doing "clean" experimental studies in a clinical context. Most clinical researchers struggle with this problem, however there are ways in which relatively strong studies can be conducted (e.g., single-case experimental methods). In other cases the shortcomings were a result of a lack of awareness of current theoretical and research issues in the field of biofeedback.

The major shortcoming of all biofeedback studies reviewed in this paper is that the researchers failed to demonstrate that the subjects trained in biofeedback actually mastered self-regulation. If one is going to evaluate the efficacy of treatment (i.e., biofeedback) on some performance measure, then it is essential that one first demonstrate that mastery of self-regulation has been achieved to a given criterion. For instance, the subject must be able to lower EMG activity to 2 microvolts on the frontal muscle or raise skin temperature one degree per minute to say 94 degrees F. This "training to criterion" is vastly superior to exposing subjects to an arbitrary number (e.g., 8) sessions of biofeedback. We urge researchers to consider this procedure in future efficacy studies.

Rather than trying to "shoe-horn" small sample clinical problems into traditional between-group experimental designs, sport psychologists studying biofeedback should consider employing single-subject experimental designs (Barlow, Blanchard, Hayes, & Epstein, 1977; Zaichkowsky, 1980). Such an approach will eliminate problems of obtaining a "large" sample of experimental and control subjects who have characteristics in common (e.g., elite gymnasts with high performance anxiety). Baseline periods can more readily be established and treatment can be monitored more carefully. Likewise the possibility of conducting important follow-up is greatly enhanced. In virtually all studies which we reviewed the researchers did not do a follow-up. Although single-case studies are a distinct advantage in clinical contexts they present the problem of generalizability of findings. The answer is obviously replication. If researchers do have the good fortune of obtaining sufficient researcher "power" using a between-subjects design then this is certainly a more desirable design. Nevertheless care needs to be taken to ensure proper baseline recording, clearly defined treatment (with training to criterion) and adequate follow-up.

Biofeedback researchers should also be careful to articulate whether they are studying the efficacy of biofeedback (solely) or biofeedback as an adjunct to other related self-regulation techniques such as self-hypnosis, autogenic training, and progressive muscle relaxation. In the studies we reviewed some combination of intervention was usually employed. There is nothing inherently wrong with studying multi-model intervention; however, the point here is that one must be careful not to say that the intervention used was solely biofeedback.

There are certainly other "problematic" research areas associated with the study of biofeedback, such as therapist variables, training procedures, and the interpretation of findings. The interested reader is referred to Kewman and Roberts (1983) for an excellent discussion of research problems in biofeedback.

SUMMARY

The purpose of this chapter was to review the literature concerning the role of biofeedback training in the management of "stress" in sport. We described biofeedback, the various modalities used, the purpose for its use and its efficacy. Research findings in the field of sport behavior and psychophysiology of exercise indicated that psychological stress during training and performance can be reduced by biofeedback training and thus enhance performance. Furthermore, cardiovascular and respiratory stress can be self-regulated while maintaining the same work loads. However, biofeedback procedures employed for strength training, flexibility training and reduction in muscle soreness due to exercise, have received limited experimentation, and thus need additional research to determine efficacy. It appears that biofeedback training has some promising potential in managing psychological and physiological stress in athletic performance and should be recommended for sport psychologists, coaches and athletes as an integral part of a holistic approach to training.

REFERENCES

Barlow, D. H., Blanchard, E. B., Hayes, S. C., Epstein, L. H. (1977). Single-case designs and clinical biofeedback experimentation. *Biofeedback and Self-Regulation, 2,* 221–239.

Basmajian, J. V. (1979). Introduction: Principles and Background. In J. V. Basmajian (Ed.), *Biofeedback: Principles and Practice for Clinicians.* Baltimore: Williams & Wilkins.

Bennett, B., & Hall, C. R. (1979). *Biofeedback training and archery performance.* Paper presented to the International Congress in Physical Education. Trois Rivierres, Quebec.

Blais, M., & Orlick, T. (1977). Electromyographic biofeedback as a means of competition anxiety control: Problems and potential. In *Proceedings of the 9th Canadian Sports Psychology Symposium,* Banff, Alberta.

Carroll, D., & Rhys-Davies, L. (1979). Heart rate changes with exercise and voluntary heart rate acceleration. *Biological Psychology, 8,* 241–252.

Clemens, W. J., & Shattock, R. J. (1979). Voluntary heart rate control during static muscular effort. *Psychophysiology, 16*(4), 327–332.

Cohen, M. D., & Knowlton, R. G. (1981). *The effects of short term biofeedback training on the metabolic response to submaximal exercise.* Paper presented at the 12th annual meeting of the Biofeedback Society of America meeting, Louisville, Kentucky.

Cummings, M. S., & Wilson, V. E. (1981). *Flexibility development using EMG biofeedback and relaxation training.* Paper presented at the 12th annual meeting of the Biofeedback Society of America, Louisville, Kentucky.

Daniels, F. S., & Landers, D. M. (1981). Biofeedback and shooting performance: A test of disregulation and systems theory. *Journal of Sport Psychology, 3,* 271–282.

DeWitt, D. J. (1980). Cognitive and biofeedback training for stress reduction with university athletes. *Journal of Sport Psychology, 2,* 288–294.

Dorsey, J. A. (1976). *The effects of biofeedback assisted desensitization training on state anxiety and performance of college age male gymnasts.* Unpublished doctoral dissertation, Boston University, Boston.

Engel, B. T. (1979). Behavioral applications in the treatment of patients with cardiovascular disorders. In J. V. Basmajian (Ed.), *Biofeedback: Principles and Practice for Clinicians.* Williams and Wilkins, Baltimore.

French, S. N. (1978). Electromyographic biofeedback for tension control during gross motor skill acquisition. *Perceptual and Motor Skills, 47,.* 883–889.

French, S. N. (1980). Electromyographic biofeedback for tension control during fine motor skill acquisition. *Biofeedback and Self-Regulation, 5,*(2), 221–228.

Goldstein, D. S., Ross, R. S., & Brady, J. V. (1977). Biofeedback heart rate training during exercise. *Biofeedback and Self-Regulation, 2,* 107–125.

Goodspeed, G. A. (1983). *The effects of comprehensive self-regulation training on state anxiety and performance of female gymnasts.* Unpublished doctoral dissertation, Boston University, Boston.

Kewman, D. G., & Roberts, A. H. (1983). An alternative perspective on biofeedback efficacy studies: A reply to Steiner and Dince. *Biofeedback and Self-Regulation, 8,* 487–497.

Kirkcaldy, B. D., & Christen, J. (1981). An investigation into the effect of EMG frontalis biofeedback on physiological correlates of exercise. *International Journal of Sport Psychology, 12,* 235–252.

LeFevers, V. A. (1971). *Volitional control of heart rate during exercise stress.* Unpublished doctoral dissertation, Texas Women's University, Texas.

Lo, C. R., & Johnston, D. W. (1984a). Cardiovascular feedback during dynamic exercise. *Psychophysiology, 21*(2), 199–206.

Lo, C. R., & Johnston, D. W. (1984b). The self-control of the cardiovascular response to exercise using feedback of the product of interbeat interval and pulse transit time. *Psychosomatic Medicine, 46*(2), 115–125.

Lucca, J. A., & Recchiuti, S. J. (1983). Effect of electromyographic biofeedback on isometric strengthening program. *Physical Therapy, 63*(2), 200–203.

Magnusson, E. (1976). The effects of controlled muscle tension on performance and learning of heart rate control. *Biological Psychology, 4,* 81–92.

McGlynn, G. H., Laughlin, N. T., & Filios, S. P. (1979). The effect of electromyographic feedback on EMG activity and pain in the quadriceps muscle group. *Journal of Sports Medicine and Physical Fitness, 19*(3), 237–244.

McGlynn, G. H., Laughlin, N. T., & Rowe, V. (1979). Effects of electromyographic feedback and static stretching on artificially induced muscle soreness. *American Journal of Physical Medicine, 58*(3), 139–148.

Middaugh, S. J., Miller, M. C., Foster, G., & Ferdon, M. B. (1982). Electromyographic feedback: Effects of voluntary muscle contractions in normal subjects. *Archives of Physical Medicine and Rehabilitation, 63,* 254–260.

Mize, N. J. (1970). *Conditioning of heart rate under exercise stress.* Unpublished masters thesis, Texas Women's University, Texas.

Peper, E., & Schmid, A. B. (1983). *Mental preparation for optimal performance in rhythmic gymnastics.* In *Proceedings of the fourteenth annual meeting of the Biofeedback Society of America.* Wheat Ridge, Colorado.

Perski, A., & Engel, B. T. (1980). The role of behavioral conditioning in the cardiovascular adjustment to exercise. *Biofeedback and Self-Regulation, 5,* 91–104.

Pinel, J. P., & Schultz, T. D. (1978). Effect of antecedent muscle tension levels on motor behavior. *Medicine and Science in Sports, 10*(3), 177–182.

Powers, C. J. (1981). The psychophysiological effects of biofeedback open focus self-regulation training upon homeostatic efficiency during exercise. *Dissertation Abstracts International, 41*(10), 2927-B.

Teague, M. (1976). *A combined systematic desensitization and electromyograph biofeedback technique for controlling state anxiety and improving gross motor skill performance.* Unpublished doctoral dissertation, University of Northern Colorado.

Tsukomoto, S. (1979). *The effects of EMG biofeedback assisted relaxation on sport competition anxiety.* Unpublished master's thesis, University of Western Ontario, London, Ontario.

Wenz, B., & Strong, D. (1980). An application of biofeedback and self regulation procedures with superior athletes: The fine tuning effect. In R. Suinn (Ed.), *Psychology in sports: Methods and application.* Minneapolis, MN: Burgess.

Wilson, V. E., & Bird, E. I. (1981). Effects of relaxation and/or biofeedback training upon hip flexion in gymnasts. *Biofeedback and Self-Regulation, 6,* 25–34.

Wolf, S. L. (1980). Electromyographic biofeedback in exercise programs. *The Physician and Sportsmedicine, 8*(11), 61–69.

Zaichkowsky, L. D. (1975). Combating stress: What about relaxation training and biofeedback? *Mouvement* 309–312.

Zaichkowsky, L. D. (1980). Single case experimental designs: Application to motor behavior research. In G. Roberts & W. Halliwell (Eds.), *Psychology of Motor Behavior.* Champaign, IL: Human Kinetics Press.

Zaichkowsky, L. D. (1982). Biofeedback for self-regulation of competitive stress. In L. D. Zaichkowsky & W. E. Sime (Eds.), *Stress Management for Sport,* pp. 55–64. Reston, VA: AAHPERD.

Zaichkowsky, L. D., & Fuchs, C. Z. (1986). Biofeedback: the psychophysiology of motor control and human performance. In L. D. Zaichkowsky and C. Z. Fuchs (Eds.), *Motor Behavior: Development, Control, Learning and Performance. New York: Mouvement Publishers.*

Zeigler, S. G., Klinzing, J., & Williamson, K. (1982). The effects of two stress management training programs on cardiorespiratory efficiency. *Journal of Sport Psychology, 4,* 280–289.

16

Training To Reduce Anxiety and Fear in Top Athletes

Vaclav Hosek and Frantisek Man

THEORETICAL APPROACH

Increasing pressure for achieving top sports performance brings about an increase in anxiety and fear of failure on the part of sportsmen. These problems have traditionally been dealt with two areas of research: test anxiety [see Spielberger & Sarason (Eds.), 1975, "Stress and Anxiety," Vol. 1 and Vol. 9, Spielberger, Sarason & Defares (Eds.), 1985, and "Advances in Test Anxiety Research," e.g., Vol. 1 Schwarzer, van den Ploeg, Spielberger, (Eds.), and Vol. 4 (1985), van der Ploeg, Schwarzer, & Spielberger, (Eds.), Krohne & Laux (Eds.), 1982, and in sports, Hackfort & Schwenkmezger, 1980] and achievement motivation (McClelland et al., 1953; Atkinson & Raynor, 1974; Heckhausen, 1980; Vanek, Hosek, & Man, 1982). These two different approaches have given rise to different strategies recommended to reduce anxiety and fear in sports. While for the adherents of test anxiety coping is in this context a basic concept (Krohne & Rogner, 1982; Krohne, 1984; Topman & Jansen, 1984) the other approach usually stresses achievement motivation training (McCleland & Winter, 1969; Krug & Heckhausen, 1982; Man & Hosek, 1984). It seems worthwhile to try to integrate the variety of variables in the areas of motivation and anxiety by using such models as the ones recently introduced by Heckhausen (1977) and Schwarzer, Jerusalem and Lange (1981). They interpret the chain of "situation"—"action"—"outcome"—"consequences" in terms of subjective hierarchies of expectations. Within these expectational hierarchies such concepts as subjective probabilities of success or failure, worry and the valency of goals for action should be anchored. While taking into account both these approaches, our

The authors thank H. Heckhausen, K. Hagtvet, and H. M. van der Ploeg for their comments on earlier drafts of this chapter.

own is based on Heckhausen's (1977) extended model of achievement motivation.

We agree with Hagtvet's opinion (1983) that the concept of fear of failure stands higher than the concept of test anxiety. We base our concept of fear of failure (FF) on Schmalt's concept (1976a, 1982). FF appeared to be a two-factor score: FF_1 and FF_2. "The first motive component (FF_1) describes a self concept of low ability, as well as worry about the correctness of one's performance. The second one (FF_2) describes rather emotional components of fear of failure and its social consequences" (Schmalt, 1982, p. 51). According to Heckhausen (1980, p. 266), these dimensions can be compared with the division of test anxiety into cognitive and emotional components (Liebert & Morris, 1967; Spielberger, 1980). Considerations of our study are based on this rough assumption; we suppose that FF_1 is worry and FF_2 is emotionality and we take into account that these concepts are not completely identical. We shall try to explain the relationship between FF_1 and worry on the one hand and FF_2 and emotionality on the other hand in the discussion of our article. In agreement with the psychometrically excellent studies of Hagtvet (1983, 1984) we accept that fear of failure has no direct effect on performance. A subject high in fear of failure will primarily engage in irrelevant self-perception of affective emotional arousal. Only worry cognitions are assumed to interfere with best performance. Thus fear of failure will influence cognitive performance primarily indirectly, via worry cognitions (cf. also Heckhausen, 1982; Sonntag, 1984). But in this respect it is difficult to find proof in the area of top sports. It seems to us, conversely, that emotionality in the period preceding an important sports event is rather high, especially because of the possible social consequences of failure. Its further increase in the period immediately preceding a contest, caused by increasing mental stress, must necessarily lead to a decline of sports achievement or even to total failure (Hosek, 1981). This is empirically confirmed by Schlicht and Wilhelm (1985). For this reason it would be also useful to decrease fear of social consequences (or to use the terminology of the test anxiety approach, emotionality) by motivational training. This would produce not only an increase in hope of success, which was the aim of the first training programs in this area, but also bring attention to the social context of the given activity. Existing studies of achievement motivation training programs we have surveyed (Man & Hosek, 1984) have been successful in explaining those problems to which they have been applied, i.e., school physical education. However, it now appears that such motivation programs (Krug & Heckhausen, 1982; Vanek, Hosek, & Man, 1982; Krug, 1983) seem to be useful also for young, contest-labile sportsmen whose achievement potential is high, but who do not assess themselves realistically.

Our approach considers achievement motivation to be a fixed achievement set, according to the Georgian (USSR) psychological school (cf. Uznadze, 1961; Norakidze, 1966). In forming achievement motivation according to our approach, the first step calls for making the ineffective achievement orientation to the subject which regulates behavior at an unconscious level (impulsive behavior) more objective. In the course of the second stage a change in motivation orientation itself takes place. In the third stage the aim is to strengthen newly acquired behavior so that it becomes a fixed set at the impulsive level, but of a changed quality. The theoretical basis for practical training is based on Linhart's functional system of activities (Linhart, 1976), which is very close to Vorwerg's approach (1977). Cognitive references have a decisive role to play in the program.

Their assessment function influences the whole cognitive organization and thus directly influences the regulation of the activity carried out and indirectly also regulates external stimuli (selective functions). Essentially they are based on causal attribution processes and on the utilization of success and failure in the regulation of aspiration level. Ability is the most frequently cited causal attribution in sport. However, in academic situations, effort is the most frequently used attribution (cf. Frieze et al., 1976). The difficulty of the task in sports usually depends on the competence or performance ability of the opponent (cf. Roberts, 1982). In this definition, difficulty is no longer an external and stable factor as it is in Weiner's concept (cf. Weiner & Kukla, 1970). The ability of the opponent becomes an unstable external factor, since it can vary from competition to competition (Roberts, 1982). Existing skepticism (see Roberts, 1984) as far as the use of an attribution approach is concerned, can be overcome by taking into consideration a wider utilization, where besides the classical Weiner's approach, we have also made use of causal interpretation, hence also the S-C relationship and not only C-R. According to our experiences, such strategies are possible above all with young sportsmen who have achievement prerequisites which they do not, however, consider on a sufficiently realistic level. These are mostly contest-unstable sportsmen whose failure to a certain extent can be ascribed to a lack of extended effort. Recently we have begun to implement to a greater extent in our programs fruitful ideas which integrate the sportsman's self-concept of ability into the concept of achievement motivation (Meyer, 1984; Nicholls, 1984).

The outcome of most of the achievement motivation programs in the field of sports has been a certain decrease in fear of failure and worry in the sense of the anxiety theory, but at the same time also an increase in fear of social consequences (emotionality) of failure when the Schmalt's Achievement Motivation Grid (AMG) was applied (Krug, 1983; Wessling-Lünnemann, 1983; Man & Hondlík, 1984). This was probably caused by the fact that in achievement motivation programs such patterns of behavior were adopted which were based on imitation of correct behavior and supplemented by explanations and critical assessments. This can be overcome by acquisition of psychological patterns, as in learning behavior strategies. For this purpose for instance Vorwerg (1982) recommends the sue of role playing, a method which we have recently used with young sportsmen with substantial success. On the basis of these standpoints we were able to formulate our chief hypothesis: Applied motivation training will lead to an increase in the hope of success (HS), as well as to a decrease in fear of failure (FF_1) and especially to a decrease in fear of social consequences (FF_2) of failure among young sportsmen.

METHOD

Subjects

Our experimental group was formed by 5th and 7th form swimmers, aged 11 to 13 years who regularly practice and compete as talented sportsmen. Only those were chosen for the experimental group whom coaches assessed as contest-unstable with predominating fear of failure (FF set). The coaches assessed the achievement prerequisites of these swimmers in a highly positive manner, but as was later demonstrated, the swimmers themselves did not perceive them in a sufficiently realistic light. The selection was carried out on the basis of Vorwerg's "Siebtestrating zur Beurteilung der Leistungsmotivation" (1978). Of the total of 148 pupils designated by coaches it was found that 68 had a predominating fear of failure. These pupils were divided into the experimental sample (ES) and control sample (CS) in such a way that each group was homogenous from the viewpoint of sex, age and personality traits. Finally two comparable groups were formed with 28 members each, 14 boys and 14 girls.

Training Program

The achievement motivation training program was carried out from September 1983 in weekly intervals (i.e., in 10 training units between 60 and 90 minutes each) some of them in a classroom, some in a gym, and some in a swimming pool. On the basis of our theoretical viewpoint and the objectives of our work, the achievement motivation program was divided in the following manner:

1. The first and second training units were devoted to making originally impulsive behavior more objective, that is, transfer it into the conscious level. The young swimmers were led to understand the ineffectiveness of their hitherto existing regulation patterns in an achievement situation. In the interests of their own success they agreed that it was necessary to acquire new patterns of behavior and strategies. The sportsmen were told the reason for their selection into the training group which was based on an assessment made by their coaches, concerning their very high abilities and their negative fear orientation in an achievement situation. Training motivation was further extended on the basis of examples from the lives of sports stars who had been helped by achievement reorientation. The two basic concept variables of achievement motivation—hope of success and fear of failure—were acceptably clarified in the course of a discussion.
2. The 3rd to 6th training periods were devoted to the training of conscious guidance of warranted behavior in an achievement situation. The following served this purpose:
   a. training of distinction between causal attribution and causal interpretation on the basis of the example of people motivated by hope of success and fear of failure. First, trainees on the basis of recorded case histories learned only to distinguish the relevant attributive bias. Also a classification schema for perceived determinants of achievement behavior by Weiner and Kukla (1970) was used for instruction, which in training situations was filled in by members of the group. The tendency to ascribe success predominantly to ability and failure to lack of effort was supported. On this basis changes in the interpretation model of an achievement situation occurred. Information processing is of course contaminated by the interaction between a person and his or her environment. In an attempt to overcome this random determinant the trainees were led to concentrate not on the outcome of their own activities and social consequences, but rather on the process of the activity itself (cf. Horst, 1982; Kuhl, 1983; Roberts, 1984; Nicholls, 1984).

b. Task-oriented achievement behavior. Here it was stressed and demonstrated that feeling of insecurity and anxiety were dependent on a transfer of attention on the part of the person solving a problem to its outcome and social consequences (cf. Roberts, 1982; Horst, 1982). In a manner similar to the development of a causal schema here also we began with the modification of cognition; recorded case-histories were assessed and then a group discussion followed.

c. The training of an adequate goal setting (level of aspiration). This stage was carried out in a gym and pool, on the basis of the study of sports hyperaspiration (Hosek, 1969). These were composed of sports motivities made up of chains of measurable attempts, where changes in aspiration have a significant impact (aiming a ball at a basket, darts at a target, a ring toss game, the swimming of short distances with timing, etc.).

3. The 7th to 9th training units were devoted to making the newly learned patterns of behavior and strategies more impulsive in an achievement situation. For this purpose role-playing and a group discussion were used. The 10th training period was devoted to an effectiveness check of the training.

This training program was undertaken with the experimental sample. The control sample underwent regular swimmers training.

Effectiveness Check

Before the beginning of the training, as well as after its termination and 4 months after its termination both the experimental and the control samples were administered Schmalt's Achievement Motivation Grid (1976). It is a semiprojective test for children which enables us to obtain scores of Hope of Success (HS_1) and of Fear and Failure (FF). FF appeared to be a two-factor score. FF_1 shows inhibiting processes in achievement action connected with the concept of missing personal ability (Schmalt, 1976a, p. 119) i.e., it is close to the original Heckhausen's concept of FF. The measure of FF_2 intermediates rather "emotional components of failure anticipation" (Schmalt, 1976a, p. 121). FF_1 is also supported by the independency of HS while between HS and FF_2 high correlation coefficients were found. Other scores can be derived from these basic ones, i.e., Total Motivation (TM) (Equation 1) and Net Hope (NH) (Equation 2).

$$TM_1 = HS_1 + FF_1 \text{ and } TM_2 = HS_1 + FF_2 \qquad (1)$$

$$NH_1 = HS_1 - FF_1 \text{ and } NH_2 = HS_1 - FF_2 \qquad (2)$$

When using the AMG we assumed that the variable of FF was related to the variable of test anxiety (see Heckhausen, 1980; Schmalt, 1982).

It is possible to determine by means of this test not only the total score of these variables of achievement motivation, but also the same variables of achievement motivation in the following six areas: manual activities, musical activities, school activities, independent activities, help-giving activities, sport activities.

From the viewpoint of our aims we utilized only variables of sport activity.

RESULTS AND DISCUSSION

A two factor ANOVA model with repeated measures of one factor and a Newman-Keuls test (Wiener, 1970), were utilized for the statistic evaluation of the experiment.

The findings document the differences between the experimental and control samples which can be interpreted as the outcome of motivation training. An especially significant increase in motivation parameters occurred immediately after the completion of the training program. The changes were not, however, permanent and four months after the training course they could no longer be proved. The lack of more permanent effect can be explained by the fact that the aim stage of making activities more impulsive was not achieved. Probably only the stage of objectivization at a conscious level was achieved and the trainees did not have the time to adopt the required strategy of achievement behavior. In agreement with Krug (1976, p. 224) we can consider the motivation training program successful when the trainee has possibilities of renewing his behavior repertory in achievement situations. Whether training interventions into the areas of sports are sufficient to influence the motivation structure of young people is of course open to discussion. It seems to us that specifically the area of sports is undergoing warranted changes, but still we cannot expect a deeper disposition of young swimmers to permanently and correctly distinguish and interpret relevant achievement stimuli to develop under the influence of this training. Especially a transition of these dispositions to other areas, for instance school activities, remains only in the category of wishes.

The consequences of motivation training for fear of failure are very interesting. The variable FF_1, which we consider to be similar to the worry component in test anxiety terminology, was not influenced by the training program. But on the other hand there was a permanent and marked decrease in fear of the social consequences of failure (FF_2) which we consider to be a component of emotionality in test anxiety terminology. In our previous research we have never yet encountered such a situation, nor have we encountered it in the literature (cf. also Krug, 1983). At the same time our training program did not differ from the point of view of concept from our previous programs. Only role playing was used to a greater extent and according to Vorwerg (1982) this is the most effective method of teaching strategies. We highly value the change which occurred in a decline in emotional anxiety because this variable is an unpleasant component of current mental states of sportsmen.

The achievement motivation training programs which were carried out in the field of school physical education lasted for a longer period than our training program with young sportsmen (cf. Krug, 1983; Wessling-Lünnemann, 1983; Man & Hondlík, 1984). Perhaps it was this brevity of our program and the elements more closely related to sports demands which were the reasons why the necessary increase in impulsiveness did not occur and hence also more permanent effects were not achieved.

The fact that we have not been able to decrease FF_1 (worry), but only FF_2 (emotionality), can be interpreted by the following points:

1. The great majority of studies on this subject cite a negative relationship between worry and performance; as far as emotionality is concerned, the findings

are less unequivocal and more inconsistent (cf. "Advances in Test Anxiety Research, Vol. 1 and Vol. 4"). Deffenbacher (1980, p. 117) shows that when worry is at a low level, emotionality does not have a negative influence on performance. Conversely, when worry is high, then emotionality has a debilitating effect on performance. Worry develops when a person feels a threat to his or her Ego; this produces a stress situation, regardless of whether the test already took place, is running its course or immediately before it. Emotionality is directly connected with danger (with a threat) at the beginning of the stress creating (critical) situation and it is during this period that it achieves its culmination. Deffenbacher (1980, p. 124) puts these facts into the context of state-anxiety. On the other hand a number of authors (i.e., Hodapp, 1982; Hagtvet, 1983, 1984) point out that such a distinction is possible also at the trait-anxiety level, since both levels mutually intersect each other.

In the area of sports competitions it seems evident that the more important the competition is, the more strongly and earlier the athlete experiences a threat to his Ego (i.e., worry and that gradually) with the approach of the competition, his emotionality increases and achieves a maximum immediately before the start of the competition. It also seems evident, that especially among unstable athletes (who are contest-labile), a decrease in emotionality in such a situation will tend to have a facilitating, rather than a debilitating effect on sports performance. This hypothesis of ours, as far as top sportsmen are concerned, was confirmed empirically by Schlicht and Wilhelm (1985).

2. It seems that FF_1 and FF_2 are two different types of cognitive anxiety components. Both components are obviously related to emotionality. Hagtvet's opinion is that FF_1 and FF_2 may, to some unknown degree, be a mixture of both cognitive and emotional aspects. The distinction between cognitive and emotional aspects of anxiety is hard to define empirically, but is nevertheless sensible. It should be noted that FF_1 and FF_2 were defined by exploratory factor analysis and were not designed to measure the constructs of worry and emotionality; we decided here to deal with emotionality on the basis of Heckhausen's comment that these dimensions can be compared with the division of test anxiety into cognitive and emotional components (cf. Heckhausen, 1980, p. 266).

3. Our uniform approach to individual athletes seems to offer an explanation of why FF_1 did not decline. The achievement motivation training used was the same for all. It is true that such an approach produced a number of positive results in experiments carried out under conditions of physical education in schools with children around 10 years of age (cf. Krug, 1983; Man & Hosek, 1984). But it was only after the completion of this experiment with young top sportsmen that we arrived at the conclusion, which is in agreement with Heckhausen (1986), that our approach to overcome anxiety and fear of failure in top sportsmen must delve deeper into its aetiology in the individual and that we cannot be satisfied with the situation where coaches identify certain athletes as contest-labile, either on the basis only of a qualified impression or a rating scale which is suitable for determining fear of failure under the conditions of the teaching process in school.

Another source of inspiration as far as further interpretations of motivation research are concerned, are studies by Samulski (1985) and his structured interviews with 30 high level athletes. According to these methods, which were evaluated on the basis of content analyses, the following motivation problems were identified: undermotivation, overmotivation, unstable motivation, motive-fixation, goal-fixation, negative motivation, unrealistic expectation and goal setting, extrinsic motivation, inadequate self-reinforcement and inadequate causal attribution for success and failure. Samulski (1985) of course offers a much broader range of modification strategies than those included in our program for decreasing anxiety and fear of failure. These strategies essentially strive to influence worry on the one hand and emotionality on the other. In agreement with Nitsch (1984) (cited according to Samulski, 1985), Samulski speaks of intention control and activation control.

4. To interpret the fact that FF_1 was not reduced in our experimental group we can also make use of the approach used by Heckhausen (1986); he distinguishes motivation and volition, and his basic criterion for this distinction is the making of a decision, which he designates as the Rubicon. Before crossing the Rubicon we are dealing with motivation and after crossing the Rubicon with volition. Motivation requires an accurate view of reality in order to evaluate incentives and probability of success and failure. But volition needs to focus only upon how to act to bring success into existence. It seems to us that for top level sports this approach is very fruitful, even if internal links with related mental processes cannot be overlooked. The fact that Heckhausen is at present working with sports psychologists in Kiel (Strang, Janssen et al.) in verifying his concept is very positive. In the future it will be necessary to find suitable diagnostic methods, which will be economical as far as time is concerned, to determine precisely whether an athlete is failing in the motivation or volition stages. If we are successful in doing this, it will also simplify our intervention strategy and increase its effectiveness. Kuhl's scale on action vs. state orientation (cf. Kuhl, 1985, pp. 125–128, "The Action-Control Scale) in Heckhausen's opinion (1986) makes it possible to determine quite reliably volition process on the basis of action orientation scales, while state orientation seems to determine fear of failure. Heckhausen (1986) does not cite an economical tool for measuring motivation processes. If the cited hypotheses are verified, it will certainly be interesting to determine the concurrent validity of STAI (Spielberger et al., 1970), TAI (Spielberger, 1980), SCAT (Martens, 1977) and Kuhl's approach to state orientation and action orientation. In top level sports even the best of diagnostic instruments will always have to be supplemented with an interview.

In our opinion the high quality of theoretical and empirical work in the area of achievement motivation and in the area of anxiety should not be the cause of avoiding a confrontation between both these concepts, which might lead to their mutual enrichment. Much has already been done in this area. It is sufficient to recall the very close cooperation which existed in creating the first methods of measuring fear of failure with the use of the content-analysis system for measuring McClelland's achievement motives. The mutual influencing of both approaches should exist not only in the area of diagnostics, but also in influencing behavior in the direction of higher performance with the aid of modification strategies, either for decreasing fear of failure or test anxiety. In spite of the fact that their theoretical points of departure are not identical, the objectives and modification strategies of both are very close.

When using modification strategies for decreasing anxiety and fear of failure in top level sports, some general strategies of successful action in achievement situation can be learnt in groups, especially in groups of athletes formed on the basis of the same anxiety and fear of failure etiology. But in specific stages of modification strategies used in groups, it will still be necessary to work with some athletes individually, in view of their individual specific aetiology of anxiety and fear of failure. The diagnostic tools developed for instance by Spielberger, Martens and Kuhl can be of great help, especially in research (i.e., how changed stability in these test variables would relate to changed stability in the actual ability performance of sportsmen).

In practical sports we are interested in achieving an excellent performance regardless of the experimental or methodological unequivocalness of an intervention strategy. Such a situation arose already with the first Harvard achievement motivation training sessions with managers (cf. McClelland & Winter, 1969). In these Harvard achievement motivation programs the greatest possible number of variables were influenced, in order to achieve a positive change. When a change occurred, nothing was known about which training variables (or combinations of training variables) actually causes this positive change (cf. Krug, 1983).

In conclusions we should like to stress that the theoretical concepts of both achievement motivation and test anxiety are highly relevant for top level sports and on the basis of their diagnostic and modificational procedures we can help athletes to achieve a performance in harmony with their real abilities. The fact is, however, that at the same time both these approaches have much to gain from a highly competitive sports environment, in the form of a number of incentives for developing the theory. For this reason in our opinion diagnostic methods and the relevant modification strategies for dealing with anxiety and fear of failure should be developed on the basis of a theoretical concept.

PRACTICAL CONCLUSIONS

Our applied training program was based on our positive experiences with overcoming anxiety and fear of failure in school conditions and conditions of school physical education. Also some of the specific aspects of top level sports were taken into account whenever they were in contrast to school physical education. On the basis of our experience and the most recent literary references concerning training to reduce anxiety and fear of failure in top athletes we recommend that:

1. The attribute of ability, not effort, should be considered basic in relation to failure. For this reason when using modification strategies we recommend stressing task-oriented achievement behavior and concentrating not on the outcome, but on the action itself.

2. Group training should be supplemented by the individual treatment of sportsmen with markedly different aetiologies of anxiety and fear.

3. The motivation stage should be distinguished from the volition stage. The final decision (Rubicon) represents a line of demarcation. This is important both from a diagnostic and a modification point of view.

4. The strength of diagnostic methods such as Kuhl's scale on action vs. state orientation, Spielberger's TAI, STAI and Martens' SCAT should be verified. It is absolutely necessary to supplement these methods with an interview. Schmalt's Achievement Motivation Grid has not proven to be a suitable method for measuring fear of failure in young top athletes, while it has proven to be quite suitable for school physical training.

5. In working with coaches it should be explained that when they deal with young athletes they should stress task-orientated achievement behavior and concentration, but towards the action itself.

Implementing these recommendations will perhaps lead to optimum strategies for overcoming anxiety and fear of failure in top level athletes and thus make possible the full realization on an individual's ability in sports activities.

SUMMARY

Achievement motivation training was experimentally verified with 56 contest-unstable 11 to 13 year-old swimmers divided into homogenous experimental and control samples. The program was composed of 10 sixty to ninety minute weekly training units. From the theoretical point of view the program stressed causal attribution and reality related causal interpretation, task orientation, the adequacy of aspirations and intraindividual relation standards. In comparison to previous programs, role playing in the form of psycho-dramas and socio-dramas were used to a greater extent. The effect of the training was assessed by means of Schmalt's technique (1976).

Achievement Motivation Grid was administered before the program, immediately and four months after the termination of the program. Comparisons with the control sample indicate different (non-parallel) changes in motivation variables. Due to the training program a significant and permanent decrease in fear of the social consequences of failure occurred, which from the viewpoint of test anxiety concept is interpreted as a decline in the emotional component of anxiety.

REFERENCES

Atkinson, J.W., & Raynor, J. O. (Eds.) (1974). *Motivation and achievement.* Washington, DC: Winston.

Deffenbacher, J. L. (1980). Worry and emotionality in test anxiety. In I. G. Sarason (Ed.), *Test anxiety: Theory, research and applications.* Hillsdale: Erlbaum.

Freeze, I. H., McHugh, M., & Duquin, M. (1976). *Causal attributions for women and men in sports participation.* Paper presented at the annual meeting of the American Psychological Association, Washington, 1976.

Hackfort, D., & Schwenkmezger, P. (1980). *Angst und Angstkontrolle im Sport.* Köln: bps.

Hagtvet, K. A. (1983). A construct validation study of test anxiety: A discriminant validation of fear of failure, worry and emotionality. In H. M. van der Ploeg, R. Schwarzer, & C. D. Spielberger (Eds.), *Advances in test anxiety research* (Vol. 2). Lisse: Swets and Zeitlinger.

Hagtvet, K. A. (1984). *A three dimensional test anxiety construct: Worry and emotionality as mediating factors between negative motivation and fear behavior. Paper prepared for the Symposium Cognitive Processes in Anxiety.* International Congress of Psychology, Acapulco, Mexico, Sept. 2–7, 1984.

Heckhausen, H. (1977). Achievement motivation and its construct: A cognitive model. *Motivation and Emotion, 1,* 283–329.

Heckhausen, H. (1980). *Motivation und Handeln.* Heidelberg: Springer.

Heckhausen, H. (1982). Task-irrelevant cognitions during an exam: incidence and effects. In H. W. Krohne & L. Laux (Eds.), *Achievement, stress and anxiety*. Washington, DC: Hemisphere.

Heckhausen, H. (1986). Why some time out might benefit achievement motivation research. In J.H. L. van den Bercken, Th. C. M. Bergen, & E. E. J. De Bruyn (Eds.), *Achievement and task motivation*. Lisse: Swets and Zeitlinger.

Hodapp, V. (1982). Causal inference from non-experimental research on anxiety and educational achievement. In H. W. Krohne & L. Laux (Eds.), *Achievement, stress and anxiety*. Washington, DC: Hemisphere.

Horst, H. (1982). *Effektorientierte und aufgabenorientierte Leistungseinstellungen*. Jena: Friederich-Schiller-Universitat (unveröff. Diss.).

Hosek, V. (1968). Anxiety in top sportsman and how to handle it. *Activitas Nervosa Superior, 10*, 300–301.

Hosek, V. (1969). Recherches experimentales du niveau d'aspiration des sportifs. *Kinantropologies, 1/2*, 139–149.

Hosek, V. (1981). Stupnovani motivace ve sportu. *Acta Universitatis Carolinae Gymnica, 17*, 1, 19–29.

Krohne, H. W. (1984). Coping with stress: Dispositions, strategies and the problem of measurement. *Mainzer Berichte zur Persönlichkeitsforschung, 2*.

Krohne, H. W., & Laux, L. (Eds.) (1982). Preface. In *Achievement, stress and anxiety*. Washington, DC: Hemisphere.

Krohne, H. W., & Rogner, J. (1982). Repression-sensitization as a central construct in coping research. In H. W. Krohne & L. Laux (Eds.), *Achievement, stress and anxiety*. Washington, DC: Hemisphere.

Krug, S. (1976). Föderung und Änderung des Leistungsmotivs: Theoretische Grundlagen und deren Anwendung. In H. D. Schmalt & W. U. Meyer (Hrsg.), *Leistungsmotivation und Verhalten*. Stuttgart: Klett.

Krug, S. (1983). Motivförderungsprogramme: Möglichkeiten und Grenzen. *Zeitschrift für Entwicklungspsychologie und Pädagogische Psychologie, 15*, 317–346.

Krug, S., & Heckhausen, H. (1982). Motivförderung in der Schule. In F. Rheinberg (Hrsg.), *Bezugsnormen zur Schulleistungsbewertung: Analyse und Intervention*. Düsseldorf: Schwann.

Kuhl, J. (1983). *Motivation, Konflikt und Handlungskontrolle*. Heidelberg: Springer.

Kuhl, J. (1985). Volitional mediators of cognition-behavior consistency: Self-regulatory processes and action versus state orientation. In J. Kuhl & J. Beckman (Eds.), *Action control: From cognition to behavior*. Heidelberg: Springer.

Liebert, R. M., & Morris, L. W. (1967). Cognitive and emotional components of test anxiety: A distinction and some initial data. *Psychological Reports, 20*, 975–978.

Linhart, J. (1976). *Cinnost a poznavani*. Praha: Academia.

McClelland, D. C., Atkinson, J. W., Clark, H. A., & Lowell, E. L. (1953). *The achievement motive*. New York: Appleton-Century-Crofts.

McClelland, D. C., & Winter, D. G. (1969). *Motivating economic achievement*. New York: Free Press.

Man, F., & Hondlik, J. (1984). Use of compulsory lessons of physical training for the stimulation of achievement motivation of pupils at an elementary school. *International Journal of Sport Psychology, 15*, 259–270.

Man, F., & Hosek, V. (1984). Motivacni vycvik—historie, souscasny stav a perspectivy v oblasti telesne vychovy a sportu. *Teorie a Praxe Telesne Vychovy, 31*, 16–26.

Martens, R. (1977). *Sport competition anxiety test*. Champaign, IL: Human Kinetics Publishers.

Meyer, W. U. (1984). *Das Konzept von der eigenen Begabung*. Bern: Huber.

Nitsch, J. (1984). Psychoregulatives Training. *Lehre der Leichtatletik, 35*(48), 1709–1720.

Nicholls, J. G. (1984). Conception of ability and achievement motivation. In R. E. Ames & C. Ames (Eds.), *Research on motivation in education* (Vol. 1). Orlando: Academic Press Inc.

Norakidze, V. G. (1966). *Tipy charaktera i fiksirovannaja ustanovka*. Tiblisi: Mecniereba.

van der Ploeg, H. M., Schwarzer, R., & Spielberger, C. D. (Eds.) (1983). *Advances in test anxiety research* (Vol. 3). Lisse: Swets and Zeitlinger.

Roberts, G. C. (1982). Achievement motivation in sport. In R. Terjung (Ed.), *Exercise and sport science review* (Vol. 10). Philadelphia: Franklin Institute Press.

Roberts, G. C. (1984). Children's achievement motivation in sport. In J. G. Nicholls (Ed.), *The development of achievement motivation*. Greenwich: JAI Press Inc.

Samulski, D. (1985). Analysis of self motivation techniques of high level athletes. In *Abstr. VI. World Congress in Sport Psychology,* 23–27, June 1985, Copenhagen (Denmark).

Schlicht, W., & Wilhelm, A. (1985). The effects of self-directed cognitions on performance in team-handball. In *Abstr. VI. World Congress in Sport Psychology,* 23–27, June 1985, Copenhagen (Denmark).

Schmalt, H. D. (1976a). *Die Messung des Leistungsmotivs.* Götttingen: Hogrefe.

Schmalt, H. D. (1976b). Das LM-Gitter. Ein objektives Verfahren zur Messung des Leistungsmotivs bei Kindern. Handanweisung. Göttingen: Hogrefe.

Schmalt, H. D. (1982). Two concepts of fear of failure motivation. In R. Schwarzer, H. M. van der Ploeg, & C. D. Spielberger (Eds.), *Advances in test anxiety research* (Vol. 1). Lisse: Swets and Zeitlinger.

Schwarzer, R., van der Ploeg, H. M., & Spielberger, C. D. (Eds.) (1982). *Advances in test anxiety research* (Vol. 1). Lisse: Swets and Zeitlinger.

Sonntag, D. (1984). *Motivationale Determination; von Problemöseprozessen: Struktur und Funktionsanalyse der Misserfolgsfurcht.* Leipzig: Karl-Marx-Universität (unveröff. Diss.)

Spielberger, C. D. (1980). *Preliminary professional manual for the Test Anxiety Inventory.* Palo Alto: Consulting Psychologists Press.

Spielberger, C. D., Gorsuch, R. L., & Lushene, R. E. (1970). *Manual for the State-Trait Anxiety Inventory.* Palo Alto: Consulting Psychologists Press.

Spielberger, C. D., & Sarason, I. G. (Eds.) (1975). *Stress and anxiety* (Vol. 1). Washington, DC: Hemisphere.

Spielberger, C. D., Sarason, I. G., & Defares, P. B. (Eds.) (1985). *Stress and anxiety* (Vol. 9). Washington, DC: Hemisphere.

Topman, R. M., & Jansen, T. (1984). "I really can't do it anyway": The treatment of test anxiety. In H. M. van der Ploeg, R. Schwarzer, & C. D. Spielberger (Eds.), *Advances in test anxiety research* (Vol. 3). Lisse: Swets and Zeitlinger.

Uznadze, D. N. (1961). *Experimentalnyje osnovy psichologii ustanovki.* Tiblisi: Mecniereba.

Vanek, M., Hosek, V., & Man, F. (1982). *Formovani vykonove motivace.* Praha: Univerzita Karlova.

Vorwerg, M. (1977). Adaptives Training der Leistungsmotivaiton. *Zeitschrift fur Psychologie, 185,* 230–236.

Vorwerg, M. (1978). *Siebtestrating zur Beurteilung der Leistungsmotivation (Skala, L. M.)*—*Vorläufige Mitteilung.* In Psychologie und Psychodiagnostic-Tagungsbericht der Gesellschaft fur Psychologie der DDR.

Vorwerg, M. (1982). Lernpsychologische Grundlagen der Trainings zur Verhaltensmodifikation. In K. Hock, J. Ott, & M. Vorwerg (Hrsg.), *Klilnische Psychologie und soziales Verhalten,Psychotheraepie und Grenzgebiete* (Bd. 3). Leipzig: Barth.

Weiner, B., & Kukla, A. (1970). An attributional analysis of achievement motivation. *Journal of Personality and Social Psychology, 15,* 1–20.

Wessling-Lünnemann, G. (1983). Motivationsförderung im Unterricht. In R. Erdmann (Hrsg.), *Motive und Einstellungen im Sport.* Schorndorf: Hofmann.

Wiener, B. J. (1970). *Statistical principles in experimental design.* New York: Graw-Hill.

IV

PERSPECTIVES IN SPORT PSYCHOLOGY

17

Sport-Related Anxiety: Current Trends in Theory and Research

Dieter Hackfort and Charles D. Spielberger

A coach who asks an athlete if he feels "anxious" is, as a matter of course, simply inquiring about the intensity of a particular feeling state, but s/he is also doing something quite remarkable as well. In posing this question, it is assumed that the athlete intuitively knows the meaning of "anxiety" and is able to give a meaningful response. The coach empathically understands the athlete's response on the basis of her/his own past experience. Given the complexity of anxiety phenomena and the underlying network of assumptions, such common sense communications are based on interpretations of private experience within a framework of naive concepts about the nature of anxiety. Such communications are also implicitly linked to assumptions about the relationship between anxiety and performance (Hackfort, 1980).

While communications about an athlete's subjective emotional experience of anxiety are rich in meaning and understanding, they also present a remarkable paradox. In common-sense terms, most people "know" what anxiety is, but find it extremely difficult to describe feelings of anxiety in the objective empirical language of observation. While the term "anxiety" refers to an emotional state that everyone experiences from time to time, efforts to specify the meaning of anxiety as a scientific construct have resulted in markedly different conceptual definitions and a wide variety of operational assessment procedures (Spielberger, 1966).

The general orientation of sports-anxiety research has been markedly influenced by theoretical and methodological developments in the United States, but there have also been important innovations and advances in Europe. Many of these new developments, especially, in applied research with top athletes and in investigations of techniques for anxiety control, are described in this volume. The experimental strategies and research findings reported by the contributors to this volume are examined in the context of current trends in theory and research on sport-related anxiety. Trends in international sport psychology publications and relevant anxiety theory and research in personality, social, clinical, and health psychology are also briefly reviewed in order to provide perspective regarding trends in sport-related anxiety research.

THEORETICAL TRENDS IN ANXIETY RESEARCH

Anxiety has been defined as an emotional state consisting of feelings of tension, apprehension, nervousness and worry, and activation or arousal of the autonomic nervous system (Spielberger, 1972). Since the nature and the intensity of state anxiety is directly accessible only to the person who experiences it, researchers must use indirect approaches in assessing its phenomenological and physiological properties. Consequently, as a scientific construct, S-Anxiety is operationally defined by the specific procedures and inventories that are used in its measurement. On the basis of extensive empirical research over the past 40 years, three major components of S-Anxiety have been identified for investigation: Emotional feelings, cognitive representations of threat, uncertainty, and worry, and physiological arousal.

Feelings of anxiety that may vary in intensity are perhaps the most unique and palpable manifestation of anxiety phenomena. The concept of threat and its relation to anxiety was introduced by Freud (1936) in his Danger Signal Theory. This concept was subsequently elaborated by Lazarus (1966) as an essential component of stress as a transactional process. According to Lazarus, the other components of the stress process are the objective forces or pressures that impinge upon an individual (stressors) and the emotional states that result when a stressor is perceived or interpreted as threatening.

Nitsch's (1981a) justification for differentiating the concept of uncertainty from the broader concepts of stress and threat seems equally applicable to definitions of anxiety. In Nitsch's view: "The problem is much less to find the 'right' definition (but to find) a useful one in theoretical and practical respects" (Nitsch, 1981b, p. 40). From this perspective, various concepts and definitions of anxiety can be evaluated in terms of their contribution to clarifying theoretical and practical problems.

One of the most important theoretical advances in anxiety research subsequent to Freud's articulation of his Danger Signal Theory was the differentiation between anxiety as a transitory emotional state (S-Anxiety) and anxiety proneness as a personality disposition or trait (T-Anxiety). Although the importance of the state-trait distinction was recognized in early German psychology (e.g., see Herrmann, 1969), the efforts of Cattell and Scheier (1961) and Spielberger (1966, 1972) to conceptualize and measure state and trait anxiety have provided the necessary empirical foundation. Now reflected in anxiety research around the world, this conceptual distinction has been extended to other emotions such as anger and curiosity (Spielberger, 1979).

The concepts of state and trait anxiety are operationalized in the State-Trait Anxiety Inventory (STAI; Spielberger, Gorsuch & Lushene, 1970; Spielberger, 1983)), which has been translated and adapted in 39 languages and dialects (Spielberger &: Diaz-Guerrero, 1976, 1983, 1986). Currently widely used to assess anxiety in sport psychology research in Europe and the United States (e.g., Apitzsch, 1983; Hackfort & Schwenkmezger, 1980; Spielberger, Chapter 1, this volume), the STAI has become the standard international measure of anxiety (Spielberger, 1984).

TRENDS IN SPORT PSYCHOLOGY RESEARCH

Historically, the influence of exercise and sports participation and competition on personality development has been a central area of research interest in sport psychology. An important derivative of this interest focuses on the impact of exercise and sports participation on anxiety. Investigations testing the anxiolytic effects of exercise generally use a "consequent design" research paradigm, as Morgan and Ellickson point out (Chapter 11, this volume). In contrast, "antecedent design" research paradigms are typically used to investigate the effects of anxiety on performance, the most popular topic in sport-related anxiety research.

Of the many theoretical orientations that have guided investigations of anxiety-performance relationships, the following six approaches are considered in this volume: Drive theory, threshold theory, quiescence theory, optimal arousal theory, reversal theory and the inverted-U hypothesis. The latter hypothesis, which was derived by Yerkes and Dodson (1908) more than eighty years ago from animal studies of habit formation, is probably the framework most often used in sport psychology for interpreting anxiety-performance relationships. There are two important limitations of research guided by the inverted-U hypothesis: (a) The findings generally focus on physiological arousal as an index of motivation; feelings of anxiety tend to be ignored. (b) Only descriptive analyses of the data are typically reported; no explanations of the observed relationships are given.

Weinberg (Chapter 7, this volume) examines the utility of the inverted-U hypothesis for explaining the effects of anxiety on performance in sports psychology. His research focuses on the "patterning of neuromuscular energy," individual differences in trait anxiety, and the quality of movement in stressful situations. In the context of a person-by-situation interaction model, Weinberg's process-oriented investigations generally employ three levels of the inverted-U hypothesis.

Psychophysiological methods are also widely used in investigations of anxiety-performance relationship, as can be noted in Weinberg's studies. Such methods are also used by Zaichkowsky (Chapter 5, this volume), in his research on self-regulation, anxiety control, and the efficacy of biofeedback strategies. Both Weinberg and Zaichkowsky consider muscular tension, as measured by electromyographic (EMG) responses, as an index of arousal in research on exercise and motor behavior.

Kerr (Chapter 9, this volume) outlines a "theory of psychological reversal" as a framework for stimulating and evaluating research in sport psychology. A basic assumption of Reversal Theory is that "human behavior is intrinsically inconsistent." Kerr's application of this theory to sports psychology is especially relevant as an alternative to optimal arousal theory, which assumes that the optimal level of physiological and psychological arousal facilitating performance differs from person to person. Hanin (Chapter 2, this volume) employs a variant of optimal arousal theory in his concept of "Zone of Optimal Functioning" (ZOF), which defines the range of variation in the intensity of state anxiety that facilitates performance for a particular individual.

The integration of cognitive, affective, and psychophysiological approaches is a major challenge for sports psychologists. The "cognitive-developmental" approach of Mahoney and Meyers (Chapter 6, this volume) emphasizes the personal meaning of a sports situation in determining the effects of anxiety on performance. Similarly, Nideffer (Chapter 8, this volume) has developed instruments that call attention to the meaning of task relevant cues. His "Test for Attentional and Interpersonal Style" (TAIS) and "Inventory of Concentration and Communication Skills" (ICCS) are widely used in the practice of sport psychology, especially by coaches. Thus, Nideffer's measures have contributed to applied sport psychology in bridging the gap between research and practice.

It is essential that applications of anxiety control techniques in sport-related anxiety research be accompanied by evaluative studies (Machac & Machacova, Chapter 14, this volume). Interventions designed to facilitate sports performance with techniques based on the drive properties of anxiety as a motivating agent must also be carefully evaluated. Such strategies are often used by coaches, and by teachers in physical education programs (Hackfort, 1980), but are rarely evaluated with appropriate control groups. While many coaches and teachers use techniques designed to induce anxiety in order to increase motivation, these naive strategies are generally inappropriate. Such techniques have relatively little beneficial impact on performance, and often lead to poor coach-athlete and/or teacher-student relationships.

Hypotheses regarding anxiety as a motivator of learning and as an inhibitor of behavior have been derived from learning theory and, especially, from Miller's (1948) animal studies of fear as an acquirable drive. Experiments with humans reveal that high-anxious individuals condition faster than persons with low anxiety, but such findings are limited to very simple learning tasks such as eyelid conditioning (e.g., Taylor, 1951). Since the motor behavior involved in athletic performance is very intricate, it is obviously mediated by more complex learning mechanisms. The findings in investigations of learning to swim, for example, indicate that high anxious subjects initially perform more poorly than low anxious subjects. However, as learning progresses, these differences were reduced and both groups eventually achieved the same results (Karbe, 1968).

Investigations of anxiety and motor learning have important implications for training top athletes, and for instructors and students enrolled in physical education classes. Hackfort and Schwenkmezger (1982) evaluated the anxiety of physical education (PE) teachers and identified anxiety-provoking demands in their daily work. A major source of anxiety was the lack of recognition of PE teachers as specialists in motor behavior, which often resulted in loss of self-respect and self-esteem.

Hackfort (1986) also investigated the competence of PE teachers in diagnosing the sport-related anxiety of their students. He compared students' self perceptions of anxiety with the social perceptions of anxiety of other students. The main findings in this study were: (1) Teachers' ratings tended to underestimate the sport-related anxiety of their students; and (2) Teachers' ratings of student anxiety differed significantly from students' self-ratings, and from the evaluations of other students. These findings have practical relevance for teachers of physical education classes, and demonstrate the value of conducting anxiety research in school settings.

Traditionally, sport-psychology research has been concerned primarily with negative emotions. However, future research in this field should consider the positive and negative effects of both positive and negative emotions (Hahn, Chapter 10, this volume; Hackfort, 1986). More specifically, as noted by Hahn, research on elite athletes should investigate the impact of "positive" emotions (e.g., pride, satisfaction, joy, and challenge) in improving performance. Future research should also investigate the role of emotions in youth and school sports, adult leisure-time sports, and rehabilitative sports programs. In addition, we must endeavor to learn more about the costs of negative emotions and the benefits of positive emotions in exercise and sports.

SPORT–RELATED TRAIT ANXIETY

Test anxiety has been defined as a situation-specific anxiety trait (Spielberger, Gonzalez, Taylor, Algaze, & Anton, 1978). In evaluative situations, high test-anxious persons, relative to individuals low in anxiety, generally perform more poorly on examinations (Sarason, 1960, 1972). They are also more self-centered and more likely to experience personalized, derogatory cognitions which interfere with task-oriented attention and performance (Sarason, 1972; Wine, 1971). Since sports are almost always achievement-oriented and sports situations generally include both self evaluation and evaluations by other persons, sport-related anxiety, like test anxiety, may be regarded as a situation-specific anxiety trait (Schwenkmezger 1986).

The distinction between task relevant and task irrelevant cognitions in test anxiety research may also have important implications in analyzing sport-related anxiety. In empirical investigations of top-class handball players, Schwenkmezger (1980) found that high anxious athletes experienced more task-irrelevant cognitions, and felt more disturbed by them, than low anxious individuals. Such cognitions were also experienced more often by the less successful athletes. Thus, the task-irrelevant cognitions of athletes who experience high levels of sport-related anxiety appeared to interfere with their performance.

The interdependent processes of threat and coping appraisal, as outlined by Lazarus (1966; Lazarus & Folkman, 1984), are critical factors in understanding the nature of sports-related anxiety as a situation-specific trait. The phenomena of burnout, for example, which is typically viewed as chronic, inappropriate, and ineffective coping reactions to stress, is examined by Smith (Chapter 12, this volume). After outlining his cognitive-affective model of stress and anxiety, Smith describes two intervention strategies that operate on different phases of the stress process. The first involves an environmental modification strategy aimed at providing increased social support to reduce stress. The second strategy focuses on coping responses, which combine relaxation exercises and adaptive self-statements. Self-instruction (e.g., "Relax!") and self-suggestions e.g., "I am in the best condition of my life and have to fear nobody") when employed with appropriate cognitive interventions to be effective for controlling anxiety in competitive sports (see Hackfort & Schwenkmezger, 1982).

Biofeedback also seems to provide an effective self-regulation strategy for the management of stress and anxiety. Zaichkowsky (Chapter 15, this volume) characterizes biofeedback as providing information about biological processes of which the individual is not normally aware, nor able to voluntarily control. From a process-oriented perspective, cognitive and physiological events are not only consequences of anxiety, but also starting points for anxiety prevention and control.

METHODOLOGICAL TRENDS IN SPORTS–RELATED ANXIETY RESEARCH

In sport psychology, single-case studies of top athletes are especially appropriate because, by definition, there are very few "top" athletes. Large group studies are most useful in obtaining information about general orientation, attitudes and group differences, for example, research on sport related attitudes and motivation. But the usefulness of large-group techniques for data collection, along with classical statistical strategies for data aggregation, has been questioned in sport psychology research (see Hackfort & Schwenkmezger, Chapter 5, this volume).

Large group studies are generally based on questionnaire data obtained with instruments such as the State-Trait Anxiety Inventory (STAI: Spielberger, Gorsuch, & Lushene, 1970; see also Spielberger, Chapter 1, this volume). The STAI has been used in numerous investigations of sports-related anxiety, as previously noted. The STAI T-scale measures individual differences in the disposition to experience anxiety in social-evaluation situations involving threats to self-esteem (ego-threats), but does not measure anxiety proneness in danger situations in which a person's physical well-being is threatened (physical harm situations). In comparative studies with different situational backgrounds, general measures of T-Anxiety are quite adequate (Hackfort & Schulz, Chapter 3, this volume), but situation-specific trait measures are especially useful in situations involving physical danger, as has already been pointed out (see Hackfort & Schwenkmezger, Chapter 5, this volume).

Research on sport-related anxiety will be facilitated by the development of situation specific instruments for improving predictions of elevations in state anxiety in pre-start and competitive situations. Moreover, as has been shown in research on test anxiety, instruments designed to assess the content of task-irrelevant cognitions and worries that are experienced in sports situations would be especially useful in predicting performance deficits in such situations.

REFERENCES

Apitzsch, E. (Ed.) (1983). *Anxiety in sport.* Magglingen: FEPSAC.
Cattell, R.B., & Scheier, J. H. (1961). *The meaning and measurement of neuroticism and anxiety.* New York: Ronald.
Freud, S. (1936). *The problem of anxiety.* New York: Norton.
Hackfort, D. (1980). Techniken der Angstkontrolle von Trainern. *Leistungssport, 10,* 104–110.
Hackfort, D. (1986). Theoretical conception and assessment of sport-related anxiety. In C. D. Spielberger & R. Diaz-Guerrero (Eds.), *Cross-Cultural Anxiety* (Vol. 3). Washington, DC: Hemisphere.
Hackfort, D., & Schwenkmezger, P. (1980). *Angst und Angstkontrolle im Sport.* Köln: bps.
Hackfort, D., & Schwenkmezger, P. (1982). Psychologische Aspekte zur Angst im Sportunterricht. *Sportunterricht, 31,* 409–419.
Herrmann, T. (1969). *Lehrbuch der empirischen Persönlichkeitsforschung.* Göttingen: Hogrefe.

Karbe, W. W. (1968). The relationship of general anxiety and specific anxiety concerning the learning of swimming. *Dissertation Abstracts, 28,* 3489.

Lazarus, R. S. (1966). *Psychological stress and the coping process.* New York: McGraw-Hill.

Lazarus, R. S., & Folkman, S. (1984). *Stress, appraisal, and coping.* New York: Springer.

Miller, N. E. (1948). Studies of fear as an acquirable drive. Fear as motivation and fear reduction as reinforcement in the learning of new responses. *Journal of Experimental Psychology, 38,* 89–101.

Nitsch, J. R. (1981a). Zur Gegenstandsbestimmung der Streßforschung. In J. R. Nitsch (Hg.), *Streß.* Bern: Huber.

Nitsch, J. R. (1981b). Streßtheoretische Modellvorstellungen. In J. R. Nitsch (Hg.), *Streß.* Bern: Huber.

Sarason, I. G. (1960).Empirical findings and theoretical problems in the use of anxiety scales. *Psychological Bulletin, 57,* 403–415.

Sarason, I.G. (1972). Experimental approaches to test anxiety: Attention and the uses of information. In C. D.Spielberger (Ed.), *Anxiety: Current trends in theory and research* (Vol. 2). New York: Academic Press.

Schwenkmezger, P., & Laux, L. (1986). Trait anxiety, worry, and emotionality in athletic competition. In C. D. Spielberger & R. Diaz-Guerrero (Eds.), *Cross-Cultural Anxiety* (Vol. 3). Washington, DC: Hemisphere.

Spielberger, C. D. (1966). Theory and research on anxiety. In C. D. Spielberger (Ed.), *Anxiety and behavior.* New York: Academic Press.

Spielberger, C. D. (1972). Anxiety as an emotional state. In C. D. Spielberger (Ed.), *Anxiety: Current trends in theory and research* (Vol. 1). New York: Academic Press.

Spielberger, C. D. (1979). *Preliminary manual for the State-Trait Personality Inventory (STPI).* Unpublished manuscript, Tampa, FL: University of South Florida.

Spielberger, C. D. (1983). *Manual for the State-Trait Anxiety Inventory (STAI)* (Revised). Palo Alto, CA: Consulting Psychologists Press.

Spielberger, C. D. (1984). State-Trait Inventory: A comprehensive bibliography. Palo Alto, CA: Consulting Psychologists Press.

Spielberger, C. D. (1985). Assessment of state and trait anxiety: Conceptual and methodological issues. *The Southern Psychologist, 2,* 6–16.

Spielberger, C. D., & Diaz-Guerrero, R. (Eds.) (1976). *Cross-Cultural Anxiety* (Vol. 1). Washington, DC: Hemisphere.

Spielberger, C. D., & Diaz-Guerrero, R. (Eds.) (1983). *Cross-Cultural Anxiety* (Vol. 2). Washington, DC: Hemisphere.

Spielberger, C. D., & Diaz-Guerrero, R. (Eds.) (1986). *Cross-Cultural Anxiety* (Vol. 3). Washington, DC: Hemisphere.

Spielberger, C. D., Gonzalez, H. P., Taylor, C. J., Algaze, B., & Anton, W. D. (1978). Examination stress and test anxiety. In C. D. Spielberger & I. G. Sarason (Eds.), *Stress and Anxiety* (Vol. 5). Washington, DC: Hemisphere.

Spielberger, C. D., Gorsuch, R. L., & Lushene, R. E. (1970). *Manual for the State-Trait Anxiety Inventory (STAI).* Palo Alto, CA: Consulting Psychologists Press.

Taylor, J. A. (1951). The relationship of anxiety to the conditioned eyelid response. *Journal of Experimental Psychology, 41,* 81–92.

Wine, J. (1971). Test anxiety and direction of attention. *Psychological Bulletin, 76,* 92–104.

Yerkes, R. M., & Dodson, J. D. (1908). The relationship of strength of stimulus in rapidity of habit formation. *Journal of Comparative Neurology and Psychology, 18,* 459–482.

Index